The Learning Project

Rites of Passage

Lincoln Stoller

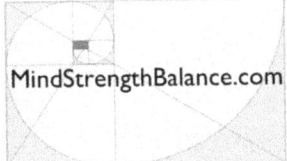

First Edition.
Published 2019 by Mind Strength Balance, Victoria, British Columbia, Canada
http://www.mindstrengthbalance.com

Copyright © 2019 Lincoln Stoller, All rights reserved.

Except for brief excepts in reviews, no part of this book may be reproduced in any form, or by any means, electronic or mechanical, including photocopying, recording, or by any information storage and retrieval system, without the written permission of the publisher.

Publisher's Cataloging-In-Publication Data
(Prepared by The Donohue Group, Inc.)

Names: Stoller, Lincoln, 1956- author.
Title: The learning project : rites of passage / Lincoln Stoller.
Description: First edition. | Victoria, British Columbia, Canada : Mind Strength Balance, 2019.
Identifiers: ISBN 9781775288008 (paper) | ISBN 9781775288046 (hard cover)
    ISBN 9781775288015 (mobi) | ISBN 9781775288022 (epub)
    ISBN 9781775288039 (pdf)
Subjects: LCSH: Learning. | Education. | Mentoring. | Thought and thinking. | LCGFT: Interviews.
Classification: LCC LB1060 .S76 2019 (print) | LCC LB1060 (ebook) | DDC 370.15/23—dc23

Front cover illustration: Narcissus, by John William Waterhouse.
Back cover illustration: Windflowers, by John William Waterhouse.

To Chiron.

PRAISE FOR
The Learning Project

"In a society deeply committed to time-wasting, Lincoln Stoller has given us something of a miracle in his *Learning Project*, a window out of our own claustrophobic darkness into the consciousness of others, a momentary intimacy with the essences which animate flesh. What learning project could match this one?"

— John Taylor Gatto, twice New York State Teacher of the Year, recipient of Alexis de Tocqueville Award for Excellence in Advancement of Educational Freedom, author of *Dumbing Us Down* and *The Underground History of American Education.*

~

"*The Learning Project* provides a Rosetta Stone for living a self-made, satisfied life; an intuitive understanding worth more than its weight in gold. With brilliant glimpses into fascinating lives, Stoller shows life's answers lie in people. I highly recommend this book to anyone in the process of pursuing their dreams – that should mean everyone."

— Alexander Khost, founder and facilitator of Voice of the Children NYC.

~

"Authentic learning comes from living as much with passion as with intellect. This is a wonderful collection of choices, risks, doubts, struggles, failures, and triumphs from widely differing backgrounds, personalities, chosen paths, and ages – from 15 to 93 – of remarkable, adventurous lives. Lincoln Stoller has a great knack for inviting the revelation of basic life truths, and the learning that has occurred along the way. I recommend this book to anyone, but especially to people thinking about how they themselves might leave a well-worn path for something new and heartfelt."

— Peter Gray, PhD, Department of Psychology, Boston College, and President of Alliance for Self-Directed Education. Author of *Psychology* and *Free to Learn.*

~

"The sheer diversity of the stories in this massive work, from individuals who forged their own trails, shows there are so many more ways to learn than the model our culture currently supports. How wonderfully inventive we are, we humans – our differences are our strength. Message to all: accept yourself as you are, take yourself seriously, and keep going!"

— Wendy Wolosoff-Hayes, psychotherapist, energy healer, and founder of spaciousheartguidance.com.

~

"*The Learning Project* explores processes of learning through a fascinating variety of interviews with people diverse in age, experience, and social standing. The transformative power of learning and knowledge are recurring themes. This informative, entertaining book should benefit readers from any discipline."

— Raymond C. Russ, PhD, Department of Psychology, University of Maine. Editor of *The Journal of Mind and Behavior*.

~

"A physicist by training and philosopher by inclination, Lincoln Stoller asks a fascinating collection of people about how they make key decisions in their lives. With simple questions like, "I don't know, tell me..." he opens discussions about deep life experiences. This book, intended for young people reflecting on how to live, is relevant for anyone considering their personal narrative and life philosophy."

— Rachel Harris, PhD, psychologist. Co-author of *Children Learn What They Live,* and *Teenagers Learn What They Live*.

~

"*The Learning Project* is a powerhouse of intellectual and humanistic insights from special individuals of all ages and backgrounds. Lincoln opens up his speakers' inmost thoughts and feelings, their highest potential, inspiration, unique abilities, goals, and dreams. An intimate look at what it means to be human, masterfully captured by a brilliant curator. An amazing book, well worth reading more than once."

— Kate Jones, artist, dance teacher, writer, philosopher, founder, and President of Kadon Enterprises, Inc. at gamepuzzles.com.

~

"Anyone interested in the actual mechanics of lifelong changes, success, and growth will realize that *The Learning Project* offers an unprecedented, invaluable key to achievement that no growth-oriented learner should bypass."

— D. Donovan, Senior Reviewer, Midwest Book Review

CONTENTS

Praise for The Learning Project			iv
Acknowledgments			ix
Introduction			x
Preface	I	Persephone's Learning	xii
	II	The Education of Achilles	xv
	III	Melencolia I	xviii

ART

1	Life Stage: Early	William Ashburton	2
2	Middle	Phantom Street Artist	12
3	Late	Crista Dahl	21

BIOLOGY

4	Early	Sonya Peters	31
5	Middle	Gudrun Sperrer	43
6	Late	Jerome Lettvin	55

COMPUTERS

7	Early	Andrew Reese Crowe	69
8	Middle	Michelle Murrain	77
9	Middle	Esther Dyson	90

FILM

10	Early	Oliver Pierce	102
11	Middle	Simon James	110
12	Middle	Tom Hurwitz	121

MEDICINE

13	Early	MaryAnn Manais	132

14	Early	Dave Williamson	141
15	Middle	George Plotkin	162
16	Late	Nancy White	178

OUTDOORS

17	Early	Ella Gazka	190
18	Middle	Lynn Hill	202
19	Late	Fred Beckey	210

PHYSICS

20	Early	Hamilton Shu	223
21	Middle	Neil deGrasse Tyson	229
22	Late	Charles Hard Townes	238

SOCIETY

23	Early	Jessica Henry	251
24	Early	Lotus Bringing	260
25	Early	Jaz Lin	269
26	Late	Phyllis Schlafly	281

TRADE

27	Middle	Tom Kellogg	293
28	Late	Clarence See	305
29	Late	Donald Dubois	313

WRESTLING

30	Early	Make Short	324
31	Middle	Paul Widerman	335
32	Late	Lou Giani	348

WRITING

33	Early	Caitlin McKenna	360

| 34 | Early | Alice Placert | 369 |
| 35 | Middle | Matt Forbeck | 378 |

POSTSCRIPT

| 36 | Middle | Lincoln Stoller | 392 |
| | | Afterword | 396 |

ACKNOWLEDGMENTS

Thanks to my ancestors, without whom gaining this knowledge would not have been possible; to my descendants, without whom passing it on would not be important; and to the people who will benefit from this project – hopefully you will help others.

And thanks to the bad teachers I have had – which is to say most of them – for developing my sense of purpose and for helping make the wrong paths clear. Thanks to the good ones too.

INTRODUCTION

I have written this book for young people interested in taking control of their lives. It addresses learning in a general sense by interviewing different people and asking them to describe their learning process: why it's important, how they do it, and what it's done for them.

The interviews are with young, middle-aged, and older people working or interested in either of 11 different fields. For some people school is important, for others it isn't. Curiosity, determination, and self-confidence keep coming up in these stories, as do the teachers people have had and the discoveries they have made. Judgment is critical. Learn to trust your judgment, your own judgment.

> "The greatest act of rebellion anyone can ever hope to achieve… is to actually break the mold and THINK for yourself: to open your eyes."
> — Jamie Stuart, from "Eyes Wide Shut"

What It Contains

The Learning Project makes deep insights available through interviews on the subject of learning, collected from people in different fields. The interviews come from young people of school age, people in their middle age who are pursuing a career, and established elders.

All the people interviewed in the project are asked:
- What are the most important things you've learned?
- How did you learn them?
- What do you hope to accomplish?

The Learning Project weaves a dialog on the subject of learning, where "learning" is used in the sense of building one's life; learning to grow up human. This is a kind of learning that each person must define and execute for themselves.

How It Started

The Learning Project combines my experiences from learning as a young person through and beyond middle age. I was independent-minded from childhood. I began rock climbing at 13 and, without anyone's help, I was planning major mountaineering expeditions at 16. These early projects taught me that important questions were not easy to find or to answer.

I was interested in science in high school but didn't know what it involved. I went to speak to the best scientist I could find: Eugene Wigner, 1963 Nobel Laureate in quantum physics. He was tremendously excited to hear from me, though he'd never heard from me before. From him I began to learn the usefulness of good advice; forty-five years later I appreciate how important good advice is… and it's largely unavailable.

How It Ends

This book is about following your heart. Consider how these insights might be of use to you. It's your journey. It doesn't end.

PREFACE I: PERSEPHONE'S LEARNING

Narcissus, by John William Waterhouse, 1912

Persephone was a legendary Greek maiden who picked an enchanted Narcissus flower from the fields of Nysia, whereupon the earth split open, and from it emerged the Lord of the Underworld, riding a chariot drawn by four black horses. Hades then took Persephone, willingly or otherwise, on a tour of the world and a journey to find her destiny, which included her becoming his queen, among other things.

The Mysteries

The character of Persephone is one of three archetypes appearing in this myth, and which together represent the cycle of human development. She is the youth who is compelled, by curiosity and divine force, to begin a journey of completion. The other two archetypes are The Giver of Life, represented by her mother, Demeter, and The Seer of Wisdom, represented by the crone, Hecate.

The ancient Greek ceremony and cult built around Persephone, called the Eleusinian Mysteries, played a central, spiritual role in Greek society. Greeks of any social rank could be initiated into these mysteries, but it required a year or more of preparation, an oath of secrecy, and imbibing a visionary entheogen known only as the Kykeon. Divulging the Greater Secrets of Persephone – the Rites of Transformation, as it were – was punishable by death. Socrates revealed the Secrets to some extent, though nothing was recorded, and as a result the authorities compelled Socrates to kill himself. The Secrets were ultimately lost with the coming of Christianity in 400 AD, and remain unknown to this day.

This myth is debased in its modern telling partly because it was distorted by Homer when it was chronicled around 700 BC. Homer, who was basically The Walt Disney Company of his day, did not convey the central teaching of the myth, which came from the story of Inanna, the Sumerian goddess who preceded the Greeks by 4,000 years. In these times people did not eschew the bad and seek only the good, a point of view developed around the time of Christ, they worked to integrate light and dark. This is Persephone's story.

> "Inanna… epitomized the essence of contradiction, of the unimaginable variety and possibility in the created world… she introduced the possibility of the individual who thinks for herself/himself… Through the choices we make, we build the unique individuality of ourselves… As the goddess of paradox, she is the model of unity in multiplicity. Each of us reflects a bit of her discordance in ourselves. Each of us is burdened with the chore of gathering our many conflicting pieces together into a semblance of order and congruence."
>
> — Betty De Shong Meador, from *Inanna, Lady of the Largest Heart*

Persephone's story is an icon for *The Learning Project* because it represents the most mysterious of the three processes of learning. These three processes are acquisition, reconstruction, and transformation. Acquisition means the growth of knowledge through learning new things, such as facts or skills. Reconstruction – which could also be called "discovery" – means the appreciation and remediation of flawed knowledge through insight and re-conception. Transformation refers to accomplishing a change in oneself that admits new levels of perception and understanding. Transformation gives a person a new understanding, not of things, but of knowledge itself.

> "Risk brings its own rewards: the exhilaration of breaking through, of getting to the other side, the relief of a conflict healed, the clarity when a paradox dissolves. Whoever teaches us this is the agent of our liberation. Eventually we know deeply that the other side of every fear is a freedom. Finally, we must take charge of the journey, urging ourselves past our own reluctance and misgivings and confusion to new freedom. Once that happens, however many setbacks or detours we may encounter, we are on a different life journey. Somewhere is that clear memory of the process of transformation: dark to light, lost to found, broken to seamless, chaos to clarity, fear to transcendence."
>
> — Marilyn Ferguson, from *The Aquarian Conspiracy: Personal and Social Transformation in the 1980s*

The interviews in *The Learning Project* reflect all three forms of learning to varying degrees. A useful oversimplification is that young people, like Persephone, face transformation; middle-aged people, like Demeter, are busy acquiring; and old people, like Hecate, seek to discover meaning. But don't take my word for it. Read the interviews yourself.

> "Blessed is he among mortals who witnesses these things, but whoever is not initiated into them or dies without them descends unblessed into the gloomy darkness…"
>
> — from "The Hymn to Demeter," seventh century BCE

> "(Human beings) don't use the knowledge the spirit has put into every one of them; … and so they stumble along blindly on the road to nowhere – a paved highway which they themselves bulldoze and make smooth so that they can get faster to the big empty hole which they'll find at the end."
>
> — Lame Deer, Lakota Shaman

PREFACE II: THE EDUCATION OF ACHILLES

The Education of Achilles by Chiron, by Pompeo Batoni, 1746

Chiron and the Education of Achilles

Batoni's painting shows the mythological centaur Chiron teaching Achilles, whom he raised and mentored from infancy. Beyond that, the story gets complicated.

King of the Centaurs

To understand what Chiron represents, you must recognize that Greek mythology is not just a set of stories, it's a cosmology that describes the origin and detail of human character. The stories are interconnected because the elements of human thought, character, and culture are interconnected, and Chiron is one of the most interconnected characters of all.

Chiron was born from the unwilling union of the mortal sea nymph Philyra with Cronus, father of Zeus and the Greek primordial god of time. His centaur form, with a human head and torso and the body of a horse, derived from his mother's attempt to escape rape by his father by shifting into a mare. In this origin he was different, and his legacy was opposite in the extreme from all the other centaurs who were famous for depravity and barbarism.

Chiron was immediately rejected by both his parents and taken into the care of the sun god Apollo, the god of prophecy and oracles, healing, plague and disease, music, song and poetry, archery, and the protection of the young. Apollo passed these skills on to Chiron, who consequently came to embody the integration of human culture and intellect with our bestial instincts and brute force.

Chiron was the Greeks' original teacher and raised many of the Greeks' most famous heroes, including Jason (barely out of his teens when he led the Argonauts to recover the Golden Fleece), Asclepius (god of medicine), Aristaios (god of shepherds, cheese-making, bee-keeping, olive growing, medicinal herbs, and the Etesian winds), Theseus (to become the king of Athens), Ajax (to become king of Salamis), and both Peleus and his son Achilles (hero of the Trojan war).

Chiron was honored by all, something uncommon in Greek mythology, so it was ironic his demise came accidentally when he was grazed by a poisoned arrow shot by his friend Hercules. Because he was immortal, the magic poison caused him endless, debilitating torment but could not kill him. From this, Chiron is recognized as the original wounded healer, an archetype central to the work of therapists, counselors, prophets, and shamans.

Hercules eventually secured a divine bargain in which Chiron's immortality was forfeit to secure the liberation of Prometheus, who was more or less Chiron's cousin, thereby granting Chiron his wish to die and consigning his spirit to the underworld. Yet even that was not to last, as his universal esteem led his half-brother Zeus to intervene one last time by raising him to the celestial realm in the form of the constellation Sagittarius (*sagitta* is Latin for "arrow"), thereby restoring to him an immortality of sorts. In this way Chiron ultimately found his cure beyond death and, in both myth and astrology, he lies as a bridge between the physical and spiritual worlds.

Approach to Education

While Chiron appears throughout Greek mythology to raise and mentor those destined to be gods and heroes, we don't know much about his personality or educational philosophy. As this is a book about learning, these are the things we are most interested in: just how does one learn to be a mythical hero? Luckily, Odysseus asked this same question of Achilles when Odysseus met him later in his life, and this is what he answered:

> "Then he taught me to go with him through pathless deserts, dragging me on with mighty stride, and to laugh at the sight of the wild beasts, nor tremble at the shattering of rocks by rushing torrents nor at the silence of the lonely forest. Already at that time weapons were in my hand and quivers on my shoulders. The love of steel grew apace within me, and my skin was hardened by much sun and frost; nor were my limbs weakened by soft couches, but I shared the hard rock with my master's mighty frame.
>
> "Scarce had my youth turned the wheel of twice six years, when already he made me outpace swift hinds and Lapith steeds, and running overtake the flung dart; often Chiron himself, while yet he was swift of foot, chased me at full gallop with headlong speed o'er the plains. And when I was exhausted by roaming over the meads he praised me joyously and hoisted me upon his back. Often too, in the first freezing of the streams, he would bid me go upon them with light step not to break the ice.

"These were my boyhood's glories... Never would he suffer me to follow unwarlike does through the pathless glens of Ossa, or lay low timid lynxes with my spear, but only to drive angry bears from their resting-places, and boars with lightning thrust; or if anywhere a mighty tiger lurked or a lioness with her cubs in some secret lair upon the mountain-side, he himself, seated in his vast cave, awaited my exploits, if perchance I should return bespattered with dark blood; nor did he admit me to his embrace before he had scanned my weapons.

"And already I was being prepared for the armed tumults of neighboring folk, and no fashion of savage warfare passed me by... Scarce could I recount all my doings, successful though they were. Now he instructs me to climb and grasp the airy mountain-peak, with what stride to run upon the level, how to catch flung stones in mimic battle on my shielded arm, to pass through burning houses, and to check flying four-horse teams on foot.

"Spercheus, I remember, was flowing with rapid current, fed full with constant rains and melted snows and carrying on its flood boulders and living trees, when he sent me in, there where the waves rolled fiercest, and bade me stand against them and hurl back the swelling billows that he himself could scarce have borne, though he stood to face them with so many a limb. I strove to stand, but the violence of the stream and the dizzy panic of the broad spate forced me to give ground. He loomed o'er me from above and fiercely threatened, and flung taunts to shame me. Nor did I depart till he gave me word, so far did the lofty love of fame constrain me, and my toils were not too hard with such a witness.

"For to fling the Oebalian quoit far out of sight into the clouds, or to practice the holds of the sleek-wrestling bout, and to scatter blows with the boxing-gloves were sport and rest to me: nor labored I more therein than when I struck with my quill the sounding strings, or told the wondrous fame of heroes of old.

"Also did he teach me of juices and the grasses that succor disease, what remedy will staunch too fast a flow of blood, what will lull to sleep, what will close gaping wounds; what plague should be checked with a knife, what will yield to herbs. And he implanted deep within my heart the precepts of divine justice, whereby he was wont to give revered laws to the tribes that dwell on Pelion, and tame his own twy-formed folk [the Kentauroi]. So much do I remember, friend, of the training of my earliest years, and sweet is their remembrance."

— Pablius Papinius Statius, from *Achilleid* Book 2. p.96ff (Latin Epic ca. 1st century AD)

Chiron taught the strength to embrace struggle, engage paradox, and prevail in challenge and, though we've forgotten his teachings, we still seek this for ourselves.

PREFACE III: MELENCOLIA I

Melencolia I, by Albrecht Dürer, 1514

Wikipedia says this 16th century engraving by Albrecht Dürer "has been the subject of more modern interpretation than almost any other image in art." I've used it here for three reasons reflecting the importance of judgment. The first relates to the angel, the second to five objects on the left side, and the third to its title. My understanding of the picture's elements comes from my friend David Finkelstein, without whom this work would remain poorly understood.

The Angel

I see the angel as a learner; she is divine and so is learning. Learning is the process of attaining godliness, and all learning is part of this process. The angel contemplates the geometric solid whose meaning is enigmatic. The solid refers to the mind, and it may refer to the soul as well. A detailed view of the fine lines defining the solid reveal what appear to be a multitude of human faces, not unlike this text. The angel has her hand in a position for writing, but the implement she's holding is a compass; compasses measure.

We interpret images according to objects familiar to us, and it is natural for us to ascribe separateness and identity to them. This was just the beginning of what Dürer had in mind. As well as conveying meanings by portraying meaningful objects and by juxtaposing objects meaningfully, he also superimposed hidden images within the objects. These form layers that tell complementary and conflicting stories. These relationships, many yet undiscovered, fuel the controversy about the picture's meaning. Of the dozens of layers in this work I'll consider only one: the Arab. One must consider the Arab to better understand what the angel is doing.

The Arab

The picture shows two events important in the 16th century, and still important today: these are the emergence of logical thinking and the conflict between Eastern and Western cultures. Both conflicts require judgment – and the angel, who connects the two, may be the key to understanding them. The emergence of logical thinking, later to dominate European culture in the Enlightenment of the 18th century, is represented by the geometric solid discussed below. The conflict between East and West is represented by the Arab.

The Arab is a kneeling figure hidden in the folds of the angel's dress. The oddly serrated saw, or sword, he's reaching for with his left hand is being held down by the angel's right foot, while his right hand is reaching back toward where she is stabbing him with the point of her compass. She seems to have him hostage while she contemplates the situation. And it appears her contemplation of rationalism (the geometric solid) as a replacement for religion (the millstone) bears on this conflict.

Was Dürer portraying the Arab's struggles as a philosophical reflection on changing culture? Was he referring to the Crusades, the three centuries of war that defined relations between Europe and the Middle East up until his time? Or was he directed by, in Dürer's words, "the fear of invasion by the Turks, which gripped all of central Europe," which also conveyed his personal and family struggles living at the edge of the expansion of Islam? He had reason to do all of these, and he probably was. These themes play a dominant part in what might be called the picture's historical story.

Five Objects

Five objects gain their importance from their referential meaning and relative placement. These objects are the globe, the dog, the solid, the millstone, and the comet. The picture uses these objects, supported by many of the smaller items, to present Dürer's philosophy. Each object deserves a dissertation of its own, but a summary will suffice. The first thing to note is their linear relationship: four of them lie on a straight line, with the millstone being displaced.

The globe is foundational in the terrestrial, spiritual, and alchemical senses. It provides the context from which humanity fashions a place in and an understanding of the world. It is the starting point for contemplation and transformation. It is blank and smooth.

The dog represents fidelity or, from the Latin origin of this word, faith. It was a common view in Dürer's time, when European culture was dominated by Catholicism, that faith sustains our connection to the divine. The dog lies between the globe and the solid in the way faith lies between the terrestrial and spiritual worlds.

Theology and the divine institution of the church, represented by the millstone, are objects to which faith applies itself to connect humanity to the spiritual realms. But the thinking that began in the Renaissance in general, and with Protestantism in particular, began the movement to supplant theology with what we now call "natural philosophy". Dürer was on the rationalist edge of these changes, as evidenced by his work in art and mathematics, and in his time it was not safe to be seen diverging from the views of the Roman Catholic Church. This explains why Dürer wrote his story in symbols rather than words, and hidden symbols at that.

The geometric solid has complex and obscure meanings. I feel it represents individual and collective rationalism, although in the 16th century this force held more mystery and promise than it does today. In those times rationalism was distinct from theology and it hinted at the renaissance of ideas to come. Today rationality has subsumed the role of religion as politicians now confer with scientists not bishops; we teach our children reason rather than religion; and we look to technology to save us.

By placing the millstone on the dog's level and out of the line leading to the comet, and at the same time placing the solid on a higher level and along the divine progression, Dürer seems to say theology and faith are much the same, while reason offers a higher truth and a more divine path. The geometric solid also carries references to gnosticism, or hidden paths to knowledge, as a top-down view of its edges presents the Shield of David inscribed within a hexagon. Both were mystical symbols used throughout the Far and Middle East.

The comet represents an aspect of God. Clearly it is distant, dynamic, and uncapturable. It may represent a power, or a message, or a messenger. No one seems to be looking at it, and the scene is not illuminated by its light, but it is tracking straight for the head of the cherub-like figure sitting against the wall who, it is fairly certain because he holds an engraver's tool, is Dürer himself.

The Title

The goal of *The Learning Project* is to encourage young people to develop judgment. The essential story of your life is knowable only by you, and only you can guide yourself. Others might claim to know what's best for you, but what is obvious to them may not be true. And so it is with the title of this engraving.

The great historians considering this work misunderstood it at the most basic level: the level of its title. It was not until David Finkelstein, a person of no special training or authority in the subject, that this key was revealed.

The title "Melencolia" is not and never was an alternate spelling of the word "melancholy," although the allusion to the word's medieval meaning of "introspective" is apposite. Nor does the "I" in the title refer to the Roman numeral "one," though this was one of Dürer's three master works. Rather, "MELENCOLIA I" is an anagram of "*CAELO LIMINE*" whose meaning in Latin can be taken as "I engrave at the wall," or "I engrave at the edge," or "at the gateway to Heaven," all of which apply to the scene. In this way, we see the engraving is about Dürer's world and philosophy.

Albrecht Dürer questioned the accepted thought of his time and wrote a symbolic discourse whose symbol-statements are hidden in plain sight. David Finkelstein deciphered some of these symbols, and from this we better understand Dürer and his times. In a similar manner, we must all question what we're told about our world, in order to find our own place in it. Like Melencholia I, *The Learning Project* also sits at the gateway to Heaven.

AUTHOR'S NOTE

Some of the names, locations, and photographs are fictional because some people requested their identities be withheld. Some transcripts were edited for focus and readability. The other transcripts are presented verbatim.

~

For additional commentary and to hear extracts from audio transcripts visit https://www.mindstrengthbalance.com/learningproject. Follow **@LincolnStoller** and **#TheLearningProject** for more information.

ART

1. WILLIAM ASHBURTON

History   Early   Born 1989, Yuma, Arizona

William struggled with his adoptive family. His issues played out through anger, which first manifested in fifth grade, and has only just finished its course now that he is 19.

His anger ran a harsh course through cigarettes, alcohol, sex, drugs, and violence. It's difficult to find solutions through anger, and it's a dangerous path – "a difficult learning tool," you might say – but anger is something we all encounter.

The phrase "love conquers all" is trite and useless. Yet William's epiphany about love saved his life when things were out of control. I am happy to say, he found a resolution and a love for his family, though they are still working to rebuild their relationships.

Excerpts

"Back then I didn't care if I was alive or dead. I wouldn't kill myself, but I'd get to scary points doing drugs that would nearly kill me…"

"I was overdosing on crystal meth, and we were… I don't know… This is where I became unconscious… so this is what Sophia told me happened. When we got to the bedroom I said, 'Please don't tell my parents! Please don't tell my parents!'… I wasn't shaking any more but my eyes were open. Then I stopped breathing…"

"So I stabbed her… with a pencil. That was bad. I'd never done anything like that before. I just got so mad so quickly that I thought it was OK (laughs… sighs), but it wasn't (sighs)… Oh, what a life…"

"I got their attention in a way I didn't want. I didn't want them to send me away or anything. But I got too deep into everything, and they thought I needed help… They arranged for me to go away to school in Utah. I went to Utah. I learned so much there. I hated my parents before I went: I hated them. I hated my sister, I hated my brother…"

"My sister and I have changed a lot. She and I are best friends now… that just came out of the blue… It was the day I came back from the treatment center… she gave me a hug for the first time ever. She had never given me a hug in my teenage years, ever. It felt like she loved me, and I started to cry. I've never gotten a hug from her. So I had to love her back…"

"It's so hard to tell stories. It is so hard."

"Knowledge must come through action; you can have no test which is not fanciful, save by trial."

— Sophocles, Greek tragic dramatist (496 – 406 BC), from *Trachiniae*

"At pettiness which plays so rough
Walk upside-down inside handcuffs
Kick my legs to crash it off
Say okay, I have had enough
What else can you show me?"

— Bob Dylan, from "It's Alright, Ma (I'm Only Bleeding)."

"There is only one happiness in this life, to love and be loved."

— George Sand, novelist (1804 – 1876).

Interview — Albuquerque, New Mexico, March 2008

We sit in the sunny weather on William's patio in the hills above Albuquerque. William is waxing his legs.

William Ashburton: Ouch, shit!

LS: All your pain is being preserved.

WA: Thank goodness! So what are we kind of looking for?

LS: The question is, what was your relationship to learning things? How did that change as you grew up?

WA: I wasn't very good at it... learning things? It's an interesting question. I've never been asked that before... I really, honestly, don't understand the question.

LS: Think about boredom. That's usually where it begins: boredom and frustration at school or at home.

WA: Yeah, I guess I could say I was bored. But at the same time I was having fun. I had a lot of friends, which made it harder, actually.

I guess it all started in elementary school. We had just watched a movie on gun violence. I started to pass notes, weird notes. I sent a note to this girl named Angela Dansala – who was my friend – and I said, "I want to blow your brains out." It was a quote from the movie. That was my first time getting suspended.

I thought being suspended was kind of cool: got to stay home, didn't do shit. I decided to get suspended more often. In fifth grade I got suspended more than seven times. Some days I just stayed home, because I didn't really give a crap.

I started smoking cigarettes in sixth grade. My parents didn't know that. They thought I started when I was 18, but I actually smoked on campus in sixth grade. I had an older friend who was in high school at the time. Her name was Stephanie Sherman. She wasn't legal age to smoke yet either, but we got cigarettes anyway. When I took that first puff, I knew I was going to be a smoker. That hurt me a lot, when it came to school.

Seventh grade was good. I didn't do anything. I did my work. It was a new school, a new environment, trying to get used to people.

When I hit eighth grade, that's when I started to ditch school. I told my parents, "Oh yeah. I'm going to go to school." But I would ditch, I would go to this place called Sugarloaf, which is here in the hills. I wouldn't drink a lot, but I didn't need to. I was really tiny in eighth grade, and a 12 oz. bottle of beer would have me on my ass. I ended up really liking drinking. I still like drinking, just not as much (laughs).

Ninth grade was pretty crazy. I wasn't quite to the age where I went to the club yet, but I got offers to go many times.

LS: What's the scene here? What's the social environment that you're growing up in?

WA: There's a lot of scenes in La Cuesta high school. I associated myself with all the different scenes: the drug scene, the dance scene – the dance scene came with the drugs. I guess that's the scene I was in, the drugs. I didn't care.

Back then I didn't care if I was alive or dead. I wouldn't kill myself, but I'd get to scary points doing drugs that would nearly kill me. A lot of stuff has happened. It's kind of hard to tell the full story, 'cause so much has happened.

LS: What were you looking for? What were you hoping to have happen?

WA: The reason why I started doing all the drugs and stuff, and smoking cigarettes and drinking, is because I wanted to get attention from my parents. I felt like my whole family didn't love me at all. Later on I found out that that wasn't true, but at the time I just felt pretty unloved. Doing drugs and drinking took that away. It just made me feel better.

Tenth grade I ditched every day. I missed half of the school year and, again, I was doing drugs.

When 11th grade came along, I was a mess. I was going to all sorts of places that I probably shouldn't have gone to, like hookah bars. I wouldn't just do hookah there.

LS: What's a hookah? Do they smoke hash?

WA: It's like flavored smoke, but it's in a bong. A hookah has a lot of leads coming off of it so people can smoke together. It's not illegal; it's only illegal if you're under 18, which I was.

We'd go there because my friend – I won't use his name because he'd get pissed – he would take us. We'd smoke meth… Not out of the same thing of course, you couldn't do that. That was 11th grade. In 11th grade I didn't go to school at all.

LS: People thought you were going to school?

WA: Yeah. They found out I wasn't going to school. This is when the story gets kind of bad.

I loved snorting crystal meth. I loved it. I had a best friend, her name was Sophia, and we went to the club. My first time doing it was at the club. I was so fucked up in there I almost got raped in the bathroom, third stall. Luckily Sophia wasn't too fucked up. She just said, like, "We just have to go. Let me call my boyfriend." And she's talking all weird, just like me.

That night we decided we needed more, because it wore off. We had this friend named Rex, who actually lives down the street, and he said he could get it for us if we went over. So we went over – ouch! – we went over, and he took us to this bridge where his parents live. They lived underneath the bridge.

That's where I did too much. I was fine at first, but when we got back here – I was walking down the driveway – I started to hyperventilate. They put me in this chair. My eyes were rolling in the back of my head. That was a very long night. It was just starting.

I got my breath back and said I was OK, but when I got to the stairs, I collapsed. So they had to lift me. Sophia's boyfriend Tom lifted me. He came from Corrales because Sophia was freaking out, and he took me to my mattress. I didn't have a bed. Back then I had a mattress on the floor.

I was overdosing on crystal meth, and we were… I don't know… This is where I became unconscious… so this is what Sophia told me happened. When we got to the bedroom I said, "Please don't tell my parents! Please don't tell my parents!" And she was, like, "OK, I won't tell your parents." And there were four of us in there: Rex, Tom, Sophia, and myself – ouch! – and I tried to sleep. I wasn't shaking any more but my eyes were open. Then I stopped breathing.

Sophia was on top of me, pounding my chest, and I woke up (laughs)! That's when my parents walked in. It was pretty noisy. So that was that night! Two days later, I went to a psychiatric hospital.

LS: Did you want to go?

WA: Hell no. Hell no! I put up a fight. I said, "Oh no, I don't need to go. I've learned my lesson. An overdose is enough." But I went anyway.

I met really interesting people at the psychiatric hospital. I made a really good friend. Her name was Delia. Her arms were probably as thin as this chair leg, and she made me realize, "Why the fuck am I here, and she's here. I didn't do anything like she did." She would do an 8-Ball – I don't know what an 8-Ball is – but she'd do an 8-Ball of coke and smoke pot every day. I wasn't like that, and I thought that I shouldn't be there because these people were crazy, and I wasn't crazy.

After we became really good friends, she got to a point that she couldn't stay any longer, so she had to leave. But she wasn't ready to leave. I started to freak out in the psychiatric hospital when she had to leave. I said, "What do you mean you have to leave?" And she's like, "You're ready to leave, but I'm not."

That made me think, hmm, maybe I should work this because I did some of the same things that she did, but not to her extent. She would talk to me about doing drugs, and I would say, "Oh, that sounds like so much fun!" I didn't feel ready to leave.

When the therapist said to me, "You get to leave in two days," I was, like, "I don't think that's a good idea." So he let me stay as an outpatient for two weeks. But I still wasn't ready.

I was doing fine for a while. I wasn't in the public high school; I was going to a continuation school because I missed so much school. I did that for about a month. Then I did something really stupid.

I slept over at my boyfriend's house, his name was Rick, and I had school the next day. He was a hard-core drug addict; I wouldn't be surprised if he's dead now. I haven't heard from him in a long time.

I did speed at his house, and then I went to school. I was really fucked up. I had a therapist at the school, and she noticed something was wrong with me. I'm usually an honest person, so I told her what I'd done. She called my parents. I got pissed… but whatever.

LS: You thought she would be confidential about it?

WA: Yeah, she's my therapist! So she told my parents, and they arranged for me to go away to school in Utah. I went to Utah. I learned so much there. I hated my parents before I went: I hated them. I hated my sister, I hated my brother.

LS: Where did that come from? Did it come from the whole growing up scene?

WA: I think so. I got their attention in a way I didn't want. I didn't want them to send me away or anything. But I got too deep into everything, and they thought I needed help. I probably did. I got help (sighs).

The school really taught me a lot to do with… about having a family. Everyone there had a problem. Again, in the beginning, I thought I didn't need to be there, and I hated my parents for sending me. For two months I didn't say anything. I didn't say anything; I didn't look at anybody.

Most of the kids in my room had a problem with their parents, and their family as well. But listening to them made me feel, "How can you hate your parents for that?"

I remember going to bed one night, and this boy named Juan, who slept above me, we had bunk beds, he was talking about how his dad is so rich, and he hates him for it. I didn't ask him, but I said in my brain, "How can you hate someone for being rich?" I don't know why, but that got me to think that being mad at my parents wasn't OK. I mean being mad at my parents was OK, but hating them wasn't OK.

The place was a year-round school, and in the third month I was there I started getting a really good GPA, which was not like me. I usually get a GPA of 2.5 or something, and now I was getting 3.9. That's when I realized that, well, I'm pretty good at school, but I just don't apply myself.

I learned a lot at that school. It's hard to talk about the school because I still don't like it, but I learned a lot. The people I met there were really interesting, even though I'll probably never talk to them again (laughs).

LS: Can you give me an example?

WA: Marshall, who was another gay. I don't know how it changed me, but he made me realize that you could find love anywhere. Marshall and I did love each other, at least that's what we think. But it changed how I looked at people. I used to be very into how people looked: if a person didn't look good, then I couldn't do anything. I wouldn't even do drugs with them.

It's so hard to tell stories. It is so hard.

Just last summer I went to visit my friend Peter, whom I met at Heritage, which is the school's name, at his house in San Francisco. I took a plane. Second night there I drink a whole bottle of cooking brandy, just 'cause I wanted to get drunk. And he took advantage of me. And then, later that night, he and I took… he took four sleeping pills, and I took 14. I had a seizure, and I went to Marin County Hospital, or something. I never heard from him again (laughs)!

That was maybe two summers ago. I don't know. It was a while ago. It was the summer after I got out. It was June 2007. I haven't done drugs since then.

LS: What's changed between now and then?

WA: Just a change in friends. Sarah has not always been my friend. In fact, in high school she said she didn't even know who I was. China is incredibly against doing any kind of drug, except for alcohol. All of us drink. I just feel like I don't need that stuff anymore. It just got old.

I had help from my friends. They're, like, "We don't want to see you go back there." I've had too many near-death situations: I don't want another heart attack, I don't want another seizure. I've stopped popping pills, and snorting, and smoking. I even stopped smoking cigarettes (laughs).

LS: Do your friends still smoke?

WA: They quit with me. They quit cigarettes with me.

LS: What's this process of learning? It sounds like for you it's very experiential.

WA: It is.

LS: Not at all intellectual. Is it emotional? Fear? Fear sounds like it's a big element. Maybe "terror" would be a better word.

WA: What do you mean "terror"?

LS: I mean terror as a palpable sense of something that's real in a world without much meaning. It's just that your story has more to do with death than life.

WA: (sighs) I've died more than I've lived.

LS: Tell me more about your family. You mentioned them before, but you didn't mention them in the story.

WA: I had a terrible relationship with my father. We fought a lot. We used to hit each other. We don't fight anymore. We kind of joke around, but it's not serious. I'm not going to say that we don't fight anymore, because everyone fights. Like my sister still fights me, and my brother still fights me. Even my mom still fights me on certain things, like taking out the garbage, but it's not as serious as it used to be.

I used to be very violent… very, very violent. One time my housekeeper, who was my babysitter at the time, wouldn't let me use the calculator for doing homework, and so I stabbed her… with a pencil.

That was bad. I'd never done anything like that before. I just got so mad so quickly that I thought it was OK (laughs… sighs), but it wasn't. My dad said I was lucky she didn't press charges. What could she have pressed charges for? I don't think it would have killed her. It was right here (pointing to his arm)… (sighs). Oh, what a life.

LS: Where are you in the scheme of things now? As you look at the past, do you see something similar in the future?

WA: I definitely don't see the same "me." I'm not going to do the same things.

LS: What are you going to do? Do you have things that you want to try out?

WA: I don't know. I know I'm not going to do drugs again! No idea yet. I'm still learning about myself.

My sister and I have changed a lot. She and I are best friends now. Best friends and siblings. And… that just came out of the blue, like I don't know how that happened.

I woke up one day and she and I were this close. I don't know. I never talked to her like I did that one day, and now that's how we talk all the time. It scared me (laughs).

It was the day I came back from the treatment center. And she just… she gave me a hug for the first time ever. She had never given me a hug in my teenage years, ever. It felt like she loved me, and I started to cry. I've never gotten a hug from her. So I had to love her back, I just wanted to be the same person that she was to me.

My brother and I still have our problems. But it's not as serious. He doesn't threaten to kill me in my sleep anymore with his weapons like he used to. "I'm going to use my flip knife," – or whatever it was called – "and I'm going to slit your throat in your sleep," (laughs).

I love them all. They're my family. I just wish some of them wouldn't do the things that they do, and I bet they wish the same thing for me.

Part of the reason why I was so violent, I think, is because my relationships were violent. I used to get hit, not just by my parents, but also by boyfriends. My friends wouldn't hit me. That's what makes me want my friends to approve of someone I like before I start talking to them seriously. My friends have a big influence in my life. Sometimes bad, sometimes good! Like this (referring to the waxing), it hurts (laughs)!

LS: What are your interests? I put everybody in this project into a bin according to their interests. For the younger people it's a bit contrived, but I do it anyway.

WA: Like what am I interested in?

LS: Yeah, like what are you going to be when you grow up?

WA: I would love to be a photographer. I love taking pictures. Actually, I just started. Most of my pictures are of myself (laughs), in different backgrounds.

LS: How do you do that? Do you hold the camera in front of you, or do you set it on a stand with a self-exposure?

WA: It's actually not a very good camera. That's why I wanted to get a better one, but it has this 10-second timer thing. I find somewhere to put it, like a branch or something.

LS: You should get a little tripod. That branch bullshit never works. I find it rarely works.

WA: (Laughs) It doesn't work, because the branches go like that, and the flash doesn't get you, it gets the branch. But some of my pictures are nice.

LS: What do you like about them, or is it the process you like?

WA: I love taking the photos, but what I love the most is putting in different effects, like decorating. I use Photoshop. I think it's fun. I think it's really fun. My friend Junior is helping me, but it's kind of awkward. He's a photographer, a professional, but his boyfriend and I had a thing, so it's kind of weird. I can't see Kelly. If I see Kelly, I'll freak out.

LS: Well, have you thought about school for photography, to take classes? They exist.

WA: Really? I know that at La Cuesta High School there's a class for photographers.

LS: Have you done other things like that: painting or drawing?

WA: I used to be very artistic. I used to paint and draw. I used to dance. I used to sing. Most of it was in school, but singing was more professional. I was hired to the Albuquerque Opera in the Albuquerque Children's Chorus. I sang a solo as Tiny Tim at the Alex Theatre. I sang "God Rest Ye Merry Gentlemen" for a Christmas production.

LS: So it was interesting at the time... but that stuff didn't touch you?

WA: I got fired! I got fired from each one for bad behavior. I was not a good boy.

LS: Well, a lot of people don't want to play along, but they usually shape-up when they're threatened with something. But I guess you didn't care. Or did it come as a surprise to you that you got fired?

WA: Ha! No, no. I knew what I was doing: I knew that if they found out, I'd get fired, and they did find out – of course they did. It was right in front of them. I was swinging on the props and breaking things, and I cussed out Ann Thompson, the Director of Albuquerque Children's Chorus.

LS: Did you cuss her out because she deserved it, or because you just enjoyed doing it?

WA: I don't think she deserved it. I felt like doing it. I just felt like cussing, and she was there.

LS: It sounds a little bit like the family situation. It fits with the whole sort of violent, angry, rebellious approach.

WA: I'm far from violent now.

LS: How about rebellious?

WA: I love rebelling.

LS: You do?

WA: Yeah.

LS: If you can imagine other people in the space where you were a few years ago, people without the clarity that you have now, what could you tell them that would help them get the kind of clarity for themselves that you have now?

WA: I'd say, "It comes from yourself," but I really can't tell them. I wouldn't want to tell them. I just want them to learn on their own. Do you mean if they were in my shoes, or what?

LS: There are different kinds of "shoes." There's some people who don't act, they just remain numb. And other people defeat themselves when they act, because they don't know what to act, or what to act on. I think most people are just bored. Nothing really grabs them. It's my impression that a lot of people stay that way for the rest of their lives.

WA: Well, I know that's why I started drugs and stuff, it was because I was bored. I wanted to see what they were like. Curious. Also, I wasn't happy. But I don't know what I could say to people to find their clarity.

LS: What about happiness? Did you find your happiness? Would it be better to say it that way?

WA: My happiness is off and on, so it's still not clear.

LS: But off and on is not the same as being unhappy. Do you mean to say that you're happy and unhappy, or happy and just sort of neutral?

WA: Happy and then neutral. I'm not sad or anything.

LS: You're not miserable.

WA: No.

LS: But you used to be?

WA: Oh yeah! I was miserable back then, but now I'm just… here. I'm OK.

LS: Say there were five people just like you at age 13, and you saw the same thing was going to happen to them that happened to you. Could you say anything to them?

WA: If I said something, it wouldn't help them. People said things to me, I didn't listen. I didn't really give a shit.

LS: But if you could say something that they would listen to… What should you have listened to?

WA: Someone told me to think about my family. They did tell me that, and I didn't think about my family for a second when I was doing those things. Maybe for a second. Maybe I was, like, "OK, maybe this will hurt Mom or something." I don't know.

Maybe I should have listened to that. That's the only thing I can ever remember anyone ever saying to me: "Think about your family. Think about yourself and your family, and who you're going to hurt." Like, I knew I hurt people, but I didn't care at the time.

I don't know what I'd say to people to help them, because they wouldn't listen. People like me: they're just not going to listen.

They might listen, keep it somewhere in their mind, and then when they're done with the process of getting clean and healthy, then they might think about it, like I did. But I still… I wouldn't know what to say in order to help somebody find happiness or clarity in the future.

2. PHANTOM STREET ARTIST

History   Middle   Born 1973, New York City, New York

I was introduced to the Phantom Street Artist by Paul Widerman, with whom he wrestled. This may seem ironic unless you understand wrestling is about coming into one's power, and this is just what an artist strives to achieve with his or her work.

The Phantom Artist grew up on the streets of New York where his option was either to learn or perish. Unlike the often incidental role that learning plays in the life of a student, learning for the Phantom Artist was the essential process of finding meaning and hope. This is learning in its most important sense.

Some of the Phantom Artist's friends did perish in his stressful and sometimes violent environment, so his reflections bear a sharp edge, similar to Dave Williamson's reflections on coming of age as a soldier in chapter 14.

If you're wondering why he has chosen to hide his identity, the answer is fairly obvious: his street art is considered vandalism.

Excerpts

"The one thing I've learned... is that the most important thing you have is your ability to change your perceptions – thoughts, feelings – into the positive. If you live in regret, you're not living in the positive, today or tomorrow. So I really don't have any regrets ..."

"And I wouldn't change anything, you know, except for the loss of great people in my life, the loss of individuals to insanity, tragedy, and murder. Those are the only things I would change..."

"My life is a living testimonial. The mentorship process has greatly influenced my life. It provided a respite, a salvation from a broken home that could not offer role models, in a world of contingent values..."

"Look for mentors; it's a very simple learning process. Look for the mentors. Channel, find purpose, and look for your destiny. Search for the moment when opportunity will knock on your door. Try to find your place in the world, and make your mark in that world either through accomplishments or through your voice. This gives things value. This is value..."

"To keep working towards that, day by day. Allow life to be the fabric of a giant, potential canvas: life as theater, to cast ourselves in new roles, to write new stories for ourselves."

Man, 24, Dies After He Is Shot In Robbery Attempt in Queens
New York Times, March 15, 1982

"A 24-year-old Queens man died early yesterday morning after being shot during an attempted burglary, the police said. According to the police, the man, Edward Glowaski, broke into the third-floor apartment of Fred Hammer at 37-68 97th Street, in the Corona section, at about 10 P.M. Saturday. Mr. Hammer, 76 years old, fired a .32-caliber revolver once into Mr. Glowaski's chest. Mr. Glowaski, who lived at 40-17 60th Street in the Woodside section, died at 2:30 A.M. yesterday in Elmhurst Hospital.

"The police said Mr. Hammer was given a summons for having an unlicensed gun. Mr. Glowaski was a self-described graffiti 'artist' who called himself Caine 1. Some of his canvases were exhibited at Graffiti: Aboveground, a gallery in Greenwich Village."

"When the story is destroyed, the feeling of historicity disappears as well. I remember the early seventies in Czechoslovakia as a time when something like a 'cessation of history' took place...

"History was replaced by pseudo-history, by a calendar of rhythmically recurring anniversaries, congresses, celebrations, and mass gymnastic events; by the kind of artificial activity that is... a one-dimensional, transparent, predictable self-manifestation (and self-celebration) of a single, central agent of truth and power.

"And since human time can only be experienced through story and history, the experience of time itself began to disappear: time seemed to stand still or go in circles, to disintegrate into interchangeable fragments. The march of events out of nowhere and to nowhere lost its story-like character and thus lost any deeper meaning as well... life became nonsense."

— Václev Havel, from "Stories and Totalitarianism," in *Open Letters, Selected Writing* 1965-1990

Interview   Los Angeles, California, March 2008

Phantom Artist: My first experience of being mentored was to a graffiti artist, who was my mentor on the streets: Eddie Glowaski, originally known as "Caine 1." Caine 1 achieved great recognition for painting his full cars top to bottom, but through a case of mistaken identity was shot and killed, while the spirit of his expression went on to receive great international recognition. That was during the great movement of graffiti artists who received international recognition in the mid 80s.

Eddie was being chased by thugs in his neighborhood. The word out on the streets was that Caine 1 was making BIG money, so the thugs wanted to jump him for his money, and they chased him through the streets of Queens. He climbed up a fire escape and began pounding on an old man's window to be let in for safety. Yet this was an old man who was previously robbed and vowed never to be taken again. What was someone actually pleading for help, to be let in for personal safety, appeared to the deaf, mute old man as someone trying to break in. The old man took a gun and, out of self-protection, shot Eddie.

Eddie was mortally wounded as a result of his being a hemophiliac. He was taken by ambulance to a local hospital, Elmhurst General in Queens, where the doctors never discovered that he was a hemophiliac. They tried to stop the bleeding, but through a series of errors they were not able to stop it. He died that morning. He was eventually buried outside of the city where his work went on to achieve great resonance in the community. People like Lady Pink and Lee Quinones knew of his work. Kenny Scharf referenced his work. Keith Haring referenced his work as well.

LS: How old were you?

PA: I was a kid. I was very young. I was one of the little kids that everybody hung out with. We were like their protégés; we were known as Tracy's kids. There were always younger kids that used to hang out with them, who were instructed, and, to some extent, would rob for them, break into things and things like that. Very much like in the film *Oliver Twist*.

LS: What was happening to you?

PA: I was a street kid interested in the arts. I was starting to spray paint. I encountered these people that were spray painting the streets and subways. I started to hang out with them, and go and hit the trains, spray painting the trains, tagging the city streets.

My mom was moving from place to place because she couldn't afford housing, so we would only stay in certain places for a certain amount of time, and then she would be served with an eviction notice. The Department of Sanitation would pack our clothing items, pick up our belongings, pack it into boxes, and take off with it. I remember it clearly since the city storage facilities were located a few blocks from the World Trade Center.

How do you like the oranges?

LS: They're good. Are they from a store or are they off trees?

PA: They're off these trees, locally. Here, have some more.

LS: Did they send you to school?

PA: In New York I never really spent any time in school. Because the schools were a really harsh environment and not conducive to learning... I was only interested in the arts. Only later on, after my experiences of being displaced – when I got into a wrestling program out on The Island (Referring to Long Island, New York, whose urban and suburban communities center around New York City. – Ed.) with people like Paul – did I become influenced by doing well in school, as a value. And that's when I really accelerated and did very well in school.

LS: At what age did that transition happen, when you started to ...

PA: Junior high school: Finley Junior High School. We were moving in and out of the city, going to different schools, you know. We were getting evicted at one location and relocating back from The Island, back and forth to the city. I encountered the wrestling program at the high school – they had a feeder program at junior high school – and eventually I got into the program of Lou Giani.

So I had a really great experience of working with the true, early, authentic, street graffiti artists; and then I had the opportunity to train in mixed martial arts, in wrestling. That altered and transcended my perceptions, my personal outlook, my existence, and my very being.

LS: Can you describe that transition? Were they two incompatible things? Did one eventually displace the other?

PA: I never saw any differences. They were complementary. To me the opposites reconciled: the arts were very much like wrestling, they were of likeness in form. I never saw them being different at all.

LS: Do you think that means your view of the arts was odd?

PA: Again, that's a subjective criteria. For me, in the arts, the greater the difference, the better.

LS: Did you recognize it as art, even in the beginning, or was it just self-expression?

PA: I think expression in the proper channel is really the important value: expression and individual pursuit. Living with your passions is an important, integral part of self-development.

LS: Can you remember when you didn't have a passion?

PA: Never.

LS: That's interesting. Most people don't have passion.

PA: Without passion, most people lack direction and purpose.

LS: So what was it? Was it the mentorship to these graffiti street artists?

PA: That's right. The mentorship to the individuals, and, mind you, I'm not even discussing the incredible adversarial condition and tragedies that I faced in my upbringing.

LS: What can you say about the family, if it's relevant?

PA: There's so much to discuss in terms of sharing my background... Well, the upbringing was about social services, in and out of foster homes. Catholicism played an important part in the upbringing; there were factors in the church that really affected our development. Eviction notices, electricity being turned off, constantly being relocated. A single, first-generation immigrant mother with kids, a lack of opportunities and forward development, a certain way of being, a lifestyle that was more about not having.

LS: Were you frightened?

PA: Well, you know you live with your fears. You live with the reality of your circumstances. That was the reality, you know, it was just, "Here it goes again."

LS: Did you feel your mother was strong?

PA: She did the best she could, considering her difficulties. It was admirable, but it was a big responsibility trying to transcend the difficult circumstances we faced. She was pretty much abandoned by her family, so we didn't have relatives. We were basically wards of the state, the welfare system, foster care.

That's why people like this, you know, in the wrestling program Lou Giani created... it really maximized the potential of the individual. He really helped out the disadvantaged, the disenfranchised, and the outsiders. I was always surrounded by a group of positive individuals who were trying to better their lives, with the understanding that they were outsiders, were marginals; perennial obstinance.

LS: How do you see this journey that you went through?

PA: I really appreciate it, and I wouldn't change anything, you know, except for the loss of great people in my life, the loss of individuals to insanity, tragedy, and murder. Those are the only things I would change. Abuse: the things that you can affect with some sort of personal change.

But for every time that I look back retrospectively, each of those individuals who provided mentorship in my life directed me to a higher sense of purpose, a greater sense of self, towards destiny.

LS: Can you think of mistakes you made, opportunities you lost?

PA: The one thing that I've learned, through all these great role models, is that the most important thing you have is your ability to change your perceptions – thoughts, feelings – into the positive. If you live in regret, you're not living in the positive, today or tomorrow. So I really don't have any regrets or loss.

Lou Giani's program was very much about working to maximize yourself, your potential self, and I walked away from the program not necessarily achieving great laurels, or great athletic achievement – like a Paul Widerman, who's one of the best people to come out of the program – but I achieved great insight, a great understanding of community, and how role models play an important part in the development of individuals' lives. That insight is something you can never really take away, and that discourse continues with me today, in all of my development, in spite of tragedies. Life teaches us to carry on.

It's very complex, and I'd love to be able to share a little bit about the background in depth as well, which I'd like to do at some time in the future. A lot to share.

LS: What can you say about it now?

PA: It would take more than the session that we're doing now, in terms of all the stories, from the earliest stories of graffiti, to the difficulties of being placed into foster care at a very early age, having my sisters taken away. One is a ward of the state for schizophrenia. Another was raped and became severely clinically depressed. She stopped talking, and she hasn't uttered a word. She hasn't spoken for over 20 years as a result of her tragedy. She actually speaks when there's music; she's able to express herself only in the solace of music.

My work is directed toward having a channel, and those great, formidable mentors. My early life impressions allowed me to find a way to vindicate, or channel my creativity, or my direction, or my commentary.

Working with bands like Rage Against the Machine, doing shows, and having my work become iconoclastic, doing great commentary by projecting images on the cathedral in downtown Los Angeles in defense of those who have been abused by the clergy; making use of political texts and statements, and now creating works of art, which challenges our society by questioning our culture.

LS: Do you think that you're still changing, and do you know how you're changing?

PA: Still changing, but don't know how. I sent you examples of the work which, if you want, we can go back to the room and I can show you more videos, or the album cover that I did about Los Angeles that was distributed all over the world and, as a result of it, I'm getting shows.

LS: I'd like to talk more; I want to squeeze out more "juice." Going to visuals is hard to follow, I mean I can, but in terms of making a text. This is a problem I often have with artists and musicians: neither work verbally. In a sense I'm pushing you through a medium that's not your primary one, so there's resistance. I have to keep pushing for stories, for tales: tales of struggle, and transformation, and passage.

PA: There was one story where I was working with my friend, my graffiti partner. We went out on the double R's – that's the way the trains were known: by their double letters, but now they've become single letters. We were painting the lay-ups in New York City with a couple of graffiti artists: Slip One, BP9.

We were set up that night. When we came back after we were done painting, we came off the railroad tracks, coming down underneath the elevated train station where we were going to exit, but the cops were waiting for us. We'd been set up.

They each tried to grab onto us, and we basically bolted out of there and ran to the next station. Little did we know, the cops had been following us, and they had already caught one of the taggers where they handcuffed him in the restroom. They were waiting for the rest of his crew to show up.

We got to the next station and they were there as well, so we had to keep running to the next elevated station, getting higher and higher, until we got to the Queensboro Plaza. Are you familiar with that station? It's right over Long Island City and its projects. The elevated stations were really tall, they got really, really tall.

I crawled underneath the platform in the station, and that's where I found a whole city of homeless people who were living with couches, like vagabonds, who were actually surviving underneath these subway platforms. Living there. I waited there for a couple of hours, until about four or five in the morning, and then I got out and caught the next train.

Unfortunately the cops had already been notified of my place and location, and they'd already been to my place. But luckily, in this particular instance, my mom was getting evicted. We were relocated to Huntington, Long Island, where I joined the wrestling program, with the great people in that program – like Gadson, Picozzi, Gafney, and Paul Widerman – developed by Lou Giani.

Through these role models, like Paul and Lou, I realized that I could maximize my potential and really do well in school and in my education. When I finally got out of high school I had a 3.46 GPA, and I got an academic scholarship to go to one of the Cal State universities where I inevitably got a degree.

LS: It sounds like that was a surprise to you.

PA: I needed role models. I needed mentors to provide guidance. I didn't have to be the angry chump, you know? I could channel that anger through the arts and through martial arts. It's directed in a manner where it affects: this Phantom Shadow figure – and that's who I'm being interviewed as, as the Phantom Street Artist – the anonymity represents everyone, it's The Everyman.

LS: Is this image you, or is it your alter-you?

PA: The image is me, the image is potential, in a world of images, in the world of ourselves, in the world of projected images, the image is everyone, and it's an archetype in the world of appearance. The shadow figure that comes in and spray paints images on the streets, with social commentary and messages. Here, I'll read it to you:

"I am the Street Phantom; the Street Phantom is the voice of our generation. It is everyone, it is Everyman, and it is the spirit of our time… The Street Phantom uses urban walls as a canvas for commentaries on political and social expression. The Street Phantom is the spokesperson of our time, effecting change through mobilizing individual activism. The artist coins political phrases that reach out to our generation in need of a voice and representation. The elusive street artist comments on our condition by voicing thoughts of a personal, intimate nature that transcends cultural prejudice."

Coming out of the difficult background that we came out of – very difficult to talk about – like we're talking about adversarial situations. It sometimes really affects people, destroys people. Some never make it out of those conditions.

LS: Some say that there's a natural inclination for people to grow and learn, and they'll find the direction they need in whatever environment they find themselves. Some people learn quicker than others. Some people are lucky. But how does a kid know?

PA: The support system is really important. The support system wasn't there for me as a youth, which is why I searched for mentors and was lucky enough to find them. I still use the mentorship process today.

LS: I've looked for mentors too, but generally I have not found them. I do like older people. I sense that a key to finding mentors lies in finding something to respect, and then you can find people who have that thing.

PA: Yeah, there's a meeting ground. And maybe that's it, it's the respectability that develops, that opens the door to teachers. It begins the initiation process, whether they're old or young. Don't you think?

LS: Yeah. My son goes to a school that is laudable in not manipulating at all, but they also don't provide mentors. They feel that kids don't need them. Part of this project, in a sense, is to argue that they do.

PA: My life is a living testimonial. The mentorship process has greatly influenced my life. It provided a respite, a salvation from a broken home that could not offer role models, in a world of contingent values. The relationship with those mentors provided a model for growth and transformation.

LS: A lot of young and angry people strike out against whoever is near them. Why didn't you strike out against those people? How did you recognize them as allies?

PA: I didn't strike out against those individuals because, I think if you really look at it, any kind of adversarial condition has to have an initiation process. Certain initiates are called into that process, and that's when you have to have respectability, and you have to work within a guideline, being chosen as initiates to that development.

LS: Did the people that you worked with know this?

PA: Did they know? No, I don't even think they knew they were creating... does Paul or Lou talk about the initiates, or the initiation? Mysticism, shamanism, those esoteric concepts are very tangible forms in my life today.

I found people that were passionate. I was lucky.

LS: Did you find them, or did they find you? You must have put your hand up, in a sense, saying, "I'll listen," or "I am listening," and they were clever enough to recognize that. Most people don't. Most people are too busy with their program: constructive, destructive, obedient, disobedient, whatever.

PA: I was lucky. When you got into the wrestling program Lou would have people write – he very much pushed self-development – he would have people write about what they thought, what they wanted from the program, what they thought about being in the program. He really got you to reflect and think about it.

LS: What could you say to kids who haven't yet found mentors?

PA: Look for mentors; it's a very simple learning process. Look for the mentors. Channel, find purpose, and look for your destiny. Search for the moment when opportunity will knock on your door. Try to find your place in the world, and make your mark in that world either through accomplishments or through your voice. This gives things value. This is value.

LS: So does that mean that you might tell people, "If you can't find a way to transform yourself, then look to culture and find your reflection in it?"

PA: It's always a question of where we place ourselves, how we're part of the fabric, how we mirror ourselves into culture and society. A great philosopher talked about being engaged in, or becoming part of a cultural discourse. You just hold up a mirror and reflect the culture of the time.

The shamans would go into the caverns of the sick, the lost, and the tragic, where there was a loss of self, a loss of identity. The shamans would carry mirrors around their necks that would provide a reflection, so that people would have a sense of connection, an identification with their own projection.

And the struggle continues. To keep working towards that, day by day. Allow life to be the fabric of a giant, potential canvas: life as theater, to cast ourselves in new roles, to write new stories for ourselves.

3. CRISTA DAHL

History   Late   Born 1934, Seattle, Washington

Crista Dahl is the mother of the partner, of the sister, of a friend, whom I bumped into on one of my trips to Vancouver. I was shocked to learn that when she was young, through complete serendipity, she knew quite well my friend Fred Beckey. There must be a deep reason for this completely implausible connection, but I have yet to find it.

Crista thinks differently. She's intensely visual, nonlinear, and inductive. In her art, her learning, and her teaching she focuses on the relationship between one's body and the world. When speaking she constantly changes tenses, topics, and points of view like a hurried teenager, except that her story always returns to the purpose of her life.

Crista has succeeded in practicing her art in spite of being a frequently impoverished single mom. She succeeded in teaching drug addicts and prostitutes to an unmatched degree, and she is one of the few people to speak directly about the prospect of her own death. There's a genius here, but it's slippery: she doesn't hit you with quotable sound bites, instead you have to reflect on her experience verbally, visually, and viscerally.

Postscript: Although she is not identified in the movie, Crista was Eric Bjornstad's girlfriend during the 1965 events at Ship Rock spire, New Mexico, seen in the 2018 movie *Dirtbag: The Legend of Fred Beckey*. Fred is interviewed in chapter 19.

Excerpts

"You should really pay attention to all of you. That's one of the difficult things with the educational system I think for some people. I've run into some people who are well educated, who have all of that, and have no relationship to their body at all…"

"A lot of my life is controlling myself. Dealing with the brain, I really like my brain. I love my brain because it's so interesting! But it's a concept-a-minute type of thing, and it doesn't seem to slow down. Well no, it doesn't slow down…"

"So the learning thing has always been by experience. Cooking, sewing, anytime I've had a chance to learn something I will learn it. I would rather do dishes than cook. I like to eat, but I don't like to cook. I collect recipes for my friend Franz and he cooks, and I clean up. I just want to eat because food is good. Food and drink is a good thing to do in life. Yeah, good food and talk with friends are probably my favorite things to do. I like that…"

"The biggest regret I have is that I'm going to die! I have a limited amount of time … I would hope I would be able to communicate some of these things that I've done in a better way, and if I do that, that would be nice, it would be really nice. The energy that I have wouldn't be so wasted, as it probably is now…"

"My skills don't have anything to do with tilling the soil, or making a bow and arrow. It has to do with if you're going to learn about this world we live in, this is a possible tool. That's the level I would put my immortality at. If I could add to that: this global thing."

"I am often shocked at the ungrown-upness of these lads and lasses stuffed with useless knowledge. They know a lot; they shine in dialectics; they can quote the classics – but in their outlook on life many of them are infants. For they have been taught to know, but have not been allowed to feel... Their textbooks do not deal with human character, or with love, or with freedom, or with self-determination. And so the system goes on, aiming only at standards of book learning – goes on separating the head from the heart."

— A.S. Neill from *Summerhill: A Radical Approach to Child Rearing*

Interview   Vancouver, Canada, August 2007

Crista Dahl: I've gotten a lot of grants for doing different art projects, and teaching, dealing with information that I have gathered and created activities for people. I've supported my children doing projects related to those things.

It started when I got accepted into the San Francisco Art Institute and couldn't get anybody in my fairly wealthy family to give me the money to go. So I asked a friend of mine and he said, "Well, all we do the first year are the semantics of art." So I began to look at the art books and decided that they weren't very good because what they did was cover from the Fertile Crescent on.

Then I thought I would paint my hands and put them on rocks (laughs), and I would make brushes out of whatever I could find, and so I proceeded doing that.

In the interim the fellow I was living with was drafted, and he didn't want to go. He tried the conscientious objector thing and that didn't work, so we talked about going to Australia, then we decided that there really wasn't enough money to do that.

I tried to get into Canada. They didn't want me: a cocktail waitress who was an artist with four children; we weren't acceptable. So he came up to Canada and got a job, and then I came up with four kids and we got married, and that's him up there (she points to a photo on the wall). I stayed.

I started working with people in the arts here. It was so different and so much more accepting. We ended up in Lund, BC (British Columbia), and I was asked to come and teach the kids art as a parent. And I went, "I don't like teaching kids art. It's just horrid!" Little kids, you know, they do what they want to do. So I just went down there and had them do what I was doing (laughs). That was great fun. We made pots and blew them up, and we did drawings over drawings.

The teacher liked what I was doing so he sent me to his professor at Simon Fraser (University). I went and talked with her, and I took the responsibility of planning a two-day session for training teachers. There was such a reaction that she applied for a Canada Council on the Humanities Grant, she thought what I was doing was incredible.

I caused great chaos at Simon Fraser campus. It was interesting. I got these adults to paint themselves, do all kinds of different things that they hadn't ordinarily done. The pièce de résistance was when I gave them sticks to fight a war (starts laughing) and they attacked another class in the building. And the people in there hid under their desks! It was good fun. The humanities grant was turned down because of my lack of academic training.

That involved me with an art organization called Intermedia, and through them I met an incredible number of women in the arts, which was impossible in the States, just practically impossible. This was really, really difficult. The classic response when I tried to get someone to handle my paintings – which took me three months to do, working with my kids and everything, I couldn't do it any faster – was, "Sorry, Crista. It's too bad you're a woman, but collectors don't buy women."

I'm taking computer lessons now. I'm going to start on a regular basis, because all this stuff isn't really out there. It's just more or less in my head.

So I did "Before People," and then I did "First People," and then "Civilization," and then "Now and Future." I would have four workshops that I would do in one day – two in the morning and two in the afternoon – there was a lot of hands-on stuff.

I had a whole series of grants from the Canadian government, even though I was a landed immigrant, to do the same sort of stuff. The reception was just incredibly good. I had lots of press, national television special, and I was making money on a regular basis, enough to support myself and the kids.

When my kids got to be teenagers – because I'd read *Summerhill* (*Summerhill, A New View of Childhood* by A.S. Neill, published in 1960. – Ed.) – they were all doing their own thing. The youngest one was looking like the most outrageous hippie you've ever seen in your life: beads, headband, doing too much dope for his age, that's for sure. One of them had mice and marijuana in the shed on the roof and was playing The Kinks full blast (laughs), another one was listening to Barbra Streisand. The oldest one was the most conservative and was playing "Greensleeves."

Poor John just couldn't deal with it anymore. So he moved into the… I had a little studio downtown, so he moved into that. And then he got a bigger one, and it got to the point where, "Do you want to spend time with me down here?" Well, I couldn't, you know I had four teenagers… it was kind of a choice I had to make, I didn't want to make, but I did. And eventually John went back to the States, and the kids managed to get through all of that, without it doing horrendous damage.

Then I got interested in clay as a mechanism to teach. I developed something where you went through history starting out with the Leatoli Beds, you know the footprints went across (The Laetoli fossil beds, in Africa's Rift Valley, preserve hominid footprints that are at least 3.6 million years old and are some of the oldest evidence known for upright bipedal walking. – Ed.), and I would have them press their hands on the clay. And it ended up going through various states showing the history of the world, and learning clay techniques at the same time. Not aiming at making anything, just working on a square piece – I wasn't interested in them making anything – I was wanting them to learn something about… that's the learning thing.

So in a funny way you were talking about learning stuff. I've learned by teaching… a lot about the world.

I've kept expanding this thing I call "Create Dino Flo." That means "creates Dinosaurs and flowers." And then "Prime," that's us, and "Gathr," that's us, "Sound," that's where we first start to get into the vocal stuff, as they can tell by the structures in the throat, and then "Bury," the first burials. They're still Neanderthals at that point.

Then comes "Mark," that's farm: marking things and farming, which is pretty much mixed food gathering, and then "War," "Peace," and it says "Real," but I first said "Being Here" and I'm happy with that … and then "Gran," "Para," and "Child," and that's just our grandparents, and us as children to come.

Then you go on to Nam, Ceca, Sam, Eura, Naf, Saf, Noca, Swas, Sas, Neas, Eas, Seas, Oce, Auspo, and Uni. All of this is based on digits. Because of my learning disability, I have always used my hands to count, one way or the other. And I figure, "Well, I'll transfer this." I just kept doing stuff dealing with this, and that's kind of where I'm at still.

The people at the Video Inn accepted Nam-Ceca-Sam, and we wrote letters to everybody in the world. We started a tabloid, and we had international information, and that's still what I'm doing. And some of that early stuff now I'm beginning to realize is probably valid. I'm just putting it together on the computer, so I'm facing the computer. I've had two computers, but I've never really been adept at the computers.

LS: Are you still intimidated, or are you excited by the prospect?

CD: Well, I'm just accepting the fact that I have… I don't think I've ever been intimidated, but my sense of it is that I couldn't get anybody to help me go through the processes so I could do something with the damn thing. Why waste my time if I can't do anything!

I took a course on the digital camera, because I realized I wasn't really using it, and the person that taught the course… I did two, three-hour sessions with him, and I learned. So I've done a couple of sessions with him, and he doesn't talk. He just does something and then, "Your turn." He was nonverbal in his teaching, and I was able to absorb that.

So I'm off and running: I'm moving pictures around, and I'm taking them off my camera and getting them out of my camera, and moving them from file to file. I already had a lot of stuff; I've always tended to use a camera. That's going to allow me to take a lot of the drawings that I did with the clay stuff and test it out in Vancouver. And then when I get a couple of things together, I'll send it all to anybody who does educational stuff and see if somebody will bite.

Then I became involved with an alternative school. I taught there one day a week. I lived there, went and took some media students to Europe, hung around for a while, and then fell in love with an African, a South African Jewish fellow. We almost got married. I went down there to get married. Let me tell you... South Africa, Cape Town: not a chance. I would have been arrested. I kept doing the wrong thing, all the time, and I didn't like their attitudes.

LS: What did you do, for example?

CD: I'd want to go into the wrong bathroom. I'd get on the wrong bus. I'd go to the wrong counter. I'd say the wrong things. I didn't fit. Not a chance, not a chance. I just got angrier and angrier. I would have ended up there with Nelson Mandela (laughs).

The pièce de résistance was when we forgot our shoes and went to some place where blacks were allowed to go, and I had to pee, and I had burned my feet to go where I could pee. Right in front of the car was a tin shack, but I had to go to this fancy stone thing down the way. I just... I left Cape Town twice. The third time I left for good. God, it was just horrendous. Love isn't everything, it really isn't (laughs).

I'm quite intense about people learning by doing things. I'm very frightened of the educational system that seems to have gotten rid of a lot of physical activity because I think there's a lot of creative people like me who can't be still most of the time. It's kind of frustrating. It really is frustrating.

I worry about the stuff designed by people who haven't moved around a lot, who design things for other people to use, because I think you have to – and this is the mind/body thing, and understand processes leverage, you know, what happens, power of whatever's – I think you have to have a sense of body/mind. Otherwise I think there's a great possibility of faulty design.

I probably would have been a good architect, but I'm not... an architect. And I probably would have been a good painter, but I haven't had enough time. So mostly what I do is concept and performance, and that seems to fit. That is what I'm doing now.

The stuff I do is "in your face," like I did a performance with a noose around my neck, with 13 things hanging there. I was sitting there and projected on the wall was a series of international headlines, just about 10 by 5, something like that, a big thing in a dark room. I called it "News Noose" (laughs). I liked it, other people did too.

I recently did a thing on John Cage where we went to three neighborhoods and we took different things. In one we went with a cart of toys and food implements and what have you, and then with business stuff in the financial district. We went and tried to get people to make sounds. We drew chalk all over hell (laughs).

LS: Tell me about when you were young, and how you learned about your own learning process?

CD: (Laughs) Well...(sighs)... I think I wasn't aware I... hmm. I just was very busy doing things. I had all of my friends, we were digging to China, and we made a huge hole in my parents' backyard (laughs). We had great fun doing that. I think I was about three.

In kindergarten I couldn't understand why everybody was drawing sticks for people. I had a horrible time in school. I got into an argument with my kindergarten teacher about not being able to play in the boys' sandbox. I shook my finger at her and told her it was wrong (laughs). I didn't like girls' toys particularly at all. So there was a compromise: I got to play with the boys' blocks, so I didn't have to go into the little house.

Reading was difficult. It was very hard for me to learn to read. They started phonics: Dick and Jane and Spot. I can see the pictures, but all I did was listen to what everybody else was doing and said what they said, as close as I could get to it. At the end of the first grade they realized that I wasn't reading. So the principal gave my mother books, and my mother taught me to read. That was a blessing.

I can't do math. Had I run around the block saying "six times seven" it might have sunk in a bit, but it doesn't work. I can't count sheep, they start coming over too fast. I can't slow my mind down to see it, or what have you, so I count on my fingers. But I can understand large numbers; I know what a million people are.

My learning is simply by experience, along with how you said most other people learn. School... I was enthusiastic, very enthusiastic, but when it came to the tests it was extremely difficult, even at university it was difficult. God, I wrote down – because I do funny things with numbers – so I wrote down the wrong time for a test. I turned up at three o'clock instead of 8 in the morning, and the guy wouldn't give me a grade. I had to fight, you know? He still gave me an incomplete. That's all I could talk him into; he was an old codger. I had definitely done really good work, and I would have done really well on his test.

Another one I had to, umm... son of a bitch... I got all dressed up in my most expensive clothes and I had to go in to say, "Look, you gave us a test that was not what we expected" – he'd sent his wife – and it was a date test. I can't remember dates, for crying out loud! And I talked him into giving me a grade by batting my eyes at him: a disgusting thing to have to do, but I needed the grade, and I knew he was susceptible to that (laughs). So, school was not fun. Not fun. My grades are interesting: I would get A's and D's, and E's, which were incompletes.

I had to take algebra over, twice. I barely made it through geometry. Foreign language was just impossible, because I had to learn the different parts of speech, and that's just like math. History was good. Architecture was good, because I could draw. That's kind of where I was at.

So the learning thing has always been by experience. Cooking, sewing, anytime I've had a chance to learn something I will learn it. I would rather do dishes than cook. I like to eat, but I don't like to cook. I collect recipes for my friend Franz and he cooks, and I clean up. I just want to eat (laughs), because food is good. Food and drink is a good thing to do in life. Yeah, good food and talk with friends are probably my favorite things to do. I like that.

LS: What age people have you been teaching recently?

CD: What I'm doing now, I'm acting as a mentor at an art organization, and they're in their 20's and 30's. I got a $25,000 grant to work with these young male and female prostitutes. It didn't take me long to figure out that these kids had had all the art experiences that anybody could ever have. They had also been taken to everything and done absolutely everything. They didn't have birth certificates. They had no health records. They had nothing.

Many of the groups that have worked with kids in the early part of the century were churches. And they set up a system where, it was secretive, you know – now they call it "people's privacy" – so you're plunked with this kid who has multiple problems and no information, and you're supposed to entertain them? Well, that's not what they need, and especially if they're fetal alcohol.

Have you ever seen pictures of fetal alcohol brains? Ugh, God! It's like slabs of liver! The worst fetal alcohol, it doesn't look like a cauliflower, it's liver slabs; they're so damaged. They have no sense of time, they have no sense of when to eat, and without those two things you can't get anyplace on time. You can't hold a job, you can't do anything, and they're like that for the rest of their life. Your brain is deformed. And a lot of the kids we had were native, and were fetal alcohol, it's degrees, like anything else.

Those were the kinds of things I was really concerned about, but I ended up having to do a questionnaire, so this is what I did: I put together a bunch of questions and it had to do with my action with the green stuff on here (Referring to "Create Dino Flo." – Ed.). I did the best I could, but I wasn't… it was only recently that I began to understand what I wanted to do in that area. More self-expression, more following one's bliss to what one does in life.

The problem I ran into is that I made it so that the kids could respond to it – you notice the big print, all of that stuff – and the kids would go through it, but the adults still wouldn't do the stuff that the kids wanted to have done.

What happened was they got the contract to do … for a school for kids. It was called ICCR, Intensive Child Care Resource. We ended up with three people – a teacher, and two social workers – just a couple of very creative people who were very good with kids – and got them a bus, and changed the whole thing around. We ended up with 30 students that were getting high school diplomas, with these difficult kids. And we were using that as a base.

So we had one person running the place and coordinating everything. And the other person going out and getting all this stuff and doing the art projects when they weren't doing school. And it was set up for them to pick, so they had three stages at the end; they could choose between 15 things they wanted to have happen.

But you know, it was just… my classic example was this jerk that was running… I mean he was a nice man but he… So this guy that was running the place actually had a friend who worked with wood, but he could never put the 2 and 2 together; even when you told him, he never would hear anything. Then we started getting ADD kids, who were refusing to take any more Ritalin, and they were different.

Then the government changed. They got rid of the school because it cost too much. It was working, but that didn't matter to them. You know there's this movement to put every kid back in a… you know: group homes don't work. Well, they work for some kids, in fact that's the only place you can put some kids. You can't put them into a family situation, they're just… they could crowbar you in the middle of the night. It's not safe for them, and it's not safe for you.

To make a long story short, I want to redo that, and I would put an enormous amount into the sorts of things that people with problems might actually be able to do. They're often creative, good cooks, they can do some things.

At this point what I would like to do is put more creative things, more expressive things in this, as opposed to gearing them all towards getting a job, which is what they want. There are really a lot of kids that could do a lot better. That's one of the major things I'd like to do before I die: take some of the stuff I've done in the past, put it into a format for people to use who have a hard time teaching difficult kids. Because my work works with difficult kids.

LS: What would you tell "normal" kids, if there is such a thing, about how they should navigate?

CD: Continue to do the things that you do well, but don't forget to use your body. Don't forget to look for what you really like to do. It's the same Joseph Campbell "follow your bliss" thing.

You should really pay attention to all of you. That's one of the difficult things with the educational system I think for some people. I've run into some people who are well educated, who have all of that, and have no relationship to their body at all.

The communication thing has been difficult for me, actually. I had a lot of testing done and I had lesions. I went to a psychiatrist about some of the problems I had, and I did also some testing when I went to university at UBC (University of British Columbia), and their response was – I got a letter saying (laughs) – that I'm an average dyslexic boy! And I have the paper proving it (laughs), which I think is very funny.

LS: You seem to be very independent. Is there a regret for being so independent?

CD: Well, that's interesting. I'm out of synch, I might have said that before, the common response of my children, after all is said and done, is: I'm weird. They all love me, in their own way. I'm hard to be around. Regrets...

LS: I don't mean to put words in your mouth...

CD: No, no. Because you do ask yourself these kinds of things. I'm always, "Well, what do I do now?" A lot of my life is controlling myself. Dealing with the brain, I really like my brain. I love my brain (laughs) because it's so interesting! But it's a concept-a-minute type of thing, and it doesn't seem to slow down. Well, no, it doesn't slow down.

The biggest regret I have is that I'm going to die! I have a limited amount of time (laughs). So, seriously, that's my biggest regret. I would hope I would be able to communicate some of these things that I've done in a better way, and if I do that, that would be nice, it would be really nice. The energy that I have wouldn't be so wasted, as it probably is now.

LS: So just like everyone else, you want immortality.

CD: (Laughs) Absolutely! Yeah... yes, I think you're absolutely right... yes, it's the pecking order in the tribe, that's what it's about (laughs). I think it's that simple.

It's the same with my own artwork. I would say my skills don't have anything to do with tilling the soil, or making a bow and arrow; it has to do with if you're going to learn about this world we live in, this is a possible tool. That's the level I would put my immortality at. If I could add to that: this global thing.

BIOLOGY

4. SONYA PETERS

History Early Born 1990, Riverdale, New York

Sonya Peters has tried every kind of schooling, from rigid Christian programs to unstructured free schools, tutors, and home schooling, but none have suited her. She suffers wide mood swings, sometimes being interested in everything, and at other times being totally uninterested and avoiding school entirely. When she's up she's unstoppable, and when she's down she's unstartable. This has made progress difficult.

Sonya sets high goals, she's smart, and she's realistic, but she moves to a rhythm that seems to conflict with every program she's tried. How does such a person get what they need? Does one really need a teacher, a program, or a school? And what if you're fully able, but entirely different? Given the obstacles that confront her, how can she succeed? Given her drive and abilities, she's bound to find success somewhere.

Excerpts

"When I was at Sudbury I would sit there going, 'Oh, there's a black spot on a white wall.' I'm staring at the white wall because there's nothing else to do. There were things to do, but I was too lazy to do them. I didn't have any interests other than animals. That was pretty cut and dry: if it has hair I like it; if it has scales I like it; if it has slime I like it… but if it's a person I don't like it. Those were my interests…"

"I didn't have interest until I left Sudbury, which is kind of weird because I'd say, 'I'm bored, there's nothing to do here. I'm bored, I'm bored, I'm bored.' Then I got home and immediately it kicked into overdrive. I got interested in solar energy, sustainable living techniques, farming, agriculture, other woodsy survival stuff…"

"It came with the realization that I could actually get something that I wanted. That I could actually learn something. 'Oh, you can sit down, and you can read this book, and you can learn it, learn what's inside.' When before I thought you needed a teacher to teach you everything…"

"I feel that one of my greatest achievements was something I said to my mom. I said to her, 'Mom, Sudbury broke my mind. I'm a free thinker now. Look at me, I'm a free thinker!'"

"Awareness is not something that just happens to us. It is a decision we must make."

— Rachel Pollock, from *The Body of the Goddess, Sacred Wisdom in Myth, Landscape and Culture*

Interview Saugerties, New York, November 2006

Sonya Peters: I started school at Cahill Elementary School in Saugerties when I was five. I was in grade school all the way to sixth grade. I was never able to stick with the structure of elementary school. Ever since kindergarten, I skipped half the school year (laughs). Monday, Wednesday, and Friday I might go to school, but Tuesday and Thursday I wouldn't.

LS: How did you get out of it?

SP: In kindergarten I was too tired to go to school and I'd sleep while being dragged down to the car or up to the bus stop, and the bus driver wouldn't take a sleeping child on the bus. In second grade I got stomach aches. The stomach aches lasted from second grade to fourth grade. And from fourth grade to sixth grade I got headaches. Somewhere in there the stomach aches would start in school and I'd go to the nurse's office, and I'd leave school that way. A lot of grade school was really spent trying to get out.

At the end of sixth grade I basically just lost it and left school, and tried to get to seventh grade. Did two weeks of seventh grade; I was enrolled for two weeks but went to school for three days (laughs). Junior High wasn't for me. Then I went to Sudbury (Hudson Valley Sudbury School – Ed.), two weeks after they first opened. I curled up on a chair and would go to sleep every day. And then they closed. And that was Sudbury!

LS: What did you get out of it?

SP: Out of the first year? Nothing. It was just a bunch of screaming kids. Actually, what I got out of that was, by the end of it there were lots of bicker battles between the staff and the parents. The parents and the staff thought they knew how the school should go and what the school was good for, and they weren't listening to the kids at all.

And these were our school meetings, they weren't their school meetings. I sat through every one of those meetings completely silent, and near the very last meeting I said, "Shut up! This is my school meeting, not your school meeting. Stop fighting. Just stop. It's not getting us anywhere." That was one of the last school meetings before the school fell apart.

After that I home-schooled – or unschooled, or whatever you call it – with Ruth (Ruth was a staff member at the Sudbury School and a former teacher. – Ed.). I went to her house every day and walked on the ice – she had a little creek by her house – and looked at the dead frogs underneath the ice (laughs). When March came we walked through the creek barefoot and felt like our feet were going to fall off because it was real cold. We ran around in the woods a lot. That's what I did.

We tried to breed mice to find out the genetics of how mixing different colored mice would give different colored babies (laughs). I didn't actually carry it through because I should have made charts and done all that stuff, but I was more interested in the baby mice. She bred snakes, and I was interested in the snakes eating the baby mice. There were cats, snakes, and mice, which kept me interested.

Then Sudbury started up again. I was 13 or 14, and I did some of the work to try to get the school going again, and I learned a lot about what we were doing. I was with the process the whole time, trying to get the school going again. I saw the new building being built. The school finally opened, and I was one of five or so kids who carried over from their first year.

School started in the spring, and then it closed for the summer after a month. I went the next year and was there for a year. But even at Sudbury I had attendance problems like, "I don't feel like going. I can learn more at home." I was constantly struggling with trying to do the structured public school thing.

I wanted to do math. I wanted to sit down with a math book and do math. I wanted to learn… whatever. I mean I didn't understand the Sudbury approach. I was confused, very confused.

LS: Can you summarize the Sudbury approach?

SP: The Sudbury approach was take a bunch of kids, stick them in a building, give them some books and some computers and some friends, and they'll figure it out. They'll figure it out. So what am I supposed to be figuring out?

I read a lot about vampires (laughs)… I lay around a lot and thought about things. Watched how the little kids played together and thought about communication between human beings and children. Watched the little kids bicker and develop in different ways. "She stole my toy," and "She didn't share her lunch with so-and-so." That was mostly what I did: communication skills. But I never understood what I was supposed to be learning.

I thought learning was ABC, English, Science, Social Studies, and so on. I didn't feel like I was getting that. Especially because I entered that school saying, "I'm going to be here a year, then I'm going to leave and go to the community college. Go to community college for two years and then leave with an associates degree at the age of 18. Be well on my way to success and go to a four-year college for the last two years, get a bachelors, and then head on to veterinary school. That didn't work (laughs)! Didn't work as planned.

I thought Sudbury was going to prepare me for Ulster Community College but it didn't. I wanted to sit down and do work. Sudbury's idea of work was something else. The system was all confused.

I stayed there another half a year and they gave me a notice that said, "You've missed 40% of the school year," and it was January or something like that, so I missed a lot of school. I said, "OK, well, Mom, either you let me leave school, or I just don't go any more and the school just kicks me out!" (Laughs) She said, "OK, you can leave school."

I left school and was home-schooled for the remainder of the year. So really, up to this point, it's been complete mush of home-schooling, and unschooling, and Sudbury schooling. It was horrible.

LS: What happened when you got out of Sudbury and went home?

SP: I just sat around and just tried to recover. I didn't have Ruth because she was working. I think I actually started playing an online video game and I didn't stop for six months. I just played on the computer. Made some good friends, that was my social group thing. My day was go to sleep at 6am, wake up at 6pm, get on the computer, stay online, go to sleep at 6am. Avoid family. That was my education for the rest of my 10th grade year.

LS: What did you get out of that, anything that people might not recognize?

SP: Socially it was very unique because you can make lots of friends, even though it's cyber all over the Internet, all text messaging and stuff. I made some really great friends, and I'd talk to people from Germany and Austria and England, Indonesia, and a really good friend from Malaysia. I ended up going on-line trying to find out what language they spoke in Malaysia.

She'd tell me, "Oh, I speak English!"

"But you're on the other side of the world! You're not supposed to speak English!"

So we talked a lot over Skype while playing the game. We'd play the game and we'd talk. It was like a party except everyone was there all the time, and you can kill them at any time by just pulling the plug (laughs)!

Then Mom said, "You have to start doing school again if you want to become a vet." So at the beginning of this year I found a private, very, very traditional German school that has 48 kids in total and is run by the Bruderhof community.

So I go from hippie kids at Sudbury, who are running around playing Digimon and Magic cards – I don't know what all they did, the little ones always had something they were doing – to this classroom full of all these Christian kids. Very Christian kids. And their views are, "Got to get an A, got to get an A, got to get an A." I went from really relaxed to perfectionistic: "You've got to do it this way."

I'm very attuned to people's facial features and stuff, like when they're talking and expressing emotion. And some of these kids would be so full of anguish when they looked at their paper that you could tell it wasn't an A. It could have been a B, but it wasn't an A. Something about being in this environment was frustrating, to say the least.

Here I am. I haven't done any school for four years. Haven't done any math – I'm doing pre-algebra right now – and I've got these dreams of vet school. You've got to do calculus to get into vet school, to even contemplate getting into vet school. So I'm in pre-algebra, I'm planning on going to college in a year and a half, and how am I ever going to catch up?

I'm in this school with a bunch of kids who are overachievers, who have been told what their careers are going to be – they didn't even choose them – they've been told what they're going to be, and they've got to work towards it.

A girl in my class was told she's going to be a nurse. She's 15 years old. I'm actually placed in the 10th grade class, although I'm an 11th grader, because it's very accelerated. And the 10th and 11th graders are together for most of the stuff, except for the sciences. So this friend works toward being a nurse. She never said she wants to be a nurse, but she's now working toward doing something because that's what she's expected to do.

LS: This is the way the Bruderhof Community works, right?

SP: Right, because you can't have everybody wanting to be doctors and nobody wanting to be plumbers. So they spread it out a little bit.

LS: They're expecting these people to stay in their community, so they're telling their members to train for the skills their community will need.

SP: So that was different. I mean here I am with dreams to be something big, something wonderful. It's my dream, and I work toward my dream. And here are these kids who are pounding away at the books trying to get A's for dreams that are not even their dreams. And I'm sitting there feeling… like… I've been dreaming my dream for eight years, since I was nine years old, and working toward it since I was nine years old.

It's just frustrating, really frustrating, to be in this environment where you're told, "This is how it works. You get the A's here, here, here, and here. Study for Regents. Study for the SATs. Memorize these words for the SATs." It's a world of tests and numbers and letters and it makes your head spin (laughs)… really, really bad.

I went to school there for two months and all of a sudden started becoming absent again: absent through elementary school, absent through Sudbury, and now I'm absent from this traditional school. I actually skipped school today, and yesterday, and the day before.

LS: Are you in control of this, or not?

SP: I, uh, I… half, only half. I don't know. Even when you have this dream, even when you have something that you really want to do, I feel like there's some stuff you can't control.

Sometimes I get really depressed because things aren't working the way I want them to. And at a certain level of being depressed I go online and look at colleges. I don't know why, but something says that if I look at colleges enough, then I'll be motivated to do the work to get to the college. It's not like I don't want to get there already, but I'm trying to find a motivation that actually makes me want to do the work.

My newest plan is, "Mom, if I go to school until February, then will you send me to South America?" Because I found a three-month high school program in South America for girls. You send your girl away to high school, and then you have to wake up and go to school, whether you like it or not, because you're in South America. And school's on top of mountains, so it's different than sitting in a classroom. I felt like that might be the middle ground between Sudbury, where there's no structure, and the Bruderhof school, which has a lot of structure. Somewhere in there I think I'm going to figure it out so that I can become a vet. I don't know how (laughs)! I'm working on it.

LS: What was it that you wanted to learn when you were nine that you still can see?

SP: I remember that I wanted to be a doctor because a doctor was looked upon as the highest profession you could be, even though it's not the richest. Other people would say, "I want to be a doctor when I grow up." But I wanted say, "Yeah, but I really am going to be a doctor when I grow up!" I felt like I was smart enough to do it and had enough will power to do it.

Then I decided that people complain too much (laughs), and I found out that I like fuzzy things more than people. So I fell in love with critters and decided I wanted to be an animal doctor.

I think it has to do with the cute factor: hamsters are cuter than people, puppies are cuter, horses are cuter (laughs). I also think there's less stress with operating on someone's cat than operating on someone. If you accidentally kill the cat, you didn't kill a human being, you just killed a cat, which is also bad but it's less stressful.

Just recently I got interested in psychiatry, watching a psychiatrist for a while, but then decided people complain too much.

LS: What pulled you into that?

SP: Lots and lots of experience with mental illness in sixth grade.

LS: So you got interested in people again?

SP: Yeah, to understand people only in order to understand myself more. I felt like maybe it was a secret puzzle and that it would help me unlock the problems that I had myself because I decided the attendance issue was really something else. First I decided I was interested in psychiatry, and then decided it wasn't for me.

I've always been interested in health and health sciences. I've been trying to convince my mom to let me become an EMT last year because there was a course to become an EMT in one semester that met every Saturday. One day a week. I said to myself, "I can do this, I can get to school one day a week." The problem is the class met from 9am to 5pm. I can do this, I can be an EMT. That's awesome! I don't know why I want to be an EMT, but why not? But I couldn't because I had to be 18 or older. So that kind of killed that inspiration. I'm still thinking about it because then I could work for Wayfinder as their wellness person.

LS: Tell me about Wayfinder.

SP: Wayfinder is a live-action role-playing camp for kids ages 6 to 19. You run around in the woods with swords and fairy wings, and it's fun. More than that, it's a community of friends. We have workshops that cover issues like trust and status and improv.

You take a kid with very little self-esteem who's giving off the "I'm shy" thing, and you teach him how to trust other people, how to read what other people are doing, and to know why people seem to have higher status than him. You teach him how to look big, how to feel big, and how to speak big for improv, then all of a sudden you've turned a kid with very low self-esteem into a kid that actually feels good about living. That's what I first got out of it: friends and becoming a person that at least pretends to be big and tough.

After that I got into story writing, writing the adventure games. That was my home-schooling for a while: it took me six months to write an adventure game based on a dream. I put it on as a production for 80 people. It was amazing, and I won awards through Wayfinder.

I almost got "Best Story of the Year," which is impressive because there are, like, 20 stories. This was my first story. I got "Best New Story Writer," which I gave up immediately to my friend so we could share it because we were both new storywriters. And "Best Story Concept," which made me feel good.

That was my home-schooling. My mom says, "You did do stuff when you home-schooled!"

"No, I just laid around."

"No," she said. "You did do stuff!"

LS: So she was supportive? Most mothers wouldn't have let you do even a small portion of what you've done. What is your attitude toward being a woman with regard to the programs you've been in? I'm wondering why you were interested in this all-girls South American high school program.

SP: Well, it was the only program I could find. I've also looked into women's programs. I've looked at a college that's only for women because for some reason I felt like being in an all-women's college would make all the other factors less, because guys are stressful. I haven't really gotten involved with many, but the ones I got involved with made my life really stressful. So I said, "Maybe if they don't exist! Maybe if they only exist off-campus."

But I connect with guys more, most of the time, as friends. So I don't know if I'd be able to deal with only interacting with women. It would be kind of traumatizing to my whole life.

LS: So what's your attitude about stress? You didn't really say it, but it seems that stress is a thread that runs through what you said. I mean with headaches and stomach aches, the whining of people and the cuddliness of animals, and the contrast between the high- and low-pressure schools. How do you deal with your own stress?

SP: Well, I'm going to bring this into an area that I call dissection, because that's what I've been calling it for the last while. At the end of sixth grade I was diagnosed with bipolar disorder, which lots of people have been diagnosed with. So I was 12 years old being diagnosed with a disorder that usually doesn't appear in people until they're 18 or 19.

There's a famous psychiatrist named K. Redfield Jameson, and she got through graduate school and wrote a book on bipolar disorder, and mostly it was coming from studying herself, which I thought was kind of interesting.

So I started relating the manic-depressive spikes with the way I learned and found that in the beginning of the school year – September, October, November – I'd go way up. So during September, October, November I'd do really well in school. Get lots of A's.

End of November stop going to school, stop getting A's, everything goes down. November, December, January everything is down, down, down. Also known as "seasonal affective disorder," so when it gets dark, I get sad.

January, February, March everything is heading back up. April, May, June I'm getting A's, A's, A's, A's. The beginning and the end of the school year is lots of A's.

On top of that, when I'm manic – when I'm really happy and really into learning – I can turn out amazing stories, amazing papers, everything. I read stuff online, do lots of research online, and do 20 times what a normal human should be doing at my age academically. But when I get depressed I stop doing everything completely.

So I've decided the days I miss are days when I'm depressed, and if I sat in school I wouldn't be able to do anything anyways. And the days I'm not depressed I actually go to school. And the days I'm manic I'm too busy thinking about wanting to go outside and look at blades of grass, rather than sitting in a room looking at a chalk board.

I like dissecting problems of interest. The problem with schools is that they say, "Here, taste this! Taste this! OK, I'm going to take that away now and give you something else." Like, "We're going to learn really minor things about the heart. Now we're taking that away and we're going to learn about the lung…" But I say, "The heart's interesting! I'm interested in the heart. I don't want to learn about the lung!" What's with this? I'm still stuck on the heart!

I found that I can learn in a structured environment if a teacher says, "This week we'll learn about the stuff in this chapter. This chapter is called 'The Heart' ". And then I leave and – in my own time – I dissect that. I go online and read about it. I find out what a blood vessel is, for example. I find out that I don't know what blood is, so I find out what blood is. I find out that there are white blood cells and red blood cells. I go all the way down, like a tree's roots, until I can understand what the word "heart" means, what that subject is.

That's the way that I took Sudbury and traditional school and put them together. I say, "OK, you tell me what I have to study so that I don't go and look at blades of grass all day, because I will (laughs)! Tell me to learn about some particular thing and I'll go and learn about it. Then I'll get back to you by the end of the week so that you can give me something else." But I can't have you tell me what to learn, because if I'm stuck thinking about something over there, then I can't learn more over here.

I've got a love/hate relationship with math. I love it when I can sit down and do it and understand it. I hate it when someone is trying to teach me and I'm not understanding what they're saying.

LS: How about when you're trying to understand something on your own and you can't understand it?

SP: Then I usually close the book, walk away, turn around, walk back, open the book and try again (laughs)! That's what I've been doing teaching myself pre-algebra. I'm saying to myself, "I don't want to sit in a classroom and learn this material one chapter at a time!" So I said to myself, "I'm going to finish this in two weeks." I sat down, and I've been doing five chapters a day. I'm trying to finish this one book, and I've 12 days left. I need to catch up (laughs)!

If I can do this, then I can do algebra by the end of this year, and then I'll be ready for Algebra-2 for 12th grade. The other idea is taking community college evening classes in basic algebra so I can catch up, and intermediate algebra over the summer. Math is an issue for me right now. I don't care about anything else. I can understand the science, I'm good at writing, I learned those naturally.

Math is the one place where I feel like Sudbury betrayed me, and traditional school is just making me mad.

LS: How do you feel like you're progressing?

SP: It depends on the day of the week. It's hard – it's always hard – but not hard because the material's hard. It's hard because I have to sit down and do it. I'm an ideas person. I'm not the one who does something with the ideas. I come up with the ideas, then you do it.

I once found a math book that I could understand, and I fell so much in love with it that I was in tears by the end of the week, because I understood! It was *The Algebra Survival Guide*. It's in the Sudbury library, but it's falling apart because I had it out from the library for seven months (laughs)!

I can't understand the numbers I need a calculator – and it's not like I didn't drill on the multiplication tables since I was in third grade. Even doing the flash cards and stuff, I'm just not a doing-the-multiplication-tables kind of person.

I think what I'm going to find when I start learning algebra is that all of my number problems will disappear. People who are good at math because they understand the numbers go to algebra and find they suck. I did the math, I could do the math, I just wasn't good with the numbers. I feel like when I go to algebra, because my mind is set up a different way, maybe it will click. That's my hope!

LS: You mean you do badly when you have to solve a problem?

SP: Right, but I can tell you how to solve the problem. I could tell you how to set up the problem and then say, "Now you do the math. You add the numbers."

What happens in school is that they throw something at you, it dangles in space, and they say, "Now I want you to stand here and throw stuff at this subject until it makes sense." They just keep adding stuff onto that glowing orb until, all of a sudden, you just understand because there's just so many things attached to the same area.

I'm just now understanding the idea of biology being different than ecology, or geology, or geography. All these different things, they just didn't make sense before. I just thought, "Science, frogs, and rocks: they can go over there." Now I understand that the study of what's inside a frog is different than the study of rocks, or the study of mixing things together and having big explosions happen (laughs)! That's a part of school I never got. I found that what I need is a teacher to say, "Chapter 1: cells. Lesson A: the nucleus. Then within that whatever, whatever, whatever… any information they want to have about the nucleus. For me to understand stuff it has to be written flat out. Or if they say, "We're going to look at things in this woods…" OK, then go (laughs)! We'll come back and talk about it later.

LS: It sounds like you're talking about context: things and how they relate to each other. They need to have relations or…

SP: … it just doesn't click.

LS: What have you done that you think was really successful. What would you tell other kids to do or not to do?

SP: Hmmm. I guess it really depends on the kid. I feel that one of my greatest achievements was something I said to my mom. I said to her, "Mom, Sudbury broke my mind. I'm a free thinker now. Look at me, I'm a free thinker!" And she said, "Yes, so?" And I said, "Exactly!"

I don't have to go to school. I feel that I can learn more outside of school. I feel that I can follow through with my thoughts and line my life up. And guess what? My friend at the Bruderhof, she wouldn't be able to do any of that because she can only do what's in the textbook. She can't learn what's outside of the textbook.

You could give me a subject, and I could go online, and I'd come back to you in an hour and say this is what I've learned, this is what's important. I'm not very good at taking notes from what someone else is saying, but Sudbury gave me the freedom of being able to pick and choose what I need, what I want to learn, putting it all together. I think that's what lots of kids don't have.

LS: How did they do that, or how did you do that, or what did that?

SP: I'd say things like, "I want to know about this. I don't know anything about that. Well, where can I find out about it? The library!" OK, I'll go to the library, or I'll go on the Internet (laughs)! Really you should learn to research at the library, which I need to do next.

People say, "I can't get Google to give me the right results." That's the first thing I learned: if I want to know something particular, then find out how Google will give me the right results. And I learned that, and now I can find things on Google faster than most people.

LS: But what came first? It's kind of a chicken and the egg problem because first you had to have an interest before you went out to look for other interesting things. How did you develop your interest? There are a lot of kids in Sudbury who don't seem to have interest, and they just play video games all day.

SP: I didn't have interest until I left Sudbury, which is kind of weird because I'd say, "I'm bored, there's nothing to do here. I'm bored, I'm bored, I'm bored." Then I got home and immediately it kicked into overdrive. I got interested in solar energy, sustainable living techniques, farming, agriculture, other woodsy survival stuff. I got involved in dog training, search and rescue, service dogs, and police work for no apparent reason other than they have horses (laughs)!

I was actually listing off all the career choices to a friend online and he went, "EMT! I thought you wanted to be a veterinarian!"

Well, I was like, "I either want to be an EMT, or a police officer with a canine unit, or a mounted police officer on a horse, or a search and rescue unit, or a park ranger, or a nurse, or a midwife, or a paramedic, or a psychiatrist, or – the list just kept going on and on – or a farmer, or a bum (laughs). Those are all interests! And depending on my mood I read about how people make food with wind power, or how to pick locks. Too many interests – now I'm getting into computer science.

LS: How do you prevent yourself from getting swept away from the field you're looking at before you can finish looking at it?

SP: That's the thing with dissection. It has a tendency to pull you out, which is how I've gotten so many interests, and how they've all tied themselves together.

LS: So you do put your foot down occasionally?

SP: I don't really put my foot down because I'm not really good at that. If I have an interest I'll start reading about it and all of a sudden I get pulled somewhere else. Eventually I have 12 interests, but that means I can pick and choose on a daily basis. "Oh, I want to go research something. OK, I'm interested in this…" I pick it up, do a certain amount of research, and then it carries me away again. And sometimes I get tired of something, and I'll do something like say to myself, "I want to learn about flying," and I'll get into paragliding or something like that. I've gotten interested in scuba diving… It's hard to stay focused when you've got too many interests.

LS: Do you feel that you're succeeding, or that you will succeed?

SP: I feel that the interests I've got now are just a landing pad. I might follow any one of these interests somewhere else, but right now they are creating my space. These are my interests, these are my areas of interest. I'm interested in health sciences, I'm interested in activism, I'm interested in the environment.

LS: And you think you'll stay in those areas?

SP: It's the hope (laughs)!

LS: If you could imagine where you'll be in five years, even if it's just a fantasy, where would you like to be, and what would you like to have happen by that time?

SP: In five years I'd like to be shooting for my first year of vet school. If all works out, if I get accepted, if I get my prerequisite classes done... and if I'm still alive (laughs)! That's where I'm hoping to be... or in China. China would be fun.

Even though I've got many interests – and I do contemplate other career tracks – the vet idea is the one thing that I'm dead set on. Eight years now, eight years.

My biggest issue with the world is trying to understand how it can be that when you meet someone and you ask, "What are your interests?" and they go, "I don't have any." That's my biggest issue: how could somebody not have any interests! And the problem is that three years ago I was one of those people.

When I was at Sudbury I would sit there going, "Oh, there's a black spot on a white wall." I'm staring at the white wall because there's nothing else to do. There were things to do, but I was too lazy to do them. I didn't have any interests other than animals. That was pretty forward, cut and dry: if it has hair I like it, if it has scales I like it, if it has slime I like it... but if it's a person, I don't like it (laughs). Those were my interests.

LS: What happened there? You're making a distinction, and I'm not seeing all the implications. You had interests: animals, but these are not the same kind of interests you have now, which are something more than just interests. What is the difference between the interests you had three years ago and now?

SP: It came with the realization that I could actually get something that I wanted. That I could actually learn something. "Oh, you can sit down, and you can read this book, and you can learn it, learn what's inside." When before I thought you needed a teacher to teach you everything.

When I got to Sudbury I thought, "I can't learn anything because there are no teachers here, and I need a teacher to teach me everything." I still feel that I need a teacher to teach me things. I'm not going to try to scuba dive without having professional instruction because that's stupid and illegal.

I think what needs to happen is that the public system and the private schools need to come to a decision that isn't this extreme or that extreme, it's a middle ground which some call experimental education.

I just got my fingers on the book *The Teenage Liberation Handbook*, after I got out of Sudbury, which is the biggest mistake I ever made because that book changed my mind completely.

What I need now is the book that says what you do in the last six months when you notice that you haven't done anything to get you into college for the last four years but you need something that looks good. That's the book I need (laughs)!

5. GUDRUN SPERRER

History Middle Born 1961, Steyr, Austria

After college Gudrun left Austria and arrived in the Amazon jungle without a penny in her pocket. She started making and selling jewelry on the street, barefoot. With a little inherited money she bought an abandoned ranch and built a zoo, a butterfly farm, and a wild animal rescue clinic called Pilpinuwasi which is open to tourists outside of the jungle city of Iquitos. In it, all the animals are free, except those who would get in trouble, like the leopard. They stay there because it's their home and because Gudrun has built them a family.

I spoke to her over lunch at a street cafe. Before we were finished she had invited three street children over to eat with us. One local referred to her as the best woman in Iquitos.

Excerpts

"Sometimes it is very sad when an animal dies. Like the last animal that was killed a few months ago – I was very, very sad – was a kinkajou, also known as a "honey bear," a night-active animal of the raccoon family. Very naughty, very active, hyper-active, but cute! I had raised it from very small, and also crippled."

"She slept in the daytime... But at one in the morning... she came in and wanted to play, and she just got into your bed and would jump on you, biting you, and whatever. But besides that she's so soft and so nice. It's the only animal that I know that is incredibly nice smelling... it smells like vanilla... so soft and so nice. And then somebody shot it..."

"I'm sometimes angry at them because they're not into learning things, which is something I hate: to be happy only with what you know. To want to change things..."

"So I remember when the guide took me (into the jungle). You cannot use power in the boat; we had to pole it because the river is not deep, and there's lots of stones. And we were going for a few hours and suddenly he stopped and said, 'OK, you get out here,' But I said, 'There is no village here?' And he said, 'No, I don't go any further'..."

"I had a strange feeling, it was around evening, I was this stupid *gringa* that was going to get lost in the jungle. So I walked, and I found lots of people in the river washing. The men use the loincloths and the women used a wrap. They didn't run away, but many of them turned away when I came..."

"Then I stopped, and a guy came up to where I was walking. He was all painted black on his arms and his face. And he asked me in Spanish... 'And what do you want?' I said I don't want much of you but I would ask if I could maybe stay with you and learn something from you. The first question then was 'Are you a missionary?' I said, 'No!' Then he said, 'OK, come on,'..."

"Believe in the good things... believe that it's worth at least to save one thing for future generations. And it's worth it, that's something important. And you don't lose that feeling. When you're an adult, and you haven't learned that, it becomes very hard to keep believing in things when you see that nobody else does, or everything's against you..."

"Muhammed says, 'I come before sunrise to chain you and drag you off.' It's amazing, and funny, that you have to be pulled away from being tortured, pulled out into this Spring garden, but that's the way it is. Almost everyone must be bound and dragged here. Only a few come of their own."

— Jalal ad-Din Rumi, 13th century Persian poet, jurist, and theologian, from *The Illuminated Rumi*, by Coleman Barks

Interview   Iquitos, Peru, July 2006

Gudrun Sperrer: What I wanted to do was a little bit similar to what I am doing, but it concerned human beings. I'm a social worker, that's what I studied, and when I came to Peru I thought I'd go around, do some tourism and, as I got a one-year ticket, the idea was doing some social work here. People need so many things; there is so little health care or security. That was the original idea when I came in 1982.

I'd finished school and worked for a few months with drug addicts and alcoholics. You want to do something, you want to do some good, and they don't want it, or the drug is stronger than you. I wanted to go away from Austria, thinking of doing some social work in South America.

From the time when I was small I had wanted to be a veterinarian, and I always walked the dogs of our neighbor who was a veterinarian, and he was actually the reason I did not study veterinary medicine. He told me, "You're not strong enough, you're a woman." I believed him. And one more reason was a guy, a friend of mine, an older student who studied veterinary medicine, who told me that in Austria after you finish studying you have to work for one year at a slaughter house.

I came to Peru with a friend of mine; she had been studying social work with me. She had quit working in a psychiatric hospital. She couldn't stand the way they treated the patients, and as we were very good friends we decided to go somewhere else. I wanted to go to South America, so I convinced her. She wanted for us to go to India. And then we didn't know where exactly to go – I was actually thinking of Mexico first. We looked at our money and the cheapest thing was a one-year ticket with Aeroflot to Peru. And that's how we came here.

She fell in love quite soon with a Peruvian guy, and I still wanted to travel and come to the Amazon. So she stayed around Cuzco, and I came here. Here I just loved the animals, and I loved nature, and I also loved the people. More than people in the Highlands or in the Coast, you might have noticed, they're just so sweet. I mean they can be a nuisance, too, because they're so curious. You have absolutely no privacy – they want to know everything. And if you give them an answer they still want to know "... but why... but WHY" (laughs)?! It's somehow like children: naive, nice, open.

That was the first impression, but now I'm sometimes angry at them because they're not into learning things, which is something I hate: to be happy only with what you know. To want to change things, that's what I miss a little bit. I notice this with my students. Everybody hates politics, and I say, "But you're in the middle of it!" But it was definitely part of the reason why I stayed here: the people and how they treated me ... well, besides nature.

I first looked for a place to stay outside of town because I couldn't afford a hotel. I spoke a little Spanish and I went to the villages where they told me there was a family with a house on the river where nobody lives… but maybe I could live there. The house was on the river, nowhere, no village nearby, nothing, and they raised pigs and hens there. They had an old Indian there taking care of the animals, but the problem was the Indian was a drunkard and – phst! – he would disappear for two days taking a chicken to sell so he could afford to drink, and meanwhile a pig was stolen. So they wanted someone to look after him, or to be there when he was gone. So I started to live there, with the guy in the house, and I started to learn Spanish.

I had seen people selling earrings, as I'd been to Cuzco before, and I had things to make earrings with, both the ceramic and the beads, so I started to do those things when I had time and exchange them for food, firewood. And I also came to Iquitos to sell them. That was in the 1980s and at that time there was nobody. It was really different: a *gringa* selling earrings in the street. I used to come barefoot because I like to go barefoot. One day somebody came by and they took me a pair of sandals, and they put them in front of me and they said, "You have to use shoes in town" (laughs).

LS: So how did you slip from taking care of chickens and pigs on the street to owning a butterfly farm and rescuing animals?

GS: I'm not an artist; I got bored just doing earrings. And when I went with the old Indian to the village where he'd get his booze, I noticed there was a school and I asked him about it. He said, "Yes, it's a school. It's a primary school with about 70 pupils, and there is one teacher."

And I come from a teacher family – my mother is a teacher and my father is a psychologist but he taught too, and I thought that's something I'd like to do: help children and maybe teach something. If it's just one guy with 70 children for up to sixth grade, they would need some help. I didn't speak much Spanish, but the teacher told me to teach fifth and sixth level. I was quite lost, and I asked him if he had any books and he told me no, he has one book for fourth to sixth grade but he used it.

I asked if they had a map, and he had a map of the world. They had never used it, and I remember when I unrolled it, it was the first time, and I showed them where Austria was just to tell them where I come from. It was useless: they had never seen a map (laughs)!

LS: But he wasn't paying you, was he?

GS: No. No, the people of the village paid me with fish or with firewood. Then I started teaching first and second grade, instead of fifth and sixth. And in the first few weeks I did a lot of walks through the village to get to know the village. That's how I learned more Spanish: the children just told me that's that, and that is that, and that is who and who, and I got to know the people, and I got to know the things. And they learned mostly to wash their hands after going to the toilet (laughs)… basic things they hadn't known before. And then I taught them writing and counting and a little bit of reading.

LS: Are you a good teacher?

GS: People say I'm a good teacher, I don't know. I'm never content with what I'm doing. They didn't learn everything I wanted them to so much. Later on, when I taught kindergarten, I'd think, "What have I done in one year? What have they learned?" And it's very little, for me it's little. For the kindergarten the only change that I thought I'd done for these children is that maybe they wash their hands after going to the toilet and they brush their teeth (laughs). At least when they had a toothbrush – normally they don't have one. That's not much.

LS: You still haven't gotten to the animals.

GS: Ahhh! Then I wanted to do something for the village, for the school, as there were no materials. I wrote to Austria to ask if they could help us, and I found an aid organization that was interested, and they told me to make a project. I wrote the project with the people of the village; they told what they wanted to do and what we could help for it. They wanted some program for vaccines, and they wanted to make money breeding pigs or hens. And our proposal was accepted.

We got the wife of the teacher to teach people so they could become nurses, public health. We got vaccines, we made a water tank, we made toilets for the school because people have no toilets. And then the people wanted to start breeding pigs, so we started breeding pigs.

I got tired, not tired but disappointed, when I noticed that with the money coming from somewhere else the people did less and less on their own initiative. They were just waiting.

For example, we had gotten money to build a big, beautiful pig sty. Really solid with declining floors so they'd be easy to wash it. We bought water pumps to make it easy to get water from the creek. Everything was perfect, but they had to plan things for the food because the grant did not include money for the feeding of the pigs. The project was working until money stopped coming from Austria, and then they let loose the pigs so that they could find their own food. Then a few pigs were killed by yucca farmers who were not integrated in the project: the pigs were going and eating their yucca.

I left then, in the middle of all this, because I had the last chance to take a paid flight to Europe, so I went away for three weeks. When I came back after three weeks I had the surprise that not only all the pigs had gone, they had sold them without even getting them big. They had also sold the water pump for less than a tenth of the price we had bought it. They got just enough so that each member of the association could get drunk once. And they had removed the water tank – which was to have drinking water for the children – and had put it into the church. It was the time of the feast of the patron of the village, and so they had filled the water tank with masato, the yucca beer.

Now I can laugh about it because if you think about it, it's really funny. It must have been great: you have a 500-liter tank, and you open the tap and *masato* comes out just like beer – great! But I was really angry at them then, I mean that wasn't the idea!

LS: Did they put it back afterwards?

GS: No, I think it's still up in the church.

And I noticed how they treat the animals, and I had raised a few and released them, and if they stayed in the area they'd be killed. Mostly wild monkeys and sloths, but also capybaras. When people kill the mothers and are left with the baby animal, they feed the baby animals water and sugar, since they don't have milk for their own children. The animals take it for a few days and then they die, or they run away. And as I don't have any children, and I had some money, I'd spend it on milk and vitamins, and I raised the baby animals I got from them.

LS: And the land, where did you get the land that you now have?

GS: The land I bought from a German lady. I had worked at that place when it was a zoo and a lodge. That was in the late 80s, a German lady started it. And then her husband left her and she married a Peruvian guy and he spent all her money; and in the end, he made I don't know how many women pregnant in the village, and she wanted to go away with him. And I had worked with her for about two months, helping her with the monkeys because she needed somebody who really cares for the animals, not just for the money.

She then tried to sell the place but she wanted US$500,000 for it because that's what she had spent. There were 12 hectares of land and I think 10 bungalows with furniture. She had lots of cages and she had the animals, she had walkways, she had a restaurant, she had a solar-energy generator. But still it was too much. I think the first time she noticed it was too much was when she started offering it for $300,000. But that was the time of terrorism in Peru and nobody was even interested. She had her mother-in-law from the next Peruvian husband in charge of the house.

There was somebody who was willing to pay $30,000 which she thought was an offense, but they told her that there wasn't much left, so she asked that I should have a look. So I went out there and there was nothing left but the house. The cages were gone, the animals were gone, the bungalows were still standing but had no more furniture. They had scavenged the materials, sold or eaten the animals, sold the furniture, taken out the toilets. Everything was gone.

And then she said, "You know what, if I sell it to somebody I would give it to you, because I know you're going to do something good with it." In the end she sold it to me for US$18,000, which I paid using money that my grandfather left for me, and now I'm not owing her anymore. So we got 12 hectares of land in 1996.

We were thinking still of only butterflies – I did not want anymore to raise any animals I get attached to. When I had the animals, a monkey and a capybara that I raised from babies to adults, and when they went away and later came back with babies of their own, then the neighbors killed them. And I was very sad and very upset.

I actually took one of the guys who had killed them to the police in Iquitos because he had killed a spider monkey that was within days of giving birth. She was like a woman, with big breasts and a big belly. She couldn't even climb up the trees anymore and that damn guy killed her on my land. First I took him to the head of the village and he told me, "Well, there's nothing we can do. Take him to town." And in town they asked him what's the reason he killed it, and he told them the same thing that my neighbors in the other village had told me before. He said that this lady's raising animals and she doesn't eat them, so what for?

My argument was that this is my business. I didn't ask you to raise them, it didn't cost you any money, that doesn't give you the right to kill them. The police told me that if I would want to make a real charge it would have to be written down, and that would cost time and money and nothing would happen.

I was very, very, very sad and very angry. I remember that I ran out crying, and then the police officer came after me: "*Gringita, gringita*, don't be sad! Don't be angry! Give me 10 soles and I'll really beat that guy up!" (Laughs) But I didn't give him the 10 soles because if he beats him, then the next time he kills another monkey.

LS: You'd have to beat him up regularly.

GS: Uh huh, well, you'd have to put him in a cage and beat him up (laughs). Treat him like he treats the animals.

So I thought, "I don't want to raise animals, but I want to do something with animals." That was in 1995, and I thought about one of my visits to Austria when I went back to the zoo in Vienna where I had volunteered when I was studying.

The new attraction was the butterfly house, and I asked the guy who was showing me around how they raised the butterflies and he said, "We cannot raise them here, we do not have the host plants, we buy the chrysalis. We buy them mostly from Costa Rica, also from Malaysia." And I thought that would be something that I could do. Butterflies are beautiful, and the whole transformation is very interesting. And I don't get attached to them, and you don't eat them; you can release them. The idea also was that I thought it would be a way of making a living, to work with those animals, to breed them, and to export the chrysalis. That was the original idea.

Then when we started to try to find the host plants it was a little bit complicated, but we finally know now how to breed 43 species.

We wanted to export them, but the problem now is that we cannot export because it takes too long to get the permit. We tried two times sending the chrysalis to Lima, because you don't get the permit here. Only Lima has the authority for giving export permits. We have to send the chrysalis there, and there they think about it. They certify after five weeks, and then we noticed that our butterflies hatch before they even get out of Lima and die in the box.

And then we said, "Well, we've got a cage now," – because we had to protect the butterflies from parasites and predators – "Let's try it with tourism."

LS: So how do you like it now that you're a zoo keeper?

GS: I like to live with animals and to be with animals. It's not something that you can imagine. It's not a question of how satisfying it is if you get an animal that is almost dead, and you see it some weeks later happily crawling in the trees and jumping around… just like a wild one. It's a big satisfaction.

LS: Well, describe it as best you can, because I have no idea.

GS: (Laughs) Well, imagine that you have a child – it's stupid to compare it but actually similar with monkeys – and you get it as a baby and it's crippled almost, and it's got injuries, and you think it might die and, if it's a monkey, you carry it around for months sitting on your back, because normally it would be on the mother's still, and you know it still really needs the contact. That's really true. I notice with the baby monkeys here at the primate center – there's a primate center where they have all the means – they have incubators and now, actually – I'm so angry at that damn vet – it's the fourth time he gets a red uacari baby (*Cacajao calvus*, an endangered monkey species – Ed.) and I told him, "Give it to me!" And again it died because he said, "But no, we've got the incubator…" He wants to be the one who rescues the baby, but he doesn't know how. It really makes me angry.

So you carry them around, and you get attached to them. What's so beautiful in some of the animals, especially the monkeys, is once they get over their injuries or their disease, it's incredibly fast how they develop. With each day you see progress. At first they can't even crawl, and then on one day he starts jumping from here to here, and on the next day already they jump from here to there. And then they get independent, and you can leave them with the other monkeys. It's great.

LS: What about ecology? What relationship do you have to that situation: the destruction of the habitat.

GS: First, too much thinking about it makes me depressive. If you think of everything that's really happening and how little you can do, you'll have to kill yourself (laughs)! That's my feeling!

LS: But you're so close to it. I wonder how you stake out a part of the world that you're going to be concerned with...

GS: Uh huh. Sometimes I still feel so bad – helpless and frustrated – I know that's not good for my health. When I come back to home on the boat from a trip into town and I see those floating rafts of cut trees, some with 50 trees that I know have lived maybe 100 years to get as big, and I know they're bringing them here to make toothpicks or to make plywood. I just hate it. I can't get used to it, but that's how it is.

LS: What's going to happen here? What do you project? Are you going to stay here and grow with the city, or is there a limit to how much you can take?

GS: The problem is, like I said to a friend, I'm living out there almost in the jungle. Like on weekends now the village has two discotheques, and the loudspeakers are outside. They turn it up to full volume and, as my house is high, I could dance the whole night (laughs)! And my friend said, "Yeah, but even if you move maybe 10 kilometers, maybe further up, in about 10 years you're going to have the same situation. So you cannot run away from it. So I just have to try to get used to it. Try to face it, or fight it. I try to fight it.

I try not to think too much about it. Some things you cannot help. But I try to do something with the students because what's frustrating really, what's sad, is how little interest the people who live here have in ecology. Well, they have no idea!

LS: What's carried you through these difficult transitions of yours?

GS: The love I get from the animals, I think. Not even the love, or the love I give them, the joy of seeing them and thinking, "You have done something small but you have done something good."

Sometimes it is very sad when an animal dies. Like the last animal that was killed a few months ago – I was very, very sad – was a kinkajou, also known as a "honey bear" (*Potos flavus*), a night-active animal of the raccoon family. Very naughty, very active, hyper-active, but cute! I had raised it from very small, and also crippled. She was a nuisance because she broke into the house every night, through the mesh. In the end we didn't fix it anymore.

She slept in the daytime. When she was grown up she slept on the roof. But at one in the morning, two in the morning, she came in and wanted to play, and she just got into your bed and would jump on you, biting you, and whatever. But besides that she's so soft and so nice. It's the only animal that I know that is incredibly nice smelling... it smells like vanilla. They have some special glands, and they produce a scent that smells like vanilla... so soft and so nice. And then somebody shot her.

LS: Really?

GS: Uh huh, in the night… on our land. Well, they eat them. She was two and a half kilos maybe. And then I was angry and sad. That's why we're making a fence now because when the water is high hunters come in with the canoe. It's easy. And my dogs are not there, my dogs are at the house or the porch, but they don't go to the end of the property.

And then when I'm very sad I think at least she had a good life… a good life. I think, "It's bad now, but she would have been dead in a day if we hadn't got her." My partner took it away from children in the port of Bella Vista because they were playing around with it like a puppy, in the daytime, an animal like this… the end is the same now: it's dead. But I think she had a really nice life.

LS: Yeah, her life was much better than she could have expected, if she could have expected anything! Do you think you're going to make a lasting impression, or do you care?

GS: I care, for sure! And I'm not sure if I do, but sometimes I think, "Yes." But it's very little, like in the village there are two children, they're actually in the same family, a girl and her little brother. When they find caterpillars now they tell us, they don't kill them. They tell us to go and get them. The other day the little boy came with this big caterpillar, he's still a little bit afraid. That's not much, but it's something. They brought a caterpillar because now it's not just a worm that you have to kill. And that's my hope: little bits of change.

LS: It's surprising to me that with all this fascinating stuff going on in the natural environment, that people don't get interested. No one gets interested, even the kids don't.

GS: Well, they're much too busy getting the food for the day. And if you look around, you notice what they do in their spare time, if they have spare time, and you see them sitting around without doing anything. And I was always asking them – typically a woman question – "What are you thinking about? What are you planning?" They answer, "Nothing," or "Just looking," which is great. I mean others go to India to learn not to think. Here people know how to relax or how to get a blank mind. I believe that really. I didn't believe it in the beginning, but they can really sit in a hammock and I can say, "What are you thinking about?"

"Nothing!"

They haven't much stimulation when they are small; they have no books. They don't tell stories anymore, like they used to do in the older culture. Like in Padre Cocha (the closest village to the animal center – Ed.), those are people from different tribes that have come to the village to be near to Iquitos, but there isn't really anymore identification with the cultures they came from.

And like with the students, sometimes I'm not even angry, I'm just surprised. I say, "How don't you know!" and "Why don't you know!" and "Why aren't you interested!" For example, "Why don't you ever go out in the country side?"

We get the biology students, and they don't even know what a tapir is (*Tapirus terrestris*). And when I asked them if they've ever been to any place outside of the town, many would say no.

A few who've visited me told me it was the first time they'd ever crossed the river. And they are 20 or 25 years old. And they've lived in Iquitos and all around is water.

Now there's a road to Nauta (a small city), a new road about 80 kilometers, but a few years ago no roads led outside of town. To go anywhere you had to go by boat. But most of the students told me that visiting my place, just two kilometers from town, was the first time they had crossed the river.

And sometimes with my German-language students, when I talk to them, and with them I am more familiar, I say, "What the hell do you know! I mean you're living there, have you never been out! Don't you have a grandfather, grandmother with a farm house?" And then one told me, "Yes," but it seems they're ashamed of it; they want to be really from town. Those who don't go out say, "Oh no, there's so many mosquitoes out there!" (Laughs)

There's much more fear than interest. Well, the fear is OK; there's some reason for it. If your grandfather has been an Indian, they were afraid a little bit of the jungle. Like the people in the village where I was first living, further up the river, and they just couldn't believe that I was swimming in the river, in the lake – they don't swim. Children swim, a little bit for fun, but adults bathe themselves in the canoe by pouring water over themselves, because in the water there might be something attacking you.

It's not so much of ignorance as it is of believing in things. Actually, now I think more about it since I've been here so long. I'm not as naïve or as brave, or whatever you want to call it, as I was before. Not just because of my age, but because I've heard so many stories (laughs)… You start thinking you don't know and what there might be in the water. The more you hear, the more you imagine.

LS: And is there anything to be afraid of?

GS: I don't really think so. I mean it would not be nice to get into contact with an electric eel because it might touch you, and it might be frightening or so shocking that you might drown, I could imagine. Besides that, there's nothing to be afraid of.

There aren't any dangerous animals around here anymore. Even in town sometimes there appear boa constrictors or anacondas, but they are not dangerous. I am not afraid of snakes.

I lived once with the Choco Indians in Columbia. I enjoyed it a lot because it was so different from being with the Peruvian people. They were really proud. The jungle goes down there more or less to the sea. I hadn't asked for permission to visit them; I had asked only how could I get there when I was on the coast. And the people of the village on the coast, the black people, told me there's a village up there, and we can take you there, but I don't know if they will receive you. They don't like foreigners, and anyway, the black people feel themselves above the Indians.

So I remember when the guide took me there. You cannot use power in the boat; we had to pole it because the river is not deep, and there's lots of stones. And we were going for a few hours and suddenly he stopped and said, "OK, you get out here." But I said, "There is no village here?" And he said, "No, I don't go any further. It's just around the next curve, and there you will see the village and you go near."

I had a strange feeling, it was around evening, I was this stupid *gringa* that was going to get lost in the jungle. So I walked and I found lots of people in the river washing. The men use the loincloths and the women used a wrap. They didn't run away but many of them turned away when I came.

Then I stopped and a guy came up to where I was walking. He was all painted black on his arms and his face. And he asked me in Spanish who I was. And then I said my name, which doesn't say much. And he asked, "Where do you come from?" And I said, "I come from Peru." And he asked, "And what do you want?" I said I don't want much of you but I would ask if I could maybe stay with you and learn something from you. The first question then was, "Are you a missionary?" I said, "No!" Then he said, "OK, come on" (laughs). They didn't want any missionaries anymore.

LS: Yes, they're lovely. I also lived with them but on the other side of the mountains in Panama. That was around 1984. But it was no paradise. They had their problems.

I remember we went down the river one day, and they saw an iguana in the top of the tree; they shot it, but it wouldn't fall because it hung on with its claws. So they cut the tree down, you know, just for their fucking lunch (laughs)! They'd spent a bullet, and a bullet is very hard to come by. They were not going to let that bullet go to waste. But the tree was wasted.

They had no idea about conservation; they all wanted to get chainsaws so they could cut more trees down. I remember we went to a congress in a larger village where the Panamanian Army brought in some people to lecture about ecology. Elders from all the villages sat there listening, and then one guy puts his hand up and says, "What's ecology?" But they could learn quickly. They noticed they can't shoot deer from their back porch anymore. That's ecology!

GS: Uh huh. That's what they notice now here, too, yeah? Like the other day one of the people who sold me the leaves for thatching my roof came from the village, and I needed some more. And he wanted to charge much more than he did 10 years ago. So I said, "Well, OK, you can charge a little bit more, but not that much!"

"Ahh, you know when I sold you the leaves before, I came back with the leaves the same day? But now we've got to go two days to find the leaves."

"Uh huh," I said, "and why?"

"Because there aren't any more!"

"Yeah," I said, "and you know WHY?"

"Because there aren't any more!" he said again.

"Yeah," I said, "but it's you who did it! Because if you would have just left two palm leaves of this palm, because it comes out of one stem and would survive if they left a couple of leaves, then the plants wouldn't have died, and you would still have some! But you had to take ALL of them because of greed!"

"Yeah, that's true," he said. "We always cut down everything. But that's because we want to bring more!" (Laughs)

So now they have to go, and they come back after five days with what they have done before in one day.

LS: It just seems like maybe the only way to teach anybody anything is ...

GS: ... by experience, by the hard way. Yeah.

LS: If you were to talk to kids, what would you tell them was the most important thing to have in order to see forward with a certain degree of success and accomplishment?

GS: That question was not what I'd expected. I'd expected you would ask how to live happy (laughs), not to live a successful life.

LS: I don't mean successful in any particular way. Happy could be a good measure of success. I'm asking what they should know, or should acquire, or should believe in.

GS: That's a good word: "believe." Also everything is against it. They should believe in the good things. They should believe that it's worth at least to save one thing for future generations. And it's worth it; that's something important. And you don't lose that feeling.

When you're an adult, and you haven't learned that, it becomes very hard to keep believing in things when you see that nobody else does, or everything's against you. Maybe if you learn it from small on. I think that's very important.

And not to think that we're the only ones on the planet. Not to take oneself as too important.

That we have to kill animals because we have to eat, that is no longer true, as an example. Or that we have to cut down trees because we have to make a house. That's no longer true in the Western world, either.

No, I don't want us all to go backwards, that's not my idea, but yet there is a sense of recognizing that what you really need in order to feel fine is much less than what you get offered in the Western world.

And that it makes you really feel good when you do something good for somebody else, even if it's an animal. It makes you feel good (laughs)!

6. JEROME LETTVIN

History   Late   Born 1920, Chicago, Illinois

Jerry Lettvin worked at the Massachusetts Institute of Technology in times when teaching and research were more flexible. He taught an afternoon class in the history of science that went on for hours because he paid no attention to the time. It was so popular that students would pack a lunch, bring their girlfriends, and spend the afternoon listening to him.

Jerry won acclaim for being the first person to measure the electric impulse from fine neurons. His work was published in a paper titled "What the Frog's Eye Tells the Frog's Brain" that has since become one of the most famous publications in the field.

I first met him in the 1970s when a friend and I walked into Jerry's office, unfamiliar and unannounced, and told him that we had heard that he could tell us something useful about science. The second time I saw him was in 2007, 25 years later, when I spoke to him and his wife, Maggie, for this interview at their home outside of Boston.

Postscript: Jerry Lettvin died on Saturday, April 23, 2011. He was 91.

Excerpts

"I started out as a poet and became a physician, then became an electrical engineer, then a neurobiologist. It was never with any sense of searching for what people wanted to know. It was just to understand the thing that I was looking at in a way that made sense. That is a far more difficult job than writing equations…"

"The interesting things were the problems: were there other ways in which you could express the problem such that analogies and concordances would pop up? It's very much like listening to music and trying to decide what is meant doing it this way rather than that way. That is essentially the way that I've worked all my life. I haven't been after prizes, just curiosity, that's all…"

"You pass out after the first two breaths… and when you wake up, it is an epiphany. Things stand out with such startling clarity that you cannot quite understand how it was that such a thing as this… was… not observed… For the next 12 hours Walter (Pitts) and I were walking in a world in which every single thing became completely clear. The clarity was the likes of which you don't experience ordinarily… It's at this point that curiosity overwhelms you…"

"You see, you're asking me how I go about things. I go about things in a way that has nothing to do with what universities teach. It's very different from what universities tell you to do, what teachers tell you to do. You make it up as you go along, and god knows how it comes out; you don't know…"

"I'm a garbage picker-upper as a mode of science: I focus on the garbage truck. I look at the parts that others choose not to pay attention to. It's interesting the number of things that are not paid attention to… absolutely astounding."

"It is only when the oppressed find the oppressor out and become involved in the organized struggle for their liberation that they begin to believe in themselves. This discovery cannot be purely intellectual but must involve action."

— Paulo Freire, from *Pedagogy of the Oppressed*

"In the race to develop a single model for understanding everything, magicians have made their universe very small... When you adhere too closely to a model, you draw strange and even potentially dangerous conclusions..."

— Jason Miller, from "Strategic Sorcery" (unpublished course notes)

"The realization of Truth and Reality can never be created by the mind; it always comes as a gift of grace. Inquiry clears away misperceptions and illusions, making one available to the movements of grace..."

— Adyashanti, from *The Way of Liberation, a practical guide to spiritual enlightenment*

Interview   Hingham, Massachusetts, May 2007

LS: I think young people are tired of listening to adults.

Maggie Lettvin: You know, they are, but it's inspiration – not how much a teacher knows – it's how much they inspire the kids to learn. At the lectures Jerry used to give at MIT he used to tell the kids that the whole point of being there was to learn how to get into more interesting trouble. The only thing you really learn when you go to school is how to find information.

Jerry Lettvin: I didn't have any ambitions at all. The only thing I was interested in was curiosities. I wasn't particularly interested in what you might call standard physics, standard neurology, or standard physiology. I looked for the corners that were unoccupied and which, for some reason or another, had escaped attention.

That's not a way in which you go about doing things, but I was fortunate enough to have had a father who was an anarchist who pointed out to me that the interesting things always lay out of the beaten path. You look for them, and when you find them you play with them.

I started out as a poet and became a physician, then became an electrical engineer, then a neurobiologist. It was never with any sense of searching for what people wanted to know. It was just to understand the thing that I was looking at in a way that made sense. That is a far more difficult job than writing equations.

The interesting things were the problems: were there other ways in which you could express the problem such that analogies and concordances would pop up? It's very much like listening to music and trying to decide what is meant doing it this way rather than that way. That is essentially the way that I've worked all my life. I haven't been after prizes, just curiosity, that's all.

Am I making any sense?

LS: Can you be more specific? Can you speak to people who have not yet had these experiences?

JL: Well, I never really had any experience. In a sense I lucked out by being present when a particular problem appeared, and then I spent a year playing with it until it got interesting. That was it. I never went to publish much. What I did publish, I did on the lowest possible level that you could do an explanation.

LS: Tell me about the problem.

ML: *Jerry, tell him about the lecture you gave at Harvard where you showed them so many holes in what they considered the theory of the moment that at the end of it they just sat there stunned.*

JL: Yeah, that is what I do like to do: to tear apart what is already accepted. It's sort of like you're confronted by a jigsaw puzzle in which the pieces fit but the picture doesn't work. What you have to do is take the pieces and rearrange them to get the correct picture.

That's a very different way of pursuing knowledge than what is current, very different. It's not the sort of thing that you teach easily. Namely, you get your fangs into a problem and you…

ML: *… you don't pay attention to what is accepted theory. You say, "Why is that hole there? Why doesn't this fit?" There has to be something wrong with accepted knowledge to explain why it doesn't fit.*

JL: That turns out to be a lot of fun. It doesn't get you anywhere, it doesn't make a great name for you, but it is gratifying to say, "Ah ha! What I smelled turned out to be the case."

ML: *That is because he keeps sifting, and sifting, and sifting.*

JL: In other words I'm a garbage picker-upper as a mode of science: I focus on the garbage truck. I look at the parts that others choose not to pay attention to. It's interesting the number of things that are not paid attention to… absolutely astounding. Let me give you an example, just as a case in point.

There was a Hungarian by the name of Laszlo Meduna (Ladislas J. Meduna, - Ed.), who was one of the psychiatrists who introduced shock therapy. Back in the old days they had shock therapy for schizophrenics.

Now Laszlo was a remarkable guy. He had a background in chemistry and physiology that was… very Hungarian! I had never come across a background like that before.

What he decided, just from regular observation – just occasional observation – was that the best thing you could do for a schizophrenic was to use carbon dioxide. Doesn't that sound weird?

He wrote a book about it, which did not get more than one printing and has disappeared from the shelves everywhere. He was a psychiatrist with a fair clientele, and the extraordinary thing about this clientele was that they would arrive in despair and come out perfectly happy, cheerful, able people capable of talking.

Walter Pitts and I sort of observed this, and both of us went to Laszlo and said, "Laszlo, why don't you try it on us, just for the hell of it." He said, "I'd be glad to!"

The procedure involved inhaling a gas that was 70% oxygen and 30% CO_2. You pass out after the first two breaths – you take no more than eight breaths – and when you wake up it is an epiphany. Things stand out with such startling clarity that you cannot quite understand how it was that such a thing as this (he points to the window sash – Ed.) and its relation to that (he points to the fastener – Ed.)… how was it not observed that there was a relationship between them? For the next 12 hours Walter and I were walking in a world in which every single thing became completely clear. The clarity was the likes of which you don't experience ordinarily.

I decided that I would try this out on schizophrenics at the state hospital in Manteno, Illinois. At that time I was a psychiatrist. I had a girl who was 17 years old, crawling on the floor like a baby, drooling. She'd been that way for the last four or five years. She barely talks at all, just mews like a sick cat and crawls along on the floor because she can't walk. I decided to give her the treatment.

Eight breaths and then she wakes up a perfectly normal 17-year-old girl. She talks very clearly and she could remember the condition she had been in. Over the period of the next 10 hours she slowly, slowly declined. It lasted about 10 hours and it raised the question: what the hell was going on? The state of Illinois forbade me ever to use that treatment again. So I was never able to test it again.

You see, nothing like that ever sits in the literature. The most you have is Laszlo's book, and nobody reads that anymore. In fact it's very difficult to find a copy. The point is that something of great importance is being completely neglected because everything in this field bears away from it.

It's at this point that curiosity overwhelms you. On the one hand nobody can make a buck on CO_2. You see (laughs), medication goes where the money can be paid. Here's a treatment that costs practically nothing. Laszlo's using it on a number of extremely depressed executives, and it's working like a dream. But there's no way of publishing or talking about it, and you have the state forbidding you from using it. This is a very different way of looking at science, or in this case psychiatry.

ML: *It wasn't just science. Jerry taught History of Science and the kids just loved it. They had to open up a larger lecture hall because so many kids wanted to attend. He'd go in there and talk for three or four hours, and the kids would bring their girlfriends, lunches, and just sit there forever. They'd miss classes, they'd miss anything. They didn't care; they loved listening to him. Because he loved what he was doing!*

JL: Relax, relax!

ML: *Most of your job – even as much as you knew – most of your job was inspiration.*

JL: Well, yeah.

The idea was to bring up strange problems. The business of strange problems, the problem that I gave you is not one that you'd think is a major problem. Yet when you think about it…

Ramón y Cajal – the anatomist who got the Nobel prize for his work on neuroanatomy – has a book on what you teach your students, and it is an extraordinary book. I strongly recommend you take a look at it. His advice to a young scientist is one of the nicest, most brilliant books you've ever come across. (*Advice for a Young Investigator* MIT Press, 2004. First published in 1897.)

ML: *Jerry, tell him about your autopsies at Manteno. You remember, there would always be people dying up there. But since there were only seven doctors for 7,000 patients, they could barely pay attention. Jerry wanted the doctors to learn what was going on with these patients, so when somebody died he'd get all of their records* *together and he'd let the doctors know that the next morning he would be doing an autopsy. And the doctors and the staff would read the records and make bets on what the person died from.*

JL: In other words, I made it very much like a horse race, in which case everybody was interested and everybody learned. You learned, but you didn't know that you learned. OK? This is very far from the dedicated approach.

ML: *No, it isn't! Everything comes into play.*

JL: Well…

When you go through the literature on nerve structure, what hits you is what's missing. That sounds a little bit silly, but what you realize is that there's a structure in the way people look at things that insists on itself being the only perspective.

It's very strange how much shit there is. Between the direct view of what's going on and what you might call the academic view. This applies all across the board; it's not only in biology and science and psychiatry, it holds practically everywhere. Conservatism is the key word.

What you have to do is find those little crevices, those corners, which are neglected. There is where the gold is. That's no way in which you can go about teaching students.

ML: *Of course it is!*

JL: Well… yes and no. On the one hand, the student has to be able to get out into the world and get a job.

ML: *Not necessarily.*

JL: Look, some of my students have had a lot of trouble.

ML: *Jerry, so have a lot of other people at MIT. The top people at MIT end up driving cabs. The best people end up going into business, and in between it's variations on a theme.*

JL: This is a very different approach to problems than you get in what's called "proper science." For example, over the last two years I found an engineering problem for which there's no scientific basis whatsoever. Because of this lack of scientific basis I said to myself, "Wait a minute. I'm going to have to smell out what is converging to give me this problem." That became a real joy.

I'm vaguely writing it up now. But it's not the sort of thing that's going to appeal much to my colleagues, nor is it going to attract a large body of acceptance, or followers, or anything else of the sort. It's a curiosity that, over time, might turn out to be interesting, or maybe not.

LS: You could describe this example a little more.

ML: *I think you should tell him about the Frog's Eye paper and what happened with that.*

JL: (Laughs) You know what a nerve fiber is, no? As you know, nerve impulses travel up axons that go from here to there. The serious question is: what is the mechanism, what is the energetic cost of the mechanism, and how sturdy is it?

There is a huge literature, an absolutely enormous literature, on the axon. Enormous. A lot of equations are written, very clear and definite, along with the evidence for the equations. But something smells strange about all of this.

If I were to ask about a computer, for example, "What is the energetic cost of a wire connecting two elements?" That is a question that usually doesn't enter into the problem because there is almost no energetic cost. You have charge flowing from here to there through a wire, and there's no unnecessary heating. You can have various junctions that can be far apart and still operate properly.

When you look at a nerve, the first question you ask is, "What is the energetic cost of the signal's travel?" In the case of axons you have nerve fibers traveling in big bundles, traveling from one part of the nervous system to another. What's the cost of this transport, and how good is the transport, how reliable is it, and what makes it reliable? These are not questions that are ordinarily asked.

People say, "Stop giving me the advertising, let's see the equations!" But the problem here is this: nature generally works in strange ways. It sort of goes to the limit of the maximum amount of operation for the least amount of work. This is almost invariably the case.

I know it sounds very bald and brutal, but the interesting point about the nervous system is that here you have connections that look like wires in a computer – extremely much like wires in a computer – yet they're operating in at least five different ways in the transport of the information. And the five different ways are very different from each other. Yet they all reflect exactly the same basic mechanism, which was first discussed in the 17th century and then fell into disrepute and hasn't really appeared again, but the smell is there.

When you talk about axonal physiology, for example, the proper questions to ask are framed in this way: Here is an axon. It's got a membrane, it's got an interior – a tri-laminar interior. One of these lamina is called the cytoskeleton and is composed entirely of actin fibers with fixed negative charges on them. The question is, how do I get an impulse to go up this fiber without any waste of energy, without any expenditure? Is there a method for it?

Curiously enough, back in 1927 there were a pair of people, Erlanger and Gasser (Joseph Erlanger and Herbert Spencer Gasser – Ed.), who published an experiment that got them the Nobel Prize and was promptly forgotten. You see no references to that work after 1952 or 1953. No references to it at all. Although in that paper they made specifications that should have raised the hair on the head of every physiologist who read it. But the alternative was to say, "That's all shit so let's put it aside." OK?

Now when you go to your colleagues and say, "Look, I would like very much for you to consider…" Your colleagues look at you and say, "Wait a minute, you're recording nerve impulses from the cut ends of axons. That's not the same as an intact fiber. You don't know what is the relation between the cut end to that of the whole fiber. This will not do!" Another one will say, "Look, you have myelin-coated fiber. Myelin does not allow anions or cations to go through. Where do you get the impulse for this thing to move…" and so forth.

If you go back to Erlanger and Gasser, they already smelt what was the case, but smell is not enough. In spite of the fact that they got the Nobel Prize, the paper disappeared as fast as it appeared.

Here you have a case where, in a certain sense prior to all of the physics and chemistry and physiology – and neurophysiology is now a very big field – nowhere in these fields is there any hint of the explanation for what Erlanger and Gasser observed.

You go back and look at Erlanger and Gasser and you say, "What the shit, this is so gorgeous! Why is everybody ignoring it!" People ignore it because, they say, "Well, you have damaged the fiber!" But cutting the fiber is like cutting a wire: the wire still works up to the cut, so what's the fuss? They say, "No, no, no, we have to be scientific!"

This is the paper that I'm producing now and, like the original Frog's Eye paper, it will excite a few people, but it will disappear. I'm in the game for the fun of it. If someone asks me, "What is science?" or "What is physiology such that you can do these things?" I wouldn't have the vaguest idea of how to talk about it.

ML: *I think you do. I think it's sifting. I think that's true for everything. It's always sifting, looking for the curiosities.*

LS: Tell me about the Frog's Eye paper.

JL: You read it?

LS: It was boring.

JL: If it was boring, then you didn't read it.

ML: *No, no. Not that he didn't read it, that he didn't understand it. Most people tell you they didn't understand it because it was too dense.*

LS: It's not a criticism. It isn't my field.

JL: You see, here's an interesting thing. Suppose somebody asks me, "How would you record from a wire in a computer that's connecting two operators?" You know very well that you're not allowed to drain the current from the wire because that will prevent anything from going through. Is there any way in which you can look at that wire to tell what's happening, to tell that this impulse is going from here to there? That's a little difficult because a wire is awful goddamned fast. Well, yeah, you can record an impulse, but the shape of it doesn't have much meaning. It will have a shape, but so what? What does that have to do with the wire?

Nature is a very interesting mother. The question is this: "How do I make a wire that doesn't act like a wire, but can substitute for a wire in the translation of information?" Is there some process in nature that you can take advantage of so that you're not using any energy? Oh boy, yeah, there is! And that's what I've been spending the last half year on.

Not that it will make a big "who-hah" when it comes out, but it will explain something that was not explained before except by a batch of equations so tiresome that by the time you finish you say, "Look, let it be! That's the way it should be. Fuck it! Now we understand!" But no, you don't understand.

In the Frog's Eye paper what we showed was that...

ML: *Jerry, let me interrupt for a minute. Did he tell you that he was laughed off the stage when he first presented it? He and his colleagues were practically suicidal, and it got to be one of the most cited papers ever published.*

JL: Suppose I asked you, as a physiologist, how you would go about knowing what it is that is being seen? Not the seeing, but what it is that is being seen.

At this point you say, "Well, I can build computers that will do this." But in nature you don't have computers, you have axons carrying impulses without transporting any energy. You say, "What? You're telling me that you can transport impulses without energy?"

Well, of course you can. A sea wave travels, keeping its velocity and keeping its height. It's not dissipating energy as it travels. So let's take a look at wave theory and ask ourselves, "Is there a way in which I can design an organic tube in which I get waves and in which I can govern sequences of waves?" If I can do this, then the cost of nerve signals is negligible. The processors – the nerve cells, the dendritic axonal formations – those are the computer parts, but I'm just talking about the wires!

So you ask yourself, "How do I build a wire such that there is no dissipation?" That's been solved in modern computers. You go and take a look at the structure of the wires, but then you realize, "Wait a minute, this is sexy. There's no dissipation by the wires, instead the dissipation is in the processors, not in the wires. Can I get the same thing organically?" And the answer is yeah, but it takes an awful lot of looking.

When we recorded from the optic nerve, nobody had ever before recorded the fine fibers, only the large axons. Large axons tell you the light switched on, the light switched off – a big signal is going across the axon – good stuff.

But the frog says, "I want to pick out that fly. That's the one I'm going to eat. How do I get that fly represented in such a way that I know exactly where to put my tongue?" This is not a trivial question. I know it sounds a little wild and weird, but it ain't a trivial question.

Most of the axons that people look at in the whole literature of axonology – and that's a very large literature indeed – these axons are invariably of the large type. But we were looking at axons two orders of magnitude smaller – two orders of magnitude smaller! In other words 1:100 smaller – these carry a lot of information. But there's no access to them in any physiological way using electrodes. On the other hand, if you cut the end of an axon you can record what's coming through from that cut end. That's all I did: to show that the cut ends of axons gave you what information was being carried by the fiber.

This irritated the shit out of everyone because it was a careful repeat of the paper by Erlanger and Gasser. It was a repeat that could be done on a live animal doing no more than cutting the axon and recording from the cut end. And it turned out to be not too difficult.

Nobody in the physiology world will record from the end of an axon on the superstition that if you cut the end you have compromised the operation coming to that end. But what you can show is that, just like a wire, the operation will work up to the cut end. That's what people refused to believe, in spite of the fact that I demonstrated over eight hours of repeated stimulation in correct places that I got the same results. People considered this to be an artifact that I had arranged!

Am I making things mildly clear?

LS: Yeah, but you haven't finished the story of what you did with the result, and how you feel about it today.

JL: Oh! I'm actually putting out a paper in which I'm reviving the whole story.

It's curious how many problems have a kind of improper approach that holds the proper approach away. That occurs everywhere in biology and in a lot of other places as well. In this particular instance what I'm trying to show is that there are particular cells in the retina, ones which respond to a particular kind of object moving in the visual field in a particular way. There's an axon that comes out of the retina, and if I record from the end of that axon I can tell you exactly what the stimuli are.

That's all it is. Nothing great. Nothing profound.

LS: Then why does it baffle people?

JL: Because the dictum is that if you're going to work on a nerve fiber, and it's a living cell of some sort, then breaking it changes its function. This is a given, you see. But nobody looks to see that you're not dealing with water, you're dealing with gels. Inside the axon you'll have gels, and that means that you're not going to have an effect that will matter that much if you cut it.

If someone says, "Prove it!" it means doing an awful lot of chemistry that is not in the books as of yet. One of the things that you come up against here is that, except for Tasaki (Dr. Ichiji Tasaki at the National Institutes of Health in Bethesda, MD. – Ed.), who is a brilliant Japanese physiologist, most people don't really realize that a nerve works by virtue of a phase change in water – a change that is quite violent.

Everybody thinks water is a fluid – it's not. There are three to five stages of water in which water acts as a switch with microsecond timing. "Microsecond timing in water?!" Yeah, microsecond timing in water.

Examples of this are gotten by looking at Tasaki's work in what he calls anionic gels. What is strange is the fact that you're not looking at the actions of ions in the water; what you're seeing is a rapidly propagating transverse change in the nature of water itself. Water goes from an expanded gel, to a contracted gel, to free water, within a few microseconds. Now that's a very different story! You have to stop looking at textbooks that tell you, "These are the way the ions move..." That's bullshit! It's not that at all!

You see, I'm giving you a few footnotes to what is a seriously expanded problem. I've spent the last six months trying to get a 20-page paper out of it. I'm going crazy because it's hard, hard work to lay the whole story out clearly. But once it's laid out clearly, it's a different story from anything anyone's ever talked about... except Tasaki.

LS: What's the paper called?

JL: I haven't called it anything because I haven't finished it.

ML: *Yeah, you did: "How the Frog's Eye Tells the Frog's Brain."*

JL: Oh, yeah (laughs). I'm playing with that as a title.

The problem is that there is no current background here. Tasaki is in his late 90's, still going to work every day. He's published at least six papers on this particular topic. Each one exceedingly difficult to read and quite baffling. Some of the analogies are extremely difficult. To imagine that water operates as a switch, not as a medium, sounds like a brand new thing... but it's not brand new, it's a century old. It's just that the literature has been forgotten.

You see, you're asking me how I go about things. I go about things in a way that has nothing to do with what universities teach. It's very different from what universities tell you to do, what teachers tell you to do. You make it up as you go along, and god knows how it comes out; you don't know.

LS: What's a young person to do?

JL: Play around. You play around.

ML: *Follow their nose. In our family what we say is, "We make ourselves up." Wherever you want to go, you go, and you'll find a way. Keep looking and you'll find a way. You can't go by what other people tell you. I went totally outside the field of physical therapy to come up with the stuff I did. I figured if Jerry could do it, I could.*

And now the kids are doing the same thing.

JL: It's actually a lot more fun than fitting in with current beliefs, current teachings. Much more fun.

LS: How does a person develop a sense of direction?

JL: They don't develop a sense of direction. The direction will occur to you once you get embedded enough.

ML: *You just start, and it happens. You get enough interest, and you keep following your nose, and it happens.*

JL: Just the way any exploration occurs.

LS: Most people don't know how to explore. It's not obvious, you know.

JL: That's right.

ML: *It is true. In fact, schools almost teach you not to explore. The minute you have another way to solve a problem they say, "No, no, you have to do it this way." And that shouldn't happen. Kids should be allowed to explore all different ways of solving problems.*

JL: Biology is interesting because when you go back and start looking at structure, the structure of cells and things of this sort, there's an amazing amount of work on it, and awfully good work, but smelling how things fit together is a different story. Now you're talking about strategy, and strategy is a very different kind of thing: the strategy of operation.

I first came up against this with that psychotic girl. There she is, drooling, crawling along the floor. Eight breaths of CO_2 later, and there she is, saying, "Oh! How are you?" Wait a minute!

What ought to be taught is a certain amount of anarchy. That has become a difficult thing now that everything is arranged by managers.

Now look, I'm not saying there are not good physicists who work in astronomy, they're wonderful, and their apparatuses are extraordinary! But, oddly enough, a lot of that extraordinary apparatus was already invented by animals. There are animals that are star-guided. It's surprising how intelligent most animals are.

I had a pet octopus when I was in Naples. He was a big one, a huge one. "Juvenile Delinquent" is what I called him. My son Jonathan would play with him. We'd come into the lab in the morning and the octopus would be waiting for us. Jonathan would climb into the tank, and instantly there would be a tug of war, back and forth.

People talk about animals not having a sense of humor; this octopus knew how to play practical jokes, and it was wonderful to watch. My octopus would play practical jokes: "What do you mean, an octopus playing practical jokes?!" you say. But it's true.

I teased JD – he was a big octopus, he had a five-foot spread of arms – I teased him by holding a fish down for him to grab, then pulling it back (laughs). JD would start going black-white-black-white, indicating a high degree of irritation. Then JD decided to play a joke on me. Let me tell you, anybody who says octopuses don't have a sense of humor… forget it; they're good.

The next morning I walk into the lab, and JD is up on the edge of his 20-foot tank. I walk in and smack! … right in my face… he let out a huge squirt of water! He had been waiting for me to come in. Jonathan is in stitches, and then Jonathan says, "Take a look!" and I turn around and there are splotches of water all around the region of where my head would be when I come in. The octopus had planned his revenge, and he had been practicing ahead of time. That sounds like a ridiculous story, eh? Well, it isn't.

It's a very different science that I teach.

LS: What would you say about failure?

JL: Such as? If something doesn't work, it doesn't work.

ML: *You know what he taught me? He taught me that that's how you find the right route, by doing one failure after another until you find there's only one route left. He used to let his students make one mistake after another, even though he knew that what they were doing was going to lead to failure. He said, "That's the way they learn." Long and tedious.*

JL: Well, it isn't tedious. It really is an adventure most of the time.

LS: What about the dangers of failure?

JL: So? What about it? Who gives a damn?

ML: *The dangers of failure, Jerry, that's where it gets to be a problem once you have a job, unless you have grant money. That's why everybody knew exactly what results they were going to get before they wrote a grant proposal. They said that they had to, because if they weren't sure of the outcome, then they wouldn't get money next time. They couldn't risk exploring something if they didn't know how it was going to work out beforehand.*

JL: Up to about 1950s there was a kind of freedom in the scientific world – certainly at MIT – that allowed you to play games of all sorts. As two or three decades went by, MIT was taken over by managers.

ML: *Ay-yi-yi-yi-yi. There have always been managers. Since the beginning of the world there have been managers. Most of them are called "Mother."*

JL: Hmmm.

My father was an anarchist in Russia, a strong follower of Kropotkin (Peter Kropotkin, Russian social philosopher, 1842-1921). It was he who taught me anarchy.

LS: Are you an anarchist educator?

JL: Damn right.

ML: *I don't think he is. I think he just teaches because he loves learning himself, so much that it just, sort of, boils over and the kids get the benefit. He can't contain himself even at home; he's constantly trying to teach people at the other table. Every good teacher I've ever had was wildly enthusiastic about their subject. They were delighted if you just learned anything.*

JL: You see, there are alternative methods of teaching and research that do not appear in the textbooks. That's all that I'm trying to tell you.

LS: Let's say you had to give advice to a kid going into college...

JL: Look for what interests you. Do not pay attention to what people tell you.

Managers have wrecked education immensely. The differences between education and research now and what was done 50 years ago is fantastic. There's a profound difference in the freedom to research and question that you could do then, and what you're not allowed to do now. I wouldn't be able to get a job now under any circumstances.

LS: An obstacle to any person's development is the illusion of being dependent. Kids encounter this, and they don't know what it is. Society used to help kids through this, but our society has taken away the initiations to becoming independent.

One of the objects of my work is demonstrate to young people that they have to navigate this transition themselves. Kids have to find ways to initiate themselves. It's a process, not a goal. It's a self-transformation, not an achievement. It's impossible to describe, and no one but you will know how to do it.

ML: *All the fun is in the process.*

Jerry's brother was a concert pianist. When the kids were young we used to go over to his house and they would lie under the piano while he gave master classes. He would go over and over the same phrase looking for the right way to express it – looking for the way he wanted it to sound. That's exactly what this whole thing is about: it's about the process.

Those master classes were so much more fun than a concert because you were with him while he was finding his way through. It was fascinating. I loved that. The process is always more fun.

JL: The process is more fun than the ending. The ending is bad, but it's the finding that's wonderful.

COMPUTERS

7. ANDREW REESE CROWE

History   **Early**   Born 1989, Gainesville, Georgia

Andrew got interested in learning partly from watching war documentaries on TV and from an independent-study early-reader program when he was in elementary school. These things piqued his curiosity and provided the fuel to start asking questions. Reading, thinking, studying, and computer game playing were major parts of his early life, and the more information he finds, the more he endeavors to put it all together.

I met Andrew at The Advanced Academy, a school that gives high school kids the opportunity to start working at a college level.

Excerpts

"(When I was younger) I was interested in facts, and I absorbed them kind of like a sponge. As I got older I got interested in why things happened, not just military history and the engineering aspect of it, but also the political aspects of it. I became less interested in facts and more interested in the reasons behind things…"

"I read fast and remembered a lot. I have this really weird thing – it's true for a lot of things – the way I learn is I accumulate this massive store of data, and then I try to figure out how it works… Once I knew enough words to understand what I was reading, my comprehension jumped from nothing – maybe it was in third grade, I know it was in fourth grade – to testing at 13th-grade level…"

"I got interested in the idea that complicated systems arise from simple forces. The idea that you can have a small number of basic forces that build upon themselves to form something complicated…"

"I've come to the conclusion that I won't live long enough to learn all… I would need (in order) to become as good as I would like to be in every one of those areas. But if I can learn to use the modeling and processing powers of the computer, then I can get a better idea of how things work."

"Though I did not cease to esteem the studies of the schools, I began to think that I had given enough time to languages, enough also to ancient books, their stories and their fables… Therefore, I entirely gave up the study of letters and employed the rest of my youth in traveling, being resolved to seek no other science than that which I might find within myself, or in the great Book of the World."

— René Descartes, philosopher (1596 - 1660), from *Discourse on Method*

"Our understanding of the world we experience is proportional to our having experiences of the world given the views we hold, multiplied by the merit of those views."

— Bayes' fundamental theorem and the marginalization condition of probability, adapted from D. S. Sivia, *Data Analysis, A Bayesian Tutorial*

Interview   **Carrollton, Georgia, October 2006**

Andrew R. Crowe: I tend to have a lot of people who are interested in me. I honestly don't know why, but I do. I seem to be the kind of person who people know my name.

Because of that, they'll all ask me questions about what do you want to do. It's convenient to come up with a simple answer rather than getting into a long discussion, so I respond by saying, "I want to become a computer programmer." It's an oversimplification, but it's convenient.

LS: What led to your interest in computers?

AC: Both my parents are accountants who ran their own business. My father is retired and my mother works part time. Because of that, my parents would still be working after school was over. So I ended up watching a lot of the History Channel when I was younger. I should also mention that I'm an only child.

From five o'clock onwards the History Channel showed this program called "Our Century," which was World War II footage. That's all it was, and it really interested me. I got to the point where I could identify when they reused the same clips in different battles. It's kind of funny actually. I don't know how they got away with it.

I also played computer strategy games. I wasn't very good but I was young and I just set the computer to the easy setting. I was interested in facts and I absorbed them kind of like a sponge.

As I got older I got interested in why things happened, not just military history and the engineering aspect of it, but also the political aspects of it. I became less interested in facts and more interested in the reasons behind things.

Early in high school I got into thinking about morality, and I'm still into it. I'll sit around and try to think about where contemporary morals come from and why they exist. What the real morals are versus what the stated morals are. You can say anything you want, but when push comes to shove things start to move around a little.

I got interested in the idea that complicated systems arise from simple forces. The idea that you can have a small number of basic forces that build upon themselves to form something complicated. You have the old story,

For want of a nail, the shoe was lost.
For want of a shoe, the horse was lost.
For want of a horse, the rider was lost.
For want of a rider, the battle was lost.
For want of a battle, the kingdom was lost.

This summer I took a course on abnormal psychology here at the University of West Georgia. Our professor was interested in how a person can express themselves in seemingly strange ways that have deep significance just to them. Psychology can be a different lens to look at the same thing, but what I'm hoping is that if I can combine enough perspectives I'll have a better view of the complicated systems around me.

That's actually why I'm interested in computer science. I've come to the conclusion that I won't live long enough to learn all of the math and all of the special formulas I would need to become as good as I would like to be in every one of those areas. But if I can learn to use the modeling and processing powers of the computer, then I can get a better idea of how things work.

LS: You've talked about methods of getting perspective, getting a handle on the computations, but what really draws you? What's the underlying motivation?

AC: I think a lot of it is curiosity. I'm really interested in how humans as a whole got to the point where we are, and how we could get to other places. How societies develop.

I've always had this interest in history, probably because I saw so much of it when I was younger. I always like to trace how events years and years ago would lead towards things happening now.

In some way it's my own weird way of answering, "Why are we here?" I'm interested in why are we here at this position, what events led us here, and where we are going.

Oddly enough it was a video game that got me interested in more serious books. My step-brother gave me a copy of the game *Red Alert* in which this scientist goes back in time, removes Hitler, and creates this alternate history. But without another power to block him, Stalin tends to take over, which may be another one of those reminders that small changes, even large changes, don't always work out the way you'd expect.

The company that made that game also made the game *Dune*. I'd never heard of the *Dune* series of books, but another student started reading it, so I checked it out of the library. I got into science fiction because of that, and then I migrated into the works of Robert A. Heinlein.

Heinlein talks a lot about morals. His morals are extremely practical. That made me start wondering a little more. Many of our morals make a lot of sense when you look at them for economic reasons, more so than just thinking of them as basic rules like, "You should do this or you're bad." For example, why is stealing wrong? The economic reason would be because it diverts a large amount of the economy towards security, that makes it inefficient. As a result, a culture in which stealing is rampant will have a lower standard of living.

When I started looking at why those things happened I was better prepared to reconsider the history that I'd learned. As I developed mentally – and I still do this to some degree – I come back to things I've done before and I find I have gotten better at them. I got better at games, not necessarily because of practice but because I'm better at multi-tasking and thinking strategically. I'm also learning new ways to approach problems.

I think that's sort of what happened to some of the questions that I'd had as a kid – the World War Two histories and the other histories that I'd looked at – they kind of got jumbled in with the moral discussion. I got interested in how history flows, and why things have ended up this way.

LS: The kind of stuff you're telling me is very mature and cerebral, but it seems too neat and orderly to believe. Where did this neat and orderly interest come from?

Here you're telling me, "My life was an attempt to order the influences of history, logic, and humanity." But what about these other things that kids do at this age: socializing, schoolwork, and just hanging out? How did you develop beyond these other things, with which most kids are overwhelmed?

AC: I'd say that the stuff I was mentioning to you was more gaps between the other stuff that kids normally do. I hit my lazy senior stage at 10th grade in high school. I think that's when laziness seeped in. I do a fair bit of procrastination and time-wasting, which is a much-vaunted pastime of anyone my age.

Part of my problem is that the practical application of the things that I've been talking about happens in business or government, and I don't have many opportunities to partake in these things. I'm now a computer science research assistant, but what I tend to do for fun is play video games.

I still play a lot of strategy-type games. The space ones: I build up my little empire and lead it through its technical evolution. The games I enjoy the most are the ones where I get to see a change, something in the game where I've started with one thing and I build it up into something else. What interests me is seeing how your little culture grows.

LS: Go back to the accelerated reader program.

AC: They got us to read a lot in elementary school because of that program. You've probably already guessed how it works: you read a book that's been assigned a point value. Then you take a test on it in order to win points. When you get to a certain number of points you get a prize. I got a gazillion points because the Hardy Boys books were five points each, and I could read one in a day and take the test.

LS: You had to take a test to get the points?

AC: Yeah, you had to take like a little 10-question quiz so that you couldn't fake it.

LS: Did you get good scores?

AC: Usually. The only one I scored badly on was *Moby Dick*. I may have read that book when I was too young, but also Captain Ahab talks to himself and can't tell if he's talking to himself or someone else. It's terrible: you sit there and read a page, and then you have to go back and read it again!

LS: Well, he didn't write that book for its testability!

AC: That's true, I noticed that (laughs)! I don't know if they expected many people to be taking an accelerated reader test on it. I probably wouldn't have except for it had a massive point score attached to it.

Strangely enough the hardest tests were tiny nonfiction books. Because they were tiny they expected you to remember the specifics. We also had a bunch of old Cold War books that were interesting because they were partially strategy books, and then they had facts, like comparing the performance of an Apache helicopter to a Hinde, and then they'd show big old diagrams of how navel amphibious units worked.

LS: It's funny; I'm trying to corral you to talk about how you developed, but it always comes back to what you were thinking. It seems that things would catch your imagination, and you would make them into these projects. Where did you get your books? Was someone helping you find them?

AC: I usually found them myself, and I was a really picky reader. I was in a good position because I scored so high. They actually tried to limit kids to what they thought was appropriate to your reading level. Since I scored so high, I could read anything in the library. That's how I got into some of the weird books.

I wouldn't say I was as active as I'm making it sound; it's just that looking back... it's difficult to determine when you came to certain realizations. Something was happening, but it was much more behind-the-scenes. I didn't start to realize a lot of things until eighth grade. I got smarter in eighth grade. I can actually tell, it's quite interesting.

Looking back it seems that I was moving somewhere at a pretty good rate through middle school. High school is where I stopped.

LS: Stopped?

AC: I wasn't really challenged by classes in high school. When I got to high school I slowed down. I'm not entirely sure why. Part of it was that I wasn't doing as much in school, but even outside school I was doing less.

LS: What were you doing?

AC: In ninth grade I got into deeper books. I got into Heinlein's *Stranger in a Strange Land*. I was bored at TIP – Duke's Talent Identification Program – and my roommate was taking a Science of Science Fiction class. I was there the summer after eighth grade. Eighth grade was when I took an economics course there, which was also interesting.

LS: Wait, you're 13 and they're sending you away to a sleep-over thing at Duke University? Isn't that, like, intense for a young kid to go away and live in a dorm room?

AC: It didn't really bother me. All of us were together, and we were all the same age. Before that I had been involved some in Boy Scouts, and I'd done some hiking and some overnight stuff. I'd gone to a lot of day camps when I was younger, so it really wasn't that big of a deal. Plus at TIP they keep you perhaps too busy. They have mandatory fun. They'd have these evening programs and you'd have to go.

I didn't think to bring anything to read, and my roommate had brought *Starship Troopers*, which is one of Heinlein's books. I read it and kind of liked it, and that's how I stumbled on *Stranger in a Strange Land*.

LS: So to boil it down to one main influence, it sounds like books were the thing.

AC: Books were a large part. Books introduced me to ideas that I wouldn't otherwise have gotten. I would never have been exposed in high school to the things that I was ready for. With books I jumped ahead. I read *Lord of the Rings* in fourth grade because it had a whole bunch of accelerated reader points. I found out later that *Stranger in a Strange Land* was a really big thing on college campuses.

LS: None of the stuff you're telling me has a teacher in it, or an adult, or a mentor, or even a club. Was it your own idea to get carried away with all this reading?

AC: Well, yes and no. I probably wouldn't have gotten into it except that the accelerated reading program was a big thing in school at the time. It was kind of expected; they wanted you either reading or in the library getting a book.

I read fast and remembered a lot. I have this really weird thing – it's true for a lot of things – the way I learn is I accumulate this massive store of data, and then I try to figure out how it works. That's what happened there. Once I knew enough words to understand what I was reading, my comprehension jumped from nothing – maybe it was in third grade, I know it was in fourth grade – to testing at 13th-grade level.

LS: It's interesting that you start out saying you're interested in computer science, yet all that we've talked about is verbal stuff.

AC: There's this weird thing: I can't make an 800 on the SAT math test (800 is the highest score. – Ed.). I don't know why, but I've made an 800 on the verbal test twice!

LS: So in spite of your interest in reading, you now shifted your interest to computers.

AC: I've always liked technology. I've always been interested in the engineering side of things, and that kind of carried on to computers because that's what I had my hands on. Like I had a computer at home, so I'd be doing games on it and doing my homework on it.

LS: It's one thing to enjoy using computers, and it's another thing to devote your life to computer science, a lot of which doesn't have to do with using computers but with studying them. How did computers end up being the thing you wanted to focus on?

AC: I've had two computer courses here, and I've enjoyed both of them. It's one of the few things that I could see myself doing as a career, although I don't necessarily want to do just a single thing as a career.

I'm more interested in applying the computer to solve practical problems, and you can work on a lot of problems if you can simplify them to some computer form.

What am I trying to say here? I'm really interested in modeling and in the practical benefits of computers. I like the way that computers solve problems, and I suspect that some computer techniques, like genetic algorithms, could be used to solve a lot more complex problems than we use them for now.

I've become convinced that a lot of really complicated events come up through small changes. Computers are really good at taking a small operation and extrapolating, and I suspect that if you utilize a computer's ability to simulate small changes in complicated systems, then you could gain a lot of understanding in a lot of different fields.

I try to steal a little bit from random subjects (laughs) – a little bit of psychology, a little bit of game theory – and work it all together into something that I could put on a computer.

I intend to come out from college with a degree where I can actually get a job. Both my parents say – and I agree with them – that you want to have a plan in case your dream solution doesn't come through. There are a lot of things that you can do with computers that businesses will pay a lot of money for.

They don't really offer any degrees in what I want to do, which is a problem that a lot of people have. I'm interested in a kind of general area that will give me the background to move into a lot of different things. But there are only so many majors and minors that you can get!

LS: I'm not really a great supporter of the whole college approach. It may come as a surprise to a lot of college students that their success after college will have little to do with their success in college.

In a job interview, for example, people are going to look at you and, as business people learn to do, they'll read your future in the way you carry yourself, the way you speak, and the way you focus yourself. They'll match what they see in you with the kind of person they're looking for. They're not perfect at this, in fact they're often poor at it, but nevertheless evaluating people is what one learns to do in the business world.

AC: It's not the best way to do it... It's just better than any other way of doing it.

LS: That's right!

AC: Now they're working on computer systems that analyze all the variables and come out with some prediction about how people behave...

LS: If that program does as bad a job as people do, then we're in for it!

AC: They got mixed results; sometimes it works and sometimes it doesn't!

LS: ...The nightmares of science fiction will someday come to pass.

AC: Computers have this weird tendency – they'll find some really obscure relationship that no one would have ever thought of, and it will turn out to work, and they'll miss the completely obvious thing that any person could see!

LS: Well, my point is much of a college graduate's future is determined by what they've accomplished and what skills they've learned, not by how well they performed according to their school's ranking system. Your work speaks for itself, and one thing colleges never seem to teach people is how to convince other people of the value of what they've accomplished.

AC: I've always thought, and I still think, that the biggest advantage of going to a place like the Academy isn't the courses you're taking, it's the people you're around. The discussions you have and things.

LS: My attitude to all structured learning is that you've got to invent it yourself. When I come back to places like this I think, "Boy, look at these old college farts sitting around studying things like geology!"

AC: My roommate loves geology (laughs)!

LS: Yeah, then he should go to the mountains! What's he doing sitting in a room studying a book (laughs)?!

I resonated with something you had said earlier. You said that you liked to understand how things got to how they are. I think that means a lot. That may sound too simple to be an explanation for anything, but in fact, it's enough to motivate a lot of people.

AC: That and just proving other people wrong. Those two things seem to get a lot of stuff done!

8. MICHELLE MURRAIN

History   Middle   Born 1959, New York City, New York

This book includes an unusual collection of unusual people, and I admit I find unusual people interesting. So I was pleased when, in the course of this interview, Michelle Murrain – whom I had never met before – turned out to be even more unusual than I expected.

    Stereotypes are stupid but often contain a grain of truth. I tried to think of a non-stereotyped way of introducing Michelle, but the stereotyped way is more fun: she's a black woman, seminary-trained Born Again Christian, Buddhist, lesbian social activist, poet and science fiction writer with a PhD in neuroscience, a one-time tenured college professor, and a full-time computer consultant. She reflects none of the attitudes these stereotypes imply.

Postscript: Michelle is now known as Maxwell Pearl.

Excerpts

"I'm an only child, and my parents were very engaged in their own lives and careers and not very engaged in my life. They were mostly not around. So for me it was like, school's not very useful, my parents were not really there… Maybe that was part of learning that the world was not just about me, because I didn't have many people who were acting as if the world was about me…"

"What you're supposed to do (is) work hard at what you don't really like very much, and then later you get time to play. I never lived my life that way, and I could never imagine doing it. I've always lived my life… I mean the decision to go to grad school… was fine… but that was the last decision I made that was not, 'Let me do what I enjoy. Let me do what makes sense for me. Let me do what I feel fulfilled in.' And that's always been the way I've been…"

"When I decided to become a consultant… I read, like, fine or six books about going into business for yourself and being a consultant and stuff. In fact I got to the point where I said, 'I can't do this!' You know they have these stupid quizzes in the beginning, like 'What kind of personality do you need to be going into business for yourself.' And of course I didn't fit any of them, right? So, it was like, 'Forget it, I can't do this…'"

"I've had small failures… but at each little failure I learned enough not to make bigger ones. I don't know. Maybe they're still to come (laughs)! That could be, you know… A lot of it has been fortuitous, but a lot of it has been following my heart, following what I feel I will enjoy, and that seems to have gotten me to the right place…"

"I think if there's one thing that I would do differently – I don't know if this would really change my decisions, but I think it's one of the threads that really took me a long time, and as I said, I'm still working on this – it's to really love who I am. And I think that I didn't always appreciate who I was…"

"There are directions that you might go in if you understand and really love who you are. There are things that you'll give yourself if you do and that you won't give yourself if you don't. And there are ways that you'll… not take as seriously what other people have to say – which may or may not be true – about who you are."

"When we look into our own hearts and begin to discover what is confused and what is brilliant, what is bitter and what is sweet, it isn't just ourselves that we're discovering. We're discovering the universe."

— Pema Chodron, from *When Things Fall Apart*

Interview   New York City, New York, October 2009

Michelle Murrain: When I was young there were moments where I understood that the world was not about me, and yet I didn't come to a real awareness of myself until quite a bit later.

In the context of learning I probably want to start with my trouble in school because school was – I mean pre-college, with a couple of really standout exceptions – almost uniformly useless for me, which is probably true of most people.

We moved to Great Neck, New York, when I was nine. It was the only relatively well-off suburb in Long Island that would accept African Americans to buy houses. We were one of the half-dozen African American families that lived in Great Neck in the late 60s.

The school I went to was a very good public school with 90 or 95% of the students going on to college. It was a very competitive school, and I was not at all in that expected place of doing well, of being into college-prep mode. I just sort of hobbled along and learned most of what I wanted to learn on my own.

LS: Were you bored?

MM: Oh yeah, totally. In grade school, junior high school, and high school I was totally bored, but I stopped being bored after that because I didn't allow myself. During high school I learned how not to be bored. I read a lot, and I learned where to get information and how to learn it on my own. Once I learned that, I wasn't bored anymore.

The one time that I can remember feeling really bored was the short period of time that I did this retreat in Western Massachusetts in the Berkshires. I took very little with me to read on purpose. It was boring for four days, but it was a really active kind of bored. It was like, "I have to get in touch with this boredom!" kind of bored. So no, I don't get bored. I don't let myself be bored.

My mother was telling me a few days ago that she came across stuff that I had taken apart, radios and watches, because that's what I did when I was young: mechanical objects. I put them back together to some extent, but obviously some things I didn't, because she still had some of the things that were taken apart.

I'm an only child, and my parents were very engaged in their own lives and careers and not very engaged in my life. They were mostly not around. So for me it was like, school's not very useful, my parents were not really there, so it was "me, myself, and I." Maybe that was part of learning that the world was not just about me because I didn't have many people who were acting as if the world was about me.

My grandmother used to take me to the Museum of Natural History, the planetarium and stuff, and it was such a great experience for me, because I would learn a lot. She was very much somebody who encouraged my learning.

I graduated from high school, and I had this weird thing where my grades were not really very good, but I got really good SAT scores and, you know, those advanced test scores. So I went to Bennington College, which was a really good experience for me. That was a useful school (laughs)! It's a small college.

My parents wanted me to be a doctor, and I sort of acceded to their wishes to become pre-med. I always had an interest in science; that was always my thing. So I was a science student at Bennington, which was sort of odd, because there aren't many of them. But it was great because I got a lot of individualized attention. Unlike in high school, I had teachers who could see, "Oh, she's pretty smart. Maybe we should figure out what's going on!"

Bennington has this thing called "Field Work Term," which is a two-month time in January-February where you're off somewhere. I worked in a hospital microbiology lab one winter. I did research in the American Red Cross Blood Lab a second winter. For the third winter I worked at Columbia University in the heart research lab doing programming. That's when I started doing programming. The fourth winter I stayed at Bennington doing my senior thesis.

Bennington had this old – well, it wasn't old at the time – PDP-11/34 mini-computer, and there were like, five people who ever used it. One of the people whom I'd become friends with said, "Hey, why don't you go check this out?" So I came by, and we just sort of hung out and taught each other stuff because there wasn't a computer science teacher at the time. There was this guy Lee Supowit, who was one of the two people on the math faculty. He was a very odd guy, but he was really cool. He was sort of a chaperone for this computer group. We just hung out, and I learned how to program with a bunch of friends.

Then I got a two-month internship at Columbia University helping with a program that was analyzing a certain kind of data… I don't even remember anymore. I really got into it. I loved doing programming. I actually never took a computer science course throughout my whole career. A lot of people haven't; it's actually pretty common. So that got me into programming.

I worked at Columbia for the winter and the following summer and, because it was in a hospital, I knew that I didn't want to be a doctor. My parents wanted me to go to grad school. I wasn't sure that I wanted to go but, I don't know… it was interesting. I had a moment when I was either going to go to grad school, or I was going to go into programming. But that was 1981, before anyone thought that programming was going to be a reasonable career. It wasn't clear that you could make a lot of money doing it. It was a really new thing, not like it was 10 years later. So I went to grad school at Case Western Reserve University and did my PhD in neuroscience.

I spent six years getting my PhD, and about half of the work of the PhD was software that I wrote to do 3-D anatomical structures. Actually, I worked on cockroaches, which is kind of a funny thing.

One of the things of neuroscience – which I think is still true – is that people think if you understand simple animals, and you can sort of figure out how their nervous systems work, it's easier to understand us. The simple animals turn out to be way more complex than anybody ever thought.

My advisor was Roy Ritzmann, who's still at Case, and he was a great guy. He was a really good advisor who was encouraging, and he gave me enough rope – luckily I didn't hang myself. His style was interesting because he assumed that I could do the work. He made the assumption that I would learn to do what I needed to do, one way or another. He provided enough structure and support to get there, but no constraints. It's a style I adopted as a professor, to some extent. That was really good experience, and he was a really good scientist.

I wanted to go into a research career because I was like, "This is cool! I can do this." So I got a post-doc with this guy Stanley B. Kater who was famous in my field. He was one of the top, top guys in the field and had, like, six post-docs and four graduate students and this huge lab. In my naiveté I figured, "He must be a really, really good scientist." I knew that my advisor was really good, but he must be amazingly good if he had that kind of lab. And he offered me a job, and I took it.

I moved to Fort Collins, Colorado, and found that he actually wasn't that great. The reason he had such a big lab was that he was a good salesman. And that was soooo disillusioning to me. I was completely disillusioned. I was like, "This is what science is about? This is what I have to do to do well in science?" I knew I couldn't do it.

I learned a lot about the realities of grant funding and that kind of stuff, but I was very disheartened. At the same time – when I was in grad school – I came out as a lesbian and started to build a social network. There was a very tight-knit lesbian community in Fort Collins, and I found myself within it. I had this sort of instant group of friends, and I was spending a lot of my time learning about who I was.

I'd been writing poetry since Bennington, and I wrote a lot of poetry when I was in Colorado. I was so engaged with my social life, with poetry, and combined with the incredible disillusionment with the job that I had, I was steering in a different direction.

You know, I almost left being a scientist. I knew that I didn't want to go into doing big university research stuff, so I ended up deciding that the right avenue was to go teach at a small college, which would be more my speed. That was when I applied for and got the job at Hampshire College. That was 1989.

Hampshire was a great place. As a faculty member there's an incredible freedom to explore what you want to explore, to teach what you want to teach, to research what you want to research. It's pretty amazing in that way. Since I'd been to Bennington I understood how a small liberal arts college without grades works. It was a style I had an appreciation for, and I had really good colleagues. I got to know faculty from everywhere in the five-college area, and I did a lot of cross-disciplinary teaching.

When I was at grad school at Case, in the last couple of years, I was on the board of the Lesbian and Gay Community Center in Cleveland. In 1985 they had been awarded a grant to do an Ohio-wide AIDS hotline. Because I was a science grad student I was considered the resident scientist and was tapped to train people on what AIDS was.

At the time they had just identified HIV and everything was very new, so much wasn't known, and there was so much rumor and innuendo. I learned everything I needed to learn and was training people on the current science and treatment options and that kind of stuff. I got very involved in doing HIV/AIDS advocacy in Cleveland.

When I went back to Massachusetts I got involved in the Hampshire County AIDS Taskforce. Then I got involved in an organization around women and AIDS because at the time West Massachusetts had large HIV drug-using communities. I was doing some advocacy work around that, and I shifted my research focus to HIV- related epidemiology. I left neuroscience behind at that point.

Hampshire was great because even though I had been hired as the neuro person – and I still taught neuroscience – I could branch out and do whatever I wanted to. There were two other people (at Hampshire) who knew neuroscience, so I wasn't pegged, but at most other schools I would have been kind of stuck. If I had changed fields they would have been like, "Why are you doing that?" And if I'd changed fields it would have been a danger to my tenure and that kind of stuff. At Hampshire I could do it and it wasn't a problem.

So I took some courses in epidemiology at U. Mass. Amherst. I was still doing computer stuff on the side, and then in 1994 this organization I had done some HIV education for wanted to get on the Internet, and they knew that I did technology stuff.

This is at a time when ISPs were exorbitantly expensive; you couldn't just go to GoDaddy and get a host, and you couldn't easily get an Internet connection either. It was expensive, and they couldn't afford it. With the assistance of a Hampshire student, we put a Linux box in my office attached to the Hampshire network, and it became their site... They were the Family Planning Council of Western Mass., and we had family.hampshire.edu. I really enjoyed doing that. It was really fun. So I got into that kind of sideways, working with nonprofits on technology.

At the same time a colleague of mine wrote this big grant, a technology education grant from the NIH (National Institutes of Health). Basically it was a big teacher-education program. Teachers would come to Hampshire and get courses in various subjects. I taught a course – some of it was neuroscience, cognitive science, and technology. This was the mid-to-late 90s, so this was how to get online, how to build web pages, really basic stuff that is sort of *de rigor* now. At the time Massachusetts had a big push to get technology in the schools, so I got roped into all kinds of stuff around that.

In 1996 to 1997 I took a year-long sabbatical. I was going to write a book, a book that was a broad overview of race and class and health in the US. I think the book has subsequently been written, but it hadn't been written then, and I was going to write it. I had an outline, and I had a publisher who was interested, and it was all ready to go. I was on sabbatical to write the book, and I didn't write it, I didn't write it...

In October I got a phone call from a local Springfield television station. They wanted to put together a technology center for teachers, and they didn't know how to go about it. They didn't know what they would need, and they didn't know whether it made sense to do it, and they were sort of like, "What should we do?" So they hired me to do a feasibility study, to spend a couple of months talking to people and laying out what might make sense. I talked to teachers, I talked to people in the field, I talked to a bunch of people, and I had a really, really good time doing the project and it's like, "This is fun!" You know?

Later in that year I got roped into working with a reproductive-rights organization, helping them with some technology planning. They're still my client now, 12 years later; it's kind of funny. And I really had a good time doing that. So I'm thinking, "Hmmm..."

At the time being an academic was sort of... you know. I'm not somebody to do one thing for a very long time, as you've probably noticed by now, and academic politics – people wanted me to be a dean – and yuck. And I'm like, "I'm really enjoying this consulting work, this is fun, I can make a living at it! Let me do that."

I'd gotten tenure at Hampshire – I got tenure in '95, and I could still be there, but I chose not to. My last semester at Hampshire was the spring of '99 when I worked half-time and formed a consulting firm, and I've been doing that, not consistently, ever since.

So I started working with nonprofits and to some extent schools, but that market dried up when the money from the state dried up, so it ended up being just nonprofits. At first I did everything from building web sites to pulling cable, but that was then (laughs). That was when people needed everything. I probably didn't pull cable for more than a year, and then I focused on web stuff. By 2000 I was just doing web stuff and nothing else: no hardware, just web.

I built websites for people from then until 2005 in various different guises. I had a business partner early on, which didn't work out, and then I went solo for a while, and then I joined a consulting firm in Boston. I didn't move, but I worked with them for a couple of years.

LS: Where were you living?

MM: I was living in Amherst the whole time. I didn't move.

What I did next isn't going to make sense without another thread of the story, which has to do with my spiritual life. Up to now if I tell you, "Then I decided to go to seminary…," you'd be like, "Seminary? Where did that come from?" (Laughs)

I was raised a Presbyterian and actually got confirmed in the Presbyterian Church. It's a process like Catholic First Communion, and you take some classes, and there's a little ceremony. It's when you're about 13, 14. The Unitarians call it "Coming of Age" – it's very common. Did that.

When I was 16 my best friend in high school started to go to this Nazarene Church, which is basically fundamentalist. There are all sorts of reasons why I got involved in it. Part of it was that I was very much a seeker – and still am – a seeker of truth, of being able to know the divine, a seeker of understanding. At the time I was 16, I had a really crappy childhood, and I was pretty confused. I was an adolescent, and I was going in a not very good direction in my life. I think it was a way for me to… because it's very black and white: there is one truth, and it is the truth.

It was a way to understand the world because everything is explained from this one truth. That was really attractive to me, and also my peer group was involved, so I became a fundamentalist Christian, and I became Born Again. I did that for four years from 16 to 20 on Long Island, and then I joined a church in Bennington, Vermont, when I went to school.

The truth is I never really bought it; I sort of went along for the ride. But it did help me structure my life because it did feel like, "Well, here's a set of things I should and shouldn't do…" behaviorally, and that was helpful. And I also had an experience of understanding the divine in ways that I hadn't before. That was important, and that was probably what kept me around for so long.

But in the end I couldn't reconcile it. There were a couple of things I began to realize I was a lesbian… and that was not going to do very well. And I couldn't reconcile that there were people that I knew, that I thought were great people, who were going to Hell because they didn't believe what I believed. It's like, "I don't think so!" So I left.

For most of the 80s, actually for all of the 80s, I was sort of wandering but not lost. I dipped into Paganism for a while and did the I Ching for a while. I explored various things. When I was at Hampshire in 1990 I did my first Vipassana Meditation retreat, and that set me on a course of having a meditation practice, which I still have now.

LS: Do you want to say what Vipassana is?

MM: It's part of the Thai Forest Buddhist tradition, which is what they do at the Spirit Rock Meditation Center. I started to go to dharma retreats and sit every day, and I still do that, but it's morphed a bit since then. It was yet another level of awakening, getting in touch with what I was feeling, what was going on inside of me. It was a critical piece of the puzzle, critical to my life.

I did that for a while, I mean I still do, but then I was actively going to retreats. And then in 1999 I went to this really great performance given in Northampton (Massachusetts) by these Tibetan monks. They were doing this nationwide tour. It was one of those things where they show people Tibetan culture and that kind of stuff.

They were doing dharma combat. I don't know if you know about dharma combat. It's this very strange and odd tradition they have. It's a very expressive way of arguing various different points of the teachings.

I'm sitting there, you know, and sort of enjoying it, but a part of me was totally not getting it. That was one of the things that was always true of my going on retreats, sitting and reading Buddhist philosophy: it would go in one ear and out the other, and it never stuck. At times the fundamentals of Buddhism would stick, and I would really "get it" as I sat. But when people told me, or I read it, it didn't stick.

And that's so weird for me because I'm a bookworm; that's how I learn, right? I can read a book and when I'm done with the book I get it. I understand the book. But I would read a book on Buddhist philosophy and I wouldn't get it, and I was like, "This is odd. I don't understand this."

So I was sitting there and I realized, "Oh, well, this isn't my culture. It isn't my tradition. It isn't what I was formed with." Which sort of made me go back and think about Christianity, because that was what I was formed with, and that's my culture. Around the same time I had read in a book by Thich Nhat Hanh who suggested that people go back to their own traditions. Not that they should leave Buddhism, but that they should explore and understand their own traditions.

At the time I wasn't ready to delve back into the Christian church, so I joined a Unitarian Universalist church in Northampton, the Unitarian Society of Northampton, and I went for about four years. In the course of going there, getting involved, and being reacquainted, I found this calling. It's funny. If you talked to me in 2005, I would have said that I felt my call to ministry.

LS: What does that mean? Does it mean to be in a ministry or to minister?

MM: Well, "call to ministry" means to be called to serve in some capacity. For some people they become chaplains, or they work in religious-based nonprofits, or whatever. Some people actually become pastors or ministers. In retrospect, the call was about a desire to reorient my life around the things that were the most important to me.

LS: How old were you at this time?

MM: I was about 44 or 45. It's classic, on some level. So I applied to the divinity schools and decided I was going to go into seminary. I ended up choosing Pacific School of Religion, which is in Berkeley (California).

LS: Was this an internet school, so that you could stay in Amherst?

MM: No, I moved. I moved to Berkeley to go to school.

I sold all my stuff; that was fun. I'd recommend that to anyone: just sell all your stuff. Everything I owned could fit in my car. It was very liberating.

By the end of the first year I realized that – well, there were a couple of things I realized – I realized that I didn't need a professional change in order to restructure my life around what was most important for me, that I could do that and still be a householder and still be a non-clergy person. I also realized that being in the clergy was not the right role for me.

Going to seminary for a year and a half was one of the most important things that I ever did in my life. I have absolutely no regrets about it, even though it didn't end in a way that most people might think was a success.

The other sidebar is that in Berkeley, in the spring 2006, I met my current partner.

When I left seminary I was just going to stay in the Bay Area, but she wanted to live somewhere quieter, so we went back to Western Mass. for a year. I was trying to figure out what I was going to do with my life, so I applied for some nonprofit executive director jobs. But I decided that I really liked what I had been doing before, so I went back to doing consulting; not the same thing exactly but sort of reformulated and reformed. In January of 2008 she moved back to Oakland and I followed in August. So now I live in Oakland.

LS: What does she do?

MM: She is a poet and a therapist. She teaches poetry as well as teaches… she's actually a shaman, so she teaches shamanism courses, shamanistic journeying, and she sees clients and stuff.

I have a new business partner: Thomas Grodin. We have a new business called OpenIssue, LLC. Still working with nonprofits doing technology stuff, building websites.

LS: Have you found your niche? Or is this a sort of a springboard to go other places?

MM: I've found my niche, I would say. I mean, we've found our niche as a company, and I'm really comfortable within the company, working with him and with a bunch of subcontractors. I'm really enjoying it, and it's nice to be within an organization.

We have synergistic skills and a pretty unusual skill set for the kind of work that we do. We're both able to speak technology and do technology, as well as speak English with clients in a way that they understand. That's relatively unusual.

We are both thinking that this is not the last thing that we're going to be doing in our lives. He's actually 10 years younger than I am. He's 40, and he wants to go to grad school at some point. So this is not a permanent "we'll-be-doing-this-forever" kind of thing. It's a moment in time and we're going to concentrate on getting some interesting things to happen, and then we'll think about what's next.

LS: It sounds like you still have quite a few loose ends, although I'm not sure you ever tie loose ends up.

MM: No, never do.

LS: The spiritual thing is on one track, and the business is on another track, and the academics are on another track, and the relationship… well it sounds like it's stable but they tend to evolve, too.

MM: Yeah. Oh yeah, my relationship is definitely evolving. I've always thought of what

I do as very much education. I think of myself as an educator in the disguise of the technology consultant. I've always felt that.

Academia in itself, I mean, I'm done. I had a pretty good 10 years, but it's just not an atmosphere that nurtures me. And the spiritual stuff is... I actually belong to a church now – which I'm very heavily involved with – called the First Congregational Church of Oakland. It's a very diverse, very progressive, very interesting place, and I'm feeling called to be fully involved in it and lend whatever energy and presence I can. That's very much my home right now.

Life for me is... yeah, it's always... I don't stand still very well. Although it's funny because I stand still very well in a moment. I can be fully committed to a task for a pretty good period of time, or to a project. I can really be focused in that way.

My mother used to tell me this story; it's a really funny story because it's so emblematic of how they are and how I'm not. They were at some party and there was this older guy playing the trumpet really well. This younger guy was looking at him in awe and said, "How did you learn to play the trumpet so well?" Because he wasn't like a professional musician, right? And the guy said, "Well, I play every day." And the younger guy asked, "Where do you get time to do that?" And he said, "Well, I worked my whole life and now I'm retired and I play every day."

And this story, from my own perspective, was what you're supposed to do: you work hard at what you don't really like very much, and then later you get time to play. I never lived my life that way, and I could never imagine doing it.

I've always lived my life... I mean the decision to go to grad school... it was fine. I'm glad I did it because getting a PhD was a really good thing in the end for me, but that was the last decision I made that was not, "Let me do what I enjoy. Let me do what makes sense for me. Let me do what I feel fulfilled in." And that's always been the way I've been.

So long as this work is fulfilling to me, and I'm enjoying it, I'll do it. And when it isn't anymore, then – which might happen in 10 years, who knows – it'll be time to do something else, and who knows what that'll be.

LS: Your story has some discrepancies. To use a neurological metaphor, there are some big holes that you don't see because they fade into the background.

MM: Well, tell me. I want to know.

LS: Where's the uncertainty? Where's the struggle, and the strife, and the failure, and the...

MM: Oh (laughs)! We haven't talked about that.

LS: It sounds like a Walt Disney life: you went from one success to another. I have a picture of a character jumping from one stone to another across a lake of flaming lava, getting to the other side unscathed. Most of us fall in the lava...

MM: That's fascinating!

LS: ... or we struggle and sweat for a long time, but you didn't speak it.

MM: That's a fascinating perspective. I didn't speak it.

Well. There's been a lot of struggle and strife, for sure. I'll tell you a little bit about my childhood, which was a real time of struggle and strife for me. Much of my adult life has been a process of healing from that time.

COMPUTERS

I was in therapy for eight years, actually more than that, for all the time that I was in Hampshire. I think part of the reason that you don't hear it is because I don't know you that well, and this is for a book, so am I going to let go of all that stuff in gory detail?

LS: Well, the reason it's important is because it's the problem that people have. No one has trouble when the going is good, that's when we just coast along. It's the bad stuff that is the mystery.

MM: Yeah, sure. I would say that for me the hardest moments, I mean aside from my childhood, the hardest moments in my life, the biggest disappointment, or one of the biggest moments of, like, "What am I going to do?" was when I was in Colorado. I hated my job the minute I understood what was going on.

It's funny. This friend of mine who had worked in the lab before, who I knew from when I was in grad school, said, "Don't work there." (Laughs) But I was enamored with the idea of working for someone who was so well known. The experience was very disheartening, and I didn't do very well as a scientist in that setting. I was very not happy in the context of that job.

At the time I came really close to leaving science altogether because I didn't feel like I fit, I didn't feel like I could find a way that made sense to me. A lot of women in science have a really hard time being a woman in science. I actually never really felt as a woman, or as an African American woman… I never felt like I wasn't taken seriously. That was really fortunate.

When I got to Colorado it was a really different atmosphere. I felt I wasn't taken seriously as a woman in the lab. And the guy I worked for, his most favorite form of conversation was argument. There would be these heated arguments about scientific findings. That was really hard for me. I mean it's like, "Why argue about this? There is no point."

In some ways you could say that landing in Hampshire was jumping across the lava, and it kind of was: making the decision to teach at a small college versus going to a university. I chose the right one.

Had I ended up at any one of those other places, I would have been much more pigeon-holed in terms of what I could have taught and researched, and I probably would have left a lot sooner. So Hampshire was very serendipitous… or not – I don't know what you think about coincidence, or serendipity, or whatever – but it was the right thing for me at the time.

LS: I get the feeling that you're careful about your decisions. You haven't talked much about the struggle that goes into your decisions, but it seems that you've made the right choices. Even in going to Colorado, the way you described it, was a set-up for what you learned: you thought that the guy was going to be good because he was famous, and you learned one of the ultimate lessons of science, which is that it's a social pursuit.

MM: Yeah, I guess that's true.

I don't know about careful. It's an interesting question. I think I am so led by what feels like it will be fun. I felt like Hampshire would be fun: like it would be a fun place to teach.

LS: Just to be practical, how did you assemble the information you needed?

MM: You mean to go to Hampshire?

LS: Not just Hampshire, but to make any decision at all. Do you get involved with the situation, do you get involved with the people? Are you intuitive, do you research things?

MM: I'm pretty intuitive, I think. I do a lot of research. It's a combination.

Like when I decided to become a consultant: that was a long and extended process of reading a gazillion books. I read, like, five or six books about going into business for yourself and being a consultant and stuff. In fact I got to the point where I said, "I can't do this!" You know they have these stupid quizzes in the beginning, like, "What kind of personality do you need to be going into business for yourself." And of course I didn't fit any of them, right? So, it was like, "Forget it, I can't do this."

But then, there's this book I found called *The Consultant's Calling*, and it's this amazingly wonderful book, if you ever come across it. It's a book about... do you know the quote by Frederick Buechner: "A vocation is where the world's great need and your great gladness meet." It doesn't use that quote, but the book is very much like that quote. Consulting as a way to meet people's needs, a way to educate people, and a way to have a balanced life. And I was like, "I can do that." That book changed my mind. It made me realize that I could do consulting. It took me a year to make that decision. I talked to people. It was a very considered decision.

The decision to teach at a college instead of going for a university position was more of a fallback. I spent two months thinking I would leave science altogether and then I was like, "What am I going to do?" Yeah, I had this PhD in neuroscience, but what am I going to do? Am I going to bus tables?

There were a lot of things I could have done, but I didn't really know enough. I was in Colorado and I didn't know about Silicon Valley. I talked to this woman that I'd gotten to know who was head of the Woman's Studies at Colorado State. I was talking to her about my dilemma and she said, "Why don't you think about this..." and she told me about *Science Magazine* that had lots of ads for positions. There were a bunch of positions at small colleges, and I thought, "Wow, I should try these out." And that was how it happened.

My decision to go to seminary was very much an intuitive decision. I talked to a few people. A good friend of mine said, "What took you so long?" I thought that was funny. So that was more intuitive.

A lot of it has been fortuitous, but a lot of it has been following my heart, following what I feel I will enjoy, and that seems to have gotten me to the right place. It's interesting. I'm just thinking about the thing that you mentioned about the holes and about the struggle. I feel like in many ways... you know, all that stuff got sort of front-loaded in my childhood.

LS: What do you mean by "front-loaded?"

MM: I guess I learned a lot about the realities of the world, about the pain of the world, when I was very young. And I think that... I don't know, somehow I learned enough that the directions I've chosen to move in have aligned with what works.

I don't know how to describe what I'm saying but, um... I mean I've had small failures, like the business that I first started when I left Hampshire. I had a business partner and we didn't work well together, and that was a little difficult to figure out what to do with. But at each little failure I learned enough not to make bigger ones. I don't know. Maybe they're still to come (laughs)! That could be, you know.

LS: That could be. I guess that depends on where you're going. Where do you think you're going?

MM: I have no idea. You know, I'm doing this work for the foreseeable future, but I know it's not the only one. I literally have no idea.

One of my other side things that I do – but I can't imagine this becoming a full-time thing, but who knows – is I write science fiction. I started writing in 2006. I have two novels that are pretty much done and a third that is all fleshed out but I haven't written it. I haven't had that much time to write.

LS: Did this displace poetry?

MM: Not really, because I stopped writing poetry regularly almost 10 years ago.

LS: This is my last question. If you were talking to a kid, someone who is like you were when you were 14, assuming that you harbored indecisions and self-doubt when you were 14, which you haven't talked about...

MM: Oh, I still harbor indecisions and self-doubt!

LS: ... how would you advise that person to overcome, get through, or prevail in the face of those kinds of obstacles.

MM: I think what I would say... two things come to mind. I would say, first, find a way to learn to love yourself, which I think I haven't gotten to yet. And second, find a way to love what you do. Or find a way to do what you love, which is a better way to say it.

I think if there's one thing that I would do differently – I don't know if this would really change my decisions, but I think it's one of the threads that really took me a long time, and as I said I'm still working on this – it's to really love who I am. And I think that I didn't always appreciate who I was.

Without that appreciation or that understanding... I don't know... it's just that there are directions that you might go in if you understand and really love who you are. There are things that you'll give yourself if you do and that you won't give yourself if you don't. And there are ways that you'll take yourself seriously and... and... I don't want to say "ignore," but not take as seriously what other people have to say – which may or may not be true – about who you are.

Although in some ways you might say that I jumped from stone to stone across the lava, if I had taken these two things to heart when I started, then I would be in a different place now. I would have taken a totally different path. I can't say what that path would be, but I don't think that it's the path that I took.

LS: That opens the whole thing up for your future.

MM: Oh yeah, it does, definitely.

9. ESTHER DYSON

History   Middle   Born 1951, Zürich, Switzerland

I thought Esther and I had a lot in common: I worked on the same physics problem as her father, Freeman Dyson, we're both interested in Eastern Europe, and are active in traveling, writing, technology, and business. But, as you can hear in this interview, we had a hard time communicating. Part of this is her reticence in revealing her feelings, but we also think differently. We have less in common than I thought.

The world of high-tech entrepreneurship has superstars, and Esther is one of them. She travels almost constantly, and her name appears in print in newsletters and Op-Ed columns all over the world. Most people are not sure what she actually does, and her description of herself as being a professional member of numerous boards of directors does little to clarify. Nor does this short but typical bio that appeared on the web:

> "Esther Dyson is editor of Release 1.0, and serves as court jester to the online world, as loving critic, angel investor, long-sighted analyst and enthusiastic participant."

For the record, Esther acts as a "meta-CEO" for 24 companies. She also acts as a large and involved shareholder in 32 others. Imagine what it would be like to have detailed knowledge of, and wield significant authority in, 56 companies simultaneously.

Rather than the court jester, as she describes herself, I'd describe her as the Pope: she exercises strategic authority with limited responsibility. She's a big advocate of leverage, but in her case it's more like "uber leverage": other people do all the work, and she has all the fun. At least she thinks it's fun; it seems like a crazy life to me.

Excerpts

"I felt my college work was fundamentally useless because I was reading stuff that had already been written, and writing stuff that people already knew… I wanted to be a journalist and to ask good questions. I didn't almost flunk out, but I definitely graduated without distinction…"

"Checking facts is God's work. Before you write stuff down you need to make sure it's accurate. I think that should be one of the Ten Commandments. There really is no better way to learn stuff than to have to write it down for other people and stand by your work…"

"I feel self-directed… I have a sense that I want to do what's useful. Not that I never sit around and experience pangs of regret, but in general I feel I'm doing things that are useful. I do things that I can learn from, and that's what I like to do…"

"I'm a court jester, which is someone close to the king but who has no formal power, except he can get the king to listen on occasion. People tell the court jester everything because they know the court jester is extremely discreet and maybe will point things out to the king, but won't tell him where he learned them…"

"You have to figure it out for yourself. A lot of unhappiness comes from people using someone else's ladder. You need to design your own ladder and climb that one. Otherwise you get to the top of someone else's mountain, and you don't really want to be there."

"Many of the students one meets graduate from these outstanding universities without any clear sense of what their life mission is. Moreover, they don't have any real idea of what is out there, of what real-world career paths look like... They don't have the vaguest notion as to how real people move from post to post."

— David Brooks, from *Making It, Love and Success at America's Finest Universities*, Vol. 8, No. 5

"Rejoice in that which is present, and be content with the things that come in season. If you see anything that you have learned and inquired about occurring, in your course of life, be delighted at it."

— Epictetus, Greek philosopher (c. 55 – 135 AD), "Discourse 4"

Interview   New York City, New York, August 2008

Esther Dyson: The best learning has always been outside of school. I worked very hard in high school in order to get out. I went to college when I was 16, and then I suddenly stopped working hard because I no longer had a goal. I wanted to graduate but that was about it.

I felt my college work was fundamentally useless because I was reading stuff that had already been written, and writing stuff that people already knew. I did have one or two classes I really liked, but I spent most of my time working at the *Harvard Crimson*. I wanted to be a journalist and to ask good questions. I didn't almost flunk out, but I definitely graduated without distinction.

Then I had these two jobs in New York that I really hated. I had a headache every day until five o'clock. Then I got a job I liked, and ever since I've been working seven days a week, learning new stuff, and sometimes writing it down.

LS: How did you find what you liked?

ED: By getting lucky. I knew I wanted a writing job, and I liked to write about stuff that was new, or that people didn't know, rather than going to the encyclopedia and recomposing something that already exists. That is the essence of news.

So I loved the job at *Forbes*. I was a reporter, actually a fact-checker, and I loved it. I checked facts, and if I came up with a story idea that was good enough, then I got to write a story instead of checking someone else's. Checking facts is God's work. Before you write stuff down you need to make sure it's accurate. I think that should be one of the Ten Commandments. There really is no better way to learn stuff than to have to write it down for other people and stand by your work.

LS: Where's the meaning in all of this?

ED: I ended up writing a newsletter that wasn't really news; it was more insight, and that's where the meaning was. Thinking, "Well, what does this mean?" Selecting the particular two facts that would make people understand the broader meaning.

I could sit and interview you for an hour, I could take accurate notes, and I could make you look like an idiot or like a brilliant man. I could make you look kind and thoughtful, or mean and careless, and quote you accurately in either case. There's a meaning, as you say. In order to tell a true story, I have to pick the right anecdotes that are indicators of your character.

LS: So, do you want to tell me your character?

ED: Umm... no.

LS: (Laughs) That's obvious, but I thought I'd ask anyway!

ED: Smart, trying to be kind and thoughtful, and self-confident but not obnoxious – I hope.

LS: I'll let you run with that one.

ED: Now you have to ask another question.

LS: Well, I'm looking for the meaning there. All those adjectives, they sound meaningful but they don't necessarily have import to a person.

ED: So you need to call for some useful anecdotes.

LS: I'd ask for anecdotes from when you were young, but maybe that's not where the insights really happened.

ED: There are things that you can learn anytime that are always true: how it pays to be nice to people, how it's better to be a sucker than a jerk, that you need to think before you talk. You can learn those kinds of things anytime, and they're always true.

And then there are things that are new, like what's happening in social media, or what's the implication of the Internet, things like that. Those things unfold, and if you see them before other people see them, then it's fun to explain them to people who say, "Oh, I knew those little things, but I never really understood what they meant." That's a second kind of learning, where you learn something that's new as opposed to learning something that people already know. Like you might watch what's going in Russia and try to figure it out.

LS: Tell me for the record, because I don't really know – do you travel a lot?

ED: I travel a huge amount. I have business interests in Russia, Europe, around the US, and I have little, odd business things in other places. I'm going to a conference in Tianjin, which is near Beijing, in the middle of September. I don't really have any business interests in China, but I'd like to know what's going on. One of the best ways to find out is to go hear what people are taking for granted, not what they say.

I just got invited to go to Kampala in the middle of November to give a talk to the Ugandan Stock Exchange. How can anybody turn that down? It's like, wow! You're not just going to see Uganda and look at the animals, you're going to go meet people who are trying to make things happen in Uganda. That's really interesting.

I'm on two particular boards of directors that are interesting in this context. One is WPP Group. They have ad agencies all over the world. They probably have some affiliate in Uganda so I can go see them when I'm there and ask, "What's happening to consumer lifestyles in Uganda? Are people buying shampoo yet, or are they still too poor and focused on getting enough to eat?"

The other board is the National Endowment for Democracy; they give grants to democracy organizations in countries that are often basket cases economically and politically.

There was this judge in Russia who just ruled on a sexual harassment case. So he says, "We need sexual harassment to keep the race going. If this didn't happen our race would die out." He let the (accused) guy off. This judge just had no interest in what the law was. I'm sure he views himself as a crusty curmudgeon with a sense of humor, but the guy's a disaster. So the National Endowment for Democracy gives grants to people who train judges, and/or help people organize politically, or run honest newspapers.

Last year I spent two and a half days in Kyrgyzstan visiting grantees – I don't think that WPP has an office in Bishkek. One way or another, I've got most of the world covered.

LS: How did you get such wanderlust?

ED: Curiosity. As I said, I've been lucky. I've got connections so that I can go do interesting things, and I'm in a position where I can travel around the world and meet interesting people.

LS: Do you remember a time when you were bored and didn't have this passion?

ED: Someone asked me just the other day if I ever get bored… I never get bored unless I'm talking to someone who's boring. If I'm alone I can think about what's interesting or watch something that's interesting. The only time you get bored is when someone distracts you from what you think is interesting.

LS: But when were you intrinsically bored, deeply bored. Were you ever?

ED: Well, yeah, when I was doing that job that was so boring.

LS: No, I mean before that. I mean as a state of mind. Are you telling me that you were always enthusiastic about something?

ED: I guess I was bored sometimes in school, but after school I was mostly reading.

LS: How did you find reading?

ED: Books.

LS: What I mean is how did you become a reader? I have a 10-year-old son. He wants me to read to him, but he hasn't realized that books are a way to travel. Didn't you grow up in a family that had lots of books?

ED: I learned how to read, and I think my parents said, "Do it yourself."

LS: What did you start reading? What caught your interest?

ED: I don't know, everything there was. I was eight, or maybe I was six, and I read books about magic, I read fairy tales, I read grown-up books. I read *The Diary of Anne Frank*.

LS: Did you read these because they were in the house?

ED: Yeah, and then I went to the library.

LS: Were you one of those people who scoured the shelves for interesting things in the library?

ED: Oh yeah. I loved the library. When I was very small I wanted a job in the library, but you had to be 14. The moment I turned 14 I went to the library and got a job as a page.

LS: What does a page do?

ED: Takes books off and put books back on the shelf; makes sure that they're in the right place.

The first year I could work only in the children's section. I loved knowing what the books were, and giving people advice. I pretty much knew every author in there, and I could give people advice on what they would like, what the books were about. That was much more fun than putting books back on the shelf. And the next year I got to do the adult section; that was fun in a different way. And then I went to college.

LS: College wasn't so good?

ED: Oh, it was great, just the class part wasn't. The *Harvard Crimson* was great. I was writing things that were new, as opposed to things that were already in a book somewhere. I did some news stories but mostly I did movie reviews, which was a lot of fun. I read some of them the other day and they were very pompous: "Catherine Deneuve, who failed to please in her last four roles, shines in this new film…" This was a 17-year-old girl writing this stuff.

LS: Do you consider yourself a journalist?

ED: Yes and no. Now: not really, but my trade is journalism. I think it's a holy calling.

LS: Funny, I would have thought you'd identify yourself as a computer person.

ED: In any context I can be anything, but the trade I have is making people see stuff. I can't program a computer, but I know the computer industry, and I invest in startups. The skill I have is seeing what's going on and explaining it to people. It may be seeing that a CEO is behaving badly and explaining it to him (laughs), or it may be seeing that the company is really great and explaining it to other investors.

Put me down somewhere and I'll figure out what's going on and explain it to everyone. I like to explain in whatever medium is appropriate. It may be by investing money, it may be by writing, it may be by giving a speech.

LS: What do you mean by "explaining by investing money"?

ED: I'm explaining this is a good company, I see opportunity here. People say I do investing, and I say investing is like having sex. The fun part is actually raising – well, the sex is fun – it's the raising the children afterwards that's the real commitment. I don't like just putting money somewhere; I like growing the thing that I put money into.

LS: Is that called "management"?

ED: No, it's called sitting on a board or being an active investor. And, of course, depending on the person and the recipient, that can be called interfering or micro-managing.

LS: That is a bizarre job description, if it is a job description: a board member.

ED: There are actually two versions of being a board member. There's a member of a board of a public company where you have a fiduciary duty to the stockholders, and you need to make sure that the laws are followed. You don't get that involved in the activities of the company. Your main job is to hire and fire the CEO on behalf of the stockholders. You can tell the CEO what to do, and if he doesn't do it, then you can fire him.

When you're on the board of a small company it's more like being a parent. You do whatever is needed: you help them write their press releases, you help them hire their sales guy, you point out to them, "You know, I think the sales guy and the marketing people don't get along. Have you considered doing this or that?" There are ways to do this effectively, and there are ways to do it badly.

LS: Can you give me an example?

ED: Oh, I can give you hundreds. First of all, I help a lot of these companies write their press releases, or I edit their position statements, or their marketing materials. I help them find people. I say, "This guy just isn't cutting it. I heard him give a pitch and he wasn't listening to the customer. You've either got to get him to listen, or you've got to let him go."

I've fired CEO's. Ideally you don't fire them; you get them to understand that they should resign. If you do it well they stay and become Chief Strategy Officers or something. I give support and encouragement and also criticism. You try not to say, "You're a stupid idiot." Instead you say, "Gee, maybe we should do blah instead of blip," or whatever.

LS: How about taking criticism yourself? It sounds like you're out of the line of fire.

ED: I got a lot of criticism when I was Chairman of ICANN (Internet Corporation for Assigned Names and Numbers), the domain name system agency. I try to be good at taking criticism; it's hard, everybody knows that.

There are things that I'm not good at and things I don't want to be good at. So if someone comes in and says, "You're not a very good singer," I wouldn't really mind. If someone said, "Your writing style is lazy," or something, if it was, and sometimes it is… Criticism is much harder to take when it's merited. If it's not merited, you can say, "Well, you're wrong." But if it's merited, and you know it, that's the hardest.

I'm not perfect, but I try to… Once, when I still had my own company, I dropped my computer or something, and it took a long time to be repaired. My computer was broken and I was kind of bad-tempered around the office. My business partner came up to me and said, "You're blaming everybody here for what's going wrong. You have to understand we're not trying to make things worse for you. We're trying to deal with this as well as we can, and you're making us all feel bad." She was absolutely right. I felt terribly ashamed.

I think I apologized, and it worked. But it was clear that they should have told me that two weeks before, and I scared them off. This is a five-person, two-bit, dinky little company, and they were scared to confront me. Imagine what it's like at the top of a big billion-dollar company.

LS: Are you now involved in those big companies?

ED: In a few….

LS: I don't understand how you went from the bottom of the barrel to the top – to over the top of the barrel – without going through the barrel. Where are the years of fighting your way up, or somehow proving yourself?

ED: Well, that's what you get to do as a journalist. You get to stay on the outside.

LS: Then how did you get hired as a board member? Is it because you distinguished yourself for your insight?

ED: Yeah, fundamentally. Yes.

I have different versions of my autobiography. In one of them I'm a court jester, which is someone close to the king but who has no formal power, except he can get the king to listen on occasion. People tell the court jester everything because they know the court jester is extremely discreet and maybe will point things out to the king, but won't tell him where he learned them. That's what I like to do.

LS: So what about computers? They seem irrelevant. They haven't come up in this whole discussion.

ED: Well, you didn't ask about it.

The computer business is, other than the unfolding of history and politics, the most interesting thing that has happened to the world in the last 40 years. I think the next 20 is probably going to be genomes and health care, and information about human bodies and minds and things. So I'm doing a lot more in that and less in computers.

You know there's a great saying, "The remainder of the proof is left as an exercise to the reader." And that's where I think the computer industry is now. There's a lot more to do in the computer business, but fundamentally the first blinding flash, the understanding that this really, really matters… it's done. Now we need to carry it forward. But I think the real visionary stuff is happening in genomes and understanding life and things like that.

LS: What else, what other things?

ED: Well, the other thing that I'm doing is space travel. Which is different, but exciting.

LS: What is space travel?

ED: It's the same as the Internet: it's the privatization of what had previously been a government enterprise. I think with privatization will come a lot more commercial energy, a lot more trial and error, and better results.

LS: What's the objective, or a couple of the big ones?

ED: Well, there's three things. One, let's have a backup world, which would be Mars.

Two, let's try stuff on Mars that we can't try on Earth, like mucking around with the climate. On Earth, first of all you have a lot of politics, and second, if we screw up the Earth we're really in trouble. But if we screw up Mars we can learn from it and try again. So, what we want to do is try climate change on Mars and learn enough to do it right on Earth.

And third, there's lots of minerals and energy and all kinds of scientific and commercial reasons to go in the short run. And there's an exciting tourism business, which is kind of like the Internet. Well, probably not to Mars very soon, but maybe to a moon of Mars. Who knows?

LS: How much of your time does this take up?

ED: It may take up four months next year, because I might go into astronaut training in Moscow, but I don't know yet.

LS: It does sound like computers were never the focus of your work; they were just the vehicle of your interest.

ED: They were what I wrote about, not the computers themselves but the things they made possible: the businesses, the people, the social change, the business models, and to some extent how people spend their day. But no, I've never written a review of a hardware product.

LS: Here's my problem: kids are not allowed to grow up. They're kept childlike forever, and Mommy and Daddy are being replaced by institutions, to which they remain beholden for the rest of their lives – if things go according to plan. But this doesn't really work because people do need to grow up.

ED: So are you thinking of employers as "*in loco parentis*"? (Latin for "in the place of a parent." – Ed.)

LS: Employers, or government. The family is weak; the parents are weak. The parents are replaced by teachers; the relatives are replaced by political institutions. Ceremonies of transformation and maturity are washed into meaninglessness and replaced by things like graduation or getting a job. Even marriage has lost its sense of community place.

What I find in talking to people, and from my own experience, is that people who've found transformation, people who have experienced transformation, find it for themselves, somehow. It's often a mysterious process.

People say, "I woke up one day..." or, "All of a sudden people took an interest in me..." and then everything shifts. You shift your environment and all of a sudden everything looks different: people relate to you differently, there are new opportunities, there is movement where previously there was no avenue for movement. It's an abrupt sort of discontinuous transition. It's like falling in a hole: you don't know what's happening as you're falling into it, but you know it as you hit the bottom. The world looks different.

I would like kids to know that there are transformations that are available to them, but perhaps impossible to describe, and to know that only they can find them.

ED: OK, everything you say is true, but I'm still not really sure what you're talking about. Are you talking about becoming a responsible adult?

LS: No, I'm talking about becoming a self-actualized person, a thinking person, a person who has a passion.

ED: OK, I'd call that a responsible adult. You're saying that not everybody reaches that, obviously.

LS: Most people don't have a passion. Put them on a desert island with a chance to start over, or give them an opportunity to forge their lives the way they want, and they wouldn't know what to do. But I think you have this – you haven't fully disclosed your character, but OK. Can you comment on that, about how a person finds this passion?

ED: I feel self-directed. I would do a lot to avoid a nuclear war, but if there was one, and if I was still alive afterwards, I would say, "OK, let's get to work." I don't know if that's what you mean, but I have a sense that I want to do what's useful. Not that I never sit around and experience pangs of regret, but in general I feel I'm doing things that are useful. I do things that I can learn from, and that's what I like to do.

LS: Does the reward come from outside? Do people need to reward you, or do you just know it?

ED: I know it. But I also like it when other people notice. I like it when people say, "Oh gee, you told me this and it turned out to be true and these nice things happened." It's nice to be noticed, but it's also nice to just watch it happen.

I mean this seriously, and people laugh, but I'm lazy in the sense that I'd much rather do something with little effort and achieve something than kill myself doing it. I don't want to get a million dollars for nothing, I wouldn't enjoy that, but if there's a way to earn a million dollars by making a machine that makes the job easier, I'll always do that. I don't see any virtue in vacuuming by hand if you can build an automatic vacuumer.

I'll tell you one of my favorite books: it's called *Danny Dunn and the Homework Machine*. (Written by Raymond Abrashkin and Jay Williams, published in 1958 – Ed.) I must have read this when I was six or seven. Danny was a nice, fair-haired American boy. He had a thin, gloomy friend called Joe Pearson, and there was this family friend called Professor Bullfinch who worked at the university. Somehow this Professor Bullfinch had a computer – although it was called something else in the book because this was in the 50s – and Danny and Joe decided that they would avoid doing their homework by programming this computer to do all their homework for them.

They had to work far harder, learn far more, and just about kill themselves to program this computer to do their homework. It was a great story, and I would always love to program a computer if after that the computer would do all the homework.

LS: But doesn't that contradict your not wanting to vacuum if there was a vacuuming machine, because it would have been easier if they just did the homework?

ED: But then the homework machine was ready to do it forever. So it's building the vacuuming machine...

LS: Have you built any of these "vacuuming machines"?

ED: Yeah. I do so with every company that succeeds: I have other people do stuff that I don't do. It's all about leverage.

LS: You know, you're different than other people; you just won't admit it.

ED: No, I admit it totally. I'm very self-directed.

LS: Let me ask this: were you always clear about what you wanted to do? When you came to decision points, were you always clear about which choice to make?

ED: Pretty much. I don't make many decisions.

LS: Well, you made a bunch between the ages of 10 and 20.

ED: Well, this is the point: I don't really feel that I did. I felt that everything was almost... Well, yes, I decided to go to Harvard over Cornell, and I decide whether to make specific investments, but, in the end, I don't really. In most important things, I feel I didn't have to make a difficult choice.

LS: So you were never at a loss for a choice.

ED: More or less.

LS: So given kids today – and all that jazz about life and work and love – can you say anything about how to find what you think is a good state of mind?

ED: You have to figure it out for yourself. A lot of unhappiness comes from people using someone else's ladder. You need to design your own ladder and climb that one. Otherwise you get to the top of someone else's mountain and you don't really want to be there.

It's very simple, and it's hard for a lot of people because they have a lot of people giving them advice. They have things that are expected of them, and they don't have the opportunity to read widely and to talk to lots of people.

In the end, you need to figure out what interests you. Then, and this is the important part, you need to have something in particular that you want to accomplish, because that's what makes you feel good.

FILM

10. OLIVER PIERCE

History   **Early**   Born 1987, New York City, New York

I've known Oliver for many years and always thought him a good student and kind of a bookworm. So I was surprised when he dropped out of school after ninth grade with no intention of returning.

    I now appreciate what he's doing and how motivated he is; not only motivated but positive, organized, and determined. Oliver wants to make films, so he's just pushed school out of the way and started doing it by independent study, networking, apprenticeship, trial and error, and sheer pluck. His latest short film has been accepted for a showing in the Woodstock Film Festival.

Excerpts

"From very early on I always knew I wanted to do film, and then it was just a question of how to pursue that. I toyed with the idea of leaving school for a while… It's not like I had any terrible, terrible experiences at (high school), I just knew what I wanted to be doing and that wasn't it…"

"The exact moment I decided to leave school was the summer between ninth and 10th grades. I was on a camping trip and I was getting close to when school was going to start again… I finally decided that I was not going to go back to public school. Then I went and threw up in the woods for about half an hour. I was really nervous about the decision. But I'm glad definitely, definitely glad I did…"

"I think you can learn pretty much anything you can learn in school, out of school. You can, that's a fact. All the information is obtainable… What you can't do out of school that you can do in school is get a piece of paper that says this is what you know… There are more things that you can learn out of school than you can learn in school. You can learn anything out of school…"

"Occasionally you always get the negative voices that come in… I just try to get them out of my head. Some days I can do it, some days I can't. If I think about it logically, I don't feel I have very much to be nervous about. I don't mean that to sound cocky at all; like I said, I'm not rich yet, so hopefully I'm right about all that I'm saying, but you never know. I feel confident enough that I'm right that I'm continuing to do what I'm doing."

"Programming your unconscious mind… you'll begin to see opportunities and chances where before you would have missed or ignored them. You'll find yourself moving toward your positive future as if it were drawing you in the same inexorable straight line that drew Newton's apple from the tree."

— Thom Hartmann, from *Walking Your Blues Away*

"Drop out of school before your mind rots from exposure to our mediocre educational system. Forget about the Senior Prom and go to the library and educate yourself if you've got any guts."

— Frank Zappa, from "Freak Out!" (Liner notes, June 27, 1966)

Interview   Shokan, New York, June 2006

Oliver Pierce: I've decided I want to be a successful filmmaker in the areas of writing and directing. Toward that end I left school after ninth grade to pursue independent study and focus on all the different aspects of filmmaking: writing, directing, acting, cinematography, editing, and producing. Those are the main seven things it takes to make a movie.

I'm not rich yet. Everything I'm working toward is just a working hypothesis, which I think is going to work. I'm pretty confident in my decision but everything I say can be taken with a grain of salt.

If I'm going to be a writer or director it's also important to understand the other things, so I worked in all of those things and I made a bunch of short films. My approach is to study with people who are active in their fields, professionally active in those different fields as opposed to just taking a course at Ulster Community College (the local community college), where the person teaching the class has no… I don't want to say they have success, but they're not working in the industry doing what I want to learn.

Through asking different people – finding the right people to work with – the people I found were, for the most part, really willing to help out, to give me their opinions and their time. In the past year I've gotten a little work: little film projects shooting ads for people or editing short films. I've done a bunch of my own films that have been in festivals, and I've started to line up some bigger projects. Now the challenge is making those happen. The next step is trying to go to Los Angeles and really make the bigger things happen.

LS: Do you know the pivotal moment when you decided to go off in this direction?

OP: Let me think. First, from very early on I always knew I wanted to do film, and then it was just a question of how to pursue that. I toyed with the idea of leaving school for a while.

The exact moment I decided to leave school was the summer between ninth and tenth grades. I was on a camping trip and I was getting close to when school was going to start again. I finally decided that I was not going to go back to public school. Then I went and threw up in the woods for about half an hour. I was really nervous about the decision. But I'm glad definitely, definitely glad I did.

LS: You didn't think of going to another school?

OP: I did think of going to another school, but I figured, what would be the point? I figured, "Why, when I know so much about what I want to do, why have someone else's curriculum?"

LS: Did you find school was annoying to you for other reasons?

OP: Well, I went to Waldorf School through eighth grade, and I liked Waldorf School for the most part. But it only went through eighth grade, and then I went to Rondout (public high school). It's not like I had any terrible, terrible experiences at Rondout; I just knew what I wanted to be doing and that wasn't it.

LS: What are the big problems you see for yourself now?

OP: I don't see any big problems, I see a lot of little problems. Anything is just a series of little problems, in a lot of ways.

LS: You don't see the lack of a degree or a certification as standing in your way?

OP: Not at all. For other people it would be, but film – and I've heard a lot of people say this – is really the last bastion where you just go in, and if you're good enough you can get a job. You don't need degrees or any formal piece of paper, which is totally different from most fields. And I'm pretty sure it is true.

I keep kind of a mental list of filmmakers I know left high school. It's a really long list; three off the top of my head are Quentin Tarantino, Jim Carey, and David Fincher. I know all three of them dropped out of high school. And many, many, many of them dropped out of college. In fact most of them, pretty much.

One of the only things I kind of missed about not going to school – which I got over and was able to do without, even though it was one of the reasons I left – was having a deadline, which can be really helpful if you're doing a project. It's really easy to put things off if you don't have a deadline. In school it was all deadlines on projects that I didn't feel were necessary. I figured I'd rather do my own projects, not have the pressure of a deadline and be forced to focus and really do it on my own, than have the luxury of that deadline pressure in order to do projects that were of no real interest to me.

LS: So how did you get the feeling that you could pursue a project to completion?

OP: I don't know. With something you want to do, that helps. I could never do it with something I don't want to do. And even with something I do want to do it's hard. But I just figured I'd take the chance, and I have, I think. I do pursue my projects to completion.

LS: How do you think you're going to find your way? Are you relying on people to reveal the landscape to you?

OP: I don't think there's any "right way." If you're trying to be a lawyer then that's what knowledge is to you: a bunch of rules. If you're trying to be an artist it's totally different. I'm not looking to be an artist, exactly. I'm looking to be really mainstream.

LS: How do you learn that?

OP: From other people who are really mainstream (laughs). From other people who do total middle-of-the-road... not boring middle-of-the-road... but TV or film stuff. I'm not trying to break the mold.

LS: You're trying to do an apprentice approach?

OP: Sort of, yeah. I'm taking a two-pronged approach in which one is to work in menial PA, production assistant, type work on sets. Taking in the whole scene. And the second prong is working on big projects that would give me a big payoff. But those are harder to get to happen.

LS: What things make you nervous?

OP: No huge things. Obviously failure in all its different forms, but it doesn't make me really nervous. Occasionally you always get the negative voices that come in, but basically I'm not that nervous.

LS: How do you deal with those voices?

OP: I just try to get them out of my head. Some days I can do it, some days I can't. If I think about it logically, I don't feel I have very much to be nervous about. I don't mean that to sound cocky at all, like I said, I'm not rich yet, so hopefully I'm right about all that I'm saying, but you never know. I feel confident enough that I'm right, that I'm continuing to do what I'm doing.

LS: That begs the question of whether you would be certain that you were right if you became financially successful?

OP: Yeah! I do measure success financially, at least for the entertainment industry, yeah.

LS: Well, it's nice to have a bench mark; it's really useful. But a failure can also be turned into a success if you can learn from it. One of the things that I do when I'm confronted with a depressing situation is to revise...

OP: ... what success is.

LS: Success can mean learning through failure. And then all of a sudden your failure is not a failure at all.

OP: Yeah, I think learning through failure is a good thing, but I don't think that's success, really. It's just learning through failure. I don't think there's anything loser-ish about failing a lot. If you fail a lot, then the odds are in your favor that the next time it will be a success (laughs)! Assuming you do learn from your mistakes and don't repeat the same mistakes. I see a lot of people that do that, too.

Another thought I'm having about the reason I left school is... I mean I suppose I could go to college and become a lawyer or a doctor now... I wanted to create a situation for myself where I didn't really have any other option other than succeeding. If I made the odds that much higher, then I'm that much more motivated to succeed. I didn't really make a backup plan specifically for the reason that I don't want to have anything to fall back on. That way I have to get where I'm trying to go.

LS: What's the great success that you'd like to achieve?

OP: I don't know (laughs). I mean I do know: some highly paid, very creative job in the film industry.

LS: That seems like some definition of Heaven. Could it be anything in that universe of filmmaking?

OP: Well, in writing or directing.

LS: What about producing?

OP: I could be a producer, but I'm not really trying to be. What I'm really focusing my energies on is writing and directing. And that's what I feel like I'm going to end up being. I'm OK at the technical part, I'm not great, but I'm more into coming up with ideas for shows and things like that, mostly writing and thinking. If you're trying to come up with a reality show that you want to sell to MTV, then you write a pitch.

LS: What's your attitude toward selling?

OP: What do you mean?

LS: One of the things that institutional learning environments don't provide you is the ability to sell: they don't teach you how to sell. They tell you, "meet this criteria and you'll go on to the next level," and you proceed forward like a cow thinking that life is just a staircase that you climb one step at a time. You never learn how to sell yourself or your ideas to a variety of different peoples. When you get thrown into the real world you realize that almost everything is selling.

OP: Yeah, in film it's like selling yourself. It's like "Oh, I'm a really, really funny guy and you should definitely hire me to write this script because it's going to be funny," something like that. You have to convince them yours are good ideas and that they're going to be profitable. There are classes where they say they'll teach you that, but I think you're either good at it or you're not.

I think I've always been – well, sometimes I am not at all, but usually – pretty good at talking to people. It's a lot about following up, which is something I'm not always good at. It's so much about knowing the right people, like almost all of it, probably. That's what I hear most, and it seems to be true.

LS: How do you get to know the right people? Is that a question of skill or luck?

OP: I think it's both. It can be luck, but even if you're not lucky but you have the skill, then you can make it happen. Some people are just lucky, some people are just born into the circle of people they need to know. Other people are born and live in a place where they're totally removed from anyone. I feel that if you want to meet the right kind of people you just have to, like, meet the right kind of people (laughs)!

LS: How do you do it?

OP: Just go places that they're going to be and, or, talk to people. Like, I'm talking to my neighbor and I'm going, "Oh, yeah, I'm trying to do this film thing." And she goes, "Oh, well, my friend is a producer for such-and-such a show. I should give you her number and you should give her a call." Then I give them a call and I go, "Hi, I'm Oliver. I just left high school to do film. I'd really, really like to meet you and talk to you about doing some sort of work for you," or something like that. Then usually the person says "yes" and you meet them and start trying to make something happen. You just do that a lot!

There are even places – and I'm talking again just about film – like, say, the Woodstock Film Festival has this youth thing every year where you go and there are 20 people in the industry and you can go and ask questions. What I did was I brought them my stuff that I thought was pretty good. I went and showed it to someone who could give me some advice, and they called me, and I ended up meeting with them.

I think anyone could go and ask people for anything. Ask them if they'll look at your work or if you can help them somehow. Offer your time for free. Sometimes you get paid, sometimes you don't. It's just trying to meet the right people, so that the people you meet eventually grows into something.

LS: Where do you think you're going to be five years from now?

OP: Ah (laughs)! I don't want to jinx myself, and I don't think that what I'll be doing five years from now is appropriate for this book. I don't think I could say it out loud (laughs), and I don't want to say it anyway, but it's pretty good!

I don't know if I've answered any of your questions. I don't know if I've been any use in this interview (laughs)! I didn't really come prepared with anything inspirational or really educational to say.

LS: OK. Can you think something up!

OP: I think the biggest tool... well, what do you mean?

LS: If you were talking to kids who didn't do what you did, what would you say to them? Are they on a different track to an equally important place, or are they missing the track?

OP: They're on a different track and some of them are going to an equally important place, some of them are not. I think there are going to be people who go through the normal educational system who are really successful, and people who are not. I don't know how doing either one of those increases or decreases your odds of success. For me, leaving school increases my odds; but I think it depends on what you do if you leave, and it depends on the career that you want.

LS: What are the most important things a person could learn if they stayed in school, versus the most important things they could learn if they didn't?

OP: I think you can learn pretty much anything you can learn in school, out of school. You can, that's a fact. All the information is obtainable. For some people who don't... let me think this through a little bit. What you can't do out of school that you can do in school is get a piece of paper that says, "this is what you know."

There are more things that you can learn out of school than you can learn in school. You can learn anything out of school, including what's in school. Now, there are some people who are not going to learn anything if they leave school because they're not motivated to learn anything, but they do realize that they want a job that might require one of those pieces of paper. Different kinds of schooling are right for different types of people.

LS: Some people say that there's a unique community and support network both in schools and universities.

OP: That's probably kind of true. When I talk about trying to meet people I'm talking about trying to create a kind of support network for myself. Whereas in school you don't get to choose who's in your support network, when you're on your own, as long as you have the will to create the support network, you can create a really good one.

LS: A typical response to that would be to say that in schools you'll find people who are great sources of something or other. Teachers who are actually paid to sit there and yak with you all day long. Whereas for you to get the same kind of attention out of school requires bringing together so many other things that the odds are against you.

OP: Yeah, the odds are that not everything you do is going to work out, no matter what you're doing. And you're right, when you're dealing with people who are busy and have lives other than being a teacher, whose job is not to teach you, you're not going to be able to get as much time getting critiqued as you would. But I think if you're dealing with the right people… I mean I'd rather get like 10 minutes with certain people than four years with others.

If it's someone I respect and I see their work and how good it is, then I really, really listen to what they say and take it to heart. Whereas if it's a teacher I'm like, "Uh huh, maybe I should listen to you, maybe not." Not that there aren't really successful people who can give really bad advice, because I'm sure there is.

One of the things that really appeals to me about film – it's not the only thing that appeals to me about film – is that it's a fun way to get money and power. It's not like being a suit who has to work, go in and scream at his secretary, do numbers all the time to get money and power. It can be fun and profitable.

11. SIMON DANIEL JAMES

History   Middle   Born 1969, Alert Bay, British Columbia

Ever since I realized that I didn't have a culture of my own, I've been interested in and involved with other cultures. I've found that people with dual experience of both Western and indigenous cultures have useful insight into learning and growing up.

Through some friends I met the artist Simon Dick, and after I described this project to him, he introduced me to his son Simon James. Simon James started as a Native artist, learned filmmaking, and now spends much of his time producing the *Raven Tales* project in which he uses tales from different North American indigenous cultures as the basis for animated children's films.

Although it seems surprising, perhaps it is only to be expected that his work is welcomed throughout the Americas, Europe, Asia, and the Middle East. He is, after all, offering wisdom from our oldest cultures through an entertaining and easily understood medium.

In this interview Simon talks about the environment in which he, his parents, and his grandparents grew up. Trained in the traditional Kwakwaka'wakw culture, as well as in modern technology, business, and politics, Simon lives in both worlds. This is harder than it sounds.

Excerpts

"Prejudice is something I live with every single day. I have been beaten. I was at a party one night when I was 18 years old, and when people found out that I was Native, six people jumped on me… I lasted for 20 minutes against six people… I was actually the one that was dragged away by the police that night…"

"I was visiting my father on my birthday. He was sick and tired of hearing me talk about how commercial fishing was dying, and… while I was sitting there he dialed the phone and then hands me the receiver and says, 'Here, make an appointment.' I didn't know who he called! I pick up the receiver and I heard, 'Vancouver Film School, how can we help you…?'"

"Honoring has a lot to do with growth. Native people are taught from very young to honor our elders, to respect our elders. I was a firm fighter against that because a lot of my elders proved they should not be respected or honored at all, and that respect is definitely earned…"

"Here I go telling you I don't like hearing it, and now I'm about to say it: I am now and have been drug- and alcohol-free for a very long time. And it isn't that I'm trying to jump in front of a camera and get some special kind of credit, it was just a personal choice. It didn't fit my career; it didn't fit my lifestyle…"

"Quit lying to people, you know? Accept responsibility for your own actions. And that's where knowledge is so much more important than schooling. These are things that aren't offered in education – it's something that you have to seek yourself."

"Successful people aren't born that way. They become successful by establishing the habit of doing things unsuccessful people don't like to do. The successful people don't always like these things themselves; they just get on and do them."

— William Makepeace Thackeray, novelist (1811 – 1863)

Interview Bowen Island, British Columbia, December 2008

Simon James: I was born on a tiny little island in the middle of British Columbia's beautiful coast. My grandfather moved the entire family to Campbell River where he thought we could get a better education. It wasn't too far away from Alert Bay, our home base, and he could still maintain his lifestyle as a commercial fisherman. I spent all of my schooling years in Campbell River, and then I moved to the mainland when I realized that I had outgrown Vancouver Island. I pretty much learned all that I could there.

I learned a little bit of everything from numerous people. I remember seeing my Grade 6 teacher at a gas station when I was 20; he was very old at this time. I walked over and thanked him and he looked at me – he remembered me after I told him who I was – and he said, "What would you thank me for? I was mean to you." And I said, "You taught me discipline. When you walked around the classroom with a 12-inch-long, one-inch-round dowel and smacked my desk, you taught me to focus, and I just wanted to thank you for that." He was also one of the only teachers who took me camping. His emphasis was on the environment. He taught biology and science, so camping was part of his course.

My grandfather was a major influence in my entire life. He taught me compassion. He taught me discipline, even though he spoiled me rotten. He taught me that it's better to earn respect than to control by causing fear. So where I had uncles that pushed me around, knocked me down and made me fear them, my grandfather just taught me unconditional love and respect. I was just a nobody at that time. I wanted more than anything to just please him, so I worked very hard to excel at everything I did.

Over the years I've learned about culture and the history of our people, where we should have pride and where we should be humble. That's one thing that a lot of people don't learn. There are times that you should be humble. There are some things in our history that we should not really focus on.

LS: Explain what you mean by humble.

SJ: Residential school, you'll constantly hear people who were victims of residential school. The very first thing they say is, "Hi, my name is blah blah. I am a victim of the residential school, and this is why I'm angry." They basically make themselves champions of a cause, which is a negative cause. When you go to Aboriginal cultural events you'll hear somebody speaking to a camera for the news, "Hi, my name is … something… and I've been drug- and alcohol-free now for 10 years." Why is that a focus? Maybe there are some things that should not be our primary focus.

LS: Most people don't know about residential school. Can you say what that was?

SJ: Residential school was a long-practiced way of control where children were taken from their parents and placed into a school system and quite often not educated. They were just placed there so that they could control the adults, and more importantly control the children. And quite often they used religion to eradicate the person's belief. And they tried to breed them out as a way of eradicating the species. This was the Canadian government's focus.

LS: "Breed them out," what does that mean?

SJ: Residential school was something that the Canadian government enacted where the children of the Aboriginal people were taken from their parents, brought in to these buildings, and beaten, molested, and treated poorly. Quite often the younger girls were raped so that they could breed them out. Then their children would not be part of our culture. It was a very wide, common practice in North America and you'll hear this constantly from Native people. The last residential school only closed 20 years ago.

LS: These were compulsory?

SJ: Yeah. It was either do, or go to jail. If you don't submit your children to the residential school and walk away, then we will forcibly come, pick up your children, and send you to jail.

LS: But you, yourself, didn't have to attend.

SJ: No, I'm not a victim of the residential school, but my father was, so I consider myself a product of it. I am a firm believer in genetic memory, so that all of the hardships that my father endured through residential school, all the difficulties that my mother endured prior to my birth, are chemically in me.

If I'm confronted by somebody who considers themselves to be an authority – and that is more than likely a white Canadian – I find myself to be timid. But then that little timid boy inside of me hits the wall and becomes aggressive. So if I'm confronted by a police officer, for example, I shy back for a few seconds and then I get aggressive. And my quick response is, "What's the problem? What is your problem with me?" It's been known to get me in trouble, that aggressiveness. My father, same attitude, my mother, same attitude: they're very shy at first, that lasts for a small moment, and then they just explode.

I am a protector, being as big as I am, I am a protector. So if I see somebody being pushed around, I can't help it: I jump in and I try to protect them. And quite often I get hurt because of that. I think my anger stems from not being able to do what I need to do, or worse yet, when I was younger I wasn't able to say what I wanted to say.

It's strange that you're in a long list of people who now want to hear what I have to say, where most of my young life I was told to keep my mouth shut. Now everyone wants to know why I was so quiet, what is it that I have to say now. People are asking advice on subjects of Aboriginal culture, Aboriginal education, why we have a 70% drop-out rate in the Aboriginal communities nation-wide. They look to me for answers.

LS: Has that change come about because you now have something to say, or because people now want something to be said? Did you grow up, or did they grow up?

SJ: They did. I always had these things to say, ever since I was a child. My grandfather was a master speaker. He spoke about Aboriginal residential schools, about the law that forbids us to speak our language, dance and perform, even give gifts. It was against the law.

My grandfather was a third-grade graduate. His explanation for that was, "I learned how to read, and I learned how to write English. That was all I needed to know in order to go out and learn." And he did. He was on a first-name basis with the Prime Minister of Canada, the ministers of Fisheries, Education, and Finance in Ottawa. He befriended all of these people, and he knew that one day that was going to benefit him.

In the late 60s my grandfather was given an opportunity to speak at the United Nations and talk about these things. He took that as an advantage. The story is that he went down to one of the museums in the US and walked in with a notepad and started writing down the stock numbers of the stuff on display. He wrote what the items were and who they belonged to. Security showed up and asked what he was doing and he says, "Well, I'm just taking a list of the things that are coming home with me. I've rented a van and I need you to open up this back door here, and I need these things put in a box and I'm taking them home."

They thought he was a nut, so they called the police. The police showed up and my grandfather was still taking numbers, and when they tried to arrest him he pulled out his United Nations diplomat card and says, "I'm a diplomat in this country. I have diplomatic immunity. You can't touch me." So he used that to get what he wanted. And what he wanted was people to finally notice that these things were stolen from us. Well, those things are now sitting in the U'mista Cultural Centre in Alert Bay.

LS: He didn't get them just then, did he?

SJ: Oh no, but he started the process. It took a while.

We are still considered third class citizens in our country because we act like third class citizens at times. I will never give excuses about Native people, and you'll hear it constantly. People will say, "I lost my language. It was taken from me." That is a lie. They never learned it in the first place. I'll be the first one to admit I never learned it. It was available to me, my grandfather spoke, my aunts and uncles spoke it; I never learned it. Quit lying to people, you know? Accept responsibility for your own actions. And that's where knowledge is so much more important than schooling. These are things that aren't offered in education, it's something that you have to seek yourself.

LS: You're not just talking about language, are you?

SJ: Anything. When I was 15 I wanted to learn to be an artist. Who better for me to learn from than my father? So I went to him, and after he taught me all that he could, I thought that I still didn't know enough, so I went out and I practiced with other artists. I studied museum collections. I spent a long time practicing my craft: painting, sculpting, glass, carving, totem poles, canoes, anything.

Two years ago I learned Styrofoam carving. I was joking the whole time saying, "You know, we as Native people have run out of Western Red Cedar so we have to carve something else!" I learned how to do Styrofoam carving by making a parade float for the Roger's Santa Claus parade. Roger's is one of the larger communications companies in Canada and they sponsor this event.

I wanted Raven Tales to have some exposure, so I found sponsors to help me, and worked in a warehouse for three months in the cold and carved a parade float using a 30-foot-long cedar dugout canoe as the base. I made the waves that it was riding on out of Styrofoam and made Raven, Eagle, and Frog sitting in the canoe, out of Styrofoam. I had a friend who works in a movie-props company in North Vancouver. I called him up, borrowed his tools, and he showed me how to use them. A two-hour lesson and I pretty much mastered it. I'm 39, about to turn 40, and I'm still learning.

I just helped Melissa put in her septic field. I built the encasement around her tank. I connected all the pipes from the tank to the field. First time I ever done that. I'll admit to you that I lied to her… a little bit (laughs)! I told her, "Oh, sure. I know how to do this!" That's been my ongoing excuse in everything I do. Well, that's how I met my wife. I had a company come to me and ask me if I've ever carved totem poles before, and my immediate response was, "Oh, yeah. Several." I never carved a totem pole in my life before that one! And that was the one that was shipped to Japan. I carved two more in Japan in front of them to prove that I did the first one.

LS: Do you use your family as resources, or do you draw on the research and study that you did?

SJ: Both. If I can I utilize my family I will, but the big thing with me is how do I compensate them. When I was carving the first totem pole I was diagnosed with Diabetes Type II. Completely devastated, I stopped work for two weeks to get back to health. I was two weeks behind schedule and I phoned up my father who hadn't spoken to me for about four months. I told him I had diabetes and he showed up the next day, no questions asked, and said, "What do you want me to do?" This is what you do as family: when somebody needs help you just drop everything and go. And that's one of the things that my father taught me.

You've met my father. He's a very passionate person. Compassionate person as well. And he's had a very hard life, but he's had a lot of education in his life. He's a world-class soccer player and internationally renowned artist. I have some big shoes to fill. Speaking at the United Nations two years ago was my first step. The only thing that I focus on is to become a better artist and learn new stuff. Computer animation was one of those things.

LS: Tell me how you got into that.

SJ: The infamous phone call. I was visiting my father on my birthday. He was sick and tired of hearing me talk about how commercial fishing was dying and how it wasn't worth investing in anymore. I poured myself a cup of coffee and while I was sitting there he dialed the phone and then hands me the receiver and says, "Here, make an appointment." I didn't know who he called! I pick up the receiver and I heard, "Vancouver Film School, how can we help you?" I said, "I'd like to make an appointment, please." So the next day I had an appointment. They looked at my résumé and said, "You need to get into animation. This is something that you really should focus on."

I never had a computer before, I didn't even have an email address. I thought I would focus on 2D animation because I can draw. After 11 months of 2D animation training I graduated with an 86% average, which was a letter of completion, which was fine. I wasn't trying to be the best, I was just trying to figure this stuff out as I went.

Then I had the option to go on to an introductory 3D animation course with a 30% discount. Why not? So I walked in to this computer animation course, sat down, and I looked at the person beside me and kind of whispered, "Please don't laugh, but how do I turn this computer on?" (Laughs) And he said, "It's in suspend mode, just move the mouse." I didn't know what suspend mode meant! So I moved the mouse and the thing came on, and I was excited, and I did the lesson.

LS: Let me interrupt. Is 2D animation strictly drawing and not based on using a computer?

SJ: It's pretty much all drawing-based. We scan the images and then use programs to manipulate everything. We do all our color on a computer, and we can do minor editing, but a majority of it is still hand-drawn. It's laborious, very laborious.

LS: And 3D is all done on a computer?

SJ: 3D is all computer: it's all Pixar and Disney kind of stuff. But if you have 2D experience prior to 3D, it's a huge benefit because you understand more about movement. The 2D world teaches you about weight, structure, and balance, more so than when you're on the computer. The computer world has no weight, no balance, no structure. In 2D we're limited to the size of the paper; in 3D there are no limits. I learned that almost on the first day when I had to use my 2D experience of weight to make the scene better.

I remember I had a truck pulling a trailer with a boat on it. And I animated this not knowing how to set rotation on tires, how to set movement on the trailer and truck, and how to attach them to each other. I just moved it according to what my eye told me to do.

When the truck came to a stop, the truck moved forward, and then it came back, which is what we do in 2D animation – you actually have a counter-movement. When the truck moved forward, the back end came up, so of course the front end of the trailer is going to move up a little bit and then come back down when it rests. The instructor was blown away and he was like, "How'd you do that?" And I said, "Well, I was just playing with it and I figured it out myself."

In my second week my instructor came to me and asked me how much 3D computer experience I had and I said, "None, this is my first time." And he said, "Well, I hope you're not insulted by this question, but how much computer experience have you had?" And I jokingly tapped the computer screen and said, "I've never touched one of these things in my life." He actually stood up and applauded... in an empty classroom. He said, "Anyone else who walked in here like you did, I think would have quit a week ago, and you're doing amazingly for someone who's never touched a computer before." And now, here I am a computer animation producer (laughs)!

LS: You've done almost a dozen of the Raven Tales episodes, haven't you?

SJ: Thirteen episodes. We're currently working on 13 more that are confirmed and fully funded. I just have to write some more stories, and Chris has to write some more stories, and we'll get those things done. And now the talk is about going for five seasons, that's 65 episodes.

LS: Tell me the spirit behind the project.

SJ: I've been quoted as to saying, "10,000 years of market research can't be wrong!" People laugh when I say it, but that basically was the whole thing. If these 10,000-year-old stories have lasted this long, there has to be a reason for it. People want to hear them again and again, generation after generation. We took that notion and created stories based around our three primary characters: Raven, Eagle, and Frog. We just called it *Raven Tales*.

LS: Are these stories from all up and down the coast? Do the cultures of the coast share the same tales?

SJ: Originally it was Northwest Coast, and I did have 13 Northwest Coast stories. After we finished episode seven, Chris, who's Cherokee, had a lot of interest in telling Cherokee stories, and Hopi stories, and Navajo stories. We ventured into it because they were interested, the Navajo people wanted it. They said, "Well, you've got to tell something from down here." And this was always the question that people asked, "How do you go down to these territories if you're Northwest Coast based?" The explanation is that Raven and Eagle can fly, and Frog is mystical anyway, so she can show up wherever she wants.

LS: I thought you were focusing on reviving cultural tales for kids, but it sounds like you have bigger goals.

SJ: Yeah, I've always loved that expression, "Think big or go home." It's a common expression up here. When we started *Raven Tales* our original idea was just to create animation for children, possibly do a few books. Definitely do some toys and T-shirts and such. Maybe we'll make some money out of this and put it into another project. We had no interest in getting into education at all.

That changed. *Raven Tales* is part of Native language programs now. *Raven Tales* is the only animated television show licensed with the provincial school board. It was something that we were not interested in at first, but it just happened.

I was invited to a First Nations education steering committee conference. I was asked to show *Raven Tales* and I showed up expecting to be in a darkened room with 50 or 60 teachers. I arrived at one of the biggest hotel banquet rooms in Vancouver and see this poster that says, "Simon James, Keynote Speaker." OK, so now I've got to come up with a speech. Luckily I'm fairly good at it, and I came up with a speech on the spot.

I walked into the room and there are 300-plus teachers with a 20-foot screen, so I was thrown. I was introduced to the Minister of Education and to people who could make things happen, and they did. They kept their promises. Now there is a whole curriculum created around the *Raven Tales* project.

The project has developed a life that is bigger than I had ever suspected, probably bigger than any of us expected. Two years ago we got a phone call: *Raven Tales* is about to be licensed with the *Al Jazeera* network. So at that point I thought, "Wow, *Raven Tales* is actually going to be like an olive branch in the Middle East," with the 50 million viewership of the *Al Jazeera* network. They're not interested in seeing Homer Simpson, a white American family; they have no interest. But they're interested in *Raven Tales* (laughs)... I thought that was so cool! I haven't been paid in five years, so that tells you that I'm in it for life.

One of the coolest things that I experience is when I'm invited to a school district to give a lecture on *Raven Tales*. I show up as the speaker and I hold up my DVD's and I say, "Hello, my name is Simon James and I would like to ask a quick question: why do you think I'm holding up these copies of *Raven Tales*?" And the answers are always the same: I bought it at a store, or it was a gift given to me. Out of the 300 students I saw in one district, only one student had it right: "You made it." It goes beyond them that a Native person that lives here, just like their parents, could have created this.

I hated school. All my teachers disliked me (laughs). I had no girl friends. My life was hell in school. But I toughed it out and I graduated. Now I can hold my head very high to know that I've never hurt anybody in any of the careers that I've had in my life. And then when I say I was born in Alert Bay, raised in Campbell River, and I went to the same schools like you're in right now, that's when their minds go, "Wow, maybe I can do it, too!"

LS: I want to ask you a question that's a little off the wall, but it's important to me. For me, the idea of prejudice has been a big issue. I see prejudice at the root of a lot of inhuman behavior. People treating other people badly cuts across all social levels, and it manifests itself in cultures treating other cultures badly. It's never spoken about, it's never identified. I would like people to recognize it and I'm wondering if you can shed any light on it. What do you think of prejudice? It's a hard question.

SJ: Oh, no. I live with racism almost every day. Being a Native person, you're subjected to racism constantly. People see us as uneducated, living on welfare, living on a reservation, alcoholic… not just uneducated but also ignorant.

I was raised within the culture of my people. My grandfather taught us how to dance and how to sing and how to drum. I've learned almost all the stories in the culture of the Kwakwaka'wakw people, because that's where I come from. I've also learned a lot about Salish, Haida, Tlingit, and Tsimshian, and now because of *Raven Tales* I've learned a lot about Hopi, Navajo, and every other culture around North America. So what does it mean to be Native? Prejudice is something I live with every single day.

I have been beaten. I was at a party one night when I was 18 years old, and when people found out that I was Native, six people jumped on me. I remember there was a New Zealand rugby team that was there visiting, and they were shocked that I lasted for 20 minutes against six people and impressed that I was actually the one that was dragged away by the police that night.

People are now starting to understand. As my grandfather said, through education will go ignorance. And hopefully one day the Canadian government and the United States government will no longer fear us and will no longer want to eradicate us.

LS: What do you see happening in the future?

SJ: I see digital technology saving the culture, but it's not going to save the DNA. We will be eradicated. And I think most cultures of the world will be subject to that. You know you always hear these stories that they've discovered a new tribe of people in South America. No, they haven't discovered them, they just finally paid attention to them. They were always there. But even they're being bred out.

We're all going to be one people at one time in the distant future. Hopefully that will be the end of racism. Maybe that's one way we could look positively at that. How can you be racist against yourself? But then again, there's a lot of people who do that as well. There are a lot of Native people who are racist against Native people.

I saw a really pretty student-film at the Vancouver Film School. It was about two triangles that were walking down the street, one triangle was yellow, the other triangle was purple, and they saw a purple rectangle. Right away they got angry and they held the rectangle down while one of them went and got a chainsaw, came back, and turned it into a purple triangle. Then the two purple triangles turned around and looked at the yellow triangle and weren't happy. So when does it end?

I think that's where animation really will help. It's an old technology; it's been around for a long time now. There was a time when a lot of people that animated were concerned about the content – they always had to be safe. Now people want to express themselves, so there are a lot more messages out there. And with Aboriginal filmmakers, and the National Geographic channel and the Cartoon Network, we have all of these ideas being expressed for the first time.

LS: Other kids, especially in the white culture, don't have grandfathers who are role models, they don't have mentors, they don't really have a culture, but they're going through the same process of growing up. What could you tell them to look for, what can help them get through that trial period?

SJ: The trial period, that's very tough. I think honoring has a lot to do with growth. Native people are taught from very young to honor our elders, to respect our elders. I was a firm fighter against that because a lot of my elders proved they should not be respected or honored at all, and that respect is definitely earned.

My grandfather and my grandmother earned my respect. But I've met a lot of elders who should be disrespected (laughs)… really!… because they continued with their victimization. When I found out that a lot of the people whom we were told to respect were hurting their own grandchildren and children in ways that they shouldn't, that's when I started to second-guess the whole notion of honoring the elders.

Definitely finding a mentor is what the children should do today. Here I go telling you I don't like hearing it, and now I'm about to say it: I am now and have been drug- and alcohol-free for a very long time. And it isn't that I'm trying to jump in front of a camera and get some special kind of credit – it was just a personal choice. It didn't fit my career; it didn't fit my lifestyle. My father is an alcoholic, my mother was an alcoholic, and I didn't want to follow in their path.

When I had no mentorship, no male or man teaching me, my grandfather stepped in and took the position. My father was never around, my uncles were too busy with commercial fishing or raising their own children to focus on this young boy that had nothing. And all of my cousins at that age were girls, so I had no maleness around me. I think even my mother was concerned that I'd become too feminine (laughs). So my grandfather stepped in, took me under his wing.

Most of my mother's family will tell you that I was his favorite, and I kept trying to think of why. I finally came to the conclusion that it was because I was there, and there was no other reason. I wasn't a straight-A student. I wasn't born with special, magical powers. I was just there on his birthday, at Christmas, on Sunday mornings, every weekend. When I rode my bike and scraped my knee, he was there to help me.

I think it was fitting that I was the only one of the family there when he died. I was in the room with him. I tried my best to save him, despite the doctors and nurses being there. I was also there with my favorite uncle. My uncle looked at me in a strange way, unable to speak, and I yelled for my aunt to come now, and two minutes later he died. And everyone looked at me in the room and said, "How did you know?" Well, you love a man that much and you know. I guess it goes back to listening and paying attention a little bit more than other people. Those were probably the two hardest times in my life. I know I'm probably destined for a lot more (laughs), because I have a large family.

LS: Well, it's service. You do a great service when you can do that for someone.

SJ: You know fathers have a difficult time telling their sons how proud of them they are, and my father is definitely one of those people. But every so often I get a shock. I was 18 when he handed me a book called *Letters to My Son*. He had tears in his eyes when he handed it to me and said, "You are already ten times more of a man than I'll ever be in my entire life. When you read this book you'll understand." And I read that book and I think I've bought eight more copies because I keep giving them away.

It's about a man who, uh… a young man who started this job in a factory because his wife was pregnant. He sat beside an old man on the manufacturing line – they were both inspectors or something – and he looks across at the old man and says, "So, you like your work?" And he's like, "No." "Well, how long you been here for?" And he says, "Twenty years." He says, "Well, why are you still here?" "Thirteen more years I get my pension." So he stood up and said, "Thank you," and walked out: quit (laughs). "There's no way I'm going to spend 40 years here waiting for my pension!" So he quit, and he went home and wrote this book, *Letters to My Son*, just in case he didn't make it, to teach his son these lessons. And he taught the difference between maleness and manhood.

I've probably known three men in my entire life, so far. The rest are just males. When you watch these football games where these guys are out there drinking beers and tossing people around, they're a bunch of males. They don't know what it's like to be a man yet.

I have a friend who drives a truck professionally. His wife doesn't work. He drives sometimes 24 hours a day, sleeps on the ferry or sleeps in the truck. Works through Christmas and drives through blizzards so he can support his two daughters and his wife. Quit smoking and drinking because his wife had a heart attack.

That, to me, is a man: a man who can make the decision to save his family. And yet he's entirely happy with everything he does. He owns his own truck; he owns his own house. He goes home twice a week to see his wife and absolutely loves her. That's a man. I had one uncle and my grandfather. That's about it so far!

12. TOM HURWITZ

History   Middle   Born 1947, New York City, New York

Friends of mine, on hearing of my *Learning Project*, told me that a friend of theirs had a family of fascinating and accomplished people, and it was through that person that I contacted Tom Hurwitz for this interview.

I don't really know Tom, his work, or his family, though I'm not surprised that our grandparents both emigrated from Eastern Europe and brought with them a similar activism. Quoting from Tom's web page:

> "Tom Hurwitz is one of our country's most honored documentary cinematographers. Winner of two Emmy Awards and a Sundance Award for Best Cinematography, Hurwitz has photographed films that have won four academy awards and several more nominations…"

> "Apart from his film career and his time with family, Hurwitz functions as a seminary-trained liturgist, and a verger at New York's Cathedral Church of St. John the Divine."

Excerpts

"My high school English teacher... was a 'bachelor'... He had all of the conflict of a person who hasn't full realized, hasn't allowed his inner self, hasn't allowed the sexuality to come out, and a lot of that came into the intensity of his teaching. We fought like cats and dogs, and he opened all of literature. It was just incredible..."

"There's a certain kind of loving severity in the teaching experience that I find most gratifying. Teachers that I remember, going back, who really gave me a lot, were both severe and loving, even if they didn't show it too much. You could tell that they loved their subject and they loved the work that you did on their subject..."

"I never took a film class. I took one film class which I wound up teaching because I'd already done a film by the time I got to be taking that class... I had a mixed time in school; I certainly hated it as much as I loved it, but I did love it, and I did love the kind of learning that one does in school, and I don't know how else to get it..."

"You had said that you wanted to find out what motivated people, and I've thought about that, and I don't think I can tell you one thing that motivates me, but certainly love motivates me, and also anger motivates me – all my life – and hope motivates me. Love, anger, and hope."

"Albert grunted. 'Do you know what happens to lads who ask too many questions?' Mort thought for a moment. 'No,' he said eventually, 'what?' There was silence. Then Albert straightened up and said, 'Damned if I know. Probably they get answers, and serve 'em right.' "

— Terry Pratchett, from *Mort*

"The presence of those seeking the truth is infinitely to be preferred to the presence of those who think they've found it."

— Terry Pratchett, from *Monstrous Regiment*

"Coming back to where you started is not the same as never leaving."

— Terry Pratchett, from *A Hat Full of Sky*

Interview   New York City, New York, May 2006

Tom Hurwitz: What I do is not at all directly relevant to my schooling; that is, I never took a film class. I took one film class which I wound up teaching because I'd already done a film by the time I got to be taking that class at Columbia (College). I had a mixed time in school; I certainly hated it as much as I loved it, but I did love it, and I did love the kind of learning that one does in school, and I don't know how else to get it.

I think that my life would be incalculably poorer if I hadn't had a liberal arts education. And as a filmmaker I wouldn't be anywhere nearly as good, even though so much of what I do is involved with the arts, things that are complete nonverbal. And even if they're verbal, my role in them is completely nonverbal, it's intuitive, reflexive.

I'm in the process of moving my office into my home, and I'm getting rid of a lot of stuff that I have from previous years. I have an entire shelf – two shelves, three feet wide – of scripts, which I broke down scene by scene into shots and lighting and all the various needs that one has when one shoots a feature. I don't do that anymore – maybe I will again, I love having a big crew – but I find it vastly less interesting than shooting documentaries, which somehow connects better with who I am as a person.

The people I meet are all very different from me, and the films that I make are very relevant, for the most part. They're much better than the films that I would make if I was shooting feature-type films, which tend to get 5 to 10 bad ones before you get one really good film. And that's a ratio that I'm not particularly interested in.

When you shoot feature films, the people you work with, although they're very, very nice... delightful often... they're all the same kind of people that I am. They all know the same things, or less, because they're more focused. If they have broader interest, then they're kind of the normal broad middle class interests. Somebody will be a jazz fanatic, interested in old tube amplifiers, or somebody will like to read, or... but I won't be in a village in Pakistan. I won't be with a band in Haiti. I won't be with soldiers from Kansas deployed to Afghanistan. I won't be interviewing soldiers who were involved in the torture at Abu Ghrab (the Iraqi military prison – Ed.). I won't be doing a film in a college that's dedicated to putting right-wing evangelical Christians into the government and high positions in the culture, all of which I did in the last nine months, and more.

I mean it's an incredibly rich life that I'm leading doing documentary films, and it's perfect for me because I have that level of ADD that I like to learn about a lot of different things.

The other part of it is that the work that I do, which used to be more plotted and carefully developed – light by light and layer by layer in terms of space, translating three-dimensional space in a two-dimensional frame and making that relevant to the story that's being told, the characters that are being evolved. Looking at the way light plays on shape and form and face and texture. Looking at the way a rectangle moves through space. To go from one thing to another, all of that stuff, which I planned very carefully over a period of 15 years of my life – I'm now working on being improvisational.

A great deal of documentary film is improvisational. The best work that I do is improvisational – catching things as they happen and making them articulate visually – and that can either be in music or dance or just in the world of society. I found that, better than being excellent, I can be a master. Not only that, but I love it. And I love it because it involves living in the moment, channeling everything I know into a very small moment, like an athlete or a performing artist.

When I'm clear and together I can produce things that are really great. And when I'm not I can produce things that are just good (laughs)! And I love that tension... after I've come through the amount of anxiety that it causes me! To do that, the more knowledge I amass the better, the better my improvisation is, the better my moment is – even though it's just the moment, even though the more I completely empty myself and just be there – the better my work is.

The paradox is the more I've prepared, the better I can do that. And part of preparing is education, and part of preparing is being taught, and the relationship that one has with a mentor who makes you do things that are not fun – that are work! – and makes you do it even if you don't know why you're doing it. And part of the process is the kind of painful education that can turn kids off – although if you do it well it shouldn't, it should do the opposite – but there is a whole bunch of it that hurts!

What I do every day hurts... hurts. When I work with a camera, especially a heavy one, I'm in pain all the time. Even one of the light ones: I'm hurting. If I do it well I'm hurting all the time. I've learned how to do that. Part of the way I've learned how to do that was by being made to do other things, things that helped me learn how to do that. One of them was sports and various disciplines I've done throughout my life. Most of them involved working with a mentor, working with somebody who makes me do things.

That's the paradox of all of this. I think that we as Americans are infantilized, but I think that our schooling isn't the thing that's doing it. I mean it might have started the process, but it hasn't finished it. I think that there are huge... forces... in our culture that are malign. I think that education is basically benign. It tries to be benign, even though our leaders, our educators, many of them have done their best to make it harmful. The process itself is benign, whereas the process of television, of mass media, all the things that I do, they're malignant. And they infantilize more.

I think television has single-handedly infantilized Americans, and I think a lot of the way entertainment is delivered to Americans – and the way we've been allowed to become dependent upon entertainment in all kinds of different ways – has turned us into a nation of idiots.

I think average Americans don't use their heads at all, they don't think. I mean I love many, many, many people who I've been with all over this country, but they don't think much. And they certainly don't think independently, and nothing has helped them do that. They can be taught in school every day, but every night the television teaches them to forget what they're taught in school. And our food turns us into sugar-jangled maniacs who can't sit still, and all the other influences on kids' lives, which happen outside of school, turn them into ADD rattled little monsters.

And the value system: you can't have a president dedicated to greed and lying without having a nation that, after a while, doesn't take that on as one of its values. I really believe that we learn a lot by example, and our politicians have been teaching us really, really bad examples for a long time. And especially (Ronald) Reagan and (George W.) Bush.

I watched the city under Reagan, the limousines piled up by the theatres. Greed became the guiding light in New York. When Reagan got out this calmed down to average greedy New York (level), and people began to write graffiti on the walls again.

Now the clubs are beginning to charge people $1,000 for an evening. With a couple of bottles that you bring to the table for $300 each, and you've got to pay $80 to get in, and stuff like that. Young adults of the under 30 or 35 age are paying $1,000 for any evening at a club to be cool. Welcome to the Bush era. Welcome to cutting taxes.

So anyway, I'm kind of being discursive… but for me, I have profited very much from being steeped in things traditional and classic. Having a classical background to a completely unclassical career has helped me tremendously.

I have two kids who did not have that background, and one kid who has, and what he gets out of any given situation he's involved in, in terms of the range of layers in a painting he stands in front of, or a joke (laughs), or anything in between. If he reads a book, or a commercial, or anything… it's so much deeper than what they see.

LS: They being the other two?

TH: The other two. And, you know, one of them was a fine student who studied all things non-white and non-male – majored in non-dead-white males in the University of Michigan – in the honors program, and is now a teacher who has to figure out what Plato said.

She has to go find out because she didn't learn. And figure out who Weber is when she goes to a concert, or something like that. We allowed her and her sister to be way too educated by her peers and not enough educated in the traditional way. And they went to public schools and private high schools, but it was our attitude while we were allowing them to be educated. They're not as rich as he's going to be.

LS: It's the last kid who's more classically trained?

TH: Yeah. It doesn't mean everything's solved with the youngest one – he'll have his own set of problems – but at least he sees the riches in the world around him, rather than entering the world with a kind of television glow where each thing in history is not related to anything else, or each event that they read in the paper or they see on the television news isn't related to anything historical. It's not like he thinks about these things all the time, but if you ask, it's there.

LS: What's the difference in his experience?

TH: The kid's learned history. I sent him to a different school, a school that wasn't that different but it had enough... he learned Latin, sang in a choir in an Episcopal church, so he learned church music, both ancient and modern. Doesn't do it anymore, (now he) plays rock and roll, but all that stuff is inside him. That rich stuff, not repressing him and making him more limited, but it makes him bigger because he's got a broader foundation.

To the extent that I had that, when I was a kid, I am deeply grateful. Some of it came from my school, some of it came from my parents and their values. Some of it came from what I went and got myself. But the stuff that helped the most was the stuff that I had to really work for, and I learned how to work.

LS: When did that start?

TH: Really young. Really young.

I'm a product of what was called at the time "progressive education." I went to progressive schools in Manhattan. So the good part of this kind of education is there; responsible for the breadth of my knowledge about the world because we learned about the entire world. A very rich kind of understanding of that. And, uh... I'm not sure I could say what was negative about it, except that I wish that my work habits had been better. I wish they'd taught me how to work so that I didn't have to go out and force myself to learn.

LS: Could they have? How could they have? They certainly tried to instill discipline, I imagine.

TH: No, I don't think so. But that's a good question. I'm not sure.

LS: I mean even in college they don't teach you.

TH: No, in college they can't.

LS: They load work on you.

TH: They load work on you, and you either do it or you don't, but they don't teach you how to budget your time, that if you get the work done in the beginning of the week, then you can look at your draft later on in the week. If you start early enough, you can teach kids how to do that; you can't force them to do it, but you can teach them how to do it.

OK, anyway... I'm only saying that there's... there's a certain kind of loving severity in the teaching experience that I find most gratifying. Teachers that I remember, going back, who really gave me a lot, were both severe and loving, even if they didn't show it too much. You could tell that they loved their subject, and they loved the work that you did on their subject, whether or not they loved you.

I feel like I've been the best teacher or mentor when I've had that kind of relationship with my student, or the person who's worked with me, and I've taught a lot of people who've been really successful, a lot of people who are both my competitors and who are making much more money than I am. We've had really great relationships.

LS: Can you tell me, in a concrete way, some example of when you were learning under the tutelage of a person who was a great teacher, how that manifested its important effect on you?

TM: Part of it was 'cuz I started kind'a late in my life, to really buckle down to making this career work, and partly because in documentary film there really weren't people at that point, although there were some masters whom I worked with. We didn't have a kind of mentor relationship... I just watched the people in my field. I simply watched. They didn't teach me in a concrete way.

I'll tell you about my (James) Joyce professor in Columbia College. It was a kind of advanced English class. I took it very early because usually if you took a class on one author you would do that in your junior or senior year. But this we were allowed to do as freshmen, the second half of my freshman year.

He had a very dry sense of humor. He was incredibly erudite in terms of his knowledge of English literature. He was a really tough grader, and he made really tough assignments. You had to work really hard for him, but every time he explicated something it was like an explosion. It was like unlocking a symbol each time. Of course Joyce is filled with symbols, (which are) relevant to all kinds of things.

Going to his class was almost a spiritual experience because there was just so much there. He was a guy who was also, I found out later, very active politically, left wing, but you would never have known it in the class. He never brought that in. At the same time there was something about his perspective where, looking back on it, you could have found it. His name was Fred Grab, and I have absolutely no idea where he is now. (Fred Grab died in 2002. – Ed.)

My high school English teacher… here's an interesting story… I now spend my summers in the house of my high school English teacher, who's dead. I had no idea it was his house when I rented it. I found this out later. I'm renting it from his nephew who lives in Finland, so it's by pure accident that I wound up in this guy's house.

He was, in the 1950s, what you'd call a "bachelor." He was a bachelor English teacher. He had all of the conflict of a person who hasn't fully realized, hasn't allowed his inner self, hasn't allowed the sexuality to come out, and a lot of that came into the intensity of his teaching. We fought like cats and dogs, and he opened all of literature. It was just incredible. I had him for two years. An incredible guy.

There was another guy in high school, a history teacher, who I loved and about half the class hated… hated! You know, both of these guys were pretty severe in one way or another, but filled with love for the subject, for knowledge. And I think that to the extent that people learn from me they find that, too, that I love what I do, and that I love transferring that to other people.

LS: Is it why you do film, or is that something that just comes across when you do film?

TH: That's a good question… Why I do film is partly because it's the job that's the most fun of anything I can think of. The other part is that I really love what comes out the other end. It turns out that I'm lucky enough to work on films that make a difference, a lot of the time, in one way or another.

You had said that you wanted to find out what motivated people, and I've thought about that, and I don't think I can tell you one thing that motivates me, but certainly love motivates me, and also anger motivates me – all my life – and hope motivates me. Love, anger, and hope.

LS: Are those all clear things to you? Are they works in progress?

TH: No, they're not clear at all! Hope is something that you – especially as a Christian – it's something that you are always gaining and losing. It's kind of a continual process. If it's not, you're not really "doing" it. You're not really walking the walk.

A lot of American Christianity is about denying this essential process, and instead delivering various kinds of absolute sureness, which doesn't have anything to do with what I believe the real project of Christianity is about, which is absolute uncertainty. So... hope, I'm always falling off and getting back on.

Anger is something that always threatens to take over, and I have to be very careful about, because I've got to be very sure that I'm angry at the right thing and not at anything else!

And love is what kind of glues it all together. I always try to keep myself inside of love. Although it's not like it isn't always there – love is always there – it's just that you have to find it inside of the situation.

And all of those things are not static. They're all continually in relationship, continually animated... Am I speaking too abstractly (laughs)? But they're all kind of moving.

LS: Well, to answer that question, of course you are. But maybe one has to speak these things, even if imperfectly, because that's the terrain where... you know... the treasure lies.

TH: Yeah.

LS: I actually don't believe that the words carry half the meaning. In the end it's the context and the equivocations, and the...

TH: (Laughs)

LS: uh... hesitations... qualifications, that carry most of the meaning. The words are infinitely elusive.

TH: I think the actions actually carry the meaning, and all the rest of it is the explanation.

LS: Can you give me an example – I'm sure you can – of actions where those treasured forces emerged clearly?

TH: Sure. In a certain sense every time... every time I pick up the camera... all of that stuff is at work. Every time I pick up the camera.

When I was 22 years old I found myself as chairman of a peace rally. Jane Fonda was speaking at the rally, along with several (members of the) Black Panthers. It was being held in the town of Oceanside, California, which sits at the gate of the biggest Marine Corps base on the West Coast.

A significant quantity of the audience were Marines. A significant quantity of the people heckling were also Marines. It's in the middle of the Vietnam War.

The police sergeant, who I had been working with to make this all peaceful, came to me and told me that we would have to vacate the stadium where this was being held, with three or four thousand people sitting out there. We'd have to leave so that they could search it because there was a bomb threat.

I knew that would be a disaster, and he knew that that would be a disaster, and he was ordered by his superiors – I'm sure – to get us scared and get us out of there. To take this bomb threat and use it in the best way possible.

I kind of paused, and I emptied myself... I did that thing that, for some reason or other, has always worked with me all my life, which was to kind of empty myself at that point.

I looked at him and I said, "Look, if I can get everybody in the bowl to search their own seats" – they were concrete seats, it wasn't like there could be things hidden under bleachers – "if I could get them to search their own seat, then would you let us stay?" And he said, "Let me see. We'll see what happens."

So when this band that was playing was done, I went out and made a little speech. I told everybody what to look for and how to look for it, and everybody looked for the bomb, and nobody found the bomb. And it was done in absolute silence, with absolute discipline in this crowd, and with total seriousness.

And when it was over there was this moment of complete elation. The whole place had turned into an entirely different group of people who were connected and who were careful, and disciplined, and filled with affection for one another.

There was this huge cheer and it was done. And I knew at this point that this was something that I would be proud of all my life. And I am. It's just one of these moments. That's an example of the confluence of all of those things, of anger, hope, and love.

I spent a lot of time in church as a kid, but I certainly had rejected it at that point, so my (sense of) hope didn't have a name, but that's what was working there. That's just a kind of obvious example of what happens. It happens a lot, actually.

The entire process of making the last film that I made, *God's Next Army*, which I made with my partner, is a very elongated example of those things. You're under trial at every moment.

LS: What's the inspiration behind that movie? Was it yours?

TH: Yeah, it began as mine, then it passed through Jed, my partner – the perfect partnership. I wanted to make a film about fundamentalism: why people become fundamentalists. I posed a film about Christian, Moslem, and Jewish fundamentalism, three monotheisms. Three studies.

We did some work on it, did some research, got a grant, spent some money, and could not get funded for either the Jewish or the Moslem parts of it. By this time we'd found a Rabbi who was fundamentalist, part of a settlement in Gaza that was about to be kicked out, and we would have been able to be with him during the expulsion of the Jewish settlers from Gaza.

It would have been an incredible film, but nobody bought it. People we'd done lots of other projects for – our normal clients – nobody was interested… or they were scared.

We hadn't gone as far on the Moslem film. That would have been about a group of women preachers. Women who preach to women in Cairo (Egypt), but we couldn't get anybody interested in that, either.

The film that was bought was a film about Patrick Henry College. My partner found the article about Patrick Henry. He kind of channeled my first inspiration into reality. Which, as we began to film, became much more in the news. There's been a big article in the *New Yorker* (magazine) about it.

I'll give you an example, OK? My inspiration was to make a film about fundamentalism. Everybody's concerned about the fundamentalisms. But for me, I had studied economics, I had a good humanities background in economics. I'd learned a little bit about development in the third world. In the 1970s I traveled in the third world, especially in Africa, and I took a look at what urbanization was doing to people in various places. I saw this was the drama in the lives of people, and this was going to be happening throughout the world.

Then there was the rise of these nationalistic fundamentalisms which, for me, were connected to the urbanization. Connected to the big kind of upheavals that were happening with people's lives in the end of the 20th century.

So the next film that we're going to try to do is another one of these big projects about the American Dream. The closing of the America Dream, a kind of closing of the American Frontier, and why that is contributing to the level of absolutist, nationalist, fascist kind of movements that are swinging back and forth across the United States. To see if there's some connection between the two.

All of this has to do with... goes right back to the way I was educated, and the kind of stuff that I learned. You know, you learn it in school, and you learn it out of school.

What's the most important? I can't say, but if I didn't read the books in school, if I wasn't forced to think about things that were uncomfortable to think about – reading Hobbes or something like that boring, uncomfortable stuff – I don't think that what I learned by myself, in my student activism, would have been so deep.

Columbia, when I was there, was the greatest place in the world to be, I'm convinced: the greatest place to be. But it was great because what was going on in the classroom was incredible, and what was going on outside of the classroom was incredible. I was very lucky, the two went hand in hand. To say that the teaching process is all destructive I think misses something, even though partly it is (laughs)!

MEDICINE

13. MARYANN MANAIS

History **Early** Born 1987, Georgia

I spoke to MaryAnn MaNais a few months into her freshman year at the University of West Georgia where she was thinking about studying to become a doctor. She's grown up in an "average" high school culture and carries attitudes about school and life that would be considered normal for someone her age.

It was clear from her having relatives with advanced degrees that she comes from a family of high achievers and has high potential herself. MaryAnn expresses the uncertainties of youth with more balance and certainty than anyone else I've spoken to, which is all the more impressive given that she's surrounded by neither.

Excerpts

> "Until I reach a mature state – they think we're supposed to be mature at this stage, just entering college, but it's not necessarily true. We're one or two years from high school – when I become a junior or senior, when I'm wiser and older, that's when I'll start to realize what I really want to do and what's there for me…"
>
> "For me, I have to find advice to look toward a future that's better for me. Right now I'm not necessarily comfortable, and I don't necessarily know. I'm confused – like most kids my age – but I would still go out there and find any grants or any loans to help me head toward my future…"
>
> "You have a weakness that you have to work on, and after you work on that it becomes a strength. So my weakness was my self-courage and my drive – I didn't have too much at first because I was a kid, I was a child then. And I still consider myself not as an adult just because I'm here at college. I'm an average teenager who's just getting into real life…
>
> "Universities are backwards. It's not that they don't know, it's just that they're not giving the right information to us at the right time. They've been stuck in this one mind frame and as time continues, nothing changes…"
>
> "I think that universities are stuck in this mind frame where they give classes according to their departments and their majors, give classes in everything besides what's going to be in life… they don't want to give you any hints, keys, success stories to life… they're not going to give you exactly what you need to know: 'This is the key to life. This is what you're going to learn in life!' No. It's not that…"

"I was born not knowing, and have had only a little time to change that here and there."

— Richard Feynman, physicist (1918 - 1988), in a letter to Garcia Armando

"The fundamental cause of the trouble is that in the modern world the stupid are cocksure while the intelligent are full of doubt."

— Bertrand Russell, logician (1872 - 1970), from "The Triumph of Stupidity"

Interview   Carrollton, Georgia, October 2006

MaryAnn MaNais: I have been given by my parents, as all kids my age, a certain set of paths or goals in which you should follow. My path or goal is probably in the medical field. Not necessarily becoming a doctor – that my mother wants me to become – but something in the medical field, which I like and am very passionate about.

I love the field of medicine and I also love to write. In choosing it's a tough decision because you have writing, and then you have the medical field. With writing there's not so much you can do with it, but I see creative writing intertwining with me as I go into the field of medicine.

Coming here is kind of confusing because there are so many different fields of study, here at the university. It's tough to decide which ones. My path for the future is kind of shaky right now... I really don't know.

I don't necessarily like the classes – they're not so much directed toward your goal, they're just the classes given. I don't like the idea of school, basically, because we each choose our own path at a point when we're ready, but here it's so "rushy."

By your sophomore year you're supposed to have a plan for your future. But what if somebody doesn't have a plan until their fourth year – the year in which they're supposed to graduate? What will they do then? Are they supposed to keep going, or are they supposed to stop whenever the university says stop? For me it's kind of different from that.

I'm not saying school is a bad thing – it's great to go to school – but to be rushed and forced to go into something that you know that you're not passionate about and later, maybe years later, you'll come back and either regret it or do the thing that you wanted to start off with, passionately.

LS: What would you like to have in order to decide what to do? Why is what's given to you not enough?

MM: Coming from high school I don't fit in here at college where someone keeps telling me, "You gotta think about this, you gotta think about what you're going to do!" It's up to me, basically. I treat college as real life.

The experience here is for me to choose a future. It's up to me. I think that most people coming out of high school feel different from the way I feel. Most kids want some guidance, and there is a system of guidance out there, but it's all about what they think you should do.

For me, I have to find advice to look toward a future that's better for me. Right now I'm not necessarily comfortable, and I don't necessarily know. I'm confused – like most kids my age – but I would still go out there and find any grants or any loans to help me head toward my future or my field of study.

As far as advice here at college, I would prefer it if they don't rush me. That's the advice that I want. I don't want to be told, "Oh, you have to finish this by such and such a time because it's required." I want to find something that I'm passionate about, or find something that relates to me, or that I love to do.

LS: What would you like to have happen, even if it's a fantasy, in the next year or so?

MM: The fantasy would be if I were to stick with the medical field of becoming a pediatrician. The fantasy would be to graduate in four years, go into medical school for another four to six years, do my internships, and go straight into a profession. Just like that. I think it's easy – it sounds easy – but when you look at it, it's a lot of work.

LS: What's standing in the way? I mean there are the obvious things like course work, but it seems like the more important thing is to know that you want to do them. Am I making it too simple?

MM: No. I can tell you what's standing in the way. It would be my thinking, or reasoning, that it is going to be hard. I'm not saying I won't go for something even if it's difficult, but I know that becoming a doctor isn't easy. I hear from people all the time, "Wow, you're in the medical field: pre-med, biology. Good luck!" And you know that brings my self-courage down because every day people tell me that.

I don't really know how hard the medical field is going to be; I try not to think about it too much. I try not to think about the difficult things, the toughness, because when I look at something I think, "I have to do that. I have to do it regardless. I have to get it over with. Just go ahead and do it." But with people telling me how hard it is brings back those difficult thoughts. That's the toughest thing.

LS: How do you think you're going to deal with those thoughts? Do you think you can get beyond them, or do you just have to ignore them?

MM: I just started college. I'm still in that mode of, "Oh my God. With the work given here, plus with the study that I want to do, it's going to be difficult." I still think that. And I don't think I'm going to stop thinking that until later in my life, or later in my college career, probably at the end of my junior or senior year. I don't know.

I think of finding something else that I can do – always thinking about finding something else – but I still want to keep my mind focused on becoming a doctor. But I also want to branch out to do other things, too.

Until I reach a mature state – they think we're supposed to be mature at this stage, just entering college, but it's not necessarily true. We're one or two years from high school – when I become a junior or senior, when I'm wiser and older, that's when I'll start to realize what I really want to do and what's there for me.

LS: Do you think this will happen automatically, as part of growing up, or do you expect special experiences will give you new insights?

MM: Can I be neutral? It can be both.

It can be both of those: your experiences and the wisdom that comes as you get older. It's experiences that you have, because when you go through them you think about what you've done in the past and how you might want to do things differently. But as you age and get wiser you certainly know, "OK, that's what I want to do. That's right. That's wrong." That's when you begin to realize what's really out there.

LS: You said that you had certain dissatisfaction with school. Will you go out and find what you need somewhere else, or will you wait until you can take upper-level classes that are more interesting?

MM: It's kind of a tough thing to address because any school that you go to, any college, has that four-year expectation where they say, "You have to do this within four years." But it doesn't have to happen like that. I know people who did four years in college and then took an extra two years to figure out what they wanted to do.

As it's up to me, with the ideas that I want to do, it's all up to me. This is like real life to me, real world, where nobody cares for me but me. Only you can pick and choose that path for you, so I think the only thing that I can do is deal with it.

I don't like the fact that in four years we have to be finished with this, but there's probably some kind of idea behind it. I'm thinking they're trying to rush life and it's not going to work for me. I don't think to avoid it, I'll keep going at it. If I see a difficult task I keep going at it.

LS: What do you think about the idea that it doesn't matter what you do because anything can be interesting. Med schools like people with science backgrounds, not necessarily pre-med backgrounds. Any angle that dovetails with medicine can help you get into med school.

MM: That's true. My auntie, she's got a degree in biology, now she's at Georgia State as a grad student studying linguistics. She speaks several different languages. Everybody in my family wanted her to go into the medical field, and they see that she didn't follow that, and they're like, "What happened?"

As far as going to med school, I found that you can get a degree in creative writing, you can get a degree in computer science, you can get a degree in linguistics. You can get a degree in just about anything and still go off to medical school. And me knowing that, I want to take that chance, but not necessarily take a different path away from the required classes that I need.

If I choose to go off that path and get a degree in one of those other fields, I can still get into medical school. I can get two degrees and still become a doctor. I know that I can do it – I can do any field of study – so it doesn't matter. But until I'm ready to do that, that's when I'll do that. I'm unsure with that.

Nobody has to commit to anything that they don't want to commit to. And I feel as though, with my mother saying, "Oh, you're going to be a doctor," or my aunts or my uncles saying, "You should… you should… you should…" The whole logic behind that is, "I think… I think… I think that you should do this." It's not what they think that I should do, it's what I think that I should do. Even though it's not necessarily given as that phrase, I know that's the phrase given, and I'm not going to listen to that until I experience it myself.

LS: You've said you could do any of these things, so tell me what makes you feel that you can.

What are your strengths?

MM: I know what I can do. I know how far I can go. I know me. One of my major strengths is my drive. I'm not a workaholic, but I know me and I know that something keeps saying, "Just keep going, just keep going." My strength is in my drive, and my courage also.

I have the self-courage to go on, even when there's an obstacle. And my weakness is probably not all the time trusting in myself, my self-courage, or my drive. I'm not trying to contradict myself, but I believe that where there's a pro there's always a con. So if you have your strengths, then your weakness comes from those strengths. How do I put this?

You have a weakness that you have to work on, and after you work on that, it becomes a strength. So my weakness was my self-courage and my drive – I didn't have too much at first because I was a kid, I was a child then. And I still consider myself not as an adult just because I'm here at college. I'm an average teenager who's just getting into real life. I'm still trying to turn those weaknesses even more into positives.

LS: Can you say how you're turning your weaknesses into strengths? Is it something that just happens as you grow, or is it something that you have to work on in order to make it happen?

MM: I don't necessarily see tomorrow. I can't say I'm going to be wiser, smarter, whatever. It takes time for anything. But in college, when you think about it, they don't give you time. Here in college I have to keep up the pace, and my drive and self-courage has to keep up with it also. As days go by, I see that I am slowly turning my weaknesses into strengths.

LS: It seems like you're saying "I'll know it when I see it," so let me put it this way: Where did you learn those things that gave you the insights that you're now using to figure things out?

MM: It's not an easy question. But I can say one thing, and that's that I learned from experiences with the people around me, such as my aunt and uncle, because they're both college graduates. My uncle has a degree in English and political science, and now he's going on to master something else.

I think that most of my experiences come from dealing with the people that surround me. What they say and what they do, and how they do it. From this I learn what to do and how to do it, and what not to do. I see how they live, how their daily lives are. You know I just work with them.

This summer I worked in an office job with people that have degrees in business and degrees from different colleges. But it's like, they're still kids. And that's like, "Wow," and that helps me understand, "Do I want this, do I want that?"

It can be from my family and it can be from those positive outsiders. Those people that try to lead you onto something that you're comfortable with, or who give you a plan. Your positive outside influences can give you a sense of being, and a sense of focus toward the future.

LS: One of the choices we always have is where to put our attention. What do you think about the importance of deciding what to pay attention to, in terms of the events that are happening around you? Like if I was going to focus on socializing...

MM: Yeah, you hit the spot right there. That's my focus: to socialize, to play. I really don't have anything to focus on.

Like I said, I'm confused about what my major is. I'm confused about what I want to study, what I want to be. I'm 50/50, half I want to hang out and socialize, and half I just want to enjoy college life. I choose to have my focus as being social, hanging out with friends, doing fun stuff after classes, instead of going to study like you're supposed to. I'm out with my friends, just socializing. You choose what you want to focus on.

I'm just enjoying college life. I just got here. I want to be social right now. And I probably won't get wiser until after I have chosen what I want to study. Right now my major focus is socializing, hanging with friends. Doing things that a freshman should be doing. And I could say that for every freshman, because I have friends that say, "I'm trying to stay focused. I'm trying to do this. I'm trying to do that. I'm trying to get my stuff together but, man, I just can't seem to do it… When are we going to that party tonight?" See?

People think that freshmen should think, "This is college, I have to do this, I have to do that," but what freshmen do is socialize, have fun, party. Me and my friends, we say we're not going to procrastinate, we say we're not going to party all night, but we do it. We say we're going to study, but we don't study. We procrastinate a lot. We don't see things now in the way we're going to see in the future. We're just here for the moment.

It's all about experience, who you know, who you hang about, how sociable you are. You choose your friends. Most of my friends, the people that I mainly hang out with, are friends I had in high school – we all came from the same high school. But I don't like to stay in one little social group; I like to branch out to other people.

Other people have things that I can learn from. People who study all the time, I can learn from them. I'm like, "Man, I'm going to get up like you one day. I'm going to study with you one day. I'm going to study!" But then I have my main friends where I just socialize, party, and talk.

Not everyone is like me that branches off to different people. That helps me in knowing what I want, to learn what's here. I see different people doing this, doing that, but I'm like, "Hey, I'm doing this. When am I going to do that? I wish I could do that, I wish I could do that." But am I doing it? No. I'm off socializing. And at the end of the day I do feel bad.

LS: You do!?

MM: Yeah, to tell you the truth, I feel bad.

You know, some friends are good at studying right now, and they've got a test tomorrow. They look good. And in order for me to get up to being a junior or senior, I'll have to study, too. I'll have to pass all my classes. So I go back and forth.

There are so many different people at college. It's diverse, it's different, it's the real world – and when I say "real world" I'm not just saying it's like the business world – it's something you have to achieve, it's something that you have to go through, you have to succeed in. You have to.

Right now I don't do any hardcore studying, and I think that's going to catch up with me. I know it's going to catch up with me! But I continue not do it because, like I said, I procrastinate.

LS: There seem to be three things here – I wonder if there really are just three things – socializing, studying, and procrastinating. Maybe you shouldn't procrastinate, just go socialize.

Cut it down to two (laughs)!

MM: Well, like you said, you're given those options. Either go with your friends and socialize – "Oh, they look like they're having fun!" – or go sit in your room with your roommate who's boring, and study. Nobody wants to study for hours! Who wants to do that! For me I give 25% to studying and to class, and another 75% to partying and socializing. I think freshmen are confused.

LS: What would happen to you if you got really involved with writing? What if you started writing a book and you got really involved because the characters were coming out of your mind and your heart. Would that be studying or socializing or procrastinating, or would it be something else?

MM: Writing for me is something else; it's not socializing, it's not procrastinating, and it's not studying. If I feel compelled to write, and I get an idea to write something – I write poetry – then I open up my book and I write poetry. That doesn't take long to do. Especially when you have that thought, when you're in that space where you can write. When I get writer's block then, heh, my time is freed up. Then I can go procrastinate and socialize and hang out with friends.

LS: I think it's interesting that there was a fourth thing, because you've given me three, but there was a fourth. But it probably just didn't come on the scene as it was so small, right?

MM: As I'm talking, yeah, right. As I'm talking, other ideas come up. Like you said the fourth thing is writing, but not every freshman can write. I basically write when I have free time…

LS: When you're not busy procrastinating (laughs)!

MM: Yeah, when I'm not busy procrastinating (laughs)! Or not busy studying or not busy socializing, and I'm just in this set where I say to myself, "Oooo, I just want to write about something!" I write. So guess it is four things.

LS: Let me tell you something, for me, and most people who are passionate about something, it ends up there is only really one thing… and you sweep all the rest away (laughs)! You just do what you're passionate about all the time! All the rest is a bother.

MM: I always hear that. Maybe if I do go on to take creative writing, that will somehow lead back to my path of becoming a doctor.

You know what – speaking of writing and those big classes: English 101 and 102 – I'm not a big fan of English, as far as learning grammar and syntax, but I'm excellent in that class! I read every book and I can analyze them. It's just not useful to me right now. But I know that when I become a creative writer, or if I do do something with medical research, then I'll have to go back to those basics of writing – which is English class – which I never cared about. What am I to do then? Go back to that boring class that I didn't like but I did so well in? It's confusing.

I think that universities, all over the US, they're stuck in this mind frame where they give classes according to their departments and their majors, give classes in everything besides what's going to be in life. The reason that they do that is because they don't want to give you any hints, keys, success stories to life. They can show you a path of how to become successful, but they're not going to give you exactly what you need to know:

"This is the key to life. This is what you're going to learn in life!" No. It's not that.

Universities are backwards. It's not that they don't know, it's just that they're not giving the right information to us at the right time. They've been stuck in this one mind frame and as time continues, nothing changes. It's all, "Study this, study that, for your one major." But they don't tell you, "Well, you need to know this in order to survive in real life." You have to find it out for yourself in doing the college thing. That's why life isn't easy, because you've got to do that stuff plus other stuff, you know? It's a balance.

I don't know what to make of that. I'm just saying things like "I see" because I think about this stuff, but I never sit down and talk to my friends about this because… well… when I sit down with my friends and socialize we talk about something totally different. It's not about life, and not about this particular part of life.

We don't go into depth about what society has given us, what we need, versus what we want. Or what we're given, versus what we need. I don't think we take the time to sit down because we don't care right now. But as far as me, speaking for myself, I care.

14. DAVE WILLIAMSON

History	Early	Born 1982, Shreveport, Louisiana

From reading *All Quiet on the Western Front* I gathered that war was a kind of learning experience. I found a veterans' chat list and asked if any combat medics would tell their story. Dave Williamson sent me back an email titled "Your Iraqi Medic."

Dave joined the Army at 19. He was enticed into training as a medic – a post for which he had no previous interest – by opportunity, ignorance, and "a lot of females." There he found something at which he is truly excellent and underwent combat experience that he is terribly proud of and also still struggling to recover from.

At 25 Dave still looks like a kid who – to use his own expression – recently fell off the turnip truck. His story is anything but innocent, and his youth belies a depth that few others can equal, no matter what their age.

Excerpts

> "My mom pretty much considered me a lost cause. She put all her time and effort and money into my sister – my parents were divorced – and just considered me to be this great, giant, enormous screwup. Even when I did something right I was still a screwup…"
>
> "Lincoln, I'm not going to lie to you or church this up to make it sound glorious, or that I did it because I wanted to go and save lives, because that was the furthest thing from my mind. But at the time I was 18 years old, and the female to male ratio at Fort Sam was 7 to 1, and I was single with no dependents…"
>
> "That was the first and last time I let a patient have a personal impact on me. When his heel fell out of his foot I'm thinking, 'He's never going to have a normal life. He's not going to be able to play soccer with his kids.' He's 17 years old. I went back to the barracks and I cried about that one…"
>
> "Just because a teacher tells you… that this is what you're going to see or do… you will most likely see the complete opposite. And what are you going to do when it comes around? Are you going to say, 'Oh, well, I never learned that.' Or are you going to say, 'OK, I acknowledge that I don't know that, and I'm going to take it upon myself to make sure I don't look like a blubbering idiot next time that rolls around…' "
>
> "And the next time it happens and you still don't know it – and it doesn't have to be in medicine – you just look like a fool. Someone is going to be there to point out, 'You've seen this before, and you didn't know what was going on then. Why don't you know what's going on now?' "

With Sgt. Crosby at Washington LZ.

MEDICINE

Shreveport Army Medic Makes Quick, Life-saving Call

The Times of Shreveport, Louisiana, February 9, 2006.

"After a tour as a combat medic in Iraq, Army Spc. David Williamson probably thought all the action was behind him as he headed home to Shreveport for a midtour family leave in early December. But then another passenger among the 329 military folks aboard the Dec. 3 flight, an Air Force master sergeant, passed out and started convulsing. 'Being previously identified by an Army major as a medic from the forward surgical team, I was called to the front of the aircraft,' said Williamson, 23, who attended Captain Shreve High School from 1998 to 2001.

"Taking the initiative, Williamson assessed the patient, recorded his vital signs, initiated two large-bore IVs and immobilized his spine... The flight was over Greenland, so with the patient drifting in and out of consciousness with a weak pulse and no signs of getting better, Williamson and the major 'made the call to divert the aircraft to land in Bangor, Maine.' There, doctors learned the man had a lacerated spleen, three fractured vertebrae and was on the verge of septic shock.

"Williamson continued home to Louisiana, but word got back to his supervisor and commanding officer back at Medical Task Force 10 in Baghdad, Iraq. Paperwork was filed, and last month, the Shreveporter was presented the Army Commendation Medal...

"Williamson, son of Shreveport Realtor Jeff Williamson and Barbara Williamson of Oklahoma City, said he just did what training dictated. 'I don't see how anything I did saved his life, considering that if you were a patient presenting with a headache or a patient with no pulse at all, I would have done the exact same thing,' he said. 'The way I see it is every patient I am responsible for is someone's father, son, mother or daughter, and I would want nothing less than the best from the soldier that would care for me should I get injured,' he said. 'Therefore, I treat my patients the same.' "

"Knowledge studies others, Wisdom is self-known;
Muscle masters brothers, Self mastery is bone;
Content need never borrow, Ambition wanders blind;
Vitality cleaves to the marrow, Leaving death behind."

— *The Way of Life According to Lao Tzu: An American Version*, translated by Witter Bynner

Interview   Tyler, Texas, December 2007

Dave Williamson: My introduction to emergency medicine was very flawed. I had absolutely no aspirations of going into the field of medicine. I didn't ever plan on having anything to do with medicine, and it wasn't because I was scared of blood or anything; it was that before I enlisted into the service, I planned a career based around either mechanics or criminal justice. I have always been fascinated by the field of criminal justice.

Well, I am color blind, which left me with, like, five career options in the military. I didn't want to sit behind a desk, which left me with about two options. One being a radio operator – they call them RATTs in the army, short for Radio Teletype Operator – and the other was a job where I would be put in a garrison environment and wear a suit all day. I had absolutely no interest in doing either, but I was offered an $8,000 bonus to go into communications. At the time I was 18, and if you dangle $8,000 in front of any late-teen they're going to jump at it. So I jumped at it, went to school, and I became a radio teletype operator.

When I came out of high school I also never anticipated ever going into the army. Even up to the point where I graduated from Basic Training, I thought that the army life just had to suck. You know, you just sit out there and train for 10, 12 hours, and too many people yelling and screaming. I had no interest in it whatsoever, but I came home and did my research and found out what an average day is like in the military. At the time I was in the Louisiana Army National Guard and had already finished up my training by graduating Basic Training and Airborne school at Fort Benning and Combat Radio Operations at Fort Gordon. I looked at the benefits of active duty and everything I had already accomplished, and I said, "This is fantastic." This is something I want to pursue.

When I went to MEPS (Military Entrance Processing Station) to figure out where I was going, they told me that I'd be assigned by the needs of the army, and that I had no say in the matter. The contract was entirely up to them because it was my choice to go into active duty. They told me that my first duty assignment was going to be Korea, and that I'd be shipping in September. I was not looking forward to being in Korea in the middle of winter and I said, "No, there's no way. I'm not going to Korea."

They said the only way that you can get out of your duty assignment of Korea is if you re-class your MOS, which is Military Occupational Specialty. So I said, "Well, what are my options?" And they said, "Per needs of the army, your only other option is 77-Lima," which is a PAC clerk...a paper pusher. And there was no way; I was not about to be a paper pusher. I was an ASE-certified mechanic before I went in, and I always enjoyed working with my hands and taking things apart, but even that was not open to me because of my color blindness.

I've got to pause right there and go back in my story. When I was at Fort Benning for basic training, almost the entire company, 250 to 300 people strong, were going to Fort Sam Houston to become combat medics. In fact, I was one of three people in a platoon of 65 that was not going to be a medic – I was going to go do radios.

Lincoln, I'm not going to lie to you or church this up to make it sound glorious, or that I did it because I wanted to go and save lives, because that was the furthest thing from my mind. But at the time I was 18 years old, and the female to male ratio at Fort Sam was 7 to 1, and I was single with no dependents.

So I said, "I'll give this combat medic thing a shot. It's a field job, it goes hand in hand with all the other work that I had enjoyed. That's what I want to do. I get to work with the infantry, and I'll be a combat medic." But my sole motivation of going to Sam Houston was because there was a lot of females there.

LS: Was this just general basic training?

DW: No. Fort Sam Houston was the AMEDD… the Army Medical Department Center of Schools, or something like that. It's a block away from Brooke Army Medical Center, which is the leading burn hospital in the country, if not the entire world. It's way, way up there. So they had a lot of officers and a lot of people who were very good at what they did. As far as medical anything for the military, not just the army, it happened at Fort Sam Houston.

So I said, "OK, I'll be a combat medic. This is going to be great!" But I had absolutely no interest in becoming a medic. And I didn't think I was going to be any good at it. I was nervous, I didn't want to have that much responsibility – I already knew radios – and I especially didn't want to go down there and train for 22 weeks.

When I got there I was really looking forward to it, but I was really just looking forward to the females. By the time I graduated I came to feel that it was something that I was really, really good at. Not only was I really good at it, but I was really interested in it.

LS: This was now 22 months later?

DW: Twenty-two weeks.

LS: Pretty quick training.

DW: It was like taking a drink from a fire hose. It was, "We're going to give it to you, and it's up to you to learn it." Now here's something that I know you're going to love to hear. To this day I have lived my entire career by this philosophy. There was an instructor, his name was Sergeant First Class Cook, and he was a real down-to-earth guy, and he'd talk to us like people first, and NCOs (Non-Commissioned Officers) second.

Well, we were being… uh… we weren't holding ourselves accountable for our own actions. We thought that since we were all prior service we were special, and Sergeant Cook told us one day – he never really yelled, he never got upset – he told us, "In no other job that you ever have does it matter if you sit through the class, daydream, doodle, or whatnot, but if you don't remember this stuff, then somebody dies, and it's your fault because…" – and he wasn't saying it to me, he was generalizing – "because you didn't want to pay attention. This truly does matter. This is life or death. No other job you have had has been a matter of life and death and this entire career field is a matter of life and death. And if you remember, then you're not even doing something that fantastic; you're just meeting the standard. That's what we're teaching you here: how to meet the standard."

Ever since then, when it came to medicine, if I heard it, then it clicked. It was almost at an autistic level, but if I heard something that had to do with medicine, then it clicked. You could have told me one thing five years ago, and if it pertained to medicine then I would remember it to this day.

I'm not going to say that I grew up in a troubled home, but my mom pretty much considered me a lost cause. She put all her time and effort and money into my sister – my parents were divorced – and just considered me to be this great, giant, enormous screwup. Even when I did something right I was still a screwup. So when I did something right, it didn't mean that much – I considered that I was doing something my sister was doing all along. So it wasn't anything big to me. It wasn't a big deal.

It wasn't until later on that I figured out that – and I'm not trying to boast – it wasn't until I started doing medical work that I realized how good I was at it. And it wasn't by my own admission because I had doctors and surgeons and nurses and PA's (Physicians' Assistants) asking me, "How do you know all of this stuff? This is medical school stuff?" Well, I'd just tell them the story about Sergeant Cook, and tell them that the stuff just sticks. I don't really know how to explain it.

So that's how my job in the medical field – which I'm absolutely in love with – came to pass. I know a lot about a lot of stuff, but I'm not truly great in any one field. After Fort Sam I took off to Fort Campbell, home of the 101st Airborne Screamin' Eagles Air Assault division.

LS: Where's Fort Campbell?

DW: Well, it's shaped like a "U," and the upper half is in Kentucky, and the lower half is in Tennessee. When I first got there I was assigned to a divisional command, which was a pretty high honor for a person of my rank. When I first went there, Major General Turner was the general... uh, as you were... the first general – I went through three generals – the first general was David Petraeus, so I actually served under General Petraeus who, you know, now is the MNFI (Multi-National Force-Iraq) Commander, and then it was Major General Turner, and then it was another guy. I don't remember his name because I wasn't in the army for very long after he took command.

My position was interesting because not only am I working with the people that run the division, they run the entire post. There were a lot of people rubbing elbows with really high brass, the folks in Washington, and all that stuff.

They put me in the 801st Main Support Battalion. I'm not sure how familiar you are with the military, but breaking it down – and this is very important to understand what I did – breaking it down you have brigades within divisions. A division usually consists of three to five brigades. Within each brigade you have three to five battalions. Third brigade was called the Rakasans. The Rakasans were commanded by Colonel Steele. Colonial Steel was Captain Steele in Mogadishu, during the conflict portrayed in the movie *Black Hawk Down*.

So you have the three brigades and HHD, which is Headquarters and Headquarters Detachment. And we have 1st Brigade, 2nd Brigade, and 3rd Brigade. All four of them are infantry, but HHD has the motor pool and the HHD guys that are in charge of the whole brigade.

Within every infantry brigade you have the ground pounders that lob the mortars and shoot the rockets and pound the ground and do all that stuff, and then you have the forward support battalion. The people that are not on the line with these guys in the infantry battalions are support: PAC clerks, finance, quartermaster, transportation, all that stuff. And medical.

Now, if you were a line medic with the infantry, you fell in under HHD and they would assign you out to different companies. But for a forward support battalion, line medics can't uphold higher echelons of care, whereas a forward support battalion can set up their own aid station that has more capabilities than the infantry medical aid station such as X ray and lab capabilities. Every brigade has a forward support battalion. Now, you take all these brigades and they fall-in under a division. Just like a forward support battalion is to a brigade, a main support battalion is to a division. Does that make sense?

LS: I guess so.

DW: I was assigned to division command. Main support meant that we were supporting the divisional command, we were supporting everybody. If one of the medics in the line units die, get sick, or go home, or if they need another medic for this or such and such, or anything, they can draw from the main support battalion, because that's what we're there for. That's where I stayed for about a year.

LS: Isn't that sort of an office job?

DW: Very much so, very much so. It kind of fell apart, and I was really upset because my skills were just steadily going down the drain. I was wasting away. You have so many people that are so eager to get just a little bit of patient contact, and here I am where my skills are useless.

The Department of the Army announces that they're forming a new division, the 506th. Now the 506th is the same brigade that was the "Band of Brothers." But I stayed in the same spot and I was getting really upset. I started to kick up a stink because I felt that I would be a greater asset to be an infantry medic with the training I had already received. And at this point I knew I was good at what I did. People had told me, and it was apparent when I did get to work. They knew that it just came second nature to me.

So I took it to my rear detachment commander and I said, "Look, all we do is sit in an office until lunch." We literally did nothing! We watched TV until lunch, and lunch was about two and a half hours, and then at around 16:00 we'd empty out the trash and go home. Naturally, I'm furious. So I said, "There's got to be something you can do so that I can keep my medical skills up." And he said, "Yes!"

They sent me to work in the clinic. The clinic was a TMC, Troop Medical Clinic, and there I picked the doctors' and the PAs' brains all the time. Picked their brains, I mean it was to a point where the docs would come find me and say, "OK, this is really rare." They knew that I'd remember it.

I worked there for a little bit, and I met a PA whose name was Lieutenant Patton-Curry, we'll call her Vickie. Vickie was so completely blown away by my skills and talent that she was rallying with my command to send me to PA school.

LS: What's a PA do? Do they work directly behind the doctor?

DW: They can pretty much practice by themselves. As a PA I would have gotten my commission, I would have been an officer, and I'd be working on patients all the time. But in the mean time I had to start taking classes. My command said, "No, you're not doing it." They decided that since I was so advanced they'd pull me out of the clinic and put some of the less advanced medics into the clinic in order to learn stuff. And I said, "That's ridiculous! I'm getting really good at what I'm doing, and just because I'm getting really good you want to pull me? That's not fair!" Well, the army's not fair.

I picked up a slot to go to EMT (Emergency Medical Technician) Intermediate School. I went and passed and everything like that, so now I'm an EMT Intermediate, which pretty much establishes that, yes, I do know what I'm doing, I'm good at it, and I'm shit-hot.

Well, after that they refused to do anything with me. They said, "You've got all the training that you need, and you're really good at what you do." And I said, "So that's it? I just wait 'til we deploy and that's it? I keep on doing the petty stuff? That's not really fair." Once again, the army's not fair.

Turns out that I stepped on a lot of people's toes doing what I did next. There was another PA that I worked for named Lieutenant Scranton who was a Special Forces PA, and he was impressed by my PT scores. And there was another PA named Major Briley, also a Special Forces PA. I worked hand in hand with the both of them.

Major Briley and Lieutenant Scranton took me up to SF (Special Forces) Recruiting and didn't tell my unit. They both believed with my knowledge in the medical field and my motivation, that I would excel as a Special Forces medic and convinced me that I had what it took. One morning I went to the clinic while everybody else was going to PT, but when I got there they took me up to SF Recruiting so I could take my PT (Physical Training) Test. I passed it with flying colors and was given orders to go to Special Forces selection. When I took it back to my unit, they got furious.

LS: Because you didn't follow the standard procedure?

DW: I didn't go through my chain of command, and they'd already told me I'd had all my training, and I was weakening the unit strength. Plus, I was their showcase EMT Intermediate, their resident subject-matter expert on combat medicine who taught the combat lifesaver program for the division's different units, which was like saying, "Look at our guys!" I wasn't about to be a statistic.

Around Christmas time of that year I get a phone call – I was home on leave – and I get a phone call from my old platoon sergeant. The platoon sergeant that I met when I went to Fort Campbell, and who managed to stay with me all the way through my army career – and I went through seven different units – he was always my platoon sergeant. He would move into a new unit, and two weeks later I would move into the same unit. It just magically seemed to happen. So he knew me really well.

He called me up and said, "Come Monday morning you're not going to fall-in with the 801st any more." I'm thinking this is my big break, this is great. I'm not going to be in support anymore and I will finally have some line time, which is where I should have been all along. I said, "Well, where am I going?" He said, "Me and you have an interview." I said, "Interview for what?" He said, "Some of the doctors and nurses up at the hospital have put you in for the forward surgical team selection-assessment." I didn't want to do that. I did not want to do that. A forward surgical team is very small. I knew very little about them, but I knew that they did nothing… or so I thought.

The med director board review was pretty much, "So, what do you know? What have you done?" They looked at my training records and they asked me basic medical questions and stuff like that. As opposed to answering them on the level that they expected a medic to answer, I answered in the most detailed and specific manner I knew how. There was certain stuff that they were asking that, quite frankly, I had no business knowing. They weren't expecting a direct, straight-to-the-point, and guided answer that leaves no room for error.

Needless to say, about two days later I got picked up. I was upset. I was very angry. So I fall-in with the forward surgical team. After that my career absolutely skyrocketed. It just took off. I found out that to be assigned on the forward surgical team you have to be in the top 1% out of every medic in the army. Not just out of every medic of your rank, out of every medic period.

To get on a forward surgical team is very, very, very elite because you're working hand in hand with the doctor, and you're essentially using your doctor's license because you're not bound by any license of your own.

LS: So were you wrong when you said that they didn't do anything?

DW: No, I was not. There was a major that joined the team that knew how to get stuff done. And our commander was probably the smartest man I ever met, and he was very socially… I mean I love that man to death, and he's just the greatest commander I've ever known, but he was a nerd.

He pretty much gave us the go-ahead to do anything that we wanted, and Major Morton, the major that came onto the team, he is blowing the roof off the budget. As a matter of fact, about nine months before combat he got us a one million dollar grant for us to do whatever we wanted to.

Our forward surgical team had 20 people on it: six were enlisted and the rest were officers. There were specialized nurses, like an OR (Operating Room) nurse, a nurse anesthetist, a flight nurse, a trauma nurse. The lowest-ranked nurse in our team was a major, which is pretty high, and the highest rank was our commander, who was a colonel, and as far as the enlisted members, our highest rank was a master sergeant. To work hand in hand with a master sergeant and a colonel every single day… I mean in bigger units the colonel is God. Colonel Steele, who's commanding an entire brigade of close to 4,000 people, was the same rank as my commander Colonel Gross, who was commanding 20.

So Major Morton – I don't know how he did it, but I'm glad he did – ends up finding us ways to do all sorts of stuff. We end up going to Special Operations Combat Medic School in Miami. We got to work at Vanderbilt, and we got to work at St. Judes.

And since we had so many people that worked in the hospital on a regular basis, it was just kind of like going to work with Dad. I mean everybody had a chance to do whatever they wanted to and learn how to do procedures or anything that interested them. I went from having to all but beg to have any sort of patient contact, to them teaching me everything that they knew. I was like a sponge. I soaked it all up. I loved it. I was so enthusiastic!

Our team graduated with the highest cumulative average from the Emergency War Surgery course. Graduating from a course in Emergency War Surgery didn't mean that I knew how to hit the books to get the right answers, it meant that I could now do these life-saving surgeries, because I'm not bound by license, and in combat it doesn't matter. We were out there to save lives using whatever means possible.

Now I'm going to put the story on pause here and go back to tell you how a forward surgical team works. A forward surgical team is primarily designed for Special Operations use so, naturally, with the training I had already received and excelled at, I fit right in and loved that aspect of the unit. They take this forward surgical team and throw them way, way, way out in front of the line, so that if somebody was injured... Have you ever heard of the "golden hour of care?"

LS: No.

DW: The golden hour of care is from the moment of injury, to sustain life for one hour until they can get into surgery. After that one hour your chance of survival drops something like 10% every minute. It's insane. Our job was to extend the golden hour to a golden eight hours.

Our team was broken down into four five-man teams. On each of those teams you had a medic, a surgeon, an OR nurse, a nurse anesthetist, and a flight nurse. So I kind of went from a combat medic to being a combat surgeon of sorts.

The way that we're supposed to operate is, from the moment that somebody gets injured, we can pull them into cover and start surgery right away. Everybody carries their own gear: the surgeon carries his gear and the OR nurse carries his gear, and it's all specific to what you're doing in the field and your role in the life-saving surgeries. The OR nurse carries a bunch of tools and sterile packs, the doc carries books and gowns and stuff that he needs, and I carry everything for immediate trauma. So you get the picture.

We'd go out with Special Forces, the people who were like, "You must be mistaken, we were never there" types of people. That's what a Special Forces Surgical Team is designed to do.

So in the time that someone would otherwise die in transit, we would operate. And this isn't an operation where we stapled their bellies shut and said, "Fine." This was like exploratory laparoscopic surgery. It was pretty intense.

As a graduate of the Emergency War Surgery course it meant that I could do whatever was needed if shit really hit the fan, the reason being that just because someone is a doctor doesn't mean that they're immune to getting shot. So pretty much we could do whatever we wanted to. I was doing stuff as a combat medic that some people had never heard of. I mean never heard of.

So we go back to Fort Campbell after Miami and we all knew that deployment was on the horizon, we just didn't know how soon it was going to come. It was August 2nd. We're all sitting in the office waiting on the commander to show up, and the commander's never late unless he's in surgery. Our master sergeant wasn't even there. The door opens and in comes our commander and we called everyone to attention. They pulled us all in and were issued our FRAGO (Fragmentary Order), we got our OP word to go to Iraq, and it was about four weeks away.

From August the 2nd to August the 12th we were pretty much closing down our lives state-side. A lot of us were nervous – I can't speak for everyone else, I can speak for my own behalf – I was nervous that I was not adequately trained. I was nervous that I was not ready for this, where everybody on my team was unrivaled. There was no medic, ever was or ever will be, as advanced as I was, but I was still – and I guess this goes back to my mom – worried that I didn't know it all. I should know more.

I wasn't nervous that we were going to get shot, or that we were going to die; I was nervous that I would freeze up, or that something was going to happen to the tune of, "I don't know what to do now." Because when everything starts coming at you, there is just too much to think about, there's just so much going on.

On August the 12th I had moved out of my apartment, I had everything up in storage, and I came back up to Shreveport for block leave. That's when I told my parents and they didn't really know what to say, but they were really, really, really scared. Really scared. On September 9th, 2006, at 12:15 in the afternoon, we boarded a DC-8 and headed for Kuwait. On the way to Kuwait we stopped at Rhine-Main, in Germany. That was our only stop.

We land in Kuwait, and it's 118 degrees. At lot of people have asked me, "So, how did that feel? How does 118 degrees feel?" When I got off the aircraft I got out on the aft, starboard side. I got off right behind two gigantic jet engines. What do you call it when you open up the stove and all that heat rushes out at you…? Back draft! The back draft was insane.

We had to get all of our gear together and we had a little formation. The most miserable, absolute sheer misery of my entire tour wasn't the heat or the fact that my life was constantly in danger – none of that compared to the misery of movement. Movement means organizing how to get in or out of the country, or going from one place to another.

I failed to mention this, but when we went over there we didn't have a definable mission. To be 100% honest, nobody, nobody knew why we were over there and, quite frankly, we really didn't have a place to stay. We didn't have a mission, we didn't know where we were going. I was told so much crap.

See, Major Morton – and I hate saying this about a United States Army officer – he was a pathological liar. He is a great, great guy and he always looked out for the troops, but… he had his grubby little fingers in a bunch of grubby little pies that didn't belong to him.

When we got there, he pretty much set all this stuff up, and the only reason that we were over there was – it was never proven, but – I didn't fall off the turnip truck yesterday – was so Major Morton could put a combat patch on his shoulder in an attempt to hype himself and his ORB (officers record brief) up and say that he had been in combat with the 101st Airborne Division. That's at least my opinion. So ultimately Major Morton knows what's going on and nobody else has a clue.

I remember staring at the aircraft, thinking, "Those after-burners, it's a good thing we shut them off when we did because it's really, really hot up here." And I was standing maybe 20 to 25 feet away from the aircraft and we're all getting our gear together and we basically had 15 or 20 minutes of down time because we'd just been up in the air for 22 hours. We were all just shell-shocked. We don't know what to think or what to do.

The plane leaves. I was so naive and I guess you could say ignorant, as to why it was still hot. It never really registered to me that it was not the back draft from the after-burner, it was the heat of the desert. And it was! It would be like you were pulling steaks off a grill, and you pulled the top of the grill up and it all went whoosh! It's like that, except that it never stopped. I remember this so vividly.

I think the part that sucked the most was that everybody was responsible for their own weight. Now, Lincoln, if I told you to pack all the stuff up that you're going to need for the next year and a half, pack it all up, but you're only allowed this much. You need to pack up not only things that I tell you to, but you've also got to pack up the things that you think are going to make your life more comfortable. I had two rucksacks, a patrol pack, two duffle bags, and a Pelican box, which is a bullet-proof, polyurethane box on wheels.

You can imagine how big of a cluster it would be if you took 323 people and called out their names one at a time to come get their multiple bags. So instead they had a baggage detail and threw everybody's junk in the middle of this huge pile. It was just a free-for-all: just go find your stuff. That was insane. From that point on, everywhere we went we were dragging our gear. It was miserable, absolutely miserable.

I lose my temper very quickly when I don't know what's going on, when I don't know what we're doing, and when there is no game plan. I have to have some sort of order and structure in my life so that I can maintain a sense of accomplishment, dedication to the mission, and focus. I need to know, "This is what's going on." We didn't have it.

I found out later – and this is factual – that Major Morton was flying by the seat of his pants the whole time. He was coming up with idea after idea, talking to people and making deals; it was insane. He was making deals for us to deploy, and I found out all he did was get us on the plane into Kuwait and that was it. After that we were homeless, had no support, no mission, and we did not know where the gear we had already sent to Iraq was. Our unit was too small to operate as a single unit but too large to piggyback with another unit. We essentially had to wait for someone to say, "You can stay with us here at this place and if we have any work for you there you are welcome to it." We were stuck between a rock and a hard place. I was so angry when I found all of this out. That is piss-poor management and planning – all so that one selfish officer could put a combat patch on his shoulder.

Major Morton knew how monotonous everything was inside of Kuwait, so he gave us the chance to go out and do stuff, to get equipment. We went over with no medical supplies. It all would have expired, it wouldn't have made it through the flight, or it wouldn't have maintained sterility, so we had to go and get all of these medical supplies in Kuwait. And that just made more gear that we had to hump across the berm. I know now that the reason we did this in Kuwait was because we had no means to get any supplies while we were in theater because we had nowhere to go.

That was when I got to see the Persian Gulf, that's south of Kuwait, and I got a chance to get out and see the country. The biggest thing that I wanted was to see a camel. I wanted to see real, true-to-life wild camels, and I did – I saw a bunch of them.

We stayed in Kuwait until September the 10th. No, as you were, the 12th. We stayed there till the 12th. And on the 12th of September we got orders that we were going across the berm. I had a small sense of relief, and at the same time, followed very abruptly by a sense of, "This is going to suck! We're moving into another country, again!"

We were able to get our own C-130 into the country, which was extremely lucky for us. A lot of our gear had been palletized, which was good because it was at the end of the aircraft, but bad in the sense that, if things went terribly wrong, we'd have to cut sling load, which means that our gear goes completely out the back of the bird, and we'd have to jump.

I don't know if you've ever jumped out of an aircraft, but there's already a lot of things going on when you have to jump, and to cut sling load and see it wheel out the back, and then everybody has to rig up their 'chute, hook up to the static line, and come flying out the back, all the while you're crash landing and the bird's going to the ground – that's not necessarily a good thing (laughs), or easy, or anything like that.

What made it worse was that you can only fly by cover of darkness. That's the only time that you can fly, at least something like a C-130. To make things even worse, the C-130 doesn't have any windows. It's got two in the front, and that's about it. I was a little upset by this because, while flying doesn't bother me and closed spaces don't bother me, the people around me didn't feel the same way.

We did a combat dive into BIAP (Baghdad International Airport), and I don't care how strong a stomach you have, or how well you can maintain yourself… You're flying and you hear the engines kill, and the nose dives down and it sloops… like it's flying straight one moment and then they kill the engines. The tail drops down first, and then the nose drops down like this (Dave gestures with his hands), and they swing high up to the left – almost 90 degrees like it's a pendulum – and then all the way to the right, and then it levels out about five seconds before it hits the ground. So you never know if you've been shot down, or if they're doing a combat dive. The reason that they do this is to evade surface-to-air missiles. Because by doing this, any surface-to-air missile would be hitting behind the plane, as opposed to hitting the actual aircraft.

So we land at BIAP and what do we do next? We hurry up and wait. We unpalletize the gear, we take accountability for ourselves and our equipment. Major Morton goes off again to beg, borrow, and steal from… anybody to get what he wanted and to see if he could pawn off our small unit onto a larger one and get us a mission. Like I told you, Major Morton really looked out for the troops. And he could get things done.

Still, nobody knows what's going on. Major Morton is the only one that thinks he knows what he's doing, but he doesn't. He doesn't have a clue. It got to the point where the master sergeant was getting pissed because we had all put our trust in Major Morton, who is not getting anything accomplished. And there are helicopters landing and taking off, landing and taking off.

Finally we had these two Chinooks (helicopters) come to pick us up. Thank god! We were using one Chinook for cargo, and one Chinook for personnel. We landed in BIAP at 05:15 that morning. At 22:45 that night the Chinooks rolled up. We hadn't been indoors yet, we hadn't eaten, we hadn't slept. We'd been awake now for going on 30-something hours.

We repalletize all of our equipment and go and sit on these Chinooks. Mind you, we are not fortunate enough to have airconditioning. So I'm sitting in all of my combat gear, and my combat load weighs 49 pounds and includes my helmet, and my flack jacket, and my rounds, and all of that. We sit there for a couple of hours and finally the crew chiefs shut down the turbines, get up, and say, "Everybody has got to get off. We can't take the aircraft anywhere."

So around 23:00 we were literally spending the night on the runway. We had taken all of our bags and made a circle, we were using our rucksacks as pillows, laying out there hoping to get some sleep. We weren't allowed to sleep, because every half hour to 45 minutes Major Morton thought that we had a lead, or a jump on something.

Around 01:45 or 02:00 the next morning here comes a Rhino, which is an armored bus. So we're taken to an airport called Washington LZ, which is a hub for helicopters and that's all: you can't land anything bigger than a helicopter on it. Then we climb on the back of a five-ton and we're taken to the combat support hospital and my thoughts were, "You have got to be kidding. We went from working in a hospital in the states to prepare for working on the fields of combat in Iraq to working in another hospital that already has all the doctors, nurses, and medics that they need. What are we here for?"

We're given rooms and everything like that. We unpack our stuff and by the time we were all done and my room was ready, it was time for breakfast. Our building was mortared twice while I was trying to sleep. And I was like, "If this is how life is going to be, then I'm going to be hating it."

The next day Sergeant Crosby, the same NCO who was my squad leader the whole time, told me that me and him were scheduled to start working the next day, but he didn't want the rest of the medics to start working yet. He wanted me to go in there and get my feet wet so that I could go back and tell the troops. He was pretty much using me to test the waters. I worked undercover, without anyone else besides Sergeant Crosby knowing that I was working, for about a week. That is when I saw my first patient.

My first patient was an E4 who was riding in a track vehicle, an APC (Armored Personnel Carrier), when they hit an IED, which is an Improvised Explosive Device. There were six people in the APC: one was DOA (Dead On Arrival), one death later on due to injuries, and then you had four patients.

Just to give you an idea of how messed up trauma is, one of these guys had a scratch underneath his eye, the guy next to him was decapitated, and the guy next to him on the other side had two or three traumatic amputations. Sitting directly across from him was a guy that was about to die, and the guy sitting next to him was fine. It's just weird how stuff rolls out.

My first patient came out of the APC and he didn't have any noticeable signs of damage. We rolled him inside and he was CPR (Cardio-Pulmonary Resuscitation) in progress; he didn't have a pulse or anything like that. This was the very first patient I ever touched in the combat zone and he didn't have a pulse, which is not good. So he dies.

I had to wheel his body to the morgue past his entire unit, and they're all looking at me like I failed them. They're all looking at me, like, "Why did this happen?" They're all looking at me like it's my fault; like I personally had failed them.

We get to the morgue and were still not sure how this man had died, and had died so quickly, so we were going to examine him further to find a cause of death. We take him out of the body bag and he has a hole about the size of a dime that's right underneath his navel. I said, "Doc, I think I found the entrance wound." The doc says, "Let's get ready to roll him." I put my hand up underneath his right arm and below his left buttocks, and I crossed arms with the NCO next to me, just like we were supposed to. I immediately, after placing my hands on his back, said, "I think I found the exit wound."

When we rolled him over we see he was filleted open and from the top of his buttocks up to about his C5 (cervical vertebrae, his neck), it was blown wide open. His lungs and his intestines stayed on the gurney, and we pretty much rolled him out of his insides. I knew there was one of our guys who would have lost it. This kid was unstable as it was. I knew that he would start crying.

LS: He wasn't there.

DW: No, no. And this was the biggest reason that Sergeant Crosby pulled me in first. He knew that I could handle dead people, he knew that I could handle all that stuff. The people who we were relieving thought that we couldn't do anything right, and that we didn't know what was going on. They had no idea that we had all graduated from Emergency War Surgery and Special Operations Combat Medic School. We just kept to ourselves. We let them act like they were the Cocks of the Walk, just let them act like they were something special and, in all fairness, they had been there almost a year and dealt with this stuff day in and day out.

LS: You were replacing these people?

DW: Yes, it was the end of their tour. We were going to be a transition force from one unit to another. One combat support hospital was leaving and another was coming in. We transitioned two months before they were supposed to leave so that when the new one came in we'd have enough experience under our belts to "right seat, left seat" them, and they could concentrate on other stuff.

The kid that I was telling you about, that was not mentally stable enough to handle this, he was a combat medic, but this just wasn't his gig. We put him on the ICW, which is Intensive Care Ward. Basically he was changing sheets and bedpans and putting diapers on people that were conscious but unable to care for their daily life needs. There was no way that he'd ever be able to handle it in the ER. We just left it at that: out of sight and out of mind. You can change diapers and never know what goes on inside the ER, and that's fine.

There was another one, his name was Matt Mitchell. Me and Mitchell were best friends; best, best friends. And the night that he was first supposed to go to work he asked me, he said, "Dave, how is it in there?" And I said, "Look, it's not pretty. It's not something that you want to be a part of. It's not something that you get really good OJT (On the Job Training)."

The one that really got to me – and I remember this to this day – was a 17-year-old Lance Corporal who got a waiver to get into the Marines, got a waiver to come to war, and was riding along in a Humvee. The Humvee hit an IED and it came straight up from underneath him and completely shredded his legs.

When we moved him from one bed to another his calcaneus fell out of his foot, which is your heel bone. His calcaneus fell out of his foot and hit the ground, and you could hear it, and it was just unnerving. That was the first and last time I let a patient have a personal impact on me. When his heel fell out of his foot I'm thinking, "He's never going to have a normal life. He's not going to be able to play soccer with his kids." He's 17 years old. I went back to the barracks and I cried about that one.

We finally brought Mallard down to the ER. Lincoln, this kid just didn't fit. I mean he just did not understand emergency medicine; he just didn't get it. We all felt bad for him, but at the same time he brought it on himself because he'd lived such a sheltered life. His parents made all the rules and all the decisions for him. We can't change him any more than he'd already been changed. Bless his heart, he tried – God, he tried – but he just didn't get it.

I really got to shine over there because I had, on average, about 28 patients a day. Out of those 28 patients a day I learned just about everything you could learn. I also noticed that the stuff we learned in Miami did not hold a candle to the stuff that we were doing in Iraq. That was mainly because in Miami we dealt with a lot of thoracic and core trauma, but in Baghdad they're all wearing flack jackets. It was all extremity stuff. They weren't teaching anything based on military experience.

As far as decision-making in Iraq, everything worked as a fine-oiled machine. Our surgeons were always up on the OR (Operating Room), and I very rarely saw anybody from my team, other than Matt, who was my best friend; me and him worked on the same shift. Sergeant Crosby worked on the shift after us, and we worked 12-hour shifts, six days a week, for a year and a half.

The best way I can explain it is… let's say I drive a Porsche, and the doc drives a Lamborghini, and the nurse drives a Koenigsegg CCR. They're all phenomenal vehicles and they all have their own pros and cons. I can go from 0 to 60 in four seconds, the Lamborghini can go from 60 to 120 in four seconds, and the Koenigsegg can go from 120 to 196 mph in another four seconds. All told we have 12 seconds and 196 miles an hour. In other words, I do my job and everything that I'm capable of doing, and when I finish my job the doc picks up right where I left off, or the nurse does. And where the nurse stops, the doc picks up.

After the kid that lost his feet I never took anything personal. Instead, I would do exactly what I was taught, exactly what I was trained: concentrate on the job at hand, and the job in front of me, as opposed to the grand scheme of things.

Anyone who is going to get caught thinking, "Oh my God, he's missing both of his legs! Crap, what do I do?" And then get all in a frenzy, while the guy not only doesn't have a pulse, but hasn't been breathing for the past 25 minutes. You're working on a dead guy. So keep a level head, and know what you're doing, and know how to do it well. That's about all that you can do.

As far as my decision-making goes, just like it says in the newspaper article here, no matter who the patient is, I treat them all the same. And I treated them as though they were somebody's brother, or father, or son, or grandson, or daughter, or granddaughter, or whatever, because they were. They were somebody's kin. I did what I knew how to do and not until later, when I looked back on it, did I realize that I had his life in my hands. Mallard walked into every situation saying, "I'm going to screw this up," and he would. He screwed up everything.

I had a sense of urgency for everybody that came through that door. If they came through the door, they don't have to ask for my help, but they're going to get it. No one comes in there and says, "Please save my life." You don't have to beg with me to do the obvious. That's my job. It would be the same as if I said to one of them, "Hey, please protect my life." For the most part my decisions were based on morals, what I believed was right.

It got to a point where it was almost muscle memory; I knew exactly what to do. It got to a point where I was doing chest tubes, intubating patients, ordering drugs. The nurses are bound by their licenses, but I'm not bound by anything. I'm bound by what the doctor knows I can do.

It's kind of a double-edged sword because if the doctor knows I can do it, and I haven't done it, or failed to do it, then it's going to come back on me, not on him. The doc's going to say, "Why didn't you do it? You recognized it? I had to stop my procedures and my critical care to go back and cover for your mistakes. I have to downshift from 196 miles an hour all the way back to 60 because you dropped the ball while you were changing gears."

And I knew it. So before I would take my hands off the patient I'd say, "I've checked, and double-checked, and triple-checked..." And if the doc came to my patient, he expected a report: he expected to know what interventions I've done, what drugs I've given, what X-rays I have ordered, and a full report of his injuries. He wanted to know exactly what was going on so that he could pick up from my work, instead of starting off at zero and going all the way up.

Like I say, it was muscle memory. I recognized things that needed to happen and I did 'em. The biggest thing – even to this day – is: "Failure to act is unacceptable." Don't sit there and do nothing, at least do something. Even Mallard, the kid that was good at computers, would do something. It was so completely off-the-wall that it had no bearing on what we were doing, but at the very least he was doing something. I taught him that so I could feel better about having a loose cannon in the ER.

LS: Tell me, did this whole experience change you for the better? How have you taken this experience for the better?

DW: Professionally it altered my career and skyrocketed me to levels I never thought possible. Personally, it had a very adverse reaction on me because when I came home I was still in survival mode, and to this day I'm still in survival mode, and I'm trying to get over it.

LS: What's it mean to be in survival mode in terms of living around here?

DW: When I drive down the street and I see a trash bag on the side of the street, I'll stop and back up and find another way to go down the street. It's like I got blinders on to the world. Through one eye I see everything from the combat-medic perspective, and in the other eye I see what I know to be the civilian world.

My biggest challenge since I came back home is people not understanding, and to make matters worse they can't understand. They're not capable of understanding. I could sit there and try to explain it to them all day long, but until you've been there and done it you just don't understand.

There are some outstanding medics in the army that do great things for the country, and great things for the military, but when that first patient comes in missing every single one of their limbs and they can't control the bleeding... they go home in a nut wagon. They can't handle it. They don't know what to do. Drugs is a very real thing over there...

LS: You mean for your own medication.

DW: Yeah, a lot of people taking sleeping pills, a lot of people are abusing sleeping pills. There's a case of a guy that was given 30 vials of morphine a week and he couldn't keep them in his aid bag because he'd shoot up before he'd go out on a mission.

As far as changing me, it's the best thing that's ever happened to me – ever. It's made me a better medic. There isn't an injury I'm going to see in Shreveport, or Bossier, or Miami that I have not seen before.

You know, coupled with Vanderbilt and the burn ward I did there, and the pediatric patient accounts I did at St. Judes, and the rescue and EMS I did in Miami, and then my trauma rotations in the Miami trauma center, and everything I did in Iraq, I'm at the top of my game. I can go into any situation with a cool, calm, and collected head and know that I've already seen it before. There's nothing that I'm going to see as a paramedic now that I haven't already dealt with. It's very easy for me to approach a trauma scenario. Somebody that's gotten nailed by a train, or someone that's been in a head-on collision, or a motorcyclist that's gone down, even though I never saw a motorcycle accident in Iraq, I saw his injuries. It's the best thing that's ever happened to me.

But personally it's had an adverse reaction on me. I've got to start weaning myself off of ideas like, "You don't have to turn around when you see a bag of garbage in the street, and you don't have to drive over the median, and you don't have to go into a situation thinking that this is one of your own guys."

It was the greatest honor of my entire life, but it's hard, because when one of your coworkers sheds blood for your safety, he becomes your brother, even if you never see him again. He's still your brother, and he's your brother for life. And even though I'm not in the military, there's still plenty of people that consider me their brother. There are plenty of people – I know this for a fact – that would take a bullet for me. Did you know that 60% of all Medal of Honor recipients are either medics or people that died trying to save the medics? Sixty percent.

The ground pounders think that doc is God. There's a lot of them that are just so obtuse, and so ignorant, that they honestly believe that if doc sees me get shot in the head it's going to be fine because he'll save my life. There are some of them that are so naïve that they think that when I take their friends off in a helicopter, and they're in a black bag, that I'm keeping them warm because of their blood loss, and they'll see them again when they get back home. "Good job, Doc!"

What kind of a bearing does that have on me? You know? I don't tell them, "Hey, sorry, but Joe Snuffy died enroute, or Joe Snuffy was dead when he got shot." I can't tell them that. It's hard for me when they think that everything's going to be OK, and it's not. I haven't lied to them, I didn't tell them a story. But I didn't tell them the truth, either.

LS: So you've got a new problem, a new issue. You've got to shift gears to take the best of what you know and jettison the baggage that's not helping. How are you going to do it? Is there anybody to help you?

DW: Not now, no. I'm torn between two things, Lincoln. I think when I tell you the latter of the two, you're going to look at me like I've been huffing paint for the last six or eight months, but I'm stuck between two things. One of the two is going to be my ultimate career goal, the one I'm going to stick with for the rest of my life. I'm either going to take my MCAT and go back to school to be a doctor – I'm two years away from my Physician's Assistant in Emergency Medicine – or I'm going to be a Wildlife and Fisheries agent, because I enjoy guns and I enjoy the outdoors.

I know that I'd be extremely good at being a doctor, or a physician's assistant. I know that it would be a cakewalk. It would be easy for me because I'm interested. But at the same time, as a Wildlife and Fisheries agent I'd get to be on a boat, get to be in a four-wheel drive, have a gun, have authority – it's all based on wildlife conservation – and being out in the woods is where I'm truly happy.

I never want to forget everything that happened in Iraq, ever. But at the same time not all of those memories are pleasant ones, and not all of those memories are easy to deal with. There are some memories that are very, very difficult for me, but I have to remember them. I have to remember them, and make sure that they stay a part of my life, so that they continue to have a positive impact on my life.

I know that may seem just absolutely absurd, but in order for me to sustain the level of professionalism I have to remember: A, where I came from; B, what I've made of myself; and C, what I'm capable of doing in the future. Between the three of those it looks like I'm taking the back door out by going Wildlife and Fisheries, but that's something that I want to do. And also, if it's something that I want to do, and I've proven myself already, nobody can ask anything more of me.

I served my country and I saved lives. I've had people come up to me and recognize me as the person that saved them, and I have no idea who they are. Even to this day I don't see any particular way that I've saved anybody's life, because everything that I did somebody else could and would have done in most cases. It might be me being modest, but I just don't see it as anything heroic or fantastic, I just see it as how I was trained. This was my job.

There were several occasions where somebody was "expectant," which means they're not going to make it. You can't admit them to a ward when they're essentially already dead, because you need the bed space, so I was put in our specialty room. That was where we stacked up all the dead or expectant. I'd sit back here and pump them full of morphine and valium until they passed naturally. You know, I don't consider it euthanasia, and I don't consider it killing or mercy killing somebody, but at the same time I don't know what to consider it, because that's exactly what it was.

I saw some pretty traumatic stuff. I worked hand in hand with a guy named Colonel Wood. Colonel Wood was the brigade commander of an MP (Military Police) brigade and we knew about 90% of their unit on a first-name basis. They brought in three or four injured people every night, and about every other night we'd lose at least one of them. Colonel Wood presented us with a Certificate of Appreciation and a Commander's Coin for our outstanding service in support of his unit while they were there. He presented us with this two days before he left country.

That night Colonel Wood came in, and he came in in two different vehicles. They flew his lower half in on a helicopter, and his upper half was driven in. The guy was going home in less than 12 hours and you sit back and think… I mean, I'm a Christian, can't say I'm a practicing Christian, but I am a Christian… and you sit back and think, "How is this fair? This is not fun. I've got all the experience that I need, so just quit, just stop giving me patients. I'm sick of seeing it. I'm sick of dealing with it."

LS: Did you feel like that, or did it just cross your mind?

DW: It was so fleeting, Lincoln, I didn't have time to think about anything while I was over there. Taking time to think about things, that takes precious seconds. I had the option of going home and thinking about it when I was off-duty, but who wants to think about it then? I went home and played Xbox, or read magazines, or worked out, or something, but I don't want to think about that. I don't want to put it at the front of my mind and go, "I'm going to think about and get all emotional about all the things that happened to me today."

Mallard was the complete opposite. He would go home and intentionally think about it. He'd always ask me, "Dave, how come you come home and you leave everything in the ER? Those guys died tonight!" "OK, well, would you rather them died, or you died?" "Well, I'd rather that neither one happened." "Well, you know what? Life isn't like that. It happened. Somebody died. You can't get it back. Leave it in the ER, don't bring it home." He just didn't understand.

LS: The inescapable truth is that your experience is unlike other people's experience.

DW: That's correct.

LS: The people that I'm interviewing are mostly normal kids that are growing up in society. What would you advise? If you could tell them something that's important in terms of getting their lives together, what would it be?

DW: In numerous different occasions I was put in a situation where it was all or nothing: "Learn all about this. This is what you're going to see. This is what you're going to be doing." But when game-time came, I didn't see any of it. But regardless, I knew it and was ready for it when it did come. Anyone can diagnose and treat the stuff that comes along all the time in civilian hospitals, but that is not how we were trained. We were trained for the freak accident, the one-in-a-million, worst-case scenario type stuff.

I'm not the type to sit and throw my cards down and say, "Oh, now I give up. I've spent the last year and a half of my life trying to figure this out, and I'm not able to use any of this, so I'm just going to suck at what I'm doing." No, I said, "OK, I obviously need to learn what I'm doing now, and be good at it."

But truth be told, Lincoln, what I have to say is this: "Don't do whatever you like, like whatever you do." If you find something that you're interested in, and this is what you want do, then do it. But you've got to understand that it's not a hit-or-miss situation. You can't learn everything there is to know, but that doesn't mean that you have to stop trying.

People will tell you, "You can't do this because you're not allowed to know this." Or, "This is too advanced for you." When someone said that I couldn't do something, or when somebody told me that it's too advanced for me, that was fuel to the fire. I wanted to prove to them that they were so wrong.

Respect and knowledge: all of that is earned. When you start learning something, do everything you can to learn about the subject. And if it's not something that you want to do, then reevaluate why you're in it.

Just because a teacher tells you something, that this is what you're going to see or do… no, medicine doesn't work like that. Life doesn't work like that either. You will most likely see the complete opposite. And what are you going to do when it comes around? Are you going to say, "Oh, well, I never learned that." Or are you going to say, "OK, I acknowledge that I don't know that, and I'm going to take it upon myself to make sure I don't look like a blubbering idiot next time that rolls around."

You start with a foundation and you build on it. After you've built on that, another problem arises and you build on that. Make that problem your cornerstone and keep building… and build, and build, and build. I don't let a problem arise where I would say, "Oh well, crap, I don't know what to do, so I'm just going to leave this alone." No, I get in there and I engage. I make sure that I have some sort of understanding about what's going on. There is no excuse, no excuse for failure to engage. Failure to act is unacceptable.

When push comes to shove it's your own damn fault if you don't know something. This day and age everyone has the means and the capabilities to have the whole world at their fingertips and the answer is out there. You just have to dedicate yourself to finding it. And the next time it happens and you still don't know it – and it doesn't have to be in medicine – you just look like a fool. Someone is going to be there to point out, "You've seen this before, and you didn't know what was going on then. Why don't you know what's going on now?"

15. GEORGE PLOTKIN

History   Middle   Born 1951, Brooklyn, New York

George was Jerry Lettvin's student after graduate school. I learned of him only because Jerry mentioned him, and all that I know of him is embedded in this interview, with one exception: he's also generous. When I called him and told him of my connection to Jerry, he immediately invited me to stay with him and his wife, at their home in Texas, so that we could do this interview.

George is a chemist, an engineer, an inventor, a doctor, a neurologist, and a director at the East Texas Medical Center. He oversees the implanting of wires in people's heads in order to stimulate deep brain structures and remediate Parkinson's disease. Like any good Texan he likes guns, and in his free time, which I saw no evidence that he had, he practices marksmanship.

Excerpts

"Mononucleosis was the biggest blessing, because otherwise I was... dying in that school. Getting sick and having people spend a little time with me and recognize that maybe I did want to learn something, that I did have an inner life, because I certainly didn't have one at school..."

"It was the first time anybody had actually said to me, 'Look, we're doing our job and we want you to meet the expectations of the system, but if you want to know what's going on, we'll teach you.'... So, all of a sudden, I had protectors. It was this weird transition, I don't know what happened, but it happened suddenly..."

"(Jerry Lettvin) took me to visit people in the ward... And I'm sitting there... realizing that this is wild, this is unbelievable! I turn to Jerry and I say, 'Have you ever seen anything like this before?!' And he says, 'No, never... anything can happen. It's the nervous system. I don't understand the nervous system, (and) I don't expect you to, either. It's an adventure.' And I realized that this is what I was looking for..."

"There are things to be done, there's danger, there's excitement, there are errors, and there are people who get hurt, and there are people who don't come back. But it's in those ages that great things are built...

"I don't have any answers anymore. I've learned that answers are things you just make up as you go along. And until it falls apart, it's reasonable enough..."

"What's eternal is knowledge... that web that grows and keeps extending to the horizon. The horizon that we can see goes further still; it's an infinity that you cannot even approximate. It is beyond logic, and it's out there... We're all Columbus. We're all setting out. The risk of drowning is real, and the risk for success is real..."

"The more firmly established, the more difficult to change.
That social organism is embryonic.
That firmly to believe is to impede development.
That only temporarily to accept is to facilitate."

—Charles Fort, in *The Book of the Damned, the collected works of Charles Fort*

"The failure of technological medicine is due, paradoxically, to its success, which at first seemed so overwhelming that it swept away all aspects of medicine as art. No longer a compassionate healer working at the bedside using heart and hands as well as mind, the physician has become an impersonal white-gowned ministrant who works in an office or laboratory. Too many physicians no longer learn from their patients, only from their professors."

— Robert O. Becker, MD, in *The Body Electric*

Interview   Tyler, Texas, December 2007

George Plotkin: I started reading very young. When I was 10 or 11, it was incredibly inspiring. I had a knack for absorbing things. My parents didn't have TV because they felt it wasn't a good thing. TV was bad. The TV was actually locked up in the attic. It was one of these things my father had built out of some sort of kit. He wouldn't let me touch it or look at it.

My father gave me my first book, which was Lewis Carroll's *Through the Looking Glass*. It had the original Tenniel illustrations, really nice. I didn't get it. I thought it was cute at times, but it didn't do much for me.

So he said, "OK, why don't you read *Treasure Island*." He hands me this really old copy of *Treasure Island* and says, "I really liked this when I was a kid." The second day he says, "So what do you think?" I said, "An utter waste of time. It stinks. I don't like it."

"All right," he says and gives me Mary Shelley's book *Frankenstein*. I'm sitting in the back seat of the car, we're driving somewhere, and he said, "Read this." And I read the thing – I was probably around 9 or 10 – and I read the book in an hour. He said, "You couldn't have read it." I said, "I read it." So they start asking me questions and he said, "So, what do you think?" I said, "I liked the movie."

Years later I realized it was much more interesting than the movie, because I started to understand how Percy Bysshe Shelley had taken courses, and had been exposed to electrification, and how dissimilar metals had caused legs to jump when dissections were being conducted. And that he had interested his girlfriend, Mary Wollstonecraft, in reanimation, and he had challenged her to write something interesting. She generates this incredible story, which really is – depending on how you want to cut it – is a feminist tract. It questions a variety of things: the Social Darwinist theories, all sorts of stuff. But I got none of that when I first read it.

The stuff that got to me was when I found my father's science fiction collection. There was "The Million-Year Picnic," by Ray Bradbury. It's part of *The Martian Chronicles* where they're stuck on Mars, and they're watching the Earth explode below them. This is at the end of the wars, and they're burning bits of papers, which are diaries and papers, in order to keep warm. There's a little stream and they look in it and see the Martians, which are themselves. And in the 1950s post-McCarthy, Cold War, Cuban Missile Crisis environment, here is this book that encapsulates it. And suddenly I was like, "This is great! I need more of this!"

I started to find other books: Sturgeon (Theodore Sturgeon), brilliant; Bradbury, a genius. These were people who could take the drama of earthly things into another realm where you handle it, sort of like it was decontaminated: clean, isolated. You didn't have to worry about the outcome – meaning something that could get you in trouble – because it's happening on another planet. It's like *The Golden Compass* (by Philip Pullman) arguments right now: "Well, that's an alternate world. Yeah, so that's OK."

This stuff really captured my attention. But they kept talking about stuff that required enormous types of technology, and I didn't have any of that stuff, so I started building things. I got old ARRL Handbooks, I bought them at used-book sales… American Radio Relay League.

I didn't have an allowance of any sort, but my parents would give me a couple of bucks every so often and I'd go to book sales. I would rummage through to find stuff that interested me: an old dictionary that looked really cool; science fiction, any time. I didn't like images – I was much more taken with the written word. I began to stockpile and read everything I could get.

The Radio Relay League stuff showed me that there were things that you could do to modify signals. So I started building radios. I'd electrocute myself 20 different ways with these power supplies. I was building tube equipment, and everything was 600 volt B+. I could make regenerative receivers and do wild stuff. I began to realize this was a language, just like the language in the books, except this was a language with materials, and I just started to manipulate materials. I was doing this all the time, not paying much attention to my schoolwork because I couldn't stand it.

I drifted off into this alternate world of exploring stuff, but there was no one to shape this. All the voices were distant voices. There was no one in the community. Like in sixth grade when I told my father I wanted to learn calculus, I said, "Look. I've done all this other stuff, and this is a book that you have here…" It was one of his calculus manuals from college. He said, "You really shouldn't read that now. It's above you, and they'll teach you that in college." There was always this organized, regimented attitude of, "That's not right for you now." It was clear that there were some things that no one was going to teach me. So I'd go off and do something else.

The transition occurred when I got sick with mononucleosis, and I was stuck at home. I was really sick. I had fevers every day. I had a spleen the size of a bathmat, and the doctors were worried that if I went to school and fell down, I'd get a ruptured spleen. It was either surgery or rest. So I stayed home for three quarters of a year, during which time they sent private tutors to work with me.

I had been a "D" student, at best. So here come these tutors figuring they're going to get a real piece of work. Mr. LaSalle was the history teacher, a very neat guy that introduced me to Chaucer – this was like, eighth grade – he writes down:

"With his shoures soote, the droghte of March hath perced to the roote, and bathed every veyne in swich licour…"

(First line of *The Canterbury Tales*, Geoffrey Chaucer, 1342-1400)

I tried to read it. He reads it poetically, and I'm going, "That sounds great! What is that?" He says, "That's Chaucer. You do this American history, and I'll teach you Chaucer."

We had this great dialog where he'd bring stuff in and I'd absorb it. He would explain that liberty and all this stuff was not quite what everybody expected it to be, that there were a lot of issues, and nothing was clear-cut, but these were the answers that people wanted to hear.

He made it clear that, yes, there were hoops that I had to jump through, but there was a lot of other interesting stuff. So when I got to these various risqué tales, which were really titillating, I started absorbing history. I really got into it. I never thought of history as being a thing I'd be particularly excited about. He got me totally psyched.

One of the English teachers came by to teach me English, same thing. They realized I was willing to compromise, to do the work, if they would give me some insight into it in exchange.

They would say, "Why aren't you doing this in school? You never do anything in school." I was honest and I said, "There's no point to doing anything. It's of no purpose. It doesn't do anything. It's meaningless work." And instead of saying, "You idiot, there's nothing meaningless about it. It's our job." They said, "OK. This is what it's supposed to do. This is why we do these things."

It was the first time anybody had actually said to me, "Look, we're doing our job and we want you to meet the expectations of the system, but if you want to know what's going on, we'll teach you." I suddenly realized that I could do this stuff, and that there were things that were expected of me – just like in any other job – but that there were rewards. It was like this massive switch was turned.

LS: But you'd never had a job before.

GP: I'd never had a job before. Not like that. All of a sudden I was doing things. I knew none of my classmates – this was the weird thing and maybe it was good – when I suddenly showed up in all of these honor-track classes, after having been in the shop class hanging out...

LS: You mean after you recovered at this point.

GP: Yeah, I came back and they basically transitioned me. I'm now going to the library and requesting stuff by interlibrary loan, and the librarian would argue with me that that's "adult material." I'd get notes from the English teacher, and she would clear the stuff as "age appropriate." I took a course in art and started drawing nudes. And they'd say, "What's the kid doing? He's drawing Matisse nudes!" And the art teacher said, "He's good at it. Leave him alone!"

So, all of a sudden, I had protectors. It was this weird transition. I don't know what happened, but it happened suddenly.

LS: So, in a sense, it was a good school. It was just that the teachers hadn't attended to you.

GP: Most of the teachers were disinterested, but there were a handful of older, very gifted teachers who realized that I was a kindred spirit. When I came back years later to visit, they were very gracious. They were delighted to see that I'd actually tried to do something. I think they felt that I had the capacity to do something. One of them said, "I always thought you could do something if you put your mind to it." That sounds like a very trite thing, but that's what happened.

That mononucleosis was the biggest blessing, because otherwise I was just careening down, dwindling down. I was dying in that school. Getting sick and having people spend a little time with me and recognize that maybe I did want to learn something, that I did have an inner life, because I certainly didn't have one at school.

When I came back, the kids in these H-tracks courses had nothing to do with me. I still hung out with kids who are now carpenters, and firemen, and policemen. Many have died of drug overdoses, or in Vietnam, but they were good people. I really liked them, and I thought they had some insight that made it worthwhile hanging out with them. More so than the kids who were doing this as a stepping stone to the right college, or to get the right husband, or to do the right job, or whatever it was they were going to do. That didn't do it for me.

I hung out with the two who seemed bitter and cynical. We were all bright, and we could do it in our sleep, but we had other things that we were interested in. At least we could speak the same language. It made it tolerable.

I didn't realize that MIT would be the same way. I never realized the world doesn't change because you leave one school for another. It took people like Jerry (Jerome Lettvin) to bring it back, because I died again at MIT, for a few years.

LS: Tell me about that, because that happened to me too. Tell me about that illusion that it was going to get better.

GP: My parents brought me up to Cambridge (Massachusetts) in an Oldsmobile '68, a bronze-colored car with a black top and reddish interior. It was a boat and it seated all of us comfortably. My grandmother was not quite as demented as she was to become, and we were staying in a motel overlooking the Charles River.

We're standing there looking out the balcony and I say, "This is my future. This is a great new horizon." I figured it was going to be so amazing. Here are people who are really thinking.

My grandmother says, "What do you think you're going to accomplish?" She actually asked some very cogent questions back then, before she started talking to the TV. "So what are you going to accomplish?" "I'm going to just take it all in, and I'm going to figure out the meaning of everything." She looks at me and she says, "Good luck!"

So I go to MIT, and after the first few weeks I realize no one could give two hoots about the meaning of anything. There was a lot of drugs, a lot of alcohol, and then there were people getting through problem sets. "Yeah, you got to get these problem sets done." It's a lot of work, and you're chugging through them.

A lot of personality disorders. We lived in these quads and there were four people in a room. My first roommates were awful. One was a severe alcoholic, another was a psychopath, and the third was a terrorized Eastern European kid whose only interest in life was crushing communism, because it had destroyed his family. It was like, "Who dealt me this mess?"

I signed up for a whole batch of interesting stuff figuring, "I know this stuff, I'm sharp." Almost everybody there was just as sharp as I was; some were much sharper. We were doing this stuff and I'd go and talk to the TAs, the Teaching Assistants – the professors didn't want anything to do with us: we were freshmen, we were useless. But the TAs were often stuck with these jobs, and they didn't want to spend any time with us, either.

I remember one Japanese physics TA who was tripping on LSD while trying to teach our section. He was out of his mind! It was hard enough trying to understand him since he was Japanese, but this was, like, way out there. I was getting this bad headache, getting this bad feeling about the whole thing, and I said, "This is garbage. I'm learning nothing. Why did I come to this place?"

And then there would be the lectures by Jerry and by other people who would give talks around campus. People would say, "Oh, you don't want to go to that stuff. That's very political." I said, "It's a damn sight better than this stuff. This stuff sucks! This is terrible."

I started going to Jerry's lectures because they were popular, but they turned out to be much more subtle. There was exciting stuff going on. I came up and told him, "This is what I want to do!" That's when he told me, "Boychick, everybody wants to do that. Come back when you're ready."

We had a guy, Danny Kemp, who was a young professor just out of his fellowship at Harvard. Danny turned chemistry into something understandable, and we got along really well. He actually saved me from freezing to death when I was walking back from my girlfriend's dormitory. I walked her home from a party and the temperature had shifted 20 or 30 degrees and I was freezing, I was in a T-shirt. He stops his car and says, "Asshole, get in." And I look over and it's Doctor Kemp. He took me back to my dorm; I got pneumonia out of it.

He was a breath of fresh air, because Danny understood how chemical reactions could be conceived of in the way that Linus Pauling had written about them. Pauling was one of the other people who turned me on when I was in high school. That happened by accident, because the high school teachers couldn't tell me what chemical bonds were. They were terrible, they made the stuff up as they went along. They obviously knew nothing about valence, so I started to look for books on valence.

This is where I got lucky, because there were people in the periphery, and if you nudged them a little, then you got things. There was a guy, Sid Thompson, who was a black man who was a chemist on the uranium 235 project – the first African American to graduate from Notre Dame with a PhD in chemistry – he developed the filters for the uranium hexafluoride. He was brilliant. He was also very radicalized: Stokely Carmichael's picture was up on his wall; a big picture. He and my father were long-standing friends from the old days. My father dragged me over to sit with Thompson because I'd asked him about chemistry. He said, "Well, go and talk to Sid Thompson. He's a chemist."

I was a teenager and Thompson drags me along to help out at this thing in Wyandanch, New York, which was an upward-bound training thing to teach kids from the inner city. I was the token white, which was great. It was a great group of people. Some were very interested in learning, others who could care less. I don't think they'd seen white people, either, where they lived; and I hadn't seen any blacks in my life. I'd never realized Sid was black – he was just like an uncle; he just hung around.

Sid handed me a copy of Linus Pauling's *General Chemistry* and said, "This is what you need to read if you want to understand chemistry. This guy Pauling understands chemistry." So I read the book. I read it like you read a novel. I didn't realize that you're supposed to look at it like it was a year's work. I just absorbed it. This was really cool stuff, so I said, "I'll become a chemist. I'll do biochemistry because I want to do biology and chemistry, I'll do it all." I actually started to understand some of it. It gave me hope that there was something to do.

Danny Kemp understood that stuff and was kind of resonant, which is why I got sucked into doing biochemistry. The trouble was that I needed to make money. My parents didn't want to give me any money, and being an undergraduate at MIT with nothing to do except go to classes was getting me really down.

I took a job working with a professor of nutrition who was doing some rat feeding experiments. I worked for him and he eventually offered me a position in the lab, which I mistakenly took. As a result I ended up spending a number of years doing incredible drudge work.

I got my degrees very quickly, but there was no content. I realized I was lost again. Here I had started to find something, and it disappeared because I was busy doing mindless laboratory work, day in and day out, seven days a week, and all summers. I would just live in the lab. I didn't understand why I was doing it. I'd forgotten.

One day I woke up and I said, "I don't want to do this anymore. I'm going to go off and do something else. I don't care what my PhD is in, I'm not doing this. I can't do this."

LS: Were you in graduate school at this point?

GP: I was doing biochemistry. I hated it. I could read the stuff, I could do the experiments, but I absolutely detested it.

Everything about it was wrong. It was like a religion. I didn't believe it. They would say, "This is how Vitamin A works." And I said, "I don't believe it!" And they said, "What do you mean you don't believe it?" I said, "It doesn't make any sense!" "Well, that's what we're researching!" I said, "No, why would God build a system this way? There is an engineer behind everything. It has to make sense. It has to be energetically efficient. It has to be reproducible. It has to be stable on a real-time basis." They looked at me like, "What are you talking about?" I said, "I'm giving you Aristotelian reasons for why this is not feasible." They'd say, "You're just crazy. You're on drugs!" I'd say, "I'm not on drugs! It's wrong! It doesn't make any sense."

This is when I started working with Jerry. Jerry's son needed to pass biochemistry, and I tutored him, saying, "This is all you have to think about." I did my best Linus Pauling and the kid passes. The next thing I know Jerry's calling me into his office to interview me.

LS: You had met Jerry before, but you never followed up?

GP: I had never followed up because I figured he had no interest. I'm very easily rejected, at least I was. I learned later that you could be like Colin Powell (General Colin Powell) and if someone says "No," you can find someone else who says "Yes." It took a long time to learn that independence. I didn't have it then, and I'm sorry I didn't, but I think everything happens for a reason.

Jerry called me to his office; I didn't know what to expect. He was very inquisitive and he was trying to figure out what I wanted to do. I said, "I want to understand things. I just want to be able to do something, anything. I'm tired of wasting my time." And he says, "Well, I can give you a position. I can't pay you much, but you'll meet interesting people and you might learn something, because you don't know shit now." He was very straightforward with me.

That was when I began to transform into a person; that time was a remarkable chrysalis because the people who came into his laboratory would be people like Carleton Gajdusek, who discovered the slow virus, the kuru; Benoit Mandelbrot, who developed fractals; Mitch Feigenbaum, who developed chaos theory. Person after person came in who had a vision and could explain themselves.

We even had the guy who wrote *The Structure of Scientific Revolutions*, Thomas Kuhn. Tom Kuhn was my patient. I took care of Tom. Remarkable guy because you could sit and talk with him and understand what the crime of Galileo actually was. He had a brilliant style, strange man but brilliant, and you knew it instantly. He walked into a room and he was delightful. I loved him.

I started teaching physics, which was not my area, but I discovered that relativistics were really neat, what little I understood. What I tried to do was – in every lecture I ever did – I tried to have a point: one key point that the kids could hold on to.

First I'd tell them, "Where's your intellectual curiosity?" I couldn't give up on Mrs. Sullivan, my English teacher who always said, "Remember, it's curiosity that expands your horizon. It's what gives you your perspective, it gives you your insight, it makes you alive." I always think about that because she's one of those people in that original marsh who really had some substance to her. She really stood out; she was amazing. I didn't appreciate her enough.

Jerry populated my world with people who were on the cutting edge in everything they did. You could sit there and talk with them, and if you asked the right questions you got phenomenal answers. It led to a transition from measuring things just because I could measure them, to thinking about why do we need to make a measurement. What is the purpose of this? And then trying to understand, for instance, how do you encode data in a neural network, because that's what it was starting to come down to.

I had always assumed, before sitting with Jerry, that the nervous system worked by the axon reflex, that the firing of the axon embodied information. But that's so far from the truth because the axon… if you measure the temperature of blood going into the brain and going out of the brain, it's up by 0.5 degrees or some trivial amount. But if nearly a trillion cells were firing, then the temperature of the fluid coming out of the brain would be incredibly high.

The point is that there are many other things happening in nerves: there are transitions in the membrane, like in semiconductors, very low-energy transitions that don't produce heat. And different things happen depending on how you pulse a membrane. In the case of a crab's claw, same nerve, if you stimulate it at one frequency it opens, and at another frequency it closes. This means that penetration of the different branches is time-dependent, and not necessarily selected down a particular pathway.

Then you get into the business of Stentor and other protozoans. If they settle on the same stalk and you touch one, they all contract. Well, the speed with which this happens is the speed of sound, and if you do birefringent pictures of those little buggers sitting together, the refractive index of them changes and travels throughout the mass. It's as if you're changing the state of the membrane.

So that's the way the nervous system may be working – and this is turning out to be true 30 years later. It made sense when I thought about it back then, and Jerry got excited about it, that the membrane is constantly undergoing semi-conductor-like state changes. And this is not what we think of as the firing of neurons because, when I stick needles in people's brains, there is no firing. The brain is very quiet when you're awake, and I do people who are awake. I stick needles in their heads and electrically look at what's going on.

LS: How do you look at it?

GP: On an oscilloscope in the operating room. I'm back to doing what I did to animals! And what you discover is that there's not much signal. So here is the person sitting, talking to me, and his brain's as quiet as a mouse.

Where is knowledge? Where is consciousness? It's not axons and axon reflexes, it's in state changes in the membranes, just like in our computers. The computer people were right all along and we never saw it. We're just a big hunk of semiconductor firing phenomenally fast: microseconds per event. State changes that have no energy above kT (thermal) noise, just like the background noise of the Big Bang. We're operating off kT!

LS: When you say we're operating above kT, you mean we're operating just above the noise?

GP: Just above the noise.

When I realized that, I realized that Bridgman was right: there's no such thing as information without a transition at an interface. It was an epiphany! I realized that everything that I had learned was wrong. Everything was wrong.

LS: Are you talking about biochemistry?

GP: In biochemistry and in neurophysiology; I realized they were all absolutely wrong.

People argued with me and said, "No, it can't be any of that. You're crazy." They basically shunned me. This is what Tsaki (Ichiji Tsaki at National Institutes of Health, Bethesda, MD. – Ed.) is now publishing, this year, in his stuff about water layers, and the Zeta-potential kind of phenomenology, which is probably the informational circuits of the nerve. I think the nerve will end up being a very different structure than we imagined it to be.

It's not the tools you use; the tools are not important. Jerry would drive people crazy because they'd come and say, "I have a great idea for a research project." And Jerry says, "Well, what is it that you want to understand?" "Oh no, I've got this piece of equipment and now I can do this, and I can do that…" He'd look at them and say, "Fuck equipment. What is it you're trying to do? Suppose you had all the equipment in the world, what is it you want to know? If there's nothing that you want to know, then I don't care about the equipment. You have nothing to interest me."

I'd sit there and be privy to these things and realize that he was demanding that people go beyond thinking about their tools, which are very much period pieces. He demanded that they think about what questions would have been asked a thousand years ago, or a thousand years in the future.

I started to realize that my feelings had been right when I'd thought my work as a graduate student was worthless. Not because I wasn't motivated or wasn't clever, but because the work was uninspired, rote, and predictable. It was the wrong trunk of the tree

I was crawling up, and I needed to find something else. Jerry understood that. He realized that, with a little bit of focusing, I could do something.

Jerry explained neurology to me. He said it was an area where you're trying to take a history from a sick device. You're trying to interrogate a faulty circuit by talking to it. He said, "How much more interesting can it possibly be?"

He took me to visit people in the ward. The first patient I saw was a woman who was 66 years old. She collapsed in the shower. Her husband comes in to see what's the matter, and she starts screaming. He calls the police, they come, and she claims this man had come into the bathroom, that he was her husband's brother, and what was he doing there?

So she gets admitted to the hospital, she's in atrial fibrillation, she's introduced to people in the room, Dr. Gershman's there, and she says, "I know your brother." Everyone was duplicated. Everyone in the room was duplicated, including me!

Her EEG showed hiccupping in her left temporal lobe. She'd gone into atrial fibrillation due to a small embolus from the heart that's lodged in her temporal lobe, an area where she is reduplicating objects in her memory. And since her brain couldn't understand why there were two of things, it explained the second one as being the relative, or the cousin, or whatever: "You're his twin."

And I'm sitting there as an engineer – as that's essentially what I am at this point – realizing that this is wild, this is unbelievable! I turn to Jerry and I say, "Have you ever seen anything like this before?!" And he says, "No, never." Just matter-of-factly: "No, never."

I said, "You've never seen this before, but you've dragged me in, and this is what they bring in?" He said, "Well, anything can happen. It's the nervous system." He looks at me and says, "I don't understand the nervous system," very matter-of-factly. He says, "I don't expect you to, either. It's an adventure." And I realized that this is what I was looking for, and it's been like that ever since.

I get to write about this stuff, I get to teach about it in the community here. They love it. I can give them vignettes. I can encapsulate and simplify the vignettes so that they get the bare bones of what it is that the person presented with, and they can take something away from it.

I just wrote this thing (he shows a recent publication), take a look at vignette number zero. These vignettes are little stories to show doctors that they often don't know what they're looking at. This was a fashion model whose boyfriend was a Mafiosi, and who brings her to the emergency room because she can't wear her high heels. I was a resident and I thought that was the wildest complaint I'd ever heard.

There's this beautiful model with this heavy Tony Soprano-kind of boyfriend, and she can't walk in high heels, and it's pissing him off: she can't walk in high heels and look good. And sure enough, she couldn't walk in high heels.

The first thing I learned from Jerry was that when somebody says they can't do something, look at what they're doing. Figure out why they can't do it. So instead of doing what my chief resident wanted me to do, which was get this person out of the ER, I ignore him – we later became fast enemies because I showed him up and he hated that intensely – and I asked the woman to walk, and she couldn't walk in high heels. She takes them off and she's walking fine. And I do her exam and she has no ankle jerks.

LS: What's an ankle jerk?

GP: A tap on the tendon, I did this (he demonstrates), but there were no reflexes. This is a young woman and her intoxication screen is negative, and I said, "This doesn't make sense." So I did the only thing I knew to do, which is to say, "We have this machine here and we can look at the nerves in your body. I'm going to hook you up to see what your nerves are doing." Her brain looked fine, she was just a little anxious.

LS: Which nerves were you looking at?

GP: I looked at the nerves in the foot and the hand. There were no reflexes off the lower spinal cord in the lower extremities, we couldn't get anything; that's not normal. I'm actually looking at an electrical reflex, I can "ping" the nerve off the spinal cord, which is really cool. I'm doing this and I'm going, "This woman's got Guillain-Barre!"

I call the head of neurophysiology, who was this really anal-retentive guy. We later had a falling out, but at the time he was impressed that I called him about this. He says, "Well, what do you got?" I said, "I think I have something odd. I want you to come and look."

He comes and looks at the data and he says, "This is Guillain-Barre." And I tell him, "You're never going to believe this story." And I tell him this story and he starts laughing, "That's a great story! Let's admit her to my service." He says, "This woman's going to get really sick."

LS: Oh, really? What is this disease? Is it a degenerative disease?

GP: No, it's an ascending auto-immune disorder where you denervate all of your muscles and become paralyzed. She was on a ventilator for three months. She ascended over the next week, lost all her function, lost all of her reflexes. Basically, if I'd sent her home she would have died.

LS: Bizarre.

GP: I see it all the time.

LS: It's common?

GP: It's misdiagnosed. That's the reason for this article. I see so many cases of this in the community, which are sent away from the emergency rooms. I had one just recently that was sent out of three emergency rooms because they thought he just had back pain. They thought he was a crank. He's sucking on a respirator as we speak. He's been in the hospital for seven months; he's slowly recuperating.

LS: What causes it?

GP: It's an auto-immune reaction against the myelin coating on the nerves. It's pretty impressive. It's MS (Multiple Sclerosis) of the peripheral nerves, that's exactly what it is. The physiology of it is fascinating.

This experience did two things: it got me an offer to stay on at Harvard, and it polarized me against this resident who basically just spent all his time being pissed off at me. This guy is now at the University of Rochester. He's very bright, there's no question that he's very gifted, but he's a very rigid individual.

He was interested in publishing anything that could get published. There was no interest in the quality of the work – he published a lot of crap. I got sick of it to the point where I actually avoided him like the plague. I thought I was getting sucked back in to what I just escaped!

People keep trying to trap you on the flypaper of mediocrity because it's doable: just roll up your sleeves and shovel. And you can do it. The journal's full of it, and I find it utterly uninteresting.

I want to know something that actually changes things, and that gives me a reason to do X or Y. We're talking about modifying human beings. If we're going to do that, then maybe we should have some solid material, versus, "Should we measure the conductance of the ulnar nerve with the bent arm or the straight arm?" This is what people publish, again and again. And your point is? Who cares!

I end up battling the same stuff. I'll tell people that something's clinical and we don't need all of these different tests, and they get offended because I'm not ordering tests. Since when did we replace reasoning and physical exams with tests? When did putting up a CAT scan mean more than actually examining the patient?

LS: Is there an answer to that question?

GP: There never will be. The companies that are comforted by management beancounters would like to see medicine reduced to numbers. Now, statistically we can make errors, and if we miss a few it's within a statistical range that doesn't matter. We can lose those people because we would have lost a few anyway.

I've started ignoring a lot of the medical literature because people don't do the clinical work, they're just quoting other people who also don't do clinical work. So those of us who are actually clinicians, who know better, go to conferences and make this known. This is what irritates me, this is why I do what I do: the gentle vengeance aspect, which means getting even with the jerks who spend their lives filling the world with misinformation because it's expedient, it's convenient.

It's very important to have a notion of what you're looking at. It's what Jerry used to call "the Aunt Tilley effect." Most of us don't know what our Aunt Tilley looks like, we couldn't draw her, but once she shows up, then no matter what she's wearing we know it's Aunt Tilley. It's the same way that we can all type, but we can't draw the keyboard because my cortex has no care or interest in the keyboard, it's long since given it to the thalamus to manage, which means the subconscious.

The subconscious doesn't get enough credit. That's where most of us live 90% of the time. The thalamus is the flashlight in the attic. It decides where you're going to look because I'm taking in a billion bits of information per second. It's that old thing: you stare across the parking lot at a sea of cars and you can see a guy breaking in to your car, you can see what you've left on your seat. But you've never changed your gaze. It's all the same picture, all that's different is how you process the data.

LS: So tell me then, what do you think teenagers should do to get on the right track?

GP: I think everything is about conflict and its resolution. Resolution is a bad thing. I think about this every day. Most of the time when things are calm we're satisfied, and nothing is happening.

The beginning of *Finnegan's Wake* (by James Joyce) goes:

"River run, past Eve and Adams, from swerve of shore to bend of bay, brings us by a commodius vicus of recirculation back to Howth, Castle and Environs."

"Howth, castle and environs," means "here comes everybody," the whole world. "Commodius vicus" comes from the Renaissance where Vicus proposed the notion of the recirculation of history; that history repeats itself, and that all of life is this constant being born and dying, rising and sleeping, which is all about Finnegan's reawakening. Marvelous work.

There are things to be done, there's danger, there's excitement, there are errors, and there are people who get hurt, and there are people who don't come back. But it's in those ages that great things are built.

This turbulence is exciting because it's a time when you have things that are not yet resolved. When things are resolved you end up with times like the Middle Ages, where people spent a lot of time putting filigree, and curlicues, and baroque forms onto staid items because there's nothing else to do, because they didn't know what to do next.

Kids are faced with the fact that there is so much to be done in so short a time, and they're not sure for what purpose. They have the Internet, which tells them about horizons, but again, there's so much information that there's no information. If I was a kid going on the Internet and typed in "what's the meaning of things," the crap you're bombarded with!

The first thing I did when I finally got "Internetted" back in the early '90s – because I was a late adopter – was that I went around the world. I basically hopped different countries just for the hell of it. Just to see what this thing would do.

I was just astonished. I began to look at museums. And then I began to look at things and pull up documents. I didn't have a passkey, but security was very weak and even a novice like me could break in. So I was looking at different libraries, and I was having a ball. I never imagined you could do that. I realized that this completely changes my need for libraries. This changes so many things.

I guess the way to look at that is… have you ever read Borges, Jorge Luis Borges? Do you remember *Funes the Memorious*? Funes: he knows everything, and he knows nothing. Because every time a tree loses a leaf it's a new tree. And this is Borges' point.

When there's so much information, then there's no information, and direction again becomes critical. So while we had stacks of libraries to curl up in – which is what I did when I needed solace in undergraduate and graduate school. I would go into the library at Harvard and hide. I would get a cubicle, I'd lock myself in, and I'd say, "Today I'm going to try to understand X." – you can fill in what X is – and I'd go and pull the stuff on that and see if it meant something. And I might stumble on something else and realize connections, which would be exciting.

Kids now have their school requirements, but they have this thing, this wide net, which is enormous. I have no idea how they can manage it. They are obviously very good at it – more so than most of my colleagues – but without direction from teachers who have some sense of it, I think they could easily get lost.

I remember reading Descartes' (René Descartes) book on reason where he explains that he'd been a bit of a ne'er-do-well, had to leave France, and go to Amsterdam because he'd gotten into trouble with the cops. And then he suddenly decided that he had to do some work.

Now, I never noticed that when I read it the first time. It wasn't until years later, reading it again, that I realized he was trying to tell me something. Something I never would have heard when I was his age, when I was young, because at that time it wasn't an issue. The issue was being drunk and disorderly. The issue was disassociating from the system. But now the issue is focusing on the realization that, "It's not about me."

There is some transition in every educated person's life – everyone who has some responsibility to his society, whatever that society entails, a political society of some sort, a righteous society where there is some ethical reason – there's some point at which you realize it's no longer about you. It's about society.

This is something that Jerry kept telling me, and I finally heard, which is that it's not about me, it's not about my creature comforts. Those are important, but that's not the main thing, because that's not eternal. What's eternal is knowledge. And it's not that I want to make a name for myself, it's that I want to contribute to that web that grows and keeps extending to the horizon. The horizon that we can see goes further still; it's an infinity that you cannot even approximate. It is beyond logic, and it's out there.

Kids can't possibly understand that. They can't understand it at that level, but what they can understand is that it is an adventure. We're all Columbus. We're all setting out. The risk of drowning is real, and the risk for success is real.

I think of having made numerous false starts, and I felt reassured when Jerry said, "Well, there were mathematicians who started in their 50s. Why are you worried? You're not old." And I'm going, "Oh gosh, I've been doing this so long, it's a mess." And he says, "No. Step back and look at what you want to do, and start over." He says, "Always reinvent. That's what you're good at. Do it."

As I get older, what delights me is that I have a thousand more questions than I have possible answers to. That keeps me amused at this point.

My patients always offer me such complicated things that I struggle every day to figure out what they're talking about, number one, and number two: can I fix it. The business of being able to plug into the human brain and reprogram it, which is somewhat akin to listening to electrical discharges on telephone lines and intuiting what's happening at the local civic center. It's still very intriguing to me. I have to admit that I enjoy it. I do it at least once a week.

LS: Are you talking about looking at an EEG (Electroencephalograph)?

GP: No, I'm talking about drilling holes, putting electrodes in people's heads, and turning it on. We can actually go in and interrupt pathologic circuits. Do we really know what we're doing? No. Can we make people better? Absolutely.

There are about 100 centers in the United States that actively correct Parkinson's electrically, through deep-brain stimulation. I couldn't do it at Harvard because I wasn't one of the select, delegated few. I had all these patients who needed it, but the people who could do it were not interested because it was risky.

We've had people who were 40 years old and who couldn't get out of a car, couldn't walk independently, were on medicines 24 hours a day, and who now have an independent life with electrical generators in their brains, pacing their deep structures.

Deep-brain stimulation has very odd effects on some other things, which is what we're trying to understand. It can cause impulse disorders, and that gets interesting. I don't have any answers anymore. I've learned that answers are things you just make up as you go along. And until it falls apart, it's reasonable enough.

There is a book called *Who Goes First?* (by Lawrence Altman) that is about famous risk takers in the history of medicine, such as Forssmann, who was a surgical intern in

Germany back in the late 20s.

Forssmann was an interesting guy. He wondered why we couldn't look at the heart using dye. He was told this could not be done because if you put dye into the heart, the coronaries would fill up and the person would die. Evolutionarily we have the heart of a fish; it doesn't have very good vasculature. It was never meant to be a high-power, energetic kind of thing, so it's got crappy circulation. If you squirt dye into it, it's going to seize up and die.

Well, he didn't buy it. So he took a Foley catheter, which is a thing you put into the urethra for keeping the bladder open, and he stuck it in his antecubital vein, pushed it back up into his heart, squirted himself with dye, and took X-ray pictures of it. He brings this picture – the first picture of angiography of the heart – to his attending physician, who promptly discharges him from practice for having done this: "You did the impossible. You're fired!"

He later gets the Nobel Prize in medicine for developing angiography, which is the basis of all modern techniques. And the question is always: "So, who goes first?"

16. NANCY WHITE

History   Late   Born 1935, San Angelo, Texas

Nancy White, Daddy's perfect girl, married at 19 and had four children before reaching her middle twenties. A series of unfortunate events left her twice widowed and with lethal lymphatic cancer at 43, but Nancy's not your usual woman.

Already familiar with the standard medical approach to cancer, she rejected surgery and chemotherapy and cured herself. She then finished college and, at the age of 50, started work on her PhD. She now runs a clinic in Houston and is a sought-after speaker as neurofeedback psychotherapy's Grand Dame, though she hardly looks it.

I met Nancy at the WinterBrain conference in January 2007, in Palm Springs, California. We were strangers up until the moment we met, but in the 90 minutes that followed she laid her life out in detail.

Excerpts

"I went through school thinking that since I was different, and since my father had taught me to think that I was so smart... there was something wrong with everybody else. Of course, in today's world people would say that something was wrong with me and it was everybody else who was OK. I was very fortunate that I missed that..."

"My father was dying... at the same time as my husband was dying. So here the two men that had taken care of me most of my life were leaving. That left me alone. For about a year after I graduated... I worked toward getting some sanity back into my life. I come from a very addictive family, so I had four teenagers on drugs and alcohol... Then two years later I was having lunch with a friend and he said, 'Oh, I'm going to go start a doctoral program next Wednesday.' I said, 'That sounds interesting... I think I'll go, too!'..."

"People come to me and say, 'I don't have any goals!' And I say, 'Uhh, I've never had any goals, either!' If I had goals, they would have acted like blinders and I wouldn't have noticed what was going on. I just notice what's happening around me, and if it interests me I go after it, and if doesn't I walk on past. That's kind of the way I've handled life..."

"Chuck Strobel... came up to me (at the Applied Psychiatry and Biofeedback conference) and said, 'You know, Nancy, you and I... we're really the pioneers of the field. We are the foundation. That's a big responsibility.' And I'm thinking, 'Who, me? I don't even have a clue what I'm doing!'..."

"I always am on the forefront of something (laughs); it's not unusual. I've often said that I feel like I'm going across the country in my covered wagon, and the Indians are shooting arrows at my back, and I get to California, and I discover that everybody's in the pool at the Hyatt Regency!"

"To intensely feel pleasure or pain is to really live. Trying to block out painful or unpleasant experiences of the day or night leads to a muting of all your feelings and to distancing from life itself... Cultivate your instinctive drive to taste all of life."

— Gayle Delaney, from *Living Your Dreams*

Interview   Palm Springs, California, October 2007

Nancy White: I would have to start my story in the womb. My birth was fairly unusual in that my parents had been married for 13 years and thought they could never have children. When my mother was pregnant they were ecstatic, and my father began programming me in the womb with the idea that I was brilliant. When I was born he immediately started teaching me, and before I was a year old I could hold a conversation.

My purpose was set in the womb, and my purpose was learning. That's always been my identity. I'm interested in so many things, and my ADD contributes to that by giving me this open focus in which everything catches my attention. I want to know about everything, and I want to do it.

As I went to school I found that I didn't function like everybody else. My learning was unique and my thoughts were unique. Luckily this was in a world before the classrooms were large and the teachers were impatient. It was before they thought teaching had to do with how well you did on a test.

I wanted to be constantly engaged and stimulated, and my ADD expressed itself by my talking and interrupting. I was faster than the other kids, so as soon as I was finished with something I started interrupting everybody else. They saw that as interruptive, but they didn't see it as bad, and they didn't think there was anything wrong with me. Instead, they would immediately find something else for me to do.

I went through school thinking that since I was different, and since my father had taught me to think that I was so smart, I figured there was something wrong with everybody else. Of course, in today's world people would say that something was wrong with me and it was everybody else who was OK. I was very fortunate that I missed that.

When I got to high school – my father was a perfectionist – if I brought home an "A," he's say, "Didn't they give A+'s?" If I brought home a score of 100, he'd say, "Didn't they give extra credit?" Nothing was ever quite enough. Being an only child and a girl – and I had a very loving father even though he was a perfectionist – I would have done anything to please him. In retrospect, when I look back, I think he was a bit depressed. I was always looking for a way to make him feel better. I worked very hard to be class valedictorian. Not so much for me, but because I thought it would really please him, which it did.

My mother had made me think that after high school a woman went to college for a couple of years, found a man, got married, and had children. It was back far enough ago that women didn't really have careers. If they did they were either nurses or teachers, and I certainly didn't want to be a nurse or a teacher. I didn't even consider a career.

I was an artist and I went to the University of Texas, at Austin, with the intention of finding a husband. I met one who was a major in the Air Force and who was stationed in Waco, which is where I grew up. So I married, fulfilling exactly what I had programmed myself to do.

I married quite young, because part of my programming was to think that once I was over 20, I was an old maid. I got married by 19 and had a child by the time I was 20. And then I had another child two years later. But then my husband was killed in a plane crash, and that wasn't part of the program. I didn't know how to take care of myself. So my next quest was to find another husband who would take care of me.

I had a friend who was teaching school in Houston and I said, "Hmm. This is a nice city. I think I'll just move here." So I went to Houston with my two little children. There I met a friend I'd gone all the way through grade school and high school with – he was kind of like a brother to me – and he said, "Oh, I have a new roommate. His wife died in childbirth, and he's a young lawyer at Baker Botts." Baker Botts is one of the finer, snobby law firms of the country who only takes the top graduates from law school. Because of that I knew that he was bright, and that he could support me and take care of my children. I decided to marry him before I met him (laughs)! So I married him, and we had two more children.

LS: Did personality play a role, or was it more a matter of willingness and convenience?

NW: Actually, yeah, it did. Bob was so bright, one of the smartest people I've known in my whole life. Before we married we had these wonderful conversations; that was really neat. And then we literally walked down the aisle, walked out of the church, and he never talked to me again.

His wife had died in childbirth and, 18 years later when we were doing a psychodrama weekend – he hated the world of psychology, and therapy and so forth, but he realized that I had about had it and that I was on my way out the door, so he agreed to go to this weekend with me – so he did a psychodrama in which he apologized to his dead wife for having betrayed her by getting remarried to me. That answered a whole lot of questions as to why we'd had such a strange relationship and why he wouldn't talk to me.

I guess that was the most… I don't know the right word… nebulous period of my life. I kept searching for things to express myself. I had been programmed that being a mother was how I was supposed to express myself.

Here I have four children by this time, and I'm raised as an only child, so I'm really confused. It's chaotic to have four children, especially when you've grown up in an absolutely quiet household as an only child. I needed some way to express myself, so I took up sewing and I made beautiful clothes: designer-type finish work. That didn't quite do it, so I decided to go back and start painting again. I had only gotten two years of an undergraduate degree…

LS: Why only two years?

NW: Because I got married; that was part of the program! I only intended to do two years (laughs)! My father made such a deal about my grades and all, but nobody ever said it was important to do anything. I was just supposed to excel so that I could talk about it.

So I said to Bob one day – at this point my youngest child was about 12 or so – "You know, I think I'll go back to school and get my degree." And he looked at me and said, "Well, in my experience people who talk about things never do them." That was the end of that conversation. But I did go back to school. I went to the University of Houston, and by this time I had gotten into therapy and was fortunate to have phenomenally talented mentors.

I was in a lot of emotional pain with the chaos of my life, so I heard about this therapist that did Rolfing. (Rolfing is a usually painful "deep-massage" technique that works to restructure both the body and the mind. – Ed.) I went to him and he did Rolfing and training; he was a clinical psychologist and he taught psychology at the University of Houston, but he was bored with it, and he got bored with his patients, so he would train you to be a therapist, or he would Rolf you. I did ten Rolfings in two and a half weeks and that was about all that I could take (laughs)! I thought, "OK, I'll get the training." I was just fascinated with therapy.

He was one of these people – this was back in the 1970s – who was way beyond his time: he was always talking about quantum physics and quoting passages from the book *Seven Arrows* (by Hyemeyohsts Storm), and it was just an amazing opening for me. He is still probably my biggest influence as a therapist.

One of the things he taught me was, "Never block process. Never block process. Then you get pathology." That is one of the reasons that I'm so adamant about medication, because medication blocks process, and then people become stuck and never fully come all the way through. And this is now beginning to come out in the literature.

I went through the training program in gestalt therapy and then thought I'd better get my "war paint" (laughs), I'd better get the credentials. That was when I started back to school. Bob was not very supportive. He looked down his nose as if I was entertaining myself. I did 66 hours in 16 months and everybody said, "What is your hurry!?" It was like, "I don't know!" It was like a compulsion.

I was about 6 weeks from graduating with my undergraduate degree when Bob, my husband – a very healthy, 47-year-old man who'd run marathons – went into convulsions and was diagnosed with a brain tumor. He lived 11 months. I suppose that intuitively this was my hurry. I immediately went to graduate school and started a master's degree in behavioral science with a focus on art therapy. In the middle of my first year in graduate school Bob died. There I was, this spoiled little – no, cancel that – I wasn't spoiled. I was Daddy's little girl who'd been taken care of. But suddenly I was the matriarch of all these people; it was a surprise.

LS: What people?

NW: Four children and my mother, because my father was dying also, at the same time as my husband was dying. So here the two men that had taken care of me most of my life were leaving. That left me alone.

For about a year after I graduated, maybe two years, I worked toward getting some sanity back into my life. I come from a very addictive family, so I had four teenagers on drugs and alcohol.

I opened a little office and started doing marriage and family therapy. Then two years later I was having lunch with a friend and he said, "Oh, I'm going to go start a doctoral program next Wednesday." I said, "That sounds interesting – where are you going and what are you going to do?" He said, "I'm going to Union Graduate School." I said, "I think I'll go, too (laughs)!"

I went back to my office, that was on Thursday afternoon, called Union Graduate School and said, "I'd like to get into the Doctoral program." And they were like, "What! There's a lot to do to apply to a Doctoral program. We have all these papers and stuff to fill out." I said, "Can't you overnight them to me?" Overnighting something was a big deal back then, but they did it. I spent the weekend writing my life's story, filling out all these papers, and sent it back on Monday. They OK'ed it and on Tuesday they called me to say, "You can come tomorrow." That's how I got into my doctoral program.

People come to me and say, "I don't have any goals!" And I say, "Uhh… I've never had any goals, either"(laughs)! If I had goals they would have acted like blinders and I wouldn't have noticed what was going on. I just notice what's happening around me, and if it interests me I go after it, and if doesn't I walk on past. That's kind of the way I've handled life.

LS: You wait until you get to an exit before deciding whether you'll take it.

NW: That's right! Whichever direction looks the most interesting (laughs)! I went to that graduate school and found it absolutely so rewarding.

LS: What happened to the kids?

NW: By this time my youngest was 16 or 17. They were a bit of a mess and I couldn't figure out what to do with them. I was totally powerless. My youngest son just told me last week, "Mom, when you thought you could take over and tell us what to do when Dad died, there was no way that was going to happen." So I had four of them against me. They were basically doing their own thing, and I had very little influence.

At Union I went to seminars and colloquiums and did a lot of work and reporting. Virginia Satir and Jean Houston were on my doctoral committee as well as other highly creative, amazing people. I was able to explore all of these wonderful things that interested me.

The stuff they were doing at Union was just so incredibly interesting and engaging that it was like such an opportunity. I loved that and worked really hard. I was working full time and going to school full time. I would work all day, then I would go home and do all the things I was planning to do for school, and then I would go to bed at around two in the morning and get up the next day and do it all again.

LS: Are you normally such a hyper-energetic person?

NW: No. I said to myself at the time, "I have really abused my body. I hope it will forgive me." I said that about a month before I graduated. I'd had a lump in my right groin, but I didn't have time to be bothered with it. After I graduated, like the next week, I went to a doctor and he said, "Oh my god, you've got to go right to the hospital." And I said, "Ehh, it's just a blocked lymph node." And he said, "No, you've got to go to the hospital."

They took the lump out. I was really picky. I wouldn't let them give me a general anesthetic; they had to do it under a local. I made them put nice music on (laughs). Then the doctor came in and he said, "I have bad news. It was malignant and it metastasized from somewhere else. We think it was from your uterus," which they had removed several years before.

I'd been through this same kind of ordeal with my husband, and I'd gotten very interested in the Simonton's and their cancer counseling center in Fort Worth. (The Cancer Counseling and Research Center of Fort Worth – Ed.) Carl Simonton was at the beginning of the mind-body approach that used imagery to heal. I had some pretty strong ideas about treating cancer and I wasn't about to let them destroy me.

LS: But the cancer was gone and so was the source of it. What were they proposing to do?

NW: They wanted to shred all of my lymph nodes in my lower abdomen, right groin, and upper right thigh. And I said, "I don't think so!" So I went to an immunology clinic in San Diego and really changed my life overnight. I became a vegetarian, I became very conscious of health and the mind-body connection. That was a real gift.

When I was in graduate school, when Bob had the cancer, I wrote a thesis on cancer as a socially accepted suicide. I ended that saying that cancer could be a gift for growth if one would allow it to be.

When I was diagnosed with metastasized lymphatic cancer – which is usually extremely serious – I just thought, "OK, this doesn't fit for me. I think I have to go by what I wrote." That's what I did.

LS: So at this point you were 32, right?

NW: No (laughs)! At this point I was old. I'd been married 18 years with my second husband. I was 43. I went back to school at 40 and then I went to Union,… I think I went into my doctoral program when I was 50.

I graduated and got my PhD and practiced for a few more years just in my little office all by myself. I was noticing that when I worked with couples that they would come in very, very angry and – if I had long enough to work with them – there was a moment in time where something just shifted. After that they were in rapport and they were fine. And I thought, "This is amazing. How can I possibly create this and measure this." The only thing I could think of was an EEG. (Electroencephalograph, a machine that measures electrical fields originating in the brain. – Ed.)

I didn't even know what an EEG was, except that it had something to do with the brain. That's all I knew (laughs)! So I went around telling everybody, "I've got to have an EEG! I've got to have an EEG!" And they were saying, "An EEG doesn't do anything! It's not that accurate. What are you going to do with an EEG?" But when I get a thought in my head, that's what I'm going to do.

I got this big white elephant EEG machine for $13,500 from Autogenics and my friends were right: it didn't do anything (laughs)! I just knew you could do something with an EEG, but there was nobody else using them.

LS: Did you keep at it?

NW: The damn thing wasn't even working. We eventually discovered that the reason it wouldn't work – computers were pretty new at this time – was because in shipping a bunch of chips had come loose. I had all of these people trying to get it to work, but it wouldn't work.

A year after I'd gotten this white elephant I was in Atlanta, Georgia, at the American Psychological Association Convention. I found the Autogenics booth and I was raising hell when I looked across the aisle of the exhibit hall and here was this color monitor – this was 1987 – and I went, "Ahhhh! What's this!?" And he said, "Well, that's brain synchrony." I said, "Maybe that's what I'm looking for (laughs)!"

I started talking to this guy, who later turned out to be Adam Crane (R. Adam Crane is the founder of many important neurofeedback organizations – Ed.) and he was telling me about research that had just come out where this fellow named Penniston, at the Fort Lyon Colorado VA Hospital, worked with alcoholics and had great success and published his research. I said, "Ahhhh! That's probably what I want to do!" He said, "We're working on hardware and software for that which should be out right away." I said, "I want to do it."

I was one of the first in the nation and I got one of the first machines with this software. We were trained by Gene Penniston in Philadelphia and started doing the Penniston Protocol. (Which uses EEG-based neurofeedback to train alcoholics to get over their addiction. – Ed.) We thought that since we had this great thing, the world was going to knock the doors down to try to get to us. Wrong (laughs)! Wrong!

LS: But that was for alcoholics. How were you using it?

NW: Well, I had intended to use it for alcoholics except that the city of Houston is probably the most conservative medical and 12-step city on the planet. (Referring to the 12-step method of Alcoholics Anonymous – Ed.) The 12-step people think that all you need is 12 steps. They wouldn't even talk about anything else, and alcoholics don't really want to get sober anyway (laughs)! When you say to alcoholics, "Here's an expensive program – don't you want to be sober and have your life working?" They say, "No, I want to decide for the next 24 hours what I want to do!"

At that time I had my office in the same building as my friend Frank, who was a psychiatrist and who knew about and believed in the Penniston work. When he had a patient that he didn't know what else to do with, he would send them to me. I got patients with all of these wonderful different diagnoses.

One guy was referred with a panic disorder. Frank had tried all these medications and nothing had helped, so he said, "Nancy, see what you can do." This guy had to drop out of college because he had Epstein-Barr virus. Three quarters of his way through his Alpha-Theta program, the Epstein-Barr virus disappeared. Alpha-Theta training seems to be great for the immune system. His panic disorder disappeared, too. It just kind of evolved: we had this one, and other patients would come in with different disorders.

LS: What were you doing at this point? The Penniston Protocol on these guys?

NW: Uh huh! Oh, the Penniston Protocol will really do a lot more than people think it will do.

LS: Did you know that, or were you just doing it because that's what you had?

NW: I was doing it because these were the people who came in, and that's what I had (laughs).

LS: There's sort of a kind of courage in that, isn't there?

NW: Well, uh, yeah! The amazing thing was that we had remarkable successes with the first few people. It gave us lots of courage that we could do anything.

About a year later I heard that they were creating software for ADD. I didn't even know what ADD was, but I said, "We've got a machine, so why not do that, too?" So, being a responsible person, I went to Barnes & Noble to look for a book on ADD to figure out what it is. They had one little tiny book, a tiny little thing, on ADD. I bought it, went home, and after about three or four pages I wanted to put it down and cry because there was my entire family: me, my father, my children. It answered so many questions (laughs)! So I started treating ADD, and it's evolved from there.

Basically, I created a wellness model. We have multitudes of things in our office, and we were busy creating this thing that's become the whole field of neurofeedback. I was in this field before it was a field. There were the original researchers – as well as Margaret Ayres out in California – and there was Nancy (laughs).

LS: Did knowing that you were on the forefront of something contribute to your enthusiasm? Or, when you look back, was it just something you enjoyed doing?

NW: I always am on the forefront of something (laughs); it's not unusual. I've often said that I feel like I'm going across the country in my covered wagon, and the Indians are shooting arrows at my back, and I get to California and I discover that everybody's in the pool at the Hyatt Regency!

I remember the first or second AAPB Conference I ever went to (AAPB is the Association for Applied Psychiatry and Biofeedback – Ed.). Chuck Strobel – whose brain synchrony I'd seen on the color monitor – came up to me in the exhibit hall and said, "You know, Nancy, you and I have a big responsibility." "What's that?" He said, "Well, we're really the pioneers of the field. We are the foundation. That's a big responsibility." And I'm thinking, "Who, me? I don't even have a clue what I'm doing (laughs)! How can I be responsible for anything!?"

It's been a remarkable journey and it's still a struggle. It's always been a struggle. I remember right after we started working with the EEG I was invited to this fancy dinner party. I was seated across the table from this man who was a doctor, probably in his mid-80s. He said, "And what do you do, my dear?" And I started explaining how I trained brains. He looked across the table, tilted his head down, and looked over his glasses and said, "Poppycock, my dear. Nobody can train brains." That was kind of the attitude that I was confronted with out there in the world. But I wouldn't give up. I have wandered along and lost tons of money, but I just wouldn't quit. I wouldn't quit because it was fascinating and it was my passion.

Every time I see anything that I think could help mankind progress a little more than the shit-hole that it's in (laughs), I want to go do that, too, so that I can do it for other people. I think you would say I'm a risk taker. I'm not sure I ever analyze consequences – I just do it. You know: if it feels right, I do it. Then I look back and I say, "Ohhhh, shit (laughs)."

LS: How do you develop this confidence in what feels right?

NW: I think I've always had a lot of intuition. I really attribute a great deal to my father and his programming. As you astutely could see, it was all for him, it wasn't for me. But as a child I had no clue that it was for him and not me. I really thought that his obsession about training me was all about me. It wasn't at all, but it had its positive effect. He taught me a confidence and a willingness to think that I could do anything. So here I am.

LS: What do you feel were your rewards?

NW: Learning in and of itself is my reward. Learning, being able to apply what I learn, and then – as I got older – being able to help others with what I've learned. Initially it was just learning for learning's sake, but it's evolved into something a little more altruistic.

LS: Can you give me an example of the kind of rewarding experience that a young person could see as a goal.

NW: I can't in the way you're asking that question because I don't function that way. When you ask me for an experience, what popped into my head was one of those "Ah ha!" moments.

I was sitting on the floor in upper New York State where I had been for a very intense two-week seminar with Jean Houston, who's the quintessential teacher. I remember her lecturing and she said, "The next frontier of evolution is… the mind." This was in the 70s and that, to me, was one of the most exciting things I'd ever heard, "Wow!" And I knew there was this other world somewhere out there. Those kinds of moments have inspired me and kept me going.

LS: I think many people are daunted. They don't pursue dreams because they think, "What could I do? How could I get there."

NW: I don't even think that way.

LS: Is that part of your "act first, think later"…

NW: Yeah!

LS: Do you see that as a strength, something that people should have?

NW: I think it's very helpful, and yet I think one also has to do one's own work. You can't just foolishly and impulsively go out and act in the world. You've got to have some kind of background, some education. I've been responsible in the way I've done it, I think. When I want to learn something, I'll go learn from the master that created it.

LS: How do you do that?

NW: I seek them out, I find them. I hear about something, I find out who created it, and I call them on the telephone.

I think I'm driven by something innate that I don't even know. I remember when I went up to New York three summers in a row. This was the summer that Bob was dying, the summer when he died, and the summer after that. I had just met Jean Houston before Bob went into convulsions, and when she started talking about her seminars in New York I thought, "I've got to go!" I'd never really done anything like that before in my life, but I committed myself: I was going to Jean Houston's thing.

But then my husband went into convulsions and it was difficult. It was like, "How the hell am I going to leave a dying husband!?" Then I decided that he was going to die whether I stayed or didn't stay (laughs), so I decided I was going.

The third summer I was there – this was after he had died – I went through two weeks of these very intense things that Jean does. It was over and everybody was packing up to leave and I was laying on the floor sobbing. This guy who I was kind of dating came over and said, "What's the matter!" And I said, "I don't know! I have something very important to do and I don't know what it is (laughs)!" It was like my heart was broken; it was just so heavy and so big.

Whatever that is, it's part of what drives me, and I can't put my finger on it because I don't know what it is. Every now and then I'll have a client who will tell me, "I don't have a purpose, I don't have this, or I don't have that." And I will say to them, "My sense is that what you're now training to get ready for what you need to do. You don't know what it is yet, and I don't know what it is, but you need to get ready. I think you're here to do something very important."

LS: Are you still sobbing at some level? Or was the sobbing just part of your realization?

NW: I think it was part of a phase that's still happening, and I think part of the sobbing was realizing there was something going on, and not understanding it – not that I can say that I understand it now. Now I'm more able to just wait to see. What is it that I'm being called to do? I don't know.

Every now and then I think we become one of the chosen people, not because we're special, but because we hear someone say, "We need your help," and we volunteer our help. I've said that to just a scattering of people, of clients, through the years.

I don't know where it's all going, but I really have this feeling that sometime within our lifetime, and maybe very soon in the very next few years, there's going to be a huge shift in reality as we know it. I think another reality will arise, but I have no idea what that reality will be.

LS: Do you think it will be better?

NW: I think it's a toss-up. My opinion is that it's going to be better, but it could be a whole lot worse. Or it could be a whole lot worse before it gets better.

OUTDOORS

17. ELLA GAZKA

History   Early   Born 1989, New York City, New York

Ella went to progressive schools, did home schooling, and traveled around the world when she was 16. Her varied interests developed out of being a teacher's helper, a musician, an active traveler through foreign lands, and a skilled outdoor's person trained in survival and exploration.

    I met Ella at a party whose main attraction was a troupe of Mongolian musicians. She was there at the invitation of the host, with whom she was learning to make jewelry. She told me of her travels and I knew her stories would be interesting.

Excerpts

"How is learning important to me? I think we all know how to learn. It's a normal thing. My curiosity really pushes me to learn. I like learning at my own pace: if I find something interesting, something I want to learn, I can learn about it…"

"I've just gotten older and the things that seemed so far away aren't so far away anymore. … The time is getting shorter and shorter. It's like you realize that life doesn't go on forever! It's not a sad realization. Maybe it's because you grow a lot when you hit your middle teens. You make a big, big leap in growth. … So I'd think, 'Oh, wow. I'm getting kind of old now'…"

"For me, my darkest hour was that night …. it was hard for me to lie in my shelter when they were in so much pain in my dream. I got through that by knowing that it was (my friends') inner battle to deal with, and not mine. I learned so much about myself from being there, just from lying in that heap of leaves…"

"Most of my life has been an alternative experience: I have never gone to a public school. It depends on the person. I guess I would say that you should just live your life. It doesn't have to go by the books, you don't have to do it a certain way. If you want to do something different, that's OK. It makes us who we are, it makes us different people."

"Whenever we dream or have a vision, a door is opening for us. If we learn something from that, that's when we actually know something. That is 'knowing'...

"We don't live in the real world here. This is a flesh and blood world, not the real world. The real world is where the spirit of osha comes and talks to me. The real world isn't in technology or all those books. It's in our visions and dreams."

— Don Enrique Salmon, quoted in *Plant Spirit Medicine*, by Eliot Cowan

Interview   New Paltz, New York, May, 2007

Ella Gazka: How is learning important to me? I think we all know how to learn. It's a normal thing. My curiosity really pushes me to learn. I like learning at my own pace: if I find something interesting, something I want to learn, I can learn about it.

I got really lucky with home schooling in math – I had such a horrible time with math, I could never do it – because I really got good at it when I did it at my own pace. I need to go at my own pace. When I was with a class doing math, it was horrible torture; I didn't like it at all. Now I like it.

LS: What's your schooling background?

EG: I went to the school I'm actually teaching at now, Dayspring Community School, a Waldorf pre-school. I went there through second grade, and then they had to stop doing the grades because there just wasn't enough people. Everyone who was in first and second grade from where I live started this big van pool to come up here to New Paltz.

Starting in third grade I went to Mountain Laurel, a Waldorf school in New Paltz. Then for ninth grade I went to a community school that was around for two years. It had teachers from all over, and there were about 10 to 15 kids in the class. I liked it, but it was hard because I lived so far away. I never went to public school.

In 10th grade I went around the world with my grandparents. When I returned, I went back to home schooling. I tried to do home schooling while I was gone – while I was traveling – but that was really hard and I didn't get much done.

LS: What was the idea behind the programs at these schools?

EG: In Waldorf schools you do blocks. A block is where you have Main Lesson for two hours each morning in which you study one thing for three weeks. So you might do math every morning for two hours for three weeks. And then you do history every morning for two hours for three weeks. Then the rest of the day you have regular classes, like math a few times a week, English few times a week, and language every day. We followed that same rhythm. I liked it, but the school was far away.

LS: Are there important things you felt you learned at the Waldorf schools?

EG: The one thing that I am so grateful for at Waldorf schools is that they had a huge impact on my life. In nursery and kindergarten you play with silks and ropes and oddly shaped pieces of wood. You play outside a lot, so it really makes your imagination work. You don't have computers at all, or those annoying plastic toys with the buttons that make electronic noises. That's why I'm teaching now, trying to give back to that.

I always wondered why, when I compared myself to my friends who went to public school, I had way, way more of an imagination than them. Way, way more! Like I would say, "You guys are so boring! Think of something more interesting!" That continues throughout the Waldorf grades – not so much in the older grades – in fouth grade they start letting it go a little bit.

Something I learned from Mountain Laurel was art. I really focused on art a lot, and music, art with your body, and painting and sculpture. In Main Lesson you make your own textbook. If I was in the history block we'd learn whatever we'd learn about, then we'd have to write something about it, and we'd usually draw with it: there's always some kind of art incorporated into it. You do that up through 12th grade in Waldorf school.

I was really glad to do the art. They teach drawing in a really interesting way: you can't use outlines. In the younger grades you just use these block crayons. I learned how to make people that way. It's just the way they teach art. I really liked it. I remember when I was younger and I used to drive with kids who went to public school. My drawings were really different compared to them.

LS: Were you ever bored?

EG: It's really weird – and I think about this a lot – it takes a lot for me to get bored. I don't get bored easily. I have to be stuck for hours with nothing to do. I think it was just how I was raised. I mean, if you're bored you find something to do! So I was never really bored in school. I can't remember really ever being… maybe there were times when I was bored, but…

LS: Are you motivated? Is that the same thing as saying you're not bored?

EG: I am motivated. I think the reason that I don't get bored easily is that I can find something to do relatively quickly. I just think of things to do. If I'm, like, sitting around with my little brother in a waiting room, we have these weird games we play. If I have a notebook with me, then I write poems. I like to draw a lot. I like to watch people and their body language.

LS: I talk to a lot of kids in public schools. They usually phrase what they do in terms of what they're supposed to do. They're busy doing this, they're supposed to be doing that… How did you decide what you wanted to do? What kind of goals did you have?

EG: Well, when I was in Mountain Laurel I was really into music, so I worked really hard at music. I was in three, sometimes four orchestras. In one it was really hard to stay in first, second, or third cello.

I started music when I was in fourth grade. I know I had goals. I think they were short-term goals, like finishing something, or getting better at something, or learning to be able to speak more. I didn't really have a long-term view; the rest of my life was sort of distant. When I was in sixth or seventh grade the thought of going to college, getting a job, getting married, and having little babies… it was so far away!

LS: How have your goals evolved?

EG: I've just gotten older and the things that seemed so far away aren't so far away anymore. I know older people who I thought of as my friends who are getting married now. They were a lot older, but we were still a lot closer than I was to any adults. The time is getting shorter and shorter. It's like you realize that life doesn't go on forever (laughs)!

LS: That's a strange thing to suddenly realize. When did you realize that?

EG: It's not a sad realization. Maybe it's because you grow a lot when you hit your middle teens. You make a big, big leap in growth. When you're younger it's spread out more. So I'd think, "Oh, wow. I'm getting kind of old now." Not that I'm getting "old," but I'm older than I was last fall! When I turned 18 I went, "Ahhh! I'm really old now!" People told me, "You can vote, you can drive, and you can buy cigarettes." And I said, "What? I can?" I don't go out and buy cigarettes often (laughs)!

LS: Tell me about this big trip thing because that seems so important.

EG: I don't really remember how it first came up. I had just turned 16 and my grandparents just mentioned in passing: "Oh, wouldn't it be great if you went around the world with us?" I didn't really think they were serious. It took a little bit of time to sink in. I think I decided to go with them because I was never going to get that chance again.

Some places I knew a little about – I was just really excited – and other parts of the trip we had to figure out where we were going to go. They had a rough draft of the places they were going to visit, but they hadn't decided how long. I didn't really have any expectations – I just wanted to learn a lot. I didn't really know what it was going to be like.

The trip was about six months long. First we went to Singapore for two or three weeks. Then down to Australia, mostly Tasmania and New Zealand. When I was in Tasmania – my grandparents were planning on moving there – we just practiced living because they wanted to see if they wanted to move there. Then I went to Thailand and some countries in Europe, but I wasn't in Europe for long.

The first thing was the shock of how different it was. We got to Singapore right when George W. Bush was about to be re-elected, and if we said we were American, no one would talk to us. It was very strange to see firsthand how upset the world was with America. If we said we were from America they would walk away from us.

That really brought in to me just how different countries are from each other. They have these little strange differences, too, like Singapore is very clean. Chewing gum is illegal – you can't even bring it into the country. Everything is so clean – there's, like, not a piece of garbage anywhere – even the leaves look like they were shined! If you jaywalk you'll be arrested. You get fined for every infraction. I saw a T-shirt that said, "Singapore is a Fine Place", and below it had lists of everything you can't do (laughs). The way people dress and talk is so different. The smallest things make a big difference when they add up.

We went bicycling around Pulau Lagoon and went to this Buddhist temple in the middle of the jungle. I had this kind of scary experience where I climbed this tree – I had gotten way ahead of my grandparents – so that I could look back over the path that I'd just come. I was sitting in this tree, not really sure if I should be there, and I heard this crashing and thrashing that sounded like there was this really huge guy wandering around in the woods. It turned out it was just some Komodo dragons. Five came and were playing around the base of the tree. They were really fun to watch. They're really huge, giant!

Then we went to Tasmania where we were housesitting for this woman. In the mornings I did school work, then had lunch, and afterwards we'd go see something. We didn't have a car, so we had to walk everywhere. We could take a bus, but we were in Hobart, the capital of Tasmania, and the town was really small. It was nice to get to walk everywhere.

Fifty-five percent of Tasmania is reserves and parks and stuff. They're really conscious about the environment. Whole towns would decide, "Oh, we're not going to use plastic bags." So if you go to the grocery store in one of these towns and you don't know that, then they'll just put your groceries on the counter and you think, like,… "OK…?" And you have to find a place to put them! There weren't any plastic bags anywhere. I really liked how they all agreed to do that. They were a lot more laid back. It was so small – it's a small island.

I was really excited about how different everything was, like, the trees were different and that smell of eucalyptus everywhere. I had never been to anywhere really different from where I live. The vegetables were HUGE in Tasmania. Celery was, like, three-feet high! This was normal celery; you could eat it for a week! I think it's because of the fertile volcanic soil.

I learned a lot about animals. I got really good at identifying birds because birds are really different there: purple and blue and bright pink, with these bizarre calls so it's not that hard to recognize them. And I bought a bird book and a plant book.

I met this really nice guy who worked at an animal rehabilitation shelter who taught me about all the animals, like wombats. Wombats are so cool! And I got to see koala bears a lot, and wallabies, which are smaller relatives of kangaroos. They're kind of like what rabbits are here: they get in people's gardens and eat things.

He showed me Tasmanian devils, which are really cute and cuddly: really small, black and white with pointy ears. They're teensy, teensy, teensy, but their jaws have the strength of a great white shark. They have this bizarre cry, which is how they got their name. When the islanders first came to Tasmania, the Westerners thought the island was haunted by the lost souls of the Aborigines that they had, like, mass-murdered. They have this really eerie scream. If you heard it you'd picture a completely different animal.

I got to hike a lot, really long hikes. My grandparents were very fit, but on the really hard hikes, the all-day hikes, I'd go by myself. The trails were pretty well marked, and you'd sign in and sign out at the bottom of the trail.

LS: You went alone? Did you know how to read maps?

EG: Yeah, I knew how to read topographical maps. I'd learned that in Vermont Wilderness School, the survival school. I'd been doing that since seventh grade.

I learned a lot about history there. Tasmania is sort of the Alcatraz of Australia. I went to a women's prison there; it was really horrible what they did to prisoners. The Aborigines were really wiped out when Westerners first colonized Australia. All the buildings are still there, in ruins. And people seemed really sad about what had happened there. I read books and articles, visited a lot of places, and talked to a lot of people.

LS: How did you reach the point of studying it at that depth? Were you encouraged to do that?

EG: Yeah, I was definitely encouraged. Some of it was really accidental – it was just cool to visit these places and my grandparents would talk about it a lot, because they knew Tasmania really well. They would tell me stuff. They gave me a lot of books, and they really encouraged me.

LS: It's unusual to have a direct experience of something that you're learning about. That makes it a lot more personal, especially if you're learning by talking to people.

EG: I really found myself wanting to learn more about all the places where I spent the most time. It was interesting; I really liked it. The people were really cool.

LS: What do you think you took away from this experience? Did it change you?

EG: The greatest effects happened when I left New Zealand. I didn't gain that much from the time in Tasmania. I was having a really hard time for the first three months. I was homesick. I didn't have any friends. I wasn't able to keep in touch with anyone. And the age difference between me and my grandparents… in some ways we just couldn't quite connect. Maybe that just wasn't my place.

In New Zealand I was much happier. It's really beautiful there, and I really liked the Maori culture. They just seemed to be my kind of people: totally down to earth. They don't ever want to go inside: they're jumping off of bridges and hiking all the time! I could see myself living there.

My grandparents didn't know so many people in New Zealand, but they'd meet people; they're good at that. It's harder for me to meet people. I'm just shy; it takes me a while to warm up to people. I've gotten a lot better at it, but at the time it would take me a long time to know someone well enough to open up to them. It's something I've tried really hard to fix.

LS: How did you work on that? Did you force yourself?

EG: I didn't try too hard. When I met someone I wouldn't feel comfortable talking with them – just talking is all that's really required – I'd have to trust them. Then, after maybe a week, I'll know that person a lot better than any of my friends will know them, friends who are really outgoing. It's just the way I am, but it does make it hard for me to make friends in a short period of time.

LS: Tell me about the wilderness school. How did you get involved with that?

EG: That started in seventh grade. One day my class was talking together, trying to think of something that we all wanted to learn, and we all wanted to learn how to survive in the woods. My teacher overheard us and knew about the Vermont Wilderness School program. At the end of the school year my teacher said, "Hey, we're going to go on a field trip on the first week of school!" It was the first of this three-part training program at the Vermont Wilderness School, and that was the first week of seventh grade.

In the first program they just teach you the basics: how to make a fire, how to build a shelter. They didn't teach us that much about food or water because those aren't really that important. The important things are first shelter, then fire, water, and food, depending on your situation.

They taught us a lot about just being in the woods. There is so much difference of being in a house and living in the woods. I know, because now some of my teachers tell me, "Becca, you complained a lot when you first came" (laughs)!

Sleeping outside for three or four days was hard enough. We did a lot of this physical stuff that I thought was, like, torture, but now I'm glad I did it. They would make us run around this huge field with water in our mouths. Running, running! It makes your lungs work really well; I actually liked doing it. And just crawling around on the ground; all this stuff that we thought was kind of weird, but actually had a point to it.

The second time we went was at the end of seventh grade. We did group survival things. When we got there they took away all our electronic stuff: our Walkman CD players, and our watches. Then they took away our primping stuff, like our hair brushes.

I actually really like it when I don't have my watch: time is so important in this world, but there, when you're hungry you eat, when you're tired you go to sleep.

We slept in the tent that night, and the next day they said, "OK, pack up your stuff." We packed it up and left it under a tree. We took our knives and our water bottles and the girls and the boys split up. We did a group survival thing where we had to build a shelter, get a fire going. We did do some basic wild-edible things, but they brought us food and water.

The third program, which was in eighth grade, was the solo. You spend the first two or three days getting ready for that, just making sure you're comfortable with your skills, and then they sit you down and say, "OK, you're going out for 36 hours. What do you think you need to bring?" And you say, "Well, I don't think I can make a fire with a bow-drill set, can I bring some matches?" And they'll say, "Why don't you bring two matches so that you push yourself." Or you might say, "I hate bugs, and I don't want to sleep in a debris shelter! Can I bring a tent?" And they'll say, "Why don't you just bring a sleeping bag, build a debris shelter, and sleep with your sleeping bag inside the debris shelter." If you didn't think you could get enough food or water for 36 hours – but you don't really need anything for that short amount of time – then they might tell you to bring a potato, which you'll have to get a fire going in order to cook, and a water bottle. So it really depended on what your skill level was. You just work it out for who you are.

Then you go out and spend that time alone, and when you come back there is a celebration honoring your journey. And the last day you just eat a lot (laughs), because you're really hungry!

LS: When did that program have an impact on you?

EG: The first second I put my foot onto the property (laughs)! I actually did this nature camp when I was younger that was taught by two Native American women. I was really little. When people see someone make a fire out of a bow-drill set for the first time… there's something about the impact that that has… you can see it in their faces. So I'd had a little of that and I just liked it; I just like being outside.

We all have it in us, that's sort of their philosophy. Everyone can go out and live in the woods – we've just forgotten how. I like being with myself, not having anyone else to rely on. I honestly think I've made the best friendships at that program because of having nothing but yourself. It's really raw, the whole thing. I was there for three summer camps, and at the last one I was actually a counselor, not as a camper. The distance between when I first came, just building a shelter with a bunch of girls, to being by myself for a few days with nothing... I really liked that.

LS: Can you describe that? Most people don't know what you're talking about.

EG: As you learn more you get more difficult challenges. From going on a 36-hour solo with matches, a potato, and a water bottle, to going for three days with no matches, food, or water, or just fasting. There are different levels, and there are different kinds of solos. There are solos to survive, and there are solos that are vision quests where you do more inner work than survival work.

When I did the vision quest I was comfortable that I could go and make a fire and have a nice, big breakfast from stuff I'd found, that I wouldn't get dehydrated, I wouldn't be cold at night, and I wouldn't get wet if it rained. I definitely can't to that for a long period of time; if I was out in the woods for over a month, I think I'd be pretty thin by the time I came back.

LS: When you say you're pretty comfortable with what you can do, what would you bring with you?

EG: I just bring my knife, shorts, shirt, and maybe a hat.

When I went on my vision quest I brought a blanket, because I wasn't really trying to test my survival skills, and maybe some water, I can't remember. I was fasting for two days, but I couldn't get a fire, it was really frustrating. The first thing you do is build your shelter because if it starts raining and all you've got is a fire, then you're still going to get wet. But if you have a shelter and no fire, then you'll be dry.

I have to say that before, in my survival solos, I would build really elaborate shelters. I really liked building debris shelters: they'd have shelves inside, these really cool doors, and they'd be totally waterproof. I spent a lot of time making them really good, spending a lot of energy, putting on tons of leaves.

But when I went on the vision quest I built this really crappy lean-to, really bad. It was a beautiful, sunny day out, a clear sky, 70 degrees. "What could go wrong?" That's what I was thinking. I just needed a shelter, so I built this really bad lean-to. And then I tried getting a fire, but I couldn't get it started in the morning, and I tried again, but still couldn't get it going in the afternoon, and in the evening I was really tired since I hadn't eaten since the night before.

I went to sleep and then next day I woke up and tried again to start a fire, but I couldn't. I was trying so hard. I remember being so frustrated! I redid my bow and drill set and just kept trying and trying. It just wasn't happening for me. Then I said, "OK, I should just let this go."

I couldn't find a place to dig a spring, and I didn't drink anything for a day and a half, and I was starting to get a little loopy. I got water another way – it's not the best way – it's using a grape vine: you cut them and they actually pump out water, but it's not good because you kill the grape vine and usually you only get a drip of water. But I put my pot under the grape vine – I'd brought a pot to boil the water I planned to get from the spring. It was like the magic grape vine, because when I came back an hour later the pot was overflowing.

Then this huge storm came, the worst storm I've seen when I was in Vermont. I was having all these really strange dreams – I still don't know what they mean. There was always this woman in them, this woman in white. In every dream I had, no matter how stupid the dream was. I remember having this dream about Godzilla and she was somehow incorporated into that.

Then that night – there was also this bunch of boys who were going on a really long vision quest – I had this dream about them. I drew a lot of pictures about them when I came back. It was just really hard. I've never had that kind of experience. That was the night of this really big storm. It was really one of the hardest things I've ever had because of that one dream. It wasn't entirely a dream because I was awake, I was conscious of what was going on around me, but I wasn't quite awake. I remember there was a lot of blood in the dream and I almost felt it on me, but it was actually the rain.

The trees were groaning, and the wind was howling, and a branch fell on my shelter and knocked it down. Knocked it down while I was sleeping in it, so now I'm soaking wet. I didn't really care, I guess. I didn't really care. I just kind of pushed myself out of it, and threw the sticks out and went to sleep in a pile of leaves. Honesty, it really didn't bother me.

The next morning, which was the morning that I was leaving, it was one of my funniest memories (laughs)! I just kind of covered myself in the leaves to keep the water off of me and I was just sleeping there. I was kind of awake and I was wondering when someone was going to come to me and tell me that it's time to leave. I was just waiting and I didn't even bother getting out. I was so tired then, I was so tired.

Then I heard this voice, "Becca? Becca?" And I kind of poke my head out of the leaves and one of my counselors, Kevin, he's just standing there staring at me in my piles of leaves because I was always famous for my skill at shelter building.

It was just a really nice moment to come out of that state of really hard-core dreaming and see a person. If you don't see another person for a real long time, then it's nice to see another face, something familiar.

When I got back they had the whole "welcome you back" ceremony where you sit and you tell your story about what you went through. They ask, "What was your darkest hour, what got you through it, and what have you learned from it?" Those are usually the three questions.

For me, my darkest hour was that night when I had that dream, because it was about people who were so close to me. They were doing their vision quest at the same time and my dream was almost about their experience. I talked about how it was hard for me to lie in my shelter when they were in so much pain in my dream. I got through that by knowing that it was their inner battle to deal with, and not mine. I learned so much about myself from being there, just from lying in that heap of leaves.

I really appreciate the space they make to welcome you back after an experience like that. How they honor you and acknowledge the fact that you've grown, and that you're a different person than you were three days earlier. It would be really hard to go through something so strong as that and not have anyone acknowledge it. Now I know that if someone's gone through something, then what I clearly need to do is just listen to them, that's what seems to help.

I give the example of the vision quest because that was the hardest for me emotionally. The survival stuff was hard, but you have survival things to help you, like the shelter, and the fire. The hardest thing might be finding food. But the vision quest was more of a change for me to go through.

LS: You consider that most kids go to public schools, and they don't have the chance for an alternative experience: private schools are expensive, and almost no one has grandparents who can take them around the world.

If you could speak to other kids who are roughly in your situation, then what would you say was the most important thing, in terms of growing and learning, that they could do for themselves?

EG: Most of my life has been an alternative experience: I have never gone to a public school. It depends on the person. I guess I would say that you should just live your life. It doesn't have to go by the books, you don't have to do it a certain way. If you want to do something different, that's OK. It makes us who we are, it makes us different people.

What I learned from Vermont Wilderness School was that no matter where I go, or what kind of problems I'm having, the wilderness is always going to be there to help me. I really got to put that into action when I traveled around the world, because I got to see what it was like being in the jungle, or the Australian desert, different mountains. I would say that you shouldn't just assume that being outside is buggy and wet and horrible, because it's really one of the most beautiful places that I've ever been.

Not being who you really are, just following along the path with everyone else, maybe taking a detour once in a while, and spending more time outside, which is really healthy for people. People who spend a lot of time outside seem really balanced – they have a whole aura about them. Do you know what I'm talking about?

LS: Ummm... I don't know. I mean sure, I could imagine. But I know a lot of people who spend a lot of time outside who seem somewhat normal. There's sort of an illusion, that I rebel against, that the outdoors can save you. There are certain problems which the outdoors can't solve and which you have to solve yourself. I knew people who were very out-doorsy, but they couldn't resolve their inner demons.

Outdoors can be destructive as well as constructive – it is what it is – and you can climb a mountain or you can throw yourself off a mountain, it's up to you, the mountain doesn't care. I know people who didn't take responsibility for themselves and played a kind of Russian Roulette game with the outdoors and got hurt or killed. But there remains a kind of romanticism about the power of the outdoors.

EG: That's almost what I was saying. I'm not saying that if you go outside, that's going to save you. Getting outside gives you a space where you can save yourself.

The reason that I think I trust being outside is because some of my most powerful experiences – experiences that helped me grow a lot – happened when I was outside. And like you said, it can be really destructive, too: I have been really hurt when I was on these programs, like badly hurt. But every time that I've been hurt it has been my fault, completely. Like I forgot something, or I was stupid about something, or I wasn't quite focused.

Some people just don't do well inside. This is just me: I thrive when I'm outside. I've honestly made the best friendships and gone through a lot of inner stuff when I was outside. And it gives me a place to go when I'm upset.

I suppose the reason I go outside is because I have, one, two... (laughs). I can't even count them... six brothers and sisters. I have a BIG family, and if everyone's home it gets really chaotic.

I really like having quiet and being outside. Sometimes when I'm at home for a really long time and haven't gotten the chance to get somewhere really quiet, and I finally do, the sound of quiet is the strangest noise to me.

18. LYNN HILL

History   Middle   Born 1961, Detroit, Michigan

At a little over five feet tall, Lynn is a small woman, and in the male-dominated world of rock climbing that's considered a disadvantage. Yet in 1993 she was the first person to climb the 3,500-foot vertical granite face of Yosemite Valley's El Capitan without the use of any artificial hand or foot holds. It set a new landmark for climbing difficulty that went unrepeated for 10 years, despite many attempts.

Climbing is Lynn's passion, and she has pursued it competitively, professionally, and culturally. A frequent winner of international climbing competitions, she is the host of her own climbing camps, a media representative for the Patagonia equipment company, and a mother.

I bumped into her once unexpectedly when I was rock climbing in the backwoods, and met her again for this interview outside of New Paltz, New York, where she was giving a public lecture and slide show. She spoke to me about what it takes to be both realistic and idealistic.

Excerpts

"There's a million ways to make it work in this world. One route would be education through traditional means: college education, trade schools, self-taught. But you still have to provide a service that somebody's willing to pay for. That's what work is, and we get paid for providing a service or product…"

"I'm a curious person. That, I think, is a quality that's necessary for education: if you're not curious then you're not interested, and if you're not interested then you're not going to learn. I got an education in biology so I could go into physical therapy – that was the original idea – or become a doctor. But I figured that doctors had to work too much…"

"When somebody is passionate about something, they create their own reality. Your positive thoughts about whatever you do brings the opportunity, it attracts the opportunity. I wasn't even conscious of that at the time, but that's what I believe now. You have more power than you're aware of just by virtue of what you think. It's an aura that you create…"

"I took advantage of the opportunities that came my way, but they came my way because of who I am and what I was doing. I didn't realize there was much value to these things; it's really hard to quantify. In the end people seem to find inspiration in the fact that through determination and focus I have been able to do things that other people haven't done."

OUTDOORS

"Until one is committed, there is hesitancy, the chance to draw back, always ineffectiveness. Concerning all acts of initiative (and creation), there is one elementary truth, the ignorance of which kills countless ideas and splendid plans: that the moment one definitely commits oneself, then providence moves too. A whole stream of events issues from the decision, raising in one's favor all manner of unforeseen incidents, meetings and material assistance, which no man could have dreamt would have come his way."

— Johann Wolfgang von Goethe

"To make any kind of gain in life – a gain of wealth, personal stature, whatever you define as 'gain' – you must place some of your material and/or emotional capital at risk. That is the law of the universe. Except by blind chance, it cannot be circumvented. No creature on earth is excused from obedience to this pitiless law. To become a butterfly, a caterpillar must grow fat; and to grow fat, it must venture out where birds are. There are no appeals. It is the law."

— Franz Heinrich, as quoted in *The Zurich Axioms*, by Max Gunther

Interview   New Paltz, New York, October 2006

LS: Tell me what you think about the alternatives available to people just getting out of school, besides those opportunities that are offered to them?

Lynn Hill: The responsibility is yours. That's all I have to say about that!

There's a million ways to make it work in this world. One route would be education through traditional means: college education, trade schools, self-taught. But you still have to provide a service that somebody's willing to pay for. That's what work is, and we get paid for providing a service or product. That's why you get money; it doesn't come off of trees obviously. You're not going to earn very much money unless you have skills that people want.

LS: When did you start thinking of your future this way?

LH: I come from a large family. I learned to be responsible for myself from the beginning because I had to be. I couldn't rely on supervision from my parents, so I figured it out for myself.

I grew up in Southern California, near Los Angeles. California has one-eighth of the nation's population, so it's crowded and expensive. Actually, I grew up in Orange County, which has an even more of an exaggerated view on things. People are really into making money, usually through traditional means, either through nepotism – giving their kid a job in the family company – or in business: doctor, lawyer, that kind of thing.

In Orange County there's a huge difference between the haves and the have-nots. When I was young, immigrants from Mexico were just starting to come over in large numbers. A lot of them were illegal aliens. They were the ones getting the low-end jobs.

Those people were competing for the jobs that I might have unless I had some skill or education, so I went to college – several colleges – because, like I said, coming from a large family I didn't get much support. I got a few hundred dollars from my parents for my entire college education. It was at a time when I was supporting my boyfriend (laughs)...

I went to four different colleges, eventually graduating from here, SUNY (State University of New York) New Paltz. I got a degree in biology because I thought, "I can't really decide exactly what I want to do." But I knew it's going to be in the health-related fields because I'm so passionate – about climbing, obviously – but also just about how the body works. I read an anatomy and physiology textbook cover-to-cover without even taking the class just because I wanted to know more.

I'm a curious person. That, I think, is a quality that's necessary for education; if you're not curious then you're not interested, and if you're not interested then you're not going to learn. I got an education in biology so I could go into physical therapy – that was the original idea – or become a doctor. But I figured that doctors had to work too much.

I like to work in my particular profession, which is fun and is climbing-related. Actually no one pays me to climb... my work is related to climbing. In any case I like my work, but I don't want to let my work make my life unbalanced, to take away from my enjoyment of life. That's the tough part: figuring out how to balance your work, your passions for other things – like climbing or whatever it is – and family life.

People usually have something going on other than work, hopefully. In my case it feels like I have three or four things that I'm juggling: climbing, traveling, Owen (her son), and the work that I do in relation to all that stuff.

Some of the travel is related to work, like this trip. Other times I travel just for myself, like my trip to Thailand to go climbing. People expect me to climb at a high level – that's my image. It's not that I feel I have to climb, but I feel that climbing is so much a part of my well-being that if I don't do it, I don't feel as good. I'm lucky that my work, my passion, and my lifestyle all fit together.

LS: What is your work?

LH: I'm an ambassador for Patagonia (the outdoor clothing company). That means that I'm an environmental activist, in part, and it involves a certain amount of public relations for them. They don't even know what I do, sometimes.

For example, tomorrow I'm going to do an interview for *Forbes* magazine, for *Forbes* TV, I don't know how it all works, but they do some kind of video stuff. Patagonia gives me a certain amount of freedom because I'm self-motivated and responsible. So I said to *Forbes*, "OK, I'll come and do that."

I'm a spokesperson, I do photo shoots, video shoots, a little bit of writing for their website and for mine. I have a website and a blog, which I don't keep up as much as bloggers are expected to, but that's not my kind of thing. It's just not me to sit there and catalog my life. It takes too much time.

What else do I do: lots of presentations. I've done that for 25 years. I became a professional in 1988 and did 30 slide shows that year.

LS: Is that how you started making money from your climbing activities?

LH: I rarely charge for the slide shows. That wasn't my income per se. I worked for Chouinard Equipment, which became Black Diamond (the climbing equipment company

– Ed.), and they were importing Scarpa climbing shoes. They wanted a vehicle for advertising, which I was. If you had to characterize what I do, you'd say it was marketing and advertising.

LS: If you think about a young person making decisions about his or her future, what kind of problems do you think he or she might run into? How have you overcome these problems in your life?

LH: I think for young people it's really hard to decide specifically what they want to do. But you have to choose something, even if it's not exactly what you're going to end up doing. It's a step in that direction.

Maybe you'll have a general idea, like I did: biology. It was a generally appropriate area, but the specifics weren't there at all. I refined it when the time came to make those decisions. I think the hardest question is, "What do I do?" and, "What am I good at?" You don't know unless you try… something.

Some people have problems with traditional learning: sitting still, listening to a lecture, taking notes. There's visual learning, there's kinesthetic learning. Maybe traditional college education or academic study is not the right path.

Maybe a person is good with their hands or can see things in three dimensions; that would fit in with some aspect of traditional college, like engineering. At the same time they may have to be disciplined in order to overcome something they lack or find support on the academic side in order to exploit their strengths.

You have to develop some sort of service or else you're going to end up having a job that doesn't bring the satisfaction and money you need. If you don't have a skill, then minimum wage is pretty minimal. And then you get stuck in a vicious cycle where you can't go out and do anything different because you don't have the time; you're too busy working in order to earn a living. That's something serious to consider.

LS: Your profession isn't traditional, and it doesn't seem to draw specifically on your college experiences; marketing and ambassadorship weren't part of your college curriculum. Did you look for opportunities outside of your intended area study, or did you see yourself on a kind of dual track?

LH: Professional climbing didn't exist at that time. I was making money through occasional TV jobs, competing on the *Survival of the Fittest* TV series that I won four years in a row. That's what paid for my college education. I was lucky that I didn't have to have a job and go to school for very long. I did work at an outdoor shop, and I started a guiding service when I lived here in New Paltz. I took people climbing. That was at the end of my college studies.

In my last year of college I didn't work at all. I took a loan out, the only loan I've ever taken other than to buy my house. I paid it back through the income I got from my guiding company that I'd started just after I graduated.

LS: You live an interesting life. Did you have to work at making this happen? I mean if you're worried about being stuck working for minimum wage, then winning extreme sports competitions is not the highway to high wages – economic security being somewhat lacking!

LH: (Laughs) At the time it was fast money. No, it wasn't really part of my thinking. I wasn't putting those two ideas together. I was pursuing a college education so that I could have a profession. The things that came along were just bonuses.

When I got a regular job it was working for minimum wage in an outdoor store that sold climbing equipment. But it drew upon things I knew, and I was interested in the activities that people were asking about. What came through for me in the end was following my passion – doing what I really wanted to do – versus doing what I was told would be the key to success.

LS: Since we've done some similar things, I have my own ideas of what resources you drew upon to get where you are. The idea of "determination" comes to mind. Do you think you were using your determination to make things happen for you, or do you think you were opportunistic in making sure you got the most out of everything?

LH: I'm not an opportunistic person, so I would have to disagree with that. When somebody is passionate about something, they create their own reality. Your positive thoughts about whatever you do brings the opportunity, it attracts the opportunity. I wasn't even conscious of that at the time, but that's what I believe now. You have more power than you're aware of just by virtue of what you think. It's an aura that you create.

I took advantage of the opportunities that came my way, but they came my way because of who I am and what I was doing. I didn't realize there was much value to these things; it's really hard to quantify. In the end people seem to find inspiration in the fact that through determination and focus I have been able to do things that other people haven't done.

(At this point Lynn's son Owen, who is three years old, comes asking for help in finding his Spider-Man gloves. – Ed.)

LS: Taking care of your son must take a lot of time. Do you have help taking care of him? Do you rely on your family? Do you take him everywhere?

LH: Yes and no. He goes to school three days a week, but that's pretty new. He was going to daycare, but now he's going to a Montessori school, which is good for him because he's got a lot of energy that needs to be directed. But it's free form and he gets to choose what he does. There's a structure, but there's choice, and I think that's the way life is, really.

The structure is that you've got to respect others, and there's a certain rhythm to the day. There's meal time, resting time, play time, and focus time. "Play" they call it, but it's really learning. Play is learning, it's just unstructured learning. Play can be extremely informative and instrumental in your learning.

I rely on the school, on Owen's dad, and on babysitters, but I've been traveling so much lately that I've lost touch with the rhythm of having somebody else available. I run a business, I run climbing camps, I'm an ambassador for Patagonia, I go on my own climbing trips and trips for photo shoots. Since my business is small, I run every aspect of it: accounting, taxes, communications, advertising. The balance is tricky, especially being a single mother as I am.

A good friend of mine is a perfect example of what can happen if you don't consider viable career options. He rebelled against everything in high school and had a hard time growing up. He had a hard time sitting down at school. He's a smart person, but doesn't do well in traditional learning situations.

He didn't develop a specific work-related skill, he didn't get an education, he didn't even graduate from high school. He lives in Boulder, Colorado, a town filled with very educated people, professionals, and athletes. He feels really insecure in this environment because he doesn't have the skills and the preparation that he could have had, had he made different choices.

He now works on cell phone towers. At least climbing provided him with a skill that pays more than minimum wage, but it's not an easy life. He doesn't have a predictable schedule and sometimes works at night when they close the cell towers. His company bids on the jobs, and sometimes they don't tell him he's needed until the day of the job, which can be a disruptive way to live.

That's a classic example of a person who didn't really understand the ramifications of the decisions he made at a critical time in his life. It's not too late to go back, but now he has a kid, and he has a job. How does he go back to school? He can't afford it. It's hard just surviving, much less have extra time and money to dedicate towards starting a new career.

LS: You're looking at your future with a lot of concern and attention. It reminds me of a pilot scanning the sky for air traffic, looking back and forth across all the sectors. Do you think about your future in a way that's different from other people?

LH: I'm a practical person. It's my temperament, my nature. My well-being depends on it. Today's generation of kids are more pampered and sheltered than I was. My parents let me go to Yosemite Valley when I was 17. I don't know many parents who would let their 17-year-old kids do that. Don't know any.

LS: Did your parents give you this freedom because they were generally permissive, or because they recognized that you could handle the responsibility?

LH: Actually, my parents got divorced when I was 16. They were having epics in their own lives and probably didn't have the ability to focus on all the things their kids were doing. That was one reason.

They were also used to their kids doing a lot of different things. They couldn't really micro-manage all of that stuff. They gave us a lot of freedom. I think they recognized value in it, and it was a good thing for us. I also think that the times were different then.

The 60s were a different era. There were a lot of beautiful things in the 60s that we've lost. Our society has become more materialistic and egocentric. I think something's been lost. The nuclear family is more isolated, and I'm not sure why. These are just things that I've seen from having traveled the world. I've seen that as Americans we don't have as much connection to our community, especially out West.

People, for whatever reason, are trying to shelter their kids, but it's not doing them a service. When kids suddenly become adults, they have to realize that they're responsible for their own choices; but if their parents have coveted and protected them, then they don't see it coming. And it goes really fast... they turn 18, they're legal adults... and then they're 21 and maybe they've finished college, or maybe not.

And their parents are pretty much like, "OK, you're done! You should be going off, having a place of your own, girlfriend, boyfriend whatever..." They don't think their kids are their responsibility anymore, and they expect their kids just to pick it up. But it's not so easy for kids if they haven't been prepared for the responsibility. It's normal, it's natural – no matter how you're raised – you're responsible for yourself when you become an adult. It's disabling to have that kind of overbearing parenting who teaches you the opposite.

LS: How does one's development in judging other people fit in?

LH: I think your choice of people is important in every aspect of your life. Working with people you get along with will produce better results. You have to really look at situations where you're not getting along with people and say, "Am I being unreasonable, or is that other person being unreasonable, or is it a combination of the two?"

It's important to choose what's appropriate in all aspects. People are certainly the key to most businesses and most occupations.

19. FRED BECKEY

History　　　　　　　　Late　　　　Born 1923, Düsseldorf, Germany

I was 16 years old, sitting at the kitchen table when the phone rang, and to my complete amazement the caller announced himself – in a now familiar rising inflection – as: "Hello, this is Fred Beckeeeey…" Fred was already a legend; why was he calling me?

He got right to the point: he had designs on the new route my friends and I were planning to attempt on Alaska's Mt. Fairweather, a mountain that rises 15,000 feet from the sea. He began his planning first, he said, so we should go elsewhere!

We wouldn't; we had too much invested in this, our first mountaineering adventure. Instead, he chose a different route, and our groups crossed paths on our way in to the mountain. Then, four weeks later, we again joined him to wander lost among the crevasses at the snout of the glacier as we all tried to reach the sea.

We were only 17, but the endless humping of 100-lb loads up and down the frozen mountainside left us broken and exhausted. When we finally reached the shore, we all dropped our packs, and our pants, to hang our numb, sorry butts over the warmth of a driftwood fire. All we could think of was food and rest, but Fred was already scheming to fly right away to the unclimbed peaks of the Stikine Icecap. Were we game? We thought he was nuts!

Fred Beckey started pioneering difficult routes up mountains as a teenager, and he has not paused since. He is reputed to have accomplished more mountaineering first ascents than anyone, anywhere, ever. The undisputed expert on North American mountaineering, Fred was 85 at the time of this interview and had to shift gears, going to Asia to put up new routes in the remote peaks in southern China.

"He was driven, like nobody I've ever met. Relentlessly, totally obsessive, that's who Fred is. Obsessive behavior can lead to absolute genius."

— Yvon Chouinard, Founder of Black Diamond Equipment, and Patagonia Clothing, from the 2018 movie, *Dirtbag: The Legend of Fred Beckey.*

FRED BECKEY

Postscript: Fred passed away peacefully on October 30th, 2017. He was 94.

Excerpts

"I've sort of figured that if I work, don't play games, and apportion my free time, then I'll have enough to go climbing, or skiing, or whatever I want to do… Most people get married and by the time they're 30 they've got a couple of kids, and then they're strapped down. Then they have to work. They'd better get a job with somebody, stay with it, and get their salary, pension, or whatever. Right or wrong, I had more flexibility. It just worked out that way…"

"Somebody told me, 'Save 10, 15, 20% of what you make and put it in the bank.' And I did that, always. I'd spend so much, and put some of it in the bank. It added up after a while, with compound interest, you know, it takes a while. I started with nothing; my folks didn't have a nickel. It sort of worked that way, you just kind of keep at it…"

"I started out being pretty good in high school math, but then I got tired of it. I'm not interested in equations and all that; it's too abstract for me. If I had to start over again, I'll tell you, I'd just as soon get a job selling printing. Easy job, drive around in a car, shake hands, talk to the pretty secretary… It's kind of fun. Give me a company car and I'd take off on Friday afternoon for the High Sierra. You could do worse…"

"You know, you get asked this, 'Why do people climb?' There's got to be a reason … I can't figure it out. It's a lot easier to play tennis or golf, bicycle; a lot less stress, not dangerous, doesn't have the risk, doesn't have the suffering. Climbing's got a lot of suffering, a lot of it…"

"I was suddenly brought to a dead stop, with arms outspread, clinging close to the face of the rock, unable to move hand or foot either up or down. My doom appeared fixed. I must fall. There would be a moment of bewilderment, and then a lifeless rumble down… to the glacier below.

"When this final danger flashed upon me… my mind seemed to fill with a stifling smoke. But this terrible eclipse lasted only for a moment, when life blazed forth again with preternatural clearness. I seemed suddenly to be possessed of a new sense. The other self… came forward and assumed control… I found a way without effort, and soon stood upon the topmost crag in the blessed light."

— John Muir, recounting his 1872 solo, first ascent of Mt. Ritter, California

Interview   New Paltz, New York, December 2007

LS: Fred, I want to get some thoughts from you for this book I'm writing. It's a book for young people, for teenagers, and it's about what learning could be…

Fred Beckey: So, have you seen Metcalf? (Peter Metcalf, CEO of Black Diamond Equipment, and my climbing partner when we were young. – Ed.)

LS: Every year he sends this one-page description that summarizes his life over the past year. He sends it to all his friends around Christmas time. It's something his father used to do. I like it, and if you know him well enough to read between the lines… you can tell what's happening. He stills climbs, and he keeps in shape.

FB: You still climbing?

LS: No, I go flying. I have a glider. I keep in shape.

FB: I have climbing friends in Canada who do that. They go paragliding and… I don't do it. I'm not brave enough. I bet it's fun.

LS: Yeah, you don't have to stay in shape for it. Well, maybe you do. So how do you stay in shape? Do you climb a lot?

FB: I just stick to skiing and climbing. That's all I do for fun.

LS: So how did you start climbing?

FB: Oh, I don't know. Just sort of got into it by accident living in Seattle. I had a lot to do with the Boy Scouts. It's hard to find exact reasons why you do things.

I don't even know why people climb. I can't figure it out. It's a lot easier to play tennis or golf, bicycle; a lot less stress, not dangerous, doesn't have the risk, doesn't have the suffering. Climbing's got a lot of suffering, a lot of it.

You know, you get asked this, "Why do people climb?" There's got to be a reason. Part of it's the beauty of the mountains, but you can get that from hiking. You go hiking and essentially get the same scenery. You don't look down a cliff, but… most of it.

LS: Did you hike? You were always climbing, right?

FB: Well, you have to hike to get to a climb. I seldom go out just to hike. I used to. But for quite a few peaks, particularly in the Cascades, you have to do a lot of hiking to get to them. So that's my hiking (laughs)!

Have you read this book of Jon Krakauer's about the guy who went hiking in Alaska: *Into the Wild*? They're making a movie of it, I guess. I saw an ad in the *New York Times*.

LS: It's not a book I'd think you'd make a movie out of.

FB: The guy got caught in big trouble in Alaska, and he didn't have enough food with him. You know, you don't go up there with three days' food and hope you can stay there 21 days; and don't go up there without fuel, hoping you can find some wood on the glacier. Sure, you're asking for trouble.

You know, Lincoln, I really fail to understand what's interesting about that story. The guy sounded like a spoiled kid from a well-to-do family who had nothing better to do but rebel against society. There are thousands of people like that around; every bum holding a sign on the street is essentially doing that.

So why is he so different or unusual? To me, everything he did seemed like he was an idealist who's rebelling, and about why? I don't know. He's taking advantage of civilization. I have friends who think it's fascinating, and other people think it's ridiculous. I don't know.

LS: I want to know more about how you learned. Was there somebody who taught you? Did you just pick it up?

FB: We were with the Boy Scouts, but the Boy Scouts were not into climbing, they were into scrambling. We put a rope on a couple of times, like on a glacier, Mt. Olympus, but I don't think anyone knew how to rescue somebody from a crevasse. I doubt it. I don't remember ever falling into one.

LS: So how did you learn? You know, I learned a lot from you, I think.

FB: Yeah, well how'd you learn? You went to Mt. Fairweather. But where did you learn to be safe on a glacier?

LS: I read books. I thought I learned something through books, but I didn't. Mostly watching other people. You taught me to always carry ascenders on my belt and to have everything ready in case I found myself hanging upside down in a crevasse.

FB: A lot of people have gotten in trouble on glaciers by not having ascenders, or whatever. I always carry them with me, you never know. You run into people who run onto glaciers and don't tie into the rope. Who was the guy who made the winter climb of Mt. McKinley, about 1970? They didn't rope-up and he fell in a crevasse, and he's still there. That's a calculated risk. Nobody else fell in, just he did.

Crevasses scare me more than anything else. You never really know. I'm sure you've stepped into them. I have a picture in the slide show – people kind of laugh when I tell them the story. We were climbing near Mt. Saint Elias; we went through a bunch of ice falls and seracs. It wasn't really difficult, but it was dangerous. Then we got up onto some easier terrain.

We were roped-up, there were four of us, and we're going up to the summit along a moderate snow ridge. Giant cornices leaned out over the ridge, so we kept away from the cornices. We took turns and I happened to be going first. It wasn't really leading, it was just a matter of kicking steps. The snow was pretty good.

We were a couple of hundred meters from the summit. All of a sudden the snow collapsed under me. There were no signs, but all of a sudden I was down about 40 feet. Wham! Just like that. The crevasse actually ran the same way as the ridge, so we weren't expecting it, and the rope kind of sawed in lengthwise, so I went down about 40 feet.

I got out eventually using prussic knots. It was a little bit cold, and it was kind of scary. I have a picture that shows the hole and the rope going down into it. And I tell people, "What you're seeing is the rope going into the crevasse, and I'm down there about 40 feet trying to get out." In the meantime my friends are having lunch and taking pictures. And the audience all laughs. I don't know what's funny about it, but something is, I guess.

LS: Tell me about being competitive. You were pretty competitive with Chouinard (Yvon Chouinard, climber and founder of Patagonia, Inc. – Ed.) and other people, in order to be the first person to do a new route.

FB: No, never with Chouinard. Ed Cooper was a little competitive in climbing. One time he jumped us on a climb on purpose. It was kind of funny. He climbed with some of the same people that I did, and sometimes you'd know that somebody's interested in doing a particular route. You'd think, "I'll get up there next weekend, before them, and beat them out." In hindsight it's kind of amusing. It's no big deal.

As I recall, I came up there with a friend, across a mountain from Seattle, and we had to hike up a couple of hours. It was called Snow Creek Wall, near Leavenworth. We got up there and they were already way up there on the route. We were probably annoyed, probably, but we did another climb. I'm not annoyed anymore, and I've climbed with him after that, in different places.

LS: You were famous for being really secretive about where you were going and what you had planned.

FB: Not really. Not that much. A little bit. It's really kind of childish. What's the psychology of it? I suppose that beneath it all there's a certain amount of ego. I suppose: vanity.

Yeah. I admit that when you're going around making first ascents, you don't go around bragging about what you're going to do to all your friends who are climbers. I suppose there's some of that.

LS: You still do that?

FB: Nah, not really. When you get down to it, I think it stems from there being a limited number of climbs that can be done. So maybe people are a little bit jealous – they want to climb some route that nobody's done yet. But in the mountains, like in the Cascades, for example, there are so many routes left to do. Canada is full of them. You fly to Alaska, and if you have good weather you can see all the peaks up there; it's mind-boggling. Unclimbed peaks. Even on the ones that have been climbed, there are potential new routes. So, who cares?

You know, everybody likes a pretty woman: "Hey, I'd like to have her as a girlfriend." But you go to a big city like New York, or LA, and there's millions of people around. You can't catch everybody. You can't catch every climb.

I actually haven't done a new route for at least three or four years. We did some climbs last year, maybe one variation of a pitch; I've gotten to the point where I'm just as happy doing a good, traditional climb.

LS: That's a change.

FB: A little bit, maybe. There's always new things to do. I've got some things in mind that I'd like to do next year.

LS: So why? Why did you change? Is it the risk? There's always more risk with first ascents.

FB: I don't know. I'm really not sure. I'd rather climb an established route here in the Gunks, than go out to look for some new route that hadn't been done yet and end up spending all my time.

LS: That's right, a person spends a lot of time doing a new route. Do you consider yourself a professional climber? Is there such a thing as a professional climber?

FB: A guide is a professional climber. There are at least half a dozen young guys who are good climbers, who are sponsored by Black Diamond. Black Diamond doesn't give me anything. I get a pro deal: 40% off.

Patagonia gave me some free clothes for the picture on their catalog, but I've got so many clothes now. I've got about five jackets like this! I mean, how many can you wear? I have jackets like this that are 20 years old and, except for maybe a little hole, they're still good. They'll last forever! How many do you need?

This whole fashion thing... A lot of people go shopping looking like they're ready to go to Mt. Everest: down jackets in New York City. They're trying to copy somebody who climbs, I guess. I really don't know. Of course the companies are pushing that real hard: that's where the money is.

LS: What's your attitude towards money? Were you ever concerned?

FB: I've never thought about it. I get by a little bit better than I used to. I guess you have your choice of trying to make money or getting involved with adventure.

The way society is now, if you don't have an education of some kind, or skill, you're going to have a tough time meeting ends. Unless the government pays you off, which sometimes happens, or you join the army and get shot at in Iraq, and come back and you probably have a pension. It seems to me like there's a huge difference in people's abilities and their luck at making money.

I've thought about teaching school. I've never really done it, but I don't think you have to be terribly smart to get a teaching degree. Just mind your own business and teach high school, or grade school. It's a sure thing. I think if I was starting over again that's what I'd do. You have a guaranteed salary, unless you molest boys or girls, which some teachers seem to do.

You've got a ticket for life: you've got a salary, a summer vacation, a few weeks off here and there. You've got retirement pay, you've got medical insurance, you've got a lot of things going for you! There's a lot of stuff you've got to do. If you've got an 11 o'clock class, then you've got to be there at 11 o'clock. You've got to play games with the administration, I suppose, but it's almost a sure thing.

I've read articles like in, oh, in the *Wall Street Journal* or some newspaper, that people that work for the government, the county, the city, they've got a surefire job. Unless they do something like cross paths with the wrong people, or swindle money or something, they come out better in the long run than somebody who's worked for a big company like Proctor and Gamble, or Ford Motor Company – they don't give pensions anymore. I don't know.

I've sort of figured that if I work, don't play games, and apportion my free time, then I'll have enough to go climbing, or skiing, or whatever I want to do. It doesn't always work that way.

Most people get married and by the time they're 30 they've got a couple of kids, and then they're strapped down. Then they have to work. They'd better get a job with somebody, stay with it, and get their salary, pension, or whatever. Right or wrong, I had more flexibility. It just worked out that way.

LS: You did a lot of temporary jobs, didn't you?

FB: I wouldn't say temporary. I got started somehow, really by complete accident, after I got out of school, being involved with marketing and selling printing out in Seattle. Kind of a fun job, really.

I worked for the Seattle newspaper for a year selling advertising space. I'd call on customers, maybe the department store J.C. Penny; they'd have a big ad in the Sunday papers selling clothing. It was a lot of running around. A lot of work, really, for what you got out of it.

Then I got involved with a big printing company called Craftsman Press. Printing is actually the seventh, eighth, or ninth biggest industry in North America. Most people don't think about it. When you think of all these catalogs, newspapers, and magazines… it's a huge business. That catalog that Patagonia prints – I believe they send out 700,000 – and with companies like L.L. Bean, there must be millions!

A big printing company like Craftsman Press, they've got contracts like printing the phone book maybe, printing big catalogs, and Boeing Annual Reports. Annual reports: you've got to get them out to millions of people. That's a big business; it's competitive.

So I got involved with selling and marketing, calling on customers. I had some free time between jobs, and that's the way it worked, not on purpose. I'd try to go climbing in Alaska, or wherever, sort of in between jobs. It just worked that way, pretty much by luck.

LS: It never seemed to get in your way!

FB: Sometimes it got in my way. Sometimes I couldn't go off climbing during the summer. But you're right. It's kind of funny, in almost every slide show I give – if we have questions and answers afterwards – someone will raise their hand and I can almost say, "I know what you're going to ask me: How did you get by with all this?" The reason they want to know is how can they do it! That's alright.

LS: So, what do you say? Can they do it?

FB: I don't know. I don't have any secret. The other secret is to be extremely brilliant at something. I know one guy who's, like, a Nobel-Prize-quality physicist. He could say, "I'll work for you for four months a year, and then I'm going to go play the rest of the year." And they'll say, "We'll be glad to have you. Please come back." Some of these computer geniuses, they can do the same thing.

There's one guy I know, he's not really a close personal friend, but I talked to him at one time about getting me a job at Microsoft. It's not my thing, really – technology. I'm computer dumb. I don't even understand how electricity works. I have a little Dell desktop just to do word processing. I know how to check email, and I know how to use Word. In fact, I find Word very handy for doing a book. Anything. I used to have a typewriter.

LS: Nah, you don't want that. Out with that.

FB: What should I know about computers that I don't know?

LS: These little Blackberrys might be convenient for you. They're like a cell phone that you can do email on.

FB: Yeah, I have a cell phone. I do everything by paper, I write everything on paper. I'm not saying it's the wrong way or the right way. I can't see myself going to work for some company like Microsoft. I don't know what I could do for them! Maybe some research. I'm fairly good at geography, spatial things, and research. The rest of it: no. I'm not interested in physics, or chemistry, or math.

I started out being pretty good in high school math, but then I got tired of it. I'm not interested in equations and all that, it's too abstract for me. If I had to start over again, I'll tell you, I'd just as soon get a job selling printing. Easy job, drive around in a car, shake hands, talk to the pretty secretary, "Here's what we can do for you. I'll get you some quotations tomorrow." That's what I did for about four years in LA. It's kind of fun. Give me a company car and I'd take off on Friday afternoon for the High Sierra. You could do worse.

LS: Why did you stop?

FB: I don't know. The company got bought out by somebody, and the job kind of fell flat. I went from there to Oregon. I was interested in doing this book, this history book. We called it *A Range of Glaciers*, but it's about the early history of the Cascades (*A Range of Glaciers: The Exploration and Survey of the Northern Cascade Range*, by Fred Beckey, Oregon Historical Society Press, 2003).

I spent two solid years in Portland. The Oregon Historical Society got some money. I went all over doing research. I spent a month in the National Archives in Washington, D.C. I went to Yale. You know, to different library archives. I put that together; it was a lot of work. I don't have a PhD, but I think this was as much work as one or two PhDs. A lot of work. It was kind of fun, but I don't want to do anything like that again.

LS: How did you learn how to do that?

FB: I don't know. I never took a course. I've never taken a course in geology, but I know more about geology than most people. I'm not a geologist, but... I know nothing about mineralogy. I can't tell you what that's made of. I know granite's made out of quartz, feldspar and biotite, but outside of that... I've always felt I worked pretty hard.

When I was going to college in Seattle, I had a job that really suited me. I worked on weekends, vacation time, and in the summers driving a delivery truck – like United Parcel, but smaller. They had maybe 20 trucks. Somebody would load the truck up and we would deliver to 20 or 30 places. You only had about three hours to do it, and then you had to come back and pick up stuff. It's kind of like, "Go, Go, Go!" You're really moving. You'd be on the clock, and you had to be on the ball. You had to hop with other drivers. Made a lot of girlfriends that way. Oh yeah! Well, not a lot, but sometimes.

Somebody told me, "Save 10, 15, 20% of what you make and put it in the bank." And I did that, always. I'd spend so much, and put some of it in the bank. It added up after a while, with compound interest, you know, it takes a while. I started with nothing; my folks didn't have a nickel. It sort of worked that way, you just kind of keep at it.

A lot of people are used to being spend-aholics. They see some car they can't afford, a $40,000 Lexus, but they don't really need that car. They need a car, but they could buy a $3,000 Ford from somebody's grandmother that's still in good shape. But that wouldn't have any prestige. People say, "Aw, I can't have people see me driving that beat-up old car!" A lot of it's vanity and ego. I don't know. I could be wrong.

LS: You used to make a show of not having vanity and ego. You used to dress in worn-out clothes and drive an old car. Was that true, or was that a show?

FB: I didn't deliberately wear old clothes! Yeah, some. Climbing trips and skiing trips?

LS: Yeah.

FB: Yeah, some.

I've always liked to travel. My brother doesn't. He hates travel. He's living in Germany now. I don't know if he's ever been to Spain. Never been to the Himalayas or anywhere. He's been nowhere!

I like to travel; some people don't. Maybe that's why I'm here instead of hanging around Seattle doing paperwork for somebody. It's kind of fun. Maybe not for everybody.

So you're working with a computer business?

LS: No, I'm moving on to ... I'm doing this book, which is about learning, and which I'm putting on the Internet, where it will be free for kids to view. They don't buy books anyway, kids under 20.

FB: Kind of like a self-help book?

LS: It's particularly for learning. It's about what learning really is, and how it's not just school.

FB: It's a "how to" book, how to learn, how to study?

LS: Not a "how to," but how people did it: like how did Fred Beckey become Fred Beckey, and how all these other people did what they did. I also talk to young people who are thinking about going into film or becoming a book writer. I get their story about what they think they need to learn. Then I talk to older people who tell me what they actually did need to learn.

I've got 10 different subjects, and in each field I talk to a young person, a middle-aged person, and an older person, all in the same field. I've got you, Lynn Hill, and a teenager whose interest in the outdoors started with going to a survival school. She talks about how wonderful it was to make her own shelter and sleep in a pile of leaves.

FB: I think it's good for people to get back some of the primitive stuff. People now are spoiled. They grow up in a house and never have to go outside. They go to Yosemite and never get out of their camper-trailer.

Supposedly John Muir (1838–1914, American naturalist, founder of the Sierra Club) climbed a tree in the Sierras somewhere and spent all night in the tree with the wind buffeting him back and forth. He didn't have to – and he could get off the tree – but he must have wanted to experience the wind: a little bit of adventure.

How did you guys get that Mt. Fairweather trip going? You guys were pretty young at that time. Did you do it through college or something?

LS: No, we were in high school.

FB: That's right! That's unbelievable. I never heard of anybody that young starting out on a major trip. That's serious mountaineering! Most high school kids, you know, they're interested in ping-pong, and chasing women, raising hell. I can't think of any high school group, or people in high school, who planned a major trip. They might go to the Tetons to climb, but not on an expedition to Alaska.

LS: We were young. We had all the time in the world. We had no jobs. We were going to school. What do you do in school? You don't do anything in school.

We didn't think it was so important at the time. It was just something that we did. But now, 35 years later, I see that it was quite a big thing. There was a lot more suffering than we expected.

FB: Did someone tell you how to get there and what to take?

LS: No. You know, it's not that hard. If you call the bush pilot, they'll get you there. There were things we didn't know about, like walking on glaciers.

FB: Yeah, you get used to the conditions in the White Mountains (in Northern New Hampshire), and you get used to winter camping and survival. But high school is pretty young. Most people don't even dream of doing something like that even in college.

LS: We dreamed of it.

FB: Well, maybe if their parents were climbers.

LS: No, our parents had nothing to do with the outdoors. We read books, we made it up. Remember that book *Mountaineering: The Freedom of the Hills*?

FB: Yeah. That's great.

LS: You started pretty young, too.

FB: Scouts first. Then I got involved with the Seattle Mountaineers, took a course; then I met people. You know, you kind of get into it.

LS: Did you have a climbing partner in the beginning whom you stuck with, like I did with Peter Metcalf?

FB: I climbed with different people. I don't remember. There were a couple of different people, but they quit. They don't stick with it. I didn't have any affiliation with anybody, really.

LS: Are you planning to go to Asia again?

FB: I hope so, maybe next year, maybe in September. China is full of unclimbed mountains. New routes to do, it's full of them. More than any place in the world.

LS: Is it difficult?

FB: Oh, yeah, and dangerous. They seem to have a lot of avalanches. A lot of snow in certain places at certain times. Pretty unknown, and it costs money. It's getting expensive. The Chinese see what's happening in Nepal, and they try to milk you for going there. India, Nepal, China, Pakistan: they see rich Westerners – French, Germans, Americans, Canadians – and they make you pay to get a permit. You almost need a trekking agency.

I don't know much about the rest of them, but in China they have a quasi-government agency called "The Chinese Mountaineering Association"; it's a racket. Everybody that goes to China has to pay them off: payola. The first time I went there, they sent an interpreter and a liaison officer along; they don't do anything except drink coffee and eat food.

Now I work with a Chinese agency that runs the trips for me. It's like Mountain Travel (Mountain Travel Sobek, based in Emeryville, California – Ed.). They organize the trip, they get the permit, and I just show up! Show up in Chengdu and they pick us up in a truck. They do all the organizing for you. They do everything except the actual climbing.

Some people go over there on their own and try to get by with Pidgin Chinese, take buses around. A lot of suffering and misery. You get stopped by the army or at some gate point: "Who are you?" You can't speak anything, it's crazy. I don't want to go through that.

Charlie Fowler did that. That's what I've heard. Maybe that had something to do with why he got killed. (Charlie Fowler was killed in an avalanche in 2006. – Ed.) I don't know. He managed to do it, but I think he knew some Chinese. That's one way to do it, but I don't personally want to do that. I'd like to go back. There are lots of great climbs to do.

LS: Can you get the information you need? Are there photos and maps?

FB: Yeah, it's like everything else: you research it. There's actually a Japanese guy named Nakamura, he's the expert in China. He knows more about the Chinese mountains than anybody in China (laughs)! It's kind of funny, eh? He really knows his stuff. He puts out a booklet once or twice a year called Japanese Alpine News, and it's all about climbing in China.

If I want to go to a certain place, I'll read what I can, and then send him an email asking, "Who do you recommend?" China is maybe like Alaska used to be in Brad Washburn's days: unclimbed stuff all over.

So why do people climb instead of playing tennis, or going to the beach, or riding a bicycle? Riding a bicycle through the Catskills or the Adirondacks: there's a little bit of an adventure in it, but it's not very dangerous... unless you hit a tree. Why do they go climbing instead of doing that?

LS: Because climbing is harder. I think it's about fear. You can make it as hard as you want.

FB: You can wrestle, or box with Mike Tyson, and get the hell beat out of you. That's hard too.

LS: I think there's something about being alone. It's just you against nature. And you can trust nature; it doesn't have an attitude. A glacier doesn't play favorites.

FB: Uh huh. You're trusting nature. You're risking your ability against nature. You see a reflection of yourself in nature. That might be it!

PHYSICS

20. HAMILTON SHU

History   Early   Born 1990

Hamilton "Ham" Shu's parents began teaching him numbers and letters using flash cards before he was three. As the son of an engineer and a teacher, he developed an interest in learning and in building things. Sometimes precocious, and at other times a pest, he has been taking apart and rebuilding telephones, remote controls, traffic lights, and whatever other machines he has been able to get his hands on. Ham wants to become an engineer and to follow in his father's footsteps.

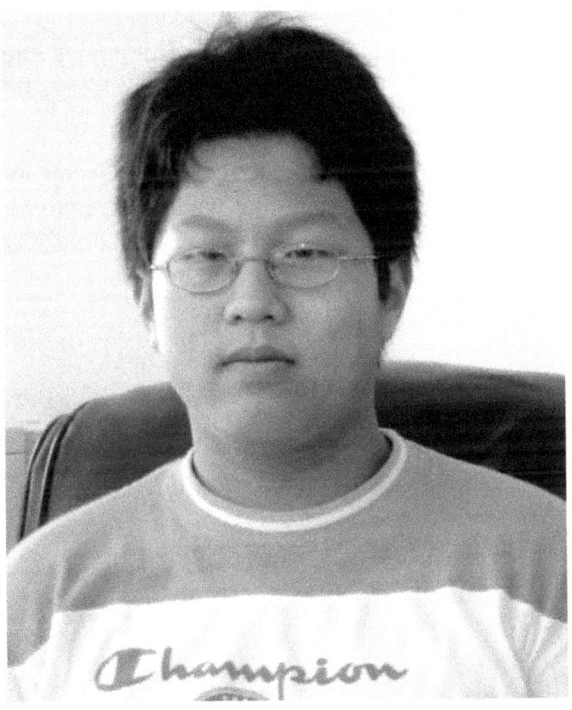

Excerpts

"School, for me, started at home... back when I was about three. I remember my parents trying to teach me numbers; they had these little cards and they'd hold them in front of me and ask me what number it was. I would answer them, and then that night I would go into their room and hide them so that I didn't have to do it the next day... The same thing with the alphabet. It finally just drilled into my head..."

"I was tired. I would stay up late and do stuff at home because I knew I could sleep at school. Like if there was something I had to solder, or something to glue that required time to cure, I'd stay up and watch it. The next day at school I'd go to sleep from 8am to 10am, switch classes, and then go to sleep again..."

"I'm very good at taking tests and making it look like I'm paying attention. I would just go, take tests, and ace 'em. Like in calculus I'd sleep, take a test, finish it, and then go back to sleep..."

"Right now I'm helping my dad with his patents... My dad wants me to do a patent on tire sensors, something I read in a magazine that made me say to him, 'Wouldn't it be easier if this?' and I drew a picture. And my dad's like, 'Just do it!' And I'm like, 'OK, I will!'"

"When vision comes to you, eternity is its black velvet backdrop. Everything else comes out on the stage to sing and dance. Some of it fits in with the grandeur of that backdrop, and some of it only clashes, looking ugly and cheap. You end up wanting to adjust your life so that it's full of stuff that fits in with eternity, and not crammed with things that don't matter."

— Grace Llewellyn, in *The Teenage Liberation Handbook*

Interview   Carrollton, Georgia, October 2006

Hamilton Shu: School, for me, started at home... back when I was about three. I remember my parents trying to teach me numbers; they had these little cards and they'd hold them in front of me and ask me what number it was. I would answer them, and then that night I would go into their room and hide them so that I didn't have to do it the next day. My parents would always find them, and then I'd have to do it all over again, every day, at least three times a day. The same thing with the alphabet. It finally just drilled into my head.

The first standard learning was in kindergarten, which I thought was useless at the time. Kindergarten didn't teach me anything except not to piss off my teacher, and not to eat Play-dough.

First grade was where I actually started learning. The teacher I had gave me all these things, because I would always do the homework and excel at it. She'd give me these second-grade things, and I'd finish them in class. She suggested that I skip to the third grade, and I skipped to the third grade.

That was when the age issue first came out. I was almost two years younger than some of the students, and there was the socializing issue. Most of my life I've had really good success socializing with older people. If I try to relate to people my age, I really don't get much across.

LS: Did that social stuff ever catch up with you?

HS: It was always really easy. Most of the places I've been to it's, like, "Wow, you're two years younger than us? That's really cool!" That's what it's been like in every single school I've ever been in.

LS: Where do you think you got that skill? Are you the youngest child of older brothers and sisters?

HS: I only have one brother; he's my older brother. It's just always been like that. With my brother it's the same way. It's never been an issue for us. It's always been really easy for us to socialize and interact with older people.

LS: What changed for you when you jumped to third grade?

HS: In third grade I learned I had incredible multitasking skills. I was able to do my homework, watch TV, listen to music, and keep a conversation going with my mom at the same time. I did the same thing in class, and I always use multitasking now. I take auditory and visual signals really well.

LS: Once you skipped ahead two grade levels, did you find school interesting or fun? Did you have enthusiasm for studying?

HS: It was with my fourth grade teacher. He was the first one that made studying fun, and that's where I got engineering from. He used to bring little toys to class and take them apart and show us what was inside while we were doing science. He'd tell us what this is and go, like, "You probably don't understand, but this is this, and that is that." It was mechanical stuff and I really liked that. He used to work for Boeing, but he quit and started teaching. That's where I decided I wanted to become an engineer.

In freshman year of high school I built my first antenna. I found out how to do it on the Internet and got all the stuff I needed to make it around the house: a Pringle's can, some coaxial cable, a little connector. I put it together and felt, like, "That was pretty easy!"

Then I went through the entire house and took stuff apart. My mom got mad at me because I would always forget to put it back together, and there would be stuff that kind of works and there's stuff that straight-up doesn't. Like our phone, our home phone.

My mom told me she wanted a way to make it ring louder because she couldn't hear it from the other room when she's watching TV. So I took it apart and hooked everything up. Now it just makes an annoying sound when the phone rings. When someone calls there's a loud, sharp-pitched sound in the house. Mom wanted me to put it back the way it was, but I forgot the process I went through to put it together.

My dad is an instrumentation engineer. That's another one of the influences I had, because my dad was always doing engineering. He was always taking me on his business trips to engineering seminars. I started going when I was 10. I started understanding when I was 15 – well, actually 13. That's when I started understanding what they were talking about.

LS: Well, you either knew what was going on or you knew how to be quiet, or was it both?

HS: It was basically my dad trying to teach me to keep quiet during the large settings where someone is talking. I always had something to do because they would hand out stuff I could play with, especially if it was an electrical engineering seminar. One time they handed out grapefruit radios; a radio powered by a grapefruit. I played with that for a good 30 minutes.

LS: Was this part of school?

HS: I learned almost nothing in school about what was happening at the seminars. My dad would teach me; he'd say, "Today, at the seminar, they were talking about this." And I'd go, "Oh! OK." And I'd ask about the parts I didn't get and he'd explain it to me.

I'm the favorite child of my dad just because I'm interested in the same stuff he is. I have my own workbench at home. I have an oscilloscope and my own voltmeter, and all that. My dad has the resources from his company, and he'd bring it home and explain it to me and I'd go, "Sweet," and I'd go stick it in outlets and my dad would go, "No, no," and pull it away from me. That was when I was younger.

When I got older I'd actually start using the tools to make stuff, like the soldering iron I have. I made a tone generator – that's the first thing I think I built.

LS: Was any of this integrated with what you were doing at school or was it all a home thing?

HS: Mostly home. To tell you the truth, I didn't learn much in public school. What I learned was all at home. That's where I learned math and science: at home.

LS: So what did you do at school?

HS: At school, I would just tolerate it and socialize. The reason my parents sent me to public school was to see how I could relate with other people, socialize.

LS: I guess they thought it was important. Did you think it was important?

HS: Pretty, yeah. Now it's a useful skill.

LS: It's surprising that you didn't get bored... to death.

HS: Oh, very much so! I slept a lot in high school.

LS: Are you good at taking tests?

HS: I'm very good at taking tests and making it look like I'm paying attention. I would just go, take tests, and ace 'em. Like in calculus I'd sleep, take a test, finish it, and then go back to sleep.

LS: You mean while the test was still going on?

HS: Yeah, like I'd finish it in 1/10th of the time of everyone else, turn it in, and go back to sleep.

LS: Why did you sleep? Were you tired, or bored?

HS: I was tired. I would stay up late and do stuff at home because I knew I could sleep at school. Like if there was something I had to solder, or something to glue that required time to cure, I'd stay up and watch it. The next day at school I'd go to sleep from 8am to 10am, switch classes, and then go to sleep again.

LS: I'm not sure I understand what was happening at school for you. Do you remember a time when you were bored?

HS: Bored as in, like, totally bored?

LS: Yeah, like nothing to do.

HS: Yeah. This summer. I would spend two hours doing nothing, just sitting there watching TV. It was mind-numbing. My parents were saying, "This is the summer before college – just take a break."

I just put everything down, I just slept, watched TV, ate, went outside. That's all I did for half the summer until I decided I just couldn't do it anymore. I just had to stop.

Before the summer, during the school year, my dad taught me some finite element analysis, and I found all that really interesting. I started doing that so that at night I would have something to keep my mind occupied and that I could think about the next day.

LS: What's finite element analysis?

HS: What it is, is... it takes a 3-D object made from a CAD program, puts it on a mesh so that you can do tests on it. Like, it will test tensile strength based on the simulation. It's material simulation, and I found that really, really interesting.

My dad said, "You want to see something cool?" And he installed the software and did some stuff. He had this cool wing, and it showed particle flow, and it was really cool. So that's what I'd do at night, and it would keep me occupied, and I learned a little bit of flow mechanics. I stopped sitting there watching TV and being bored.

LS: What's drawing you on now?

HS: Right now I'm helping my dad with his patents. He's got three patents for valve designs: two pending and one almost completely done. One's for an electrical offset seal. It's pretty cool. He's got a PVC model of his seal, and he's trying to market that right now. I help my dad with that some.

LS: What does that have to do with your next steps?

HS: It's just something to look to. He was an engineer, and now he's making his patents. My dad wants me to do a patent on tire sensors, something I read in a magazine that made me say to him, "Wouldn't it be easier if this?" and I drew a picture. And my dad's like, "Just do it!" (laughs), and I'm like, "OK, I will!"

So I went on CAD and drew basic sketches, and my Dad was saying, "This looks good, but..." and he's showing me what's wrong. And I revise it and he keeps pointing out what's wrong. And that's what I've been doing when I go home every weekend.

LS: Do you think that you're more stimulated by that than what you're doing in school?

HS: I think I'm equally stimulated because I'm learning the mechanics behind flow in physics now, I'm learning all the mechanics behind what I was doing in finite element analysis. I feel like I'm really learning some new stuff, because I never learned physics at home. I learned basic mechanics and ohms and resistance, but I didn't learn that much physics. Now I'm learning physics, and I think it's really fun. We have labs every week, springs and carts, friction pads. It's pretty fun.

LS: What are you planning to do with your college degree?

HS: I'm going to get a bachelor's in electrical engineering first. Then I'm going to get my doctorate in instrumentation and automation. My dad has the same degree. My dad's job is pretty fun. He does a lot of things: he programs, he does mechanical design, and he also does electrical design. And those are the exact three things I want to do. I just want to do what my dad does now. I think it's a really cool job.

21. NEIL DEGRASSE TYSON

History   Middle   Born 1959, New York City, New York

A person who thinks unconventionally – even something as simple as having great faith in one's self – will experience intolerance and prejudice in society and in school. Many "open-minded" teachers and administrators will only go so far in support of your open-mindedness, and in many cases they won't support it at all.

It's difficult for young people to recognize this because our educational systems support authorities in casting their discomfort as your defect. As a result many young people are pressed into inferior situations presented as the "wiser" alternative. If you aspire to great things, then the struggles Neil Tyson describes will apply to you whether or not you are black.

Hindering a passionate person often does little more than piss that person off. And while fighting and resistance are not often the best ways forward, they certainly served Neil well. But then Neil is not only passionate, he's also ambitious, smart, savvy, and charismatic. Neil is now the director of the American Museum of Natural History's Hayden Planetarium in New York City and a working astrophysicist. He has become a celebrity in his role as a public ambassador of science.

Neil and I were friends as graduate students in Texas, where his future wife Alice and I were classmates. After this interview we all met at Macy's to shop for luggage.

Excerpts

"Call it ambition or call it enchantment, but it was the source of my energy to continue to create, to continue to write. And of course I've always had a love for the universe, and that has been since I was nine years old, first visiting the Hayden Planetarium… growing up in New York City where there is no night sky… The stars came out (in the planetarium) and I thought it was a hoax. I thought it was a hoax because there are not that many stars. I said, 'I know how many stars there are and it's not that!'…"

"I would rather have someone who is inspired by their work stand in front of me and be my teacher, even if they don't know how to teach. Because – you know something – that doesn't matter. In the end what matters is the osmotic link that is made between your and their enthusiasm. Just by being in the same room at the same time…"

"Because my interest ran deep, that gave me the drive to never stop… in spite of personality mismatches between me and my first graduate school… I had a PhD committee and things were breaking down, and they just dissolved the committee, which was tantamount to them saying, 'We're kicking you out.' You know? They did not understand the depth of my interest in the subject. They did not understand my resolve with regard to that ambition. So for them to say, 'What are you going to do now? … Do you want to become a computer salesman or…' It was like 'No! No, it doesn't work that way!'…"

"There is no shortage of people telling you what you shouldn't be in life. And why is that so? Like, why do they even give a shit? Why should someone go out of their way to tell you what you can't be? …"

"I don't have patience for people who want to limit the dreams of others."

"If I accept you as you are, I will make you worse; however, if I treat you as though you are what you are capable of becoming, I help you become that."

— Johann Wolfgang Von Goethe

Interview   American Museum of Natural History, New York, August 2005

LS: How do you feel about American education, both yours and the ones that you see kids getting?

Neil Tyson: I find myself in my old age to have become quite opinionated on this matter. Not even on purpose, it just kind of descended upon me. I opened my eyes – maybe that's what it is. I opened my eyes.

LS: You had kids.

NT: Yeah, yeah... I'll give you a good example, I have a nine-year-old and a four-and-a-half-year-old. The nine-year-old goes to school, PS 234, and they're introducing this new math curriculum there called "TERC." TERC is a company in Boston, an education research, resource company, and they redid the math curriculum and have been quite influential in this reworked curriculum. But parents hate the curriculum.

I was curious what it was about. I didn't have to think about it until my kids went to school. Now I see it first-hand, and the stereotype of it is that it's turned math into this cultural relativist exercise: "Whatever way you use to solve the problem, that's OK." And if that's all you know of it you say, "Well, that's kind of stupid." Not "stupid," but there are best ways to solve problems, so why should they (the kids) not be exposed to that?

But then I looked closer at the curriculum, and I saw what it's actually trying to do. It was trying to stimulate variance in the way that you approach problems, so that when you do hit a problem that you've never seen before in real life, the fact that you've explored may different ways, not some pre-existing way that someone established for you, makes you better able to think.

So I looked at the homework sets. I'll give you one example of one set called "racing dice." On the x-axis is 2 through 12, and on the y-axis is 1 through 10, and you get a pair of dice and you roll them. (For every number that you roll you go to that number on the x-axis and mark an additional unit up y-axis.) And so you're racing (on columns) 2 through 12 to see who's going to get to the top of the page first. I thought this was brilliant.

My daughter came home and said "Daddy, I tried this and my favorite number is 10 and I wanted 10 to win but 7 kept winning, and one time 6 came in pretty close..." And I said "Holy cow, this is a brilliant exercise!" It was a race, a bit of probability and statistics was coming in here. It's making a histogram, for goodness' sake. This is in third grade!

So I came to value where they were coming from. Meanwhile the parents are saying, "But they're not learning their times tables, they're not learning the basics of the math." And I said to myself, "If she's learning things like this – and poses that kind of question to me after she's done it – then I'm happy with the kind of wiring that this is producing."

And there're other examples that I can give that are similar to this in terms of an unusual and innovative approach to thinking about a math concept. And there is never memorization. It's always "…just figure it out, figure it out…"

I found myself getting into arguments with parents who would say to me, "But your daughter is not going to get a high score on the fourth grade exam, which will prevent her from…" And I said to myself, "In the end, after you get out of school, no one gives a shit what grade you got." No one asks you after your first job what your GPA was in elementary school, junior high school, high school, or college. What matters is how your brain is wired. What is your capacity to think innovatively, to solve problems that you've never seen before? That's what matters. So I said to myself, "If this is how her brain is wired, I'm happy." I'm not even worried about the grades.

I value this feature more than I value the grade because today you have people valuing grades without regard to whether or not the person even understands the subject. In fact, they define understanding the subject in terms of having got the high grade, and then you go and ask them a question about it, and they say, "Oh, I don't know. I just memorized so I don't…" There's nothing in the head, there's no insight, there's no wisdom, there's no depth of understanding that you can tap for any later time in life to allow you to become better at whatever it is that you're doing.

I found myself to be a champion of this approach even though it's resoundingly criticized by whole generations of parents who want their kids to learn math the way they learned math, the way we learned math.

Elevating this specific case to a broad case, I see too many students who, because they got high grades, or because someone deemed them to be gifted and talented, … let me hold "talented" out of this and just stick with gifted. When I think of talented, I think of people who can play the piano, or can tap dance, or can sing. When I think of talent, I think of a craft rather than your ability to think. That's semantic, but for the purposes of this (discussion) that's how I'm using the words. So people who are deemed "gifted": someone has made this judgment, and often it's grade related. I know too many people who were straight A students who have no capacity to think innovatively at all.

The real experiment that one should do is go through society and pluck people who we would all agree are successful. Successful, but not in academia. Pick something in life that somebody's got, so pick a successful lawyer, a successful politician, a successful preacher, a successful poet, journalist, novelist, composer, artist, sculptor, comedians, actors, athletes, CEOs, inventors. Line them all up and ask them the question, "Did you get straight A's in school?" I think the overwhelming answer is going to be "No."

In fact, I'll bet the comedians were the class clowns and never did well at all. Not just didn't get straight A's but actually did poorly. I'll bet the CEOs or the politicians didn't do well, but they might have been the most popular. And so what that tells me is – and I get upset reflecting on this – it tells me that the entire educational system is streamlined to value your grade performance in a course without reference to how you might ultimately contribute to society as an adult. And since all these people on this list I just shared with you, if you're good at any of those you're actually famous, you're well known, you're well paid, you have a career. And if you only believed that grades were what mattered, then you wouldn't imagine that you would succeed without having gotten the high grades.

I'm angry because students in the class who got the teachers' affection were the students who got the best grades. That's the measure of your success in school. But what is school but a means to help you prepare to enter the real world? Most real-world jobs neither require straight A's or, in fact, straight A's preclude the expression of some talent set that you might have. I think the whole system needs to be revisited, on those grounds alone.

Then I ask, "Well, where are all the straight A students?" They're in academia, that's where they all are. That's where the valedictorians go. Just look them up, you'll see. They go back to academia and become faculty. That's fine, too. That's a successful career, but most people in the world are not university faculty. Most people are other things. So there ought to be some other way in school for me to get the attention of my teacher in ways other than showing that I got an A.

My favorite on that list are CEOs. Some percentage of CEOs on the "Fortune 500" didn't even finish high school. And the multi-millionaires (got there) because they had some clever sense, some "people sense" for those that rose up in a pre-existing company, and others had some clever idea.

One of my moments of greatest joy and frustration – emotions held simultaneously – relates to my SATs, taken twice: once as a junior and again as a senior. I remember taking them first and they said, "Oh, you're not expected to finish the test. Just work your hardest but don't rush." So I worked hard and didn't rush and got a particular score, and I saw others that had much higher scores than I did. I said, "Well, how is that possible… unless they rushed!" So I said, "There's something bogus here, so I'm gonna rush. I'm gonna like, sort of 'rev' my head, get the 'engine' running and 'pop' the clutch and hit it full bore." I did that and raised my math score a hundred and something points. Higher than what you're supposed to be able to do just by studying. The whole thing was bogus.

My verbal score was sort of average. Nothing anybody would have written home about. Nobody would say, "Hey, look, he … HEY!" It would have never happened.

So what's happened over the years? I write a column in a magazine that becomes a book. That book is now translated in ten languages. And then I wrote seven other books since then… wrote another column.

And in the middle of all that I get a letter from ETS (Educational Testing Service, administrators of the SAT and other standardized exams – Ed.). Just to show you what sway they still have over you, I'm thinking, "What (gasp) are they going to do? Are they going to nullify my SAT scores?!" You know, it's "ETS, Princeton, New Jersey," the headquarters of the purveyors of this exam.

LS: The National Security Agency of education.

NT: The NSA of education (laughs)!

It was addressed to "Dr. Tyson," so it must not have been some old record they were tapping. But I didn't know what it was, so I opened the letter and it said, "Dear Dr. Tyson, we recently read one of your essays that appeared in *Natural History Magazine* and we were impressed with its content and its writing style, and we want to excerpt it for our upcoming verbal exam in the new SAT that we're writing. Will you give us permission to do this?"

I didn't know whether to kiss the letter or burn it, because what does it MEAN if I get an average, mediocre verbal score and they're coming back to me to want to use my writing! I don't know what that means! I don't know! I'm angry just thinking about it.

There's a fundamental flaw in the system. I mean the hair stands up on my back. You are put in judgment by others based on your score, not based on the fact that I liked to write at the time.

I enjoy playing with words. Words are kind of fun. I like words the kind of way you like math brain-teaser things. Just little curiosities in the language, like, "Are there any cool sentences out there?" Like that artificial intelligence sentence which is a problem for computers. It's two sentences: "Fruit flies like a banana. Time flies like an arrow."

You hand those two sentences to a computer and ask it to understand them. They are formally identical in their structure, yet one is sort of completely metaphorical and the other is literal. So one asks, "is there a kind of fly called a 'time fly'?" ... Right? ... And is an arrow a word for a kind of food? Food has all kinds of names, so you have to check the database of world foods, and the animal database of kinds of flies. And ask if there's a kind of fly that likes a "time arrow" the way fruit flies like a banana. I just like thinking stuff like that.

Call it ambition or call it enchantment, but it was the source of my energy to continue to create, to continue to write. And of course I've always had a love for the universe, and that has been since I was nine years old, first visiting the Hayden Planetarium. You get a lot of that in astronomy because you can be an amateur astronomer and have a telescope. You can't be a nine-year-old physicist, but you can be a nine-year-old astronomer.

That level of ambition started early and it was deep. And growing up in New York City where there is no night sky, it's not a part of what you are. My first night sky was the Hayden Planetarium when I was nine years old. The stars came out (in the planetarium) and I thought it was a hoax. I thought it was a hoax because there are not that many stars. I said, "I know how many stars there are, and it's not that!"

I occasionally lay awake at night wondering, had I grown up on a farm, and had I seen the night sky in all of its majesty from birth, whether I would have had this sort of cosmic epiphany that I did. I hadn't seen the night sky until I was nine years old! It's certainly not something I could or would have ever taken for granted. Whereas if it's always up there from age zero – you go out on the porch at night and there it is... of course it's there because that's what it looks like from central Pennsylvania – the assault on who and what I was would not have been there. It wouldn't have had the singularity of impact that going to the Hayden Planetarium and seeing the sky for the first time did. I wonder whether I'd still be an astrophysicist today, had I grown up in a rural community.

But because my interest ran deep, that gave me the drive to never stop. And in spite of personality mismatches between me and my first graduate school, where they voted to dissolve the committee, and then their next question was, "So, now what are you going to do with your life?" In an attempt to try to help me with a career change.

LS: What do you mean they "dissolved the committee"?

NT: I had a PhD committee and things were breaking down, and they just dissolved the committee, which was tantamount to them saying, "We're kicking you out." You know? That's a whole other story, but my point is that they did not understand the depth of my interest in the subject. They did not understand my resolve with regard to that ambition. So for them to say, "What are you going to do now? Is there anything we can help you with? Do you want to become a computer salesman or..." It was like "No! No, it doesn't work that way (laughs)!"

So I reached down into that… that "fuel reserve," summoned it up, and re-pointed the entire operation. I end up transferring graduate schools to Columbia. I'm received with open arms. I finish the PhD there. It's another three years, so there was lost time, but there wasn't lost professional development. I remember with the PhD they kept saying, "If you go back to try to get another PhD, remember you're going to have to slog through all this again. It's a lot of years and it's…." I thought that was quite patronizing because, well, yes, a PhD is a lot of work, but it's not more work than what would be expected of you as a professional scientist. You're writing up research. Some projects are large, some projects are small, but that's what you DO! That is the entry into doing the same thing… that's what science is. So they believed they would get me to say, "You know, I hadn't thought of it that way. OK, I'm gonna leave. Gosh, you know, you're right. Why don't I just take the easy road…"

It was this life of exposure to the universe, spawned by an encounter with the Hayden Planetarium, and my time at the Bronx High School of Science where "nerd-dom" was king, at a time before nerd-dom was even a subject of playful parody, before the *Revenge of the Nerd* movies. The perseverance and the drive kept me in the game. But, you know, I had to reach for those reserves.

There is no shortage of people telling you what you shouldn't be in life. And why is that so? Like, why do they even give a shit? Why should someone go out of their way to tell you what you can't be?

It reminds me of my father; in fact, I carry this example with me to this day. My father is 5'10", lean and muscular, as opposed to bulky and muscular, a cross between a rock climber and a gymnast. He was in junior high school. He's there on the line as you line up for gym class and the gym instructor is describing what kind of body types are suitable for different activities in the track and field. That's kind of what makes track and field interesting, because you can have different kinds of talent sets that reveal themselves in different events.

So he said publicly in front of all the other students, "Take Cyril Tyson's body for example, that would not make a good running body. He's not built for running." And my father said, "Nobody's going to tell me what I can't do." So he took up running just because the guy said this. In 1946 my father had the fifth-fastest time in the world for the 600-yard run. Fifth-fastest time in the world! So if you want to talk about resolve, he did that just out of spite!

I don't have patience for people who want to limit the dreams of others. I just don't have that patience. As an educator I see it as a breach of the pedagogical contract that you have signed with your students. It's your job to get them to succeed. It's your job to alert them to how to succeed, not to find ways to tell them they can't.

It's better for a person to give up then it is for you to tell them, before they tried, that they shouldn't have attempted it. Because if they try and then give up because they fail, there's a lesson there, there's wisdom, there's insight, there's character building that goes on in that exercise. Whereas just getting in the way and saying, "Don't do it…" – you know, who gains by that? Unless the teacher is worried that the student's feelings will be hurt because they don't come in first. There's a lot of that going on today, too.

In my old age I've become a bit of a pragmatist. Part of it is my access and exposure to the current Republican administration. It flows a little bit out of that. I've been appointed by Bush three times, and one appointment is ongoing at this moment.

So, there is the "Let's have world peace," as protesters would have you want (when) protesting the Iraqi war. Or there's the attitude, "How could you be so naïve as to believe that there will EVER be world peace, when there has NEVER been world peace in the history of the species! So what, you think you live in special times? So that all of a sudden you can summon up world peace and it will happen now, and it has never happened ever before?" Let's be realistic about this. It doesn't mean intentionally wage war, it just means understand a world in which world peace is not a realistic goal. Unless you want to fundamentally believe that we are a different kind of human being in modern times.

What you do is look for solutions that are more sensible, given as who we are as humans. That's all I'm saying.

Another thing I figured out – this thing upset me to no end – I thought about it, and I said, "Who are the greatest allies that exist in the world today?" The strongest allies. Well, England and America, there's good allies right there. Uh… England and America! Wait a minute, we were mortal enemies 200 years ago. America, plus the help of France, kicked some serious British butt.

Well, how about Japan, we're like buddies with Japan? But we were, like, mortal enemies, and they were completely vanquished. So then I realized that the strongest friends in the world are people where one of them completely vanquished the other. So then I said, "OK, we'll put a pin in that fact." And then I said, "Well, let's find wars that had sustained peace from diplomatic solutions." I couldn't find one. I couldn't find one! There were none! None! None!

In other words, if you have two nations that have taken formal state-sponsored arms up against each other, and then diplomats step in and say, "Why can't we all get along?" They sit down at a table and sign a treaty. Every time that has happened, war has broken out again within half a generation. Whereas, when one country completely vanquishes the other, there is everlasting peace, some of the deepest peace you've ever seen. This upset me because I wished it weren't true. But it kinda is true.

That's what I mean when I say I've gotten pragmatic in my old age. I just look at stuff that's worked and I try to make it work again.

LS: How does that play into who you are now and where you want to be?

NT: It plays in because it's this suite of attitudes that allows me to say… rather than say, "Get A's so that you can get a good job," instead let's find people who have great jobs and see if they got A's. And the answer is that they didn't. And so we need to know their stories, not the story of the bookworm.

Harvard, as you may know, has more applicants to its freshman class who are valedictorians of their high school than there are openings to the entering class. They choose to not fill their entering class with valedictorians. Yes, in the end, there are a lot of valedictorians, but not nearly as many as they could have brought in, because there's a missing link there.

Harvard wants you to come there, go get famous, and bring more light back to them. Bookworms do not have that talent. The odd thing is that you get a valedictorian from high school who is rejected from Harvard and who says, "Why was I rejected from Harvard? I have the highest grades in the school. I have the highest grades ever here in five years!" Then they see, like, a black person got into Harvard: "Oh, well, that person got a lower grade… whata whata…" Then it becomes this issue.

I am fascinated by that dynamic! The person isn't wondering whether they would contribute to the campus life, whether they have a personality that enriches the organizations that exist, which creates partnerships, everlasting friendships, political alignments. Whatever it is that goes on that matters in the rest of the world, they don't have it.

My last bit of tirade has to do with what has become of the education establishment. It used to be that you had an expertise that you loved, then you took some education course to learn how to teach that expertise, and then you became a teacher. I'm talking about K through 12 now. But that's not what's happening now.

What's happening is people major in education, not in some subject. Well, what does THAT mean?! They learn how to administer exams, how to write the perfect exam. Where's the enthusiasm for learning about birds, or about the sky, or about particles, or about…? It's not there. The educational enterprise is being taken over by people who are experts in education, but who have no capacity to impart inspiration.

In the end, I would rather have someone who is inspired by their work stand in front of me and be my teacher, even if they don't know how to teach. Because – you know something – that doesn't matter. In the end what matters is the osmotic link that is made between your and their enthusiasm. Just by being in the same room at the same time. Once you have the enthusiasm as a student, that's what will keep you off the streets, that's what will enable you to turn off the TV – turn off *American Idol* – and go the library, rent a video on the subject. That's what drives you.

LS: Talk about your enthusiasm, what drives you. You, personally.

NT: I have an intense curiosity about how the universe works. And I'm intrigued that the public likes the universe enough so that I get tapped regularly to interpret it for them. I'm just tickled to death by that. I don't know of any other scientific discipline where that's true. Yes, the news has medical doctors to interpret the latest *New England Journal of Medicine* article, but that's because you're worried about your health, not because you have a curiosity of the knowledge, and the insight that you glean from having heard it.

That's what keeps me going. As Carl Sagan said, "When you're in love you want to tell the world." When I walk down the street and it's clear, and I see somebody looking up trying to point something out, I've got to stop. "What you looking at?" Total stranger. "Oh, this, that, that, that, that." When I see a crowd I feel this urge to run up and get my telescope, and set it up on the sidewalk so that I can show people the universe, because it's our universe, not my universe. It's our universe.

And people are intrigued. I don't twist the arms of the newscasters or the editors of the magazines. I don't twist their arms to do a cover story on Saturn, or Mars, or Venus. They do it anyway. There's something deep and fundamental about that interest factor, and I'm part of that community. It's a privilege.

Plus I gotta go. I gotta reconnect with (my wife) Alice. Where you headed now?

22. CHARLES HARD TOWNES

History   Late   Born 1915, Greenville, South Carolina

While Charles Hard Townes' public fame comes from his invention of the laser, he's equally recognized in professional circles for his work in molecular beams, radio astronomy, the discovery of interstellar organic molecules, developing the atomic clock, and many other projects. The 1998 book *1000 Years, 1000 People* ranked him in the top one thousand who shaped the millennium, next to Martha Graham and Malcolm X. Martin Luther King, who was a friend of Townes's mother, referred to him as "Ellen's boy."

    Like all great teachers Townes doesn't really teach, he just helps people join him in his work. He was surprised when I told him that he was one of my most influential teachers, because all he'd done was give me a job as an astronomer when I was an undergraduate. But what he taught me was critical, even though it came naturally to him – it was the joy of exploration and the rewards of discovery.

Postscript: Charlie Townes died on January 27th, 2015. He was 99.

Excerpts

"When I was a youngster I was very interested in natural history. I used to walk in the woods and the streams and catch butterflies, and watch birds, and look at the stars, and so on. All the universe was fascinating to me…"

"I think curiosity and discovery, and sense of discovery, and wanting to discover, and wanting to figure out things, figure out new things is great. Now, that doesn't mean that you shouldn't read what other people have done carefully. And think about them, and work problems…"

"I did experimental work with a professor who… he was a little tough. He was a nice guy, but he was tough on his students. He really made them work hard, so he didn't have many students. And I thought, 'Well, he didn't have many students so maybe I'll get a lot of attention from him…' He really gave me a lot of attention…"

"I went over to Denmark at one point… and I visited Niels Bohr and he was walking along the street with me, and he asked me what I was doing. And I told him we had this device which produced a very pure oscillation from molecules… Now Niels Bohr, one of the most famous theorists at the time, said, 'Oh no, no. That can't be. No, you must misunderstand. It can't give such pure frequencies… You must misunderstand'…"

"You have to know how to disagree with other people. If somebody disagrees with you, if it's a serious person, you want to think carefully about what he's saying. Think carefully about whether you are really likely to be right or not…"

"A friend of mine comes to me and says, uh… 'You know this has saved my eyes.' And, oh boy, that's very emotionally pleasing to me… Of all things, ah… A lot of these things I couldn't imagine at the time… I didn't know about the kind of eye trouble that's saved by lasers. I'd never heard of it! I couldn't imagine that…"

"Now I've tried some things that don't work. Well, OK… You can be wrong. Don't worry about it too much. Try hard to be right, but don't be unwilling to take some chances. And look hard for things that might be there, that you think have a reasonable chance of being there. Look, and a failure or two won't hurt you."

"I was at once confused and amazed by Theodore. First, since he was obviously a scientist of considerable repute… In fact he was the only person I had met until now who seemed to share my enthusiasm for zoology. Secondly,… he treated me and talked to me exactly as though I were his own age… but also as though I were as knowledgeable as he."

— Gerald Durrell, reflecting on Dr. Theodore Stephanides from the time when Gerald was 11, from *My Family and Other Animals*

Interview   Berkeley, California, June 2005

Charlie Townes: When I was a youngster I was very interested in natural history. I used to walk in the woods and the streams, and catch butterflies, and watch birds, and look at the stars, and so on. All the universe was fascinating to me. I thought I would probably go into some kind of science.

I had an older brother who was also interested, and we used to catch insects together, and he was two and a half years older than I. He was always better than I was, we used to compete, of course (laughs), and he went into biology. I sometimes say that's why I didn't go into biology: I felt I couldn't compete with him. But actually I didn't go into biology – even though I was fascinated by it – because biology at that time was descriptive largely. It didn't get down to basics. It was descriptive. And when I took my first course in physics, oh boy! That seemed like "it" because with physics you could pretty definitely prove whether you were right or wrong. Very specific, it was much more basic.

I took my first course in physics as a sophomore in college. I'd taken some biology, and I took some chemistry, and I took a lot of mathematics – I liked mathematics. But physics REALLY was it, because you could apply mathematics, you could make good reasoning and so on, and figure things out. And I like to know how the universe works. I like to know how things work and try to make them work. I used to tinker with things, and try to fix things. I like to… to make things work.

It was very clear to me: what I wanted to do was physics. So now the question was, "Would I be able to do it? Could I get a job in physics?" Physics wasn't very well known at that time actually. When they asked me, I told my friends I was going to go into physics and they would say, "Physics? What is that? Is that something like civics?" No (laughs)! Not at all like civics. It's a science (laughs)!

Well, physics is better known now. Much better known, partly because of what it did in World War II – it really won World War II. And of course then made the very frightening atomic bombs, but it did a lot of other things, too.

Well, I had to get some kind of help in a university to finance my graduate work, and I managed to get a teaching assistantship at Duke University. Duke was pretty good, but it wasn't one of the best. I applied to a lot of other very good schools, and I didn't get any financial help. I applied a second year, and I didn't get any financial help. Oh, dear! What should I do?

Well, I had saved up $500 – which was a lot more money than it is now – I'd saved up

$500, and I decided I'll just go to the very best place that I'd ever heard of, and that was Cal Tech at that point. At Cal Tech (Robert J.) Oppenheimer was teaching there. (Robert A.) Millikan was president of the university. Cal Tech, California Institute of Technology, that is. (Albert) Einstein went there from time to time. Linus Pauling was head of the chemistry department there. It was a wonderful place. It was a small school. And I like small schools where you can interact with everybody.

So with $500 I got on a bus and went out to California from South Carolina where I lived. I went out on the bus, and it was easy to get enrolled in graduate school then, but it wasn't easy to get financing. This was the depression years, 1936 this was. So I got enrolled, all right, and after I'd been there one semester fortunately they gave me a teaching assistantship, so then I could pay the rest of my way. That made it so that I finished my degree at Cal Tech.

Now I was also wondering at that time, "Do I want to do theoretical work or experimental work?" I was having some eye trouble. I was reading a lot and my eyes were bothering me, and a medical doctor, an oculist, worked on it, and finally he said, "Well, you had just better stop doing physics because your eyes are not going to get any better. You'll probably have to change fields. Don't do any physics…"

Well, I wouldn't want to leave physics! Oh, no (laughs)! But I decided, "Well, maybe the thing to do is to do experimental physics, instead of theoretical physics." That was a great decision. Just the right thing to do: experimental physics. I think you can do a lot more in experimental physics than in theory, generally. You want to know as much theory as you can, but a combination of good theory and experimental work is very fruitful. So I did experimental work in physics.

I did experimental work with a professor who… he was a little tough. He was a nice guy, but he was tough on his students. He really made them work hard, so he didn't have many students. And I thought, "Well, he didn't have many students so maybe I'll get a lot of attention from him." (Laughs) So that's why I went to work with him. W. R. Smythe was his name. He really gave me a lot of attention. I separated isotopes, I made pumps, vacuum pumps, to circulate gas and thereby concentrate isotopes of carbon, and oxygen, and nitrogen, and study their nuclear properties to find out what their spins were. The nucleus would spin a certain amount, and I could measure them doing spectroscopy.

I got my degree and I wanted to be in a university. What I wanted to do was think about things and understand things. I wanted to be in a university. University jobs were very scarce, and a Bell Labs representative came along and offered me a job. Well, I wasn't awfully interested; I didn't want to go into industry. I wanted to do fundamental physics and be in a university. But there weren't any jobs, so my professor said, "Well, you'd better take this." And I took it. I knew Bell Labs was a good place, it just wasn't a university, but I went there. And it was a big success, even though I was there only a year before I had to do engineering.

The war had come along and everybody had to pitch into the war, and I recognized that, and Bell Labs assigned me to work on radar. I was to design a radar bombing system for aircraft. For radar to decide where to drop bombs, and so on. And I had to work on that, design that, and for several years during the war I worked on radar of various kinds.

I learned a lot of engineering. It was very valuable to me. A combination of engineering and physics was very valuable. The engineers at that time didn't know a lot of quantum mechanics, and the physicists missed a lot of things that the engineers understood, like oscillators, and amplifiers, and things like this,... circuits. And I learned how to build all those, and how to design them, and what not. That was very helpful.

One of the last radars that I was designing was supposed to work at a rather short wavelength: 1.25 cm. That's about half an inch wavelength. And I studied this and I recognized that those wavelengths were absorbed by water vapor in the atmosphere. I tried to persuade Bell Labs and the government: "No, we shouldn't build it at that wavelength because it will probably be absorbed." Well, maybe they believed me, but they said, "Well, no. We decided to do this. We'd better go ahead. We gotta go ahead."

So we built it and put it up in the air and, sure enough, the waves were absorbed by water vapor. Well, what that meant to me was – I had studied the absorption to see how it behaved, and I realized – "Hey, this looks like a very good way for understanding water, and we can do spectroscopy and look at the absorption of microwaves." We could do very high resolution spectroscopy, get very accurate measurements of the behavior of molecules by looking at the absorption of microwaves. I recognized that ammonia would absorb nicely, and water, and a lot of others. And so right after the war I urged Bell Labs to let me do microwave spectroscopy, that is studying molecules with microwaves.

Bell Labs didn't really think that was going to pay off for them very much; they wanted me to do engineering. They said, "Look, you've learned a lot of engineering. We've got so many good things for you to do." But I said, "No, I really want to do physics. I really want to understand things. Explore new things." "Well," they said. "Well, OK. We'll let you do it. We're not going to hire anybody else in that field, but if you want to do it, OK." That was very generous of them, and that was Bell Labs in those days. It was willing to do long-term basic research and explore things. And I like to explore. That's my pleasure: to explore and find out new things.

So I did that, and it was a very promising field. After a few years I published a lot of new findings about molecules, about nuclei in molecules, and I was offered a job at Columbia University. So I got a job in university (laughs) as a result of that work!

I went to Columbia University and continued to do that kind of work. We found a lot of interesting things: the properties of nuclei, the masses, the shapes, how they were spinning. And the properties of molecules, their structure and so on. I had a lot of students that worked with me, and we had a great time of it.

But I wanted to get to shorter wavelengths. We were making these wavelengths with klystrons and magnetrons; these had been invented shortly before the war and very much developed in the war. They worked very well, but they couldn't get to wavelengths shorter than about a half an inch, a centimeter or something like that. Maybe two or three times shorter than that, but not much more.

Now, as you go down from a centimeter to, let's say, a millimeter, we begin to call that infrared – shorter than a millimeter we call infrared radiation rather than microwaves. I wanted to get on down below a millimeter in wavelength because I saw there was a lot of spectroscopy that could be done. One could study atoms and molecules still better, and many more of them. I wanted to get down there, but we couldn't make any oscillators. Well, I knew a lot of engineering then, and I worked on various kinds of oscillators, hoping to make 'em oscillate faster and faster and get to shorter wavelengths. My students worked with me. The oscillators sort of worked a little bit, but they didn't work well enough.

Now the Navy knew that I was interested in getting to short waves, so they appointed me chairman of a committee, a national committee, to see if anybody knew how to get to short waves. To get down to, or below, a millimeter. We traveled all around trying to see if anybody had any good ideas. We traveled to Europe, the United States, and we didn't find any good new ideas.

So I was going to have one last meeting in Washington, D.C., of our committee, and say, "Well, we'll wrap it up because we just haven't found any right answers." And I woke up early in the morning worrying about it. Breakfast wasn't ready yet in the hotel, so I went out and sat in the park there in Washington. A nice sunny day and I thought, "Well, why haven't we been able to get to short waves?" And I thought it, and I thought it. I thought of all the different ways that I'd considered.

Well, I knew molecules could produce short waves. Molecules and atoms can oscillate very fast to produce short waves, but the second law of thermodynamics says you can't get more than a certain amount of energy from them until you heat them up. The higher you heat them, the more energy you can get; but to get enough radiation from them, you'd have to heat them so hot the molecules would fall apart. I knew that was true, and that was too bad. And suddenly I said, "Wait a minute! Wait a minute! We can get molecules in a state that's not described by a temperature."

See, in a temperature distribution the molecules, some of them are low energy, some of them are high energy, some of them are still higher energy. The distribution in different energy states depends on the temperature.

"Wait a minute, they don't have to be described by temperature. We can pick out molecules all in a highly excited state." I knew how to do that because at Columbia University people had been working with molecular beams. As you take a gas of atoms or molecules, let it go through a small hole into a vacuum, and it's a beam then – it extends on out – and now you put an electric field, or a magnetic field nearby, and that deflects them. Atoms and molecules in one state will get deflected one way, and in another state will get deflected another way, so you'll pick out which ones you want. I knew about that because some of my friends at Columbia University were doing that kind of thing.

So I quickly wrote down… I pulled out a envelope and a pen, and I wrote down the numbers and the equations. I was very familiar with it all then, and I said to myself, "Now, could this be done? Could we pick out molecules all in an excited state, send them into a cavity, let them radiate, and the radiation would be caught in the cavity and would stimulate them to radiate still more?" That's called Stimulated Emission of Radiation.

Now Einstein first discovered that. We knew that he knew – and everybody knew – that atoms can absorb a quantum of radiation or can emit a quantum of radiation. Depending on if the atom is in the lower state it will absorb, if it's in an upper state it will emit. But what Einstein also showed is that it would also be true that if light comes along – if a photon comes along – and comes close to the atoms in an excited state, it will induce it to fall down and give up the energy. So that's induced, or stimulated radiation: stimulated emission of radiation. Einstein discovered that. Everybody knew about it – all the physicists knew about it – but they just hadn't had the idea that I had of how to use it.

I saw how to separate molecules and get a lot of them in an excited state, send them into a cavity and they would emit some, and the radiation would bounce back and forth in the cavity, and make them emit still more until we get all of the energy out of the molecules before they then passed on through the cavity. "Ah! There's a way of getting just as high a frequency of radiation as we want!" And, oh boy, I wrote down the numbers, and it looked like it would work.

But I wasn't absolutely sure it was going to work, so I didn't mention it to the committee, and we had our last meeting. I went home to Columbia University, and I persuaded a graduate student to help me work on it: Jim Gordon. He was a good student. He'd had some experience with molecular beams, and he was willing to try it. And I told him, "Well, it's a little bit chancy. I think it will work. If it doesn't work, I think that even so you can get a good thesis out of it by studying it." So he tried it.

Well, now, it's very natural that when you have a new idea, there are going to be some people that don't believe you. A breakthrough... any breakthrough kind of challenges the people in the field. And so a number of people told me, "Oh, that won't work." One of the professors at Columbia, a very well known theorist, every time he saw me in the hallway he said, "You know that's not going to work. You should stop." Well, I looked at it very carefully, I looked at the theory very carefully. I was pretty sure it would work.

My student and I had been working on it about two years – we hadn't made it work yet, but we were coming along. And then the head of the department, Professor (Isidor Isaac) Rabi, a very famous physicist, a Nobel Prize winner, came into my office, and the person who was going to be the next head, Professor (Polykarp) Kusch, who also got a Nobel Prize, came into my office. They came into my office, and they sat down and said, "Look! That's not going to work. You know it's not going to work. We know it's not going to work. You're wasting the department's money – you've got to stop."

Well, that's the picture, you see. A lot of people don't always agree with you, especially if you have a new idea. Fortunately I had tenure. That is, they couldn't fire me just because they didn't agree with me (laughs). If I did something wrong, let's say ethically wrong, they could fire, but not if I just made a mistake in physics. So I said, "No, I think that it has a good chance of working. I'm going to keep going." They marched out of my office kind of angrily. And we kept going.

Two months later, I was teaching a class, and Jim Gordon dashed into my class and says, "It's working! It's working!" Oh, boy! So we were getting oscillations produced by the molecules. We tried it first in the microwave region because we had a lot of equipment there. I thought, "Well, we want to get down to shorter wavelengths, but we'll do that later." We first tried the microwave region, about 1 cm with ammonia molecules. And it was working, made a very pure oscillation of 1 cm wavelength, very, very pure. And oh, that was great. We published it and everybody got excited about it. However, people were still skeptical because it was a new idea!

I went over to Denmark at one point, and I knew Niels Bohr's son – he was a friend of mine – and I visited Niels Bohr and he was walking along the street with me and he asked me what I was doing. And I told him we had this device which produced a very pure oscillation from molecules. We called it a MASER, which my students and I invented, a name for Microwave Amplification by Stimulated Emission of Radiation: M.A.S.E.R. for "maser."

I told him we had this thing, and it was very pure radiation. Now Niels Bohr, one of the most famous theorists at the time, said, "Oh, no, no. That can't be. No, you must misunderstand. It can't give such pure frequencies." He was thinking, I believe, of the uncertainty principle. The uncertainty principle applied, the way he was thinking of it, to single molecules. But I was studying a whole beam of molecules, a whole collection of molecules in there. "Oh, it can," I said. "Oh, yes!"

"Oh, no. You must misunderstand," he said. Well, finally he said, "Well, maybe you're right." I'm not sure he ever believed me.

And with another very famous physicist (it was) much the same. I was at a cocktail party in Princeton with John Von Neumann, a very famous mathematical physicist. And he asked me what I was doing, and I told him. He said, "Oh, no. You can't get such pure frequencies. Oh, no."

"Oh, yes! I know we can – we're doing it!"

"Oh, no. You misunderstand. Something's wrong." Well, he went off and got another cocktail and about 15 minutes later he came back. "Heh!" He said, "Hey, you're right! You're right!" He'd thought about it some more.

Now, what was the problem? They were thinking about the uncertainty principle. The uncertainty principle says if you have a molecule that's going through a cavity, and it's in there a short time only, then you can't measure the frequency very precisely. But, the point is, we had a lot of molecules that were going through there all the time – it wasn't a single molecule. And we had feedback, a feedback oscillator.

Now any engineer would know if you have a feedback oscillator you're going to get a very pure frequency. The physicists weren't accustomed to the engineering ideas, and the engineers weren't accustomed to the quantum mechanics and how molecules worked. It was just putting those together. So getting two different fields, you see, it's very good to know different fields of science and… and put them together. Engineers recognized immediately, "Oh, sure, this will give a pure frequency," but the physicists thought, "Oh, no, it can't!" (Laughs)

Well, it became very popular and very exciting. About two years later than that, we'd been working on it and having good fun with it and made the most perfect, the most wonderful amplifiers, about 100 times more sensitive than any other amplifier that anybody had ever made before. And it made a very pure frequency. We called it "an atomic clock," and we could get very pure timing with it. Lot of people all over the world were working on them, and it was exciting.

Now, before we made it work, nobody wanted to work on it… except me… and some Russians. And the Russians and I got the Nobel Prize together. Well, they worked on the idea too; they had it somewhat independently. People would come into my laboratory and see it and say, "Oh, well, that's an amusing idea, uh huh." But nobody was competing. Once it got going, then everybody was competing to make more of them, and make better ones and so on. Got very exciting for everybody.

They (still) didn't think it could get down to very short wavelengths. I wanted to get on down into the infrared, shorter than a millimeter, but they thought, "Well, maybe a millimeter, but not much shorter." And nobody worried about it. I thought, "Well, now, I want to get on down." So I just sat down and thought, "What's the best way to do it? I'm sure we can do it." And I wrote down the numbers and what to do, and I said, "Hey! Wait! It looks like we can get right on down to optical wavelengths. We could make light with this!" Get light from molecules and amplify light, of all things! Wow! So I tried to figure out just the best way to do it.

I was consulting at Bell Telephone Laboratories then, and the Bell Telephone Laboratories asked me to come talk with their scientists and just sort of try to help stimulate them, and I would learn things from it too, and that was great. So I would go out there one day every two weeks and I would visit. My brother-in-law, Arthur

Schawlow, was working there. He had worked with me as a post-doc, married my kid sister, and then gone to Bell Labs, and I talked to him about it. "Oh!" he said. "That's very interesting. I'd been wondering whether we could get to shorter wavelengths. Could we work together?" So we worked together, and we wrote a paper on it.

So Schawlow and I invented the laser. That does the same thing that I did making microwaves, but to get to shorter wavelengths it was now called "laser" for Light Amplification by Stimulated Emission of Radiation: L.A.S.E.R. Light amplification.

By that time we knew everybody would be excited about the field, but nobody had thought it would get to shorter wavelengths, so what we did was construct a theoretical paper showing how it could be done. Rather than trying to do it, we showed how it could be done and let everybody try it. So we published that paper, and then everybody jumped into the business and then tried to do it.

By now there have been, oh, 10 or 12 different people that have received the Nobel Prize using masers and lasers as a scientific tool. I'm just delighted it's so useful in science. Of course, it was very useful in industry, too, particularly in communications, fiber optics communications, also in computing and recording, recording information, and readouts, and all kinds of things. It's an enormous industry now and very, very useful.

So I'm delighted. I'm delighted to see it used, and I'm particularly pleased to see it used for medical purposes. A friend of mine comes to me and says, uh… "You know this has saved my eyes." And, oh, boy, that's very emotionally pleasing to me… Of all things, ah… A lot of these things I couldn't imagine at the time. I saw there were going to be a lot of uses, but a lot of them I didn't know at the time. I didn't know about the kind of eye trouble that's saved by lasers. I'd never heard of it (laughs)! I couldn't imagine that.

So new things are new, and it's great. You have new ideas; where do they come from? Well, you just work at it, and work at it, and sometimes an idea comes (laughs). That's about it.

LS: A student these days has a choice of following a path that's prescribed for them, often, or trying to find their own. And that's a common struggle. People try to meet a standard even if it means sacrificing their enthusiasm. People, even at a young age, trying to study for competitive tests more than going out and finding bugs.

CHT: Um, hmm.

LS: Do you know of the books of Gerald Durrell? Did you read those?

CHT: No, uh… no.

LS: He wrote these books when he was 30. He became a zoologist and he was trying to fund his own animal studies, so he wrote about his childhood on the island of Corfu, in Greece, in 1932 to 1934, when he was an incredibly curious 10-year-old.

He had an odd family because his brother was Lawrence Durrell, becoming a famous continental writer. And he describes being in the country with the Greek peasants. He got a doctor, who was a naturalist, to teach him. And they would go out together – you know, an older man – and they would go out in the bogs and collect bugs. And he wrote these stories for kids. He was very popular in the 1940s. It just reminded me of your story.

I read these to my kid, and they were read to me when I was a little boy, very young: eight. In my own fathering I find it extremely important, critically important to keep that sense of discovery alive. I want to do everything I can to avoid quenching it. What would you say about that struggle?

CHT: Well, I think curiosity and discovery, and sense of discovery, and wanting to discover, and wanting to figure out things, figure out new things, is great. Now, that doesn't mean that you shouldn't read what other people have done carefully. And think about them, and work problems.

I learned an enormous amount by working problems in a book by my professor at Cal Tech. He wrote a book on electromagnetic theory, and he had an enormous number of problems in them. And it was a new book, and I was the first one to sort of work all the problems. I learned a whale of a lot from just trying to understand and work those problems and read the book carefully, and so on. So you learn as much as you can.

On the other hand, I've always liked to go off in other directions that I feel other people are missing. For example, when I started on microwave spectroscopy, there wasn't anybody else doing that. I started on microwave spectroscopy in World War II, and it was a new field. I saw a lot of new things that could be done, and I thought people were missing that. After a while microwave spectroscopy gained popularity. Of course, I went and invented the maser and the laser, and those became very popular. I use them, we did a lot of good science with them. Then there were a lot of good people in the field.

I thought, "Well, I ought to do something that's being missed." And I went into astronomy. Infrared astronomy especially. There were very few people working in infrared astronomy at that time, and it looked like a very rich field to me. So I went into infrared astronomy. I saw ways I could use the laser to do it, too. And also radio astronomy.

Radio astronomy wasn't very much appreciated in the early part of the century. And after the war we had a lot of radar, radar equipment. We knew how to use the radio waves very well, and short waves. But, particularly in the United States, people weren't doing radio astronomy very much.

And so I went into radio astronomy and infrared astronomy – new fields that people were missing. And that's just fun, to explore new things (laughs)! Go out into new territory and try to find out new things. That's great. Well, you want to learn everything else you can, too, and the more you know the more likely you are to find out something new. You learn what other people are doing. Interact with a lot of different people, interact with different fields. Nevertheless, think of those things that are being overlooked, not recognized. New ideas, new ways of doing things, new fields that people are not really exploiting.

And I'd move from one to the other, uh… oh, about every 15 years the field I'm doing becomes popular (laughs). Once I make a success of it, it begins to become very popular, and then I move onto something else (laughs). There are enough people in the field: they don't need me anymore.

LS: Did you ever have second thoughts about your ideas? I mean, you progress into these fields against the tide of better advice. It's sort of contradictory… it's as if you're talking from the point of view of an ice-breaker as if you had no ice to break.

CHT: (Laughs)

LS: How much soul-searching did you have to do, knowing that you were out on a limb, or didn't you think you were out on a limb?

CHT: Well, I thought I saw some promising things to do. Other people disagreed with me. You have to know how to disagree with other people. If somebody disagrees with you, if it's a serious person, you want to think carefully about what he's saying. Think carefully about whether you are really likely to be right or not.

You see, Professor Rabi and Professor Kusch wanted to stop me from doing this work toward the maser and the laser. They assured me it wasn't going to work and so on. Well, I thought about it carefully, and I thought it had a reasonable chance, and I was gonna do it. You don't want to be stopped by somebody that disagrees with you if you think you're really right, but you do want to listen to them carefully.

Now that's happened to me over and over again. In radio astronomy, for example, I thought of going into radio astronomy, and I went out to see a very famous professor who was head of the two biggest observatories in the world at that time. Mr. Bowen, he was head of Mount Wilson and Mount Palomar observatories. And I said, "Well, you know, here I am with Bell Labs, and I have all this good radio equipment, and I've learned a lot of engineering. I think I'd like to do some radio astronomy. What do you think would be the best thing to do?" And Dr. Bowen looked at me, and he said, "Well, I'm sorry, but I don't think radio waves will ever tell us anything about astronomy." Well, I was sure he wasn't right, but I didn't know just what to do, so I didn't do that, and I did microwave spectroscopy instead.

Well, later I saw ways of doing radio astronomy that I thought would be good. Now radio astronomy has turned around and become somewhat popular with astronomers. Astronomers like Dr. Bowen, and most astronomers at that time, didn't think there was that much in it, but it turned out to be a very promising, rich field.

I came out to California to do astronomy, and one of the things I wanted to do was look for molecules in space. Molecules in space. Well, using microwaves I wanted to look for ammonia, for example. Now one of the very important theorists in the department at Berkeley, Department of Astronomy, told me, "Look, that's not going to be there. The molecules can't be there. I can show you they can't be there theoretically: they get torn apart by ultraviolet radiation. They can't be there."

Well, I thought I understood enough about astronomy – I thought there were ways they could be there. And he said, "Oh, no, you can't be right. You'll just waste your time." But there was an electrical engineer at Berkeley who was willing to work with me, and a good student, Al Cheung, a Chinese immigrant student. And we worked together, we looked, and we found it! We found ammonia, and then we found water. Of all things: the water was a maser. There were natural masers out in space, and nobody had recognized that.

Now I've tried some things that don't work. Well, OK. Let me tell you one of the ones that didn't work. After finding molecules in space, I wanted to look for hydrogen out there. Now hydrogen has been found in our galaxy, but I thought that maybe there was hydrogen between galaxies. A galaxy is a big collection of stars, and that's our Milky Way, and there are many other galaxies like it. I thought that between galaxies there might be some hydrogen. We should look. I wanted to look.

Well, I persuaded a student, Arno Penzias, to work with me and look for hydrogen in inter-galactic space. And he worked hard at it. We made a maser amplifier to get great sensitivity, and he looked. He didn't find it. Well, that still made a thesis for him. He got his PhD, and he got a job at Bell Labs, and he wanted to look some more. And so he made a good maser amplifier, and he had a very good antenna at Bell Labs. And he and a friend of his, Bob Wilson, looked. They didn't find hydrogen, but what did they find? They found the Big Bang, the origin of the universe. The Big Bang. They found there was radio radiation there, coming from everywhere, due to the Big Bang: the initiation of the universe 13 billion years ago. What a wonderful discovery… So he didn't find hydrogen, a great disappointment maybe, but – wow! – he made one of the most important discoveries in the world (laughs).

LS: They stumbled on it, didn't they!?

CHT: Yeah, they stumbled on it, looking for this thing which wasn't there, you see.

So it's not bad to keep looking, keep looking. No telling what you'll find. And of course he got a Nobel Prize for that, too (laughs). And we've learned a great deal about the universe: it had an origin, and we understand a great deal about it now as a result of finding these microwaves.

So, you can be wrong. Don't worry about it too much (laughs). Try hard to be right, but don't be unwilling to take some chances. And look hard for things that might be there, that you think have a reasonable chance of being there. Look, and a failure or two won't hurt you.

SOCIETY

23. JESSICA HENRY

History   Early   Born 1989, Georgia

Like most smart kids, Jessica had a hard time with school. Finding most places inadequate, she went from one disappointing school to another until she convinced her parents that she would need to leave home in order to find a program that fit her needs.

I spoke to her at the Advanced Academy, a high school that provided her access to the college classes at the University of West Georgia where she could explore her interests in media, marketing, and public speaking.

Excerpts

"In college I find that I'm running this race with people who are running faster than me, and that encourages me to run faster. And being in a dorm with high schoolers gives me a more whole experience in that I'm not lonely, and I feel that it's OK to be smart, it's OK to be working on a paper…"

"One of the cool things that I've kind of discovered in my learning has been becoming more aware of what was going on at the time – like in religion, in literature – I can relate all the different ideas together and things start flowing, and that's cool to me. I'll hear something either in British lit. or American lit. and I jump off this deep end of, 'So that's why!' Or I jump off with thoughts like, 'I wonder if he was writing this when…' and I start going on with that. That really helps me be engaged…"

"I also told you that I procrastinate. So a lot of times my public speaking is very fresh – like when I get there it's usually the first time I'm doing it. As everybody else was giving their practice speech, I was sitting in the back of the room writing my speech and trying to memorize it…"

"When I stood on stage the energy was so alive! I had the responsibility of molding that energy and bringing attention; it was just incredible. People were coming up to me afterwards while they were scoring, and kids were swarming me. I felt like this amusement park character because people were saying, 'I got goosebumps!'…"

"From that experience I really learned my bliss. Bliss meaning something that absolutely makes me feel alive, in that energy of being on stage…"

"The journeyer is at home while underway, at home on the road itself, the road being understood not as a connection between two definite points on the earth's surface, but as a particular world. It is the ancient world of the path…"

— Karl Kerény, in *Hermes Guide of Souls*

Interview   Carrollton, Georgia, October 2006

Jessica Henry: I've done just about every form of education there is. I initially went to public school until I was in seventh grade, then we moved to Maryland, and I went from a school that had somewhere around 300 kids, to a middle school that had 3,000 kids.

In the school I came from I was so involved: I knew everybody, I was the head cheerleader and the morning announcement girl. At the new school my mom was talking to the middle school counselor and the counselor said, "The pecking order has already been established. You might want to try something else."

I had been in the gifted programs all through elementary and middle school, and all that they did was give me an extra book report. That's not challenging you, that's punishing you for learning quickly. So we tried homeschooling.

Homeschooling worked for my sister, but it didn't work for me. I needed to be in a class – I didn't like doing my homework online. I didn't like doing it on a computer – I liked being where someone was talking with me, talking to me.

In ninth grade, by a series of random events, I dual-enrolled in our local community college as both a homeschooler and as a full-time college student. It was a small college with a student-teacher ratio of 13 or 14 to one. It was great. It didn't really feel like college, mainly because I was getting the highest scores out of all the kids in my classes!

I'm a very audio-visual learner, and I was really getting that experience where I was being told information. Being in a community and having peer competition helped me, especially wanting to improve myself and be better than other college students.

That's where I started to excel. It's weird because when I look back, I wasn't really, like, spending hours at my books every night; if something came up, I would do it.

We'd thought that I would go to Carol Community College for two more years, but because of my dad's job we relocated to Atlanta at the end of my ninth grade year. We found this school called the Burrow Academy, on the campus of Burrow University. It was an all-girls private school, and I was led to believe that it was a place where high-school girls could take college courses. I went there thinking, "this will be great!" I was so excited that I'd found the best of both worlds: like Carroll Community College, but I'd get to be with high-school girls.

I get there and find that only one senior is taking a night art class at the college (laughs). They tell me, "Well, we don't think college classes would really fit into your schedule, and we're only willing to give you half-credit for each one." If I took college classes, I would never have been able to graduate! So I suffered there for a year.

At the end of the year we don't know what we're going to do. Burrow doesn't work, there isn't any other private school, and at all the local colleges you had to be at least 16 in order to dual enroll.

About a month before, we had heard about the Advanced Academy. So I asked my dad, "Hey, Dad, what about one of these (sleep away) schools?" And he's, like, "No, no. It's too early for you to be leaving home." But then my mom started saying, "We need to do what's best for Jessica, not what we want." I told my dad, "It's not like I really spend that much time with you guys anyway." When I was at Burrow, I'd be at drama practice and I'd come back at 6:30, go upstairs and do homework, come down, have dinner, go back upstairs and talk on the phone, or go on the computer. "I don't spend that much time with you guys."

The Academy was the best of both worlds. I could be with kids my age and with college kids at the same time. There's just something to that. I've used this analogy once or twice: if you look at education as a race, and if you're running the race with people who are slower than you, you naturally tend to slow down and find ways to stay ahead of the group by just jogging.

In college I find that I'm running this race with people who are running faster than me, and that encourages me to run faster. And being in a dorm with high schoolers gives me a more whole experience in that I'm not lonely, and I feel that it's OK to be smart, it's OK to be working on a paper.

I found that I tend to procrastinate the most out of all my friends. My friends would always say, "Oh, Jessica always gets the best grades!" and, "Jessica is always the smartest one!" But now my roommate is a lot smarter than me, and that's a cool thing. I totally embrace that.

LS: Do you find yourself in situations with people who are more advanced than you, and you can't keep up at their level?

JH: I had this American lit. class with people who were much smarter than I, not smarter than I, but who really understood and could draw in other concepts from literature. I would sit and just listen to these two guys go back and forth with these theories. I did OK in that class, I got a B.

Then I went to my British literature class this semester and suddenly I'm the one who's presenting all the cool theories (laughs)! I'd listen to somebody else's theory and I'm like, "Yeah, you could have totally gone ten times deeper with that! What about that... and if you're looking at the same time period let's draw on this... and let's come up with some theological conclusions about that...!" It's been a cool learning experience. I almost want to tell one of those guys, "You know, I listened to you last semester, and this semester I am you. I'm the annoying kid who comes up with all the intimidating ideas, who everybody else wants to argue with!" (Laughs)

One of the coolest classes I took here was a marketing class taught by the president of the university. The second half of this class was based upon a project. We had to go out and find a local business in Carrollton and provide marketing research and analysis for them. We had to create fliers, and we had to get, like, 380 respondents to our questionnaires and then come up with all of these conclusions. For my first semester of being a junior, I did marketing research for the president of the university! That was so cool!

LS: Tell me more about that project. What did you find out?

JH: Well, our company was Bath and Body Works. We thought that, well, they're a business, and we could draw some interesting conclusions. The conclusions weren't anything too terribly remarkable, but they were things as far as customers' preferences in that… if customers are shopping for other people, then they're more likely to come into the store if the doors are open. Something like that. We had some really interesting conclusions about who they were shopping for, and when they would shop. Not as far as day of the week, but as far as if they would shop when they just got their paycheck, just different things like that.

It wasn't too terribly unforeseen, but they were conclusions that greatly helped the local business. For example, keeping the doors open, that's a huge incurred cost for them to heat and cool the store. They wanted to know whether or not that was actually making a difference and what type of shoppers it was encouraging.

LS: So think back. You have a lot of drive. Can you remember when you got it? How did you get to being so excited about stuff?

JH: When I was in the public school system, I didn't ever think of college. When I was in middle school, I was completely concerned about who my friends were and the activities I was doing. I seriously believe that if I stayed in the public school system I would have come to my senior year and said, "Wait, now I have to apply to college?" It wouldn't have been a focus; I would have been completely concerned with having fun.

I'm not sure, but I think I can attribute a lot of my drive to that transition of going to college in ninth grade. My grades were starting to go down the last month that I was in seventh grade in public school in Pennsylvania. In Maryland, where I homeschooled for all of eighth grade, I was pretty much like, "I don't care. School is completely boring and a waste of time." It was on the computer, and I didn't get it. I didn't know what they were trying to teach me.

In seventh grade I didn't care. In eighth grade I was frustrated, fed up, and therefore, I didn't care. And then in ninth grade the excitement of being in class… I don't know if it's just me or if it's people that just have this natural competitive edge, but I liked being tested to some extent. It's like a game, and when you are homeschooling, you're learning just to learn.

When I went to college there was this excitement, this cool factor of, "I'm going to go to college! It's not going to be busy work. I'm going to be in a classroom with other adults." I initially did really well: I got a 4.0 through my entire first year in college. And it's not like they were really easy courses. I took a political science class, I took music theory, I took a theatre course, I took reading, I took English, several maths – which really secured my foundation in math.

I never really talked with any of the other college students. I was very independent. From that year on I grew up a lot in terms of my maturity and my independence and my drive. It wasn't like I was learning because I had to learn: I was there because I wanted to be there. There's something in that, in that mind-set that set me forward. If I really wanted to homeschool, I probably would have flourished there; but there is just something different when it's what you want to do and do well in. I just loved it.

LS: This sort of sounds like a bit of an accident because you said you were not that interested in school in seventh grade, and then in eighth grade you kind of endured the program, and then what you went into in ninth grade was not really school as you knew it, either. Did you have an expectation that going to college in ninth grade was going to be a neat thing for you?

JH: When I say I was really excited about school, let me just clarify: I did not go home and say, "Wow, this is so interesting! I want to learn more about this!" I did not do that at all! I would just go to class, I'd listen, I'd take it in, and I was really good in memorizing, and not necessarily regurgitating, but I could just output all that I'd learned. I didn't really have to study. I don't know if it was because of a lack of distraction in class or just motivation to do well.

There was an excitement to feeling that this was a solution. My eighth grade year had been so frustrating, and we knew that something needed to change. We were dreading entering me in the local high school where they've got signs on the door that say things like "Marijuana Kills!" and they've got a big problem with drugs. I didn't want to be there with other kids who didn't want to be there. I'm so frustrated when I'm in a class with students who don't want to be in the class.

One of the cool things that I've kind of discovered in my learning has been becoming more aware of what was going on at the time – like in religion, in literature – I can relate all the different ideas together and things start flowing, and that's cool to me. I'll hear something either in British lit. or American lit. and I jump off this deep end of, "So that's why!" Or I jump off with thoughts like, "I wonder if he was writing this when…" and I start going on with that. That really helps me be engaged.

During my first two or three weeks of history, I'd sit there and just zone out. But now, even though the teacher hasn't changed, and I don't know if it's because there's 80 people in the class and 30 of them are failing and I feel this edge, and I'm, like, "Oooo, this is kind of a dog-eat-dog world. You have to prove yourself – you have to do well in this class. You can't just slack off."

LS: It sort of sounds like you really respond to being fed stuff. What do you think about these projects where people say, "OK, come back in six months and show me what you've done?"

JH: The idea of that is quite intimidating. If you had asked me the same question last year, I think I would have said, "That sounds too scary! I don't think I can do that." But this year I've taken on more independence, even in my math classes. Last year in both of my math classes I had two good friends, really good friends, and it was really easy to turn to them and go, "Hey, what did you get?" Or, "Hey, I don't get this." But this year there is a sense of independence, and I feel that if I can't get a problem, I'm not going to try to turn to a friend; instead I'm going to think on it. It's just a small baby step, but I'm tapping into that sense of complete independence and motivation.

I think it's easy to be motivated when you're with other people. Either they're motivated and therefore you're motivated, or you're motivated because they're not motivated. So it's like, "Hm, I want to be a step above them." A lot of it is competitiveness; but then when you're all alone, what are you really striving for? You're striving to get it done. There's no time for recognition – it's just you.

LS: What's your feeling about things that aren't rewarded? I'm thinking about artists and writers who just do things because they think it's important, and there's often no appreciation at the other end. Or maybe nobody understands their work. Are you repelled by that idea of doing something that no one would understand or that no one would appreciate?

JH: No. I could do that if that was what motivated me. If my motivation was purely in getting out what I felt inside, then I could do it.

I was in this speaking competition this summer. There was a national speaking contest that was kind of like a spelling bee. It was trying to find the best high-school orator in the United States. Fifteen thousand kids were invited and 250 students sent in tapes. I sent my three-minute tape in and, as I've told you, I always had this knack for public speaking.

I got into the top 10 and they flew me down to D.C. with my mom to do this competition. Everybody was given a different topic, and my topic was "My Message for America." My message was about embracing the continent of Africa by getting involved with the lives of the people, because Africa is something that's very dear to my heart, that entire continent, especially Kenya.

I also told you that I procrastinate. So a lot of times my public speaking is very fresh – like when I get there it's usually the first time I'm doing it. As everybody else was giving their practice speech, I was sitting in the back of the room writing my speech and trying to memorize it. My mom was sitting next to me going, "You should have done this last night! You should have done this weeks ago!" (Laughs)

We had to speak in front of 600 10th graders. Ann Compton was one of our judges; the 10th-ranked judge in the court system as one of our judges; and the president of George Washington University was one of our judges.

The competition was between the top 10, and they picked my name out to go first. That seriously hindered me, because the first and second place winners were the second-to-last people to go. I won third place.

When I stood on stage, the energy was so alive! I had the responsibility of molding that energy and bringing attention; it was just incredible. People were coming up to me afterwards while they were scoring, and kids were swarming me. I felt like this amusement park character because people were saying, "I got goosebumps!" The girls in front of me were sniffling and crying like, "You moved me so much!" I kept getting that and it was like, "Wow! I've already won."

From that experience I really learned my bliss. Bliss meaning something that absolutely makes me feel alive, in that energy of being on stage.

LS: Did you feel that power while you were speaking? Were you channeling that energy by being emotional, or were you working the strength of your argument?

JH: I wasn't doing an emotional thing – it was the strength, it was the dynamic. It's like this energy – even when I'm talking to you now – if you can imagine me talking about a very serious topic and feeling the truth go out and sink in.

There were speakers who were emotional, and they got different responses. I knew that there were exclamation points in my energy going out to them, and in their energy coming back. I didn't know how it was going to affect them. I didn't know if they were going to be like, "Wow. Hmmm. Cool." I didn't think I'd make anybody cry, but apparently I got three girls to cry (laughs)! And that was cool. I discovered my power as a speaker, and so that's when I thought, "Hmm, maybe I want to be a speaker for a living. Maybe I'll be an inspirational speaker." I still don't know.

There was a time in my life when I had everything planned out. I knew where I was going to go to school. I knew how long I was going to go to school, I knew what I was going to be: a broadcast journalist. I had my entire life planned out up until I was 23. This was in ninth grade.

Now I'm feeling that when I'm a certain age I know, I'll have the qualities – maybe that's not the word – I know that I'm going to be confident and happy in whatever I'm doing, because I'm confident and happy now – not in the bad kind of confident – but I'm at peace. I'm not worried, and I don't stress, and I'm cool with everything. I just have this faith that when I'm there, it'll be fine.

LS: Tell me a little about the difference between bad confidence and good confidence, since you put it in those terms.

JH: When I define confidence I think of being assured in my strengths, knowing that my strengths are supported by what I know. I think that bad confidence can be when you base your strengths on what you feel or what you feel you know, so there's not really anything supporting it. So while you're strong in those, it's questionable how strong or secure you are as a person.

I think my confidence has come from my strengths, from being challenged and being shot down and being evaluated. In ninth grade I thought I was pretty smart, pretty analytic, and that I could come up with some pretty cool conclusions for a paper, and I could, but I BS'ed a lot. It passed for a few teachers, but in this American lit. class, after I got my first paper back, I thought, "Wow, I was BS'ing, and I've BS'ed a lot of papers before." I had made these conclusions because they sounded right, but I didn't put all of my mental power into it.

After that I would sit in class and watch these two guys debate. They were putting all of what they knew, using their strengths, and they were applying it in new ways. I was listening and thinking, "Hmmm."

My confidence has become what it is today because it's been evaluated, it's been strengthened, and it's been hardened. I'm not the smartest I'm ever going to be, that's constantly growing, and I'm going to continue to be shot down, evaluated, and then built back up stronger. I have this faith that a strong foundation can be wilted down, but it will build back up even stronger. You know what I mean?

When I think about it, the one thing that I've always struggled with since beginning my education has been apathy. I'm very motivated, and I get in these situations because I was motivated, but then I became undriven.

There would be times when I wouldn't study, and I'd still pull off these amazing grades, but then I would think, "OK, I really can't save this to the last night, to the last minute. I have to focus on this." And that's something that's still growing. It's this new motivation, this motivation that I'm not doing it because I'm supposed to, I'm doing it so I can get into a good college someday.

Last year I felt that my strengths were being supported by stilts, stilts being unsecured foundations. I've been in so many situations where I was the best of the best that it kind of lifted me up, not in an ego sense, but it lifted up who I thought I was, and defined the strengths that I thought I had. Being the best of the best in ninth grade made me think I was smarter than I really was. Then, when I got here and started college classes, I started feeling, "Hold on – under construction! – this isn't really as full as I thought it was!"

My motivation stems from not wanting to be the fastest, and not wanting to be the best. I'm not driven to get things done the fastest. I don't see any benefit in that. There are kids in the program who are taking 20 hours of credits, and I just don't see how that would benefit me; it would probably make things worse. I find that growing this rock, this foundation, is more important.

24. LOTUS BRINGING

History   **Early**   Born 1987, Vancouver, British Columbia

I was visiting Victoria and looking to meet people. I signed up for a small, weekend workshop on nondual thinking held in the nearby town of Metchosin. Most of those attending were older and knew each other. I only knew one or two people.

A young, single woman appeared whom no one knew. She was quiet, attractive, somewhat nervous, and out of her element. It was a relaxed group, with handfuls of people moving between different speakers, and everything was informal. Eventually this woman explained to us why she'd come.

Unlike most others who search for new tools to deal with crisis, she was looking for tools after having recovered from crisis, which she did using almost no tools, and having almost no help. She operated on her own psyche and, in doing so, had recovered from traumas that often kill people. This was unusual.

After the conference I asked her for this interview, and she was enthusiastic to share her experience. Whereas most other learners attribute their awakening to a mentor outside themselves, Lotus found all she needed within herself.

Excerpts

> "My entire life I had an emotionally abusive father, physically abusive to my brothers, so I had a very low sense of self-worth, so I always felt like I never fit in anywhere, like the outsider… I was always trying to please everybody so they would like me…"
>
> "When I was 24 I started to do self harm. Everything seemed repetitive; it was the same every day. I felt it was never going to change… it just felt so pointless. This was one of the reasons I became suicidal…"
>
> "I went to different therapists, and they'd always ask me what was wrong, and I didn't know. I thought that was their job to help me, right (laughs)? … I found therapy quite pointless…"
>
> "I had a very backward way of looking at myself. I was thinking this negative stuff about myself, and that was making all this negative stuff happen. I realized I was validating all these negative beliefs, things that were instilled in me, making them real…"
>
> "I realized that I could stop, that I could just stop believing in those thoughts, it was like, 'I can just stop this right now!' It was a huge epiphany. That's basically what I did, … uncovering each layer, each belief, and I went through them all…"
>
> "I lost weight and I started modeling, which was something that I thought I'd never do. I met a lot of neat people. I felt free. I knew it was OK to be me. I'm lovable, I'm approachable, I'm smart, I have potential, and I realized I have all these gifts. My past was not me at all. I guess you call it a rebirth…"
>
> "For someone who's not ready, just tell them this pain is not necessary. Usually we are the cause and the creator of our own pain, and it's because of unlooked-at situations, triggers, and identifying with a past that no longer exists. We carry those thoughts and beliefs with us."

"Beliefs are physical. A thought held long enough and repeated enough becomes a belief. The belief then becomes biology."

— Marilyn Van Derbur

"If you are here today… you are a survivor. But those of us who have made it thru hell and are still standing? We bear a different name: warriors."

— Lori Goodwin

Interview Victoria, British Columbia, November 2016

Lotus Bringing: My entire life I had an emotionally abusive father, physically abusive to my brothers, so I had a very low sense of self-worth, so I always felt like I never fit in anywhere, like the outsider. I built a persona that I fit into what I thought was needed. I was the quiet, introverted type, never free to express my real self. I always felt like I was pretending, so inside I was, like, very frustrated and lost. I was always trying to please everybody so they would like me.

LS: At what age did you recognize this about yourself?

LB: I would say it was about Grade 4, when I was nine or ten. I was overweight, so I felt like that made me stick out. In middle school I tried really hard to excel, which I did, and that gave me a sense of accomplishment, but I never felt like I belonged. I had no direction, really. I was a perfectionist, but I was hurting myself, not sleeping, things like that.

It wasn't until after high school that I started to have issues with my whole identity (laughs)! I was being a perfectionist in order to please everyone. I felt like everyone was always judging me, being critical. I had an inner voice that was analyzing everything I did and always observing everyone else. I would read the group's emotions in order to blend in. I had lots of friends because I was a chameleon, able to fit into every group.

Later on I learned that was completely in my head. Inside I felt unlikeable. I wasn't good enough. I didn't have anything to offer. I was quite popular, but I never felt like I belonged anywhere. Does that make sense? I graduated in 2008, and shortly after that I had, I guess, what you would call a nervous breakdown.

LS: Were you living at home?

LB: Yeah, I was living at home. My parents were going through a nasty divorce. I was in college, but I didn't know what classes to take. All my friends moved to Vancouver and Alberta, so I lost my support group and felt alone. I suffered with depression for a few years.

When I was 24 my best friend, who I'd known since kindergarten, passed away to a brain tumor. So I lost my longest friend and the only other person who could validate my childhood memories, that was really hard. Shortly after that my grandmother passed as well.

I was feeling really trapped. I wasn't doing well at school. I was procrastinating and I had major anxiety. My grades were dropping really low, and I was getting more and more depressed...

LS: Let me just tell you, you don't have to go back there, emotionally, in case you feel yourself getting drawn back there.

LB: No, it's OK. It feels good to talk about it. It's only been the last few months that I realized how sick I was.

When I was 24 I started to do self harm. I went to different therapists, and they'd always ask me what was wrong, and I didn't know. I thought that was their job to help me, right (laughs)? I always felt like I was talking to a brick wall because there was nothing coming back at me. I found therapy quite pointless. The questions they asked were like, "How are you feeling today?" You know, I could do that on my own. They never really offered advice.

I also became bulimic. I guess that was a sense of control, because I was quite overweight. I'm not exactly sure how it developed, but I had that for seven years, from around age 20 to 27. That was a long time. It became almost normal because it was, like, an activity I did (laughs). It got so habitual.

I'm going to fast forward now to this year...

The divorce was finished, and I was staying at home with my mom. She's good, I love my mom. It's my dad that was the major issue. He's not emotionally available. He's judgmental of everything and everyone. Everyone's wrong and he's always right. To grow up in that environment was really hard because there's no way to ever please him. You felt like you could never be anything. You were always wrong, no matter what. That was really frustrating, so I isolated myself, in the house, in my room. They always sent me to my room, so I went there on my own, to escape.

So, this year I had a concussion from falling off a horse. I had to withdraw from school that semester and spend three or four months recovering. It was quite severe. I could barely write, barely talk. It was quite scary.

I started going through my "dark night of the soul," or whatever (laughs). I went to another therapist, and they were starting to help me through my depression, but they put me on medicine again. Western medicine cures the symptom but not the cause, so my depression kept popping up because I never dealt with the internal issue, which was a sense of identity.

Then, in July, a deer hit my car. It was a big crash, and the car was written off. After that I had very bad vertigo.

LS: You were hurt in that collision too?

LB: Not as bad, but I had whiplash, and it's not fun. That lasted for three weeks, and I could barely walk. Everything was really dizzy, and I had a lot of weird experiences. Everything was shaky because my eyes, and everything would be moving, constantly, everything spinning around. Not fun (laughs).

In July I decided I was done being depressed, I was done being bulimic. I was suicidal.

LS: So when you say you were "done," do you mean you became suicidal?

LB: I was suicidal when I was 22. It's called suicidal ideation: I was thinking about it. I had that for about a year and a half, and I researched ways to do it.

LS: And that passed?

LB: Yeah, I got over that, but this year it came back really bad. I needed to find something to cure me because Western medicine wasn't working. I had to find the root cause of what was going on.

I should go back two years, sorry. I was studying psychology, and I wanted to practice the stuff I was learning, to experiment, so I decided to practice on losing weight. I cut out dairy, and I cut out carbs and wheat, and gluten. I ate a lot of veggies and protein, and started exercising. I lost 100 pounds in nine months. It came off quite easily. I leveled out to 130 within a year and a half, and I maintained it.

LS: So that started two years ago, so now we're up to six months ago, so your current body type is fairly recent!

LB: Yes, my aunts didn't recognize me. They thought I was my sister. Also, I legally changed my name, about four years ago, when I was 24. My old name, Jenny, was very common and there were so many Jennys, and my last name was way too long. I kind of wanted to distance myself from my father's name.

I changed my name, and I changed my body. I was basically like a new person, except I still didn't know who I was. I felt very confused, like my soul was fractured. I felt like I had multiple personality disorder. I behaved different ways to different people, and I never felt congruent. I was always, like, limited in my behavior and stuff. I would always think before I spoke, and I was always critical of myself. It's almost like my father's voice was ingrained in my head.

After the weight loss, I tried to understand why I was depressed, what are the core reasons. I had a note pad and a piece of paper, and I wrote down all the feelings of what depression was. So I wrote loneliness, worthlessness, low self-esteem, failure, and all that stuff.

Then, from each emotion, I would link what thoughts led to it, and from those thoughts I would draw an arrow to the beliefs that supported it: "I'm a failure... because I'm stupid." Then I would write why I believed that in the first place, say because I never received any rewards, or praise, or recognition for anything.

I had a very backward way of looking at myself. I was thinking this negative stuff about myself, and that was making all this negative stuff happen. After I realized I was validating all these negative beliefs, things that were instilled in me, making them real, I started to make peace with them, or find ways to stop them.

Like, I would write them down… (writes) like this is one: self abuse. I self-abused because I thought I deserved punishment, because I was worthless. This was the self-hatred part. I was self-abusing by cutting, being bulimic, and self-sabotaging, getting into debt, a lot of stuff (laughs). I would write "self-abuse… not seeing your higher good." When I was ready, I would let go of the belief that I deserved punishment, and I deserved to suffer, and that I didn't deserve happiness or to be loved. I would work on beliefs such as deserving.

I'd stop thinking about how the past could have been different and going into the guilt about what I'd done to myself. I started to apologize to myself for behaving the way I did. The past made me who I am today, and even though there was a lot of turmoil when I was growing up, it created a strong woman. I don't want to change that.

I started watching YouTube videos about meditation and self-hypnosis for calming and relaxing. That led to understanding and self-awareness, and that's where spirituality started coming in. I started being aware of why I behaved this way. I realized I was behaving because of false beliefs, which were only in my head. I thought certain things were true, so I would feel these emotions, and the emotions created behaviors, and the behaviors created the reality. It was circular, and kept going on and on.

Once I realized that I could stop, that I could just stop believing in those thoughts, it was like, "I can just stop this right now!" It was a huge epiphany. That's basically what I did. I started practicing self-love. I kept uncovering each layer, each belief, and I went through them all, like co-dependency with my mom. It was quite freeing because, at the end, I was able to understand why I behaved the way I did.

I started automatic writing. It was almost as if there was a different person that was with me, that's what they call your higher self, or whatever. I felt I was becoming my authentic person (laughs). It was really cool.

LS: Did you feel you were getting in touch with some kind of guidance?

LB: Yes. It was definitely a kind of experience... um... you know, it was a spiritual experience, something more than yourself, right? However you want to say that (laughs).

LS: Were you surprised with what you were writing?

LB: Yeah, definitely. It wasn't me at all, so that was really cool.

LS: Who was it?

LB: I started getting synchronicities with angel signs. One of them was Archangel Zadkiel, who is related to higher learning and guidance. Because of the vertigo, I was seeing blue auras everywhere, which was also kind of weird because I don't know if it was part of the spiritual thing, or a remnant of what happened before, but it was definitely a different feeling. I felt at one with the world. I actually felt true bliss.

LS: Did this come out of automatic writing, or did you start to experience this at other times?

LB: Yeah, in my whole life. There were times when I felt my consciousness was outside of my body, which was really odd, but it only lasted about an hour or so. I felt different. I just couldn't explain it to anyone. I still don't know anything about how to go about spirituality, or the systems.

The thing that came to me on my own was oneness and togetherness in one. I was able to levitate, to have an out-of-body experience, just above my body. When I did a meditation, I was able to do a lot of... kind of weird... like you're dreaming, but you can go into your dream, and all these different visions of like dolphins and, like, weird things. I can't explain it.

I was able to do this deep meditation on my own. I put on Jason Stephenson's guided meditations and self-hypnosis. I just liked the tone of his voice. I was able to listen to him for 20 minutes, and then turn him off and do my own thing. I was able, and I'm still able, to go into this very peaceful, relaxed state, being totally at one with myself. I just push out all the noise, and that's really nice. It's like sometimes you forget you can do these things (laughs).

That lasted for about two months, and then life started to pick up again because of school and stuff. The vertigo passed around mid-August, so I was able to drive, and I went back to school.

During this time I was able to manifest a lot of things that I really wanted in my life, which was really awesome. Like I wanted things like a new car, and even though I didn't want a car crash per se, I did want to get a new car, you know… I got my horses, I got two horses. I got a lot of things, and goals in my life just worked out on their own. I kept having synchronicities, and all kinds of interesting stuff. I can still manifest things that I want, and it's fun (laughs).

It's kind of like you want something, you dream of it, you have a vision of it, and you kind of feel it out, and then those opportunities in life you're probably more perceptive to… whereas you wouldn't be otherwise. Like college courses are expensive, and I've been able to work out payment plans, and things like that, and everything just falls into place. I just had to surrender to the process. I was always trying to control everything, and I just had to let go.

I lost the weight and I started modeling, which was something that I thought I'd never do. I met a lot of neat people. I felt free. I knew it was OK to be me. I'm lovable, I'm approachable, I'm smart, I have potential, and I realized I have all these gifts. My past was not me at all.

I guess you call it a rebirth. I felt like a whole new person because I'm now able to speak out and not hold back, not criticize myself. I know who I am now, but at the same time learning who I can become. I'm learning new interests and hobbies, because I never put myself out there before. Do you want to ask me any more questions (laughs)?

LS: No, I just want to know how you got to what sounded like completion, because… I could see you thinking about it.

LB: Yeah, like one of these things I wrote was, "I accept the thoughts and emotions of self-hatred. I take responsibility, I accept this as reality, which became my reality. This is an irrational belief. I actually love myself, all of myself. These old thoughts are no longer valid. I release them now, and I no longer recognize self-hatred as my reality. They served a purpose when I was a child, but they're no longer needed."

I understand a lot about how the family dynamic worked. I have two brothers and a sister, so it's a fairly large family. I was so rolled up in it… I was not even existing. Everything seemed repetitive, it was the same every day. I felt it was never going to change, and I didn't want to get a nine to five job and have a family, it just felt so… pointless. This was one of the reasons I became suicidal.

I couldn't find happiness anywhere, but really it was because I was hating myself so much that I couldn't realize the beauty in life, you know? There is so much out there which I never picked up on. Part of me still feels regretful because I wasted so much of my life. At the same time I know that's not true. I'm still working on that.

The last time I talked to my higher self I asked her for guidance on how to heal that part of me. I asked her a lot of why questions (laughs). I'm going to read to you a little writing I have because I like how it's phrased.

"I can only recover from depression through action. I want to understand why I behaved in certain ways, why I did this to myself. I discovered I was self-sabotaging because I was afraid to succeed. Success would mean I had grown into my father's vision of me, that he won over me, or something. But I realized that he never wanted any of this for me, he actually loved me, and I let all that anger and frustration go."

You don't take the time to look deep inside yourself because of everyday happenings. You never bring it to the forefront, but if you just lie down, relax, go deep within yourself, and ask some of these hard questions, the answers come up, they do. And they guide you to the truth of why you do these things. With that you can start taking steps to let go of these emotions through acceptance and forgiveness. Forgiveness for the people who you think hurt you, and just let it go. It's in the past, and it no longer has control over you.

Once you're ready to let go, that's all you have to do. Cut the cords of the past. Those pains don't serve you, they're only causing you pain. You're causing your own suffering, so forgive them, and forgive yourself for carrying these behaviors and for hurting yourself. You don't have to hurt anymore. There's no point to it. Don't think about the future, that just creates anxiety. Live in the moment and experience life.

LS: Did these insights come first, enabling you to change yourself? Or do you think you were ready to change, and then found the insights that made sense of your new awareness?

LB: I used a technique where I went back in time and talked to my inner child. My inner child knew who I was all the time. I told her she would always be comforted and safe, so she could let go of these feelings. When I came back out from that I felt I could let her go. I no longer had to hold on to my past in order to protect her.

Feelings of pain and fearfulness. I felt like I was fractured, right? The hurt and abused child who couldn't get attention or validation, the me that I presented to everyone. I felt like I was holding on to all these parts of me, and I let those go. There was this integration of all of them coming together. She's integrated into me now. The guidance came to me because I was ready for it. If I wasn't ready, I don't think the answers would have come.

LS: Is there anything you could say to people who aren't ready? That's almost a contradiction in terms, because if they're not ready, then they're not going to hear it.

LB: Yeah, really. Like my mom. I did write something like that, so let me find it… I did automatic writing. It comes to me at night, and it's kind of mumbled. I would have this different voice in my head telling me all these fun things. It got some interesting stuff into the light.

This is what I wrote to my future self, in case this would happen again. "Face your fears," that's the first thing I would say. "Fears only grow larger if you ignore them. Fear is actually your ally because it's helping you recognize your weaknesses. Recognize that vulnerabilities create the place you are at. Awareness of your vulnerabilities leads to higher self-knowledge."

With my weight loss, one of the big things I decided was everyday I'm going to be working on weight loss, because time's passing, right? If I didn't do that, I could look back two years from now and regret never taking action, and I'd be the same weight I was then. Do it for yourself, don't do it for anyone else, that's the most important thing. You need to be tired of being in pain. For me it was death or get better. I really had no choice. I had nowhere else to go.

For someone who's not ready, just tell them this pain is not necessary. Usually we are the cause and the creator of our own pain, and it's because of unlooked-at situations, triggers, and identifying with a past that no longer exists. We carry those thoughts and beliefs with us.

I was the creator of my own pain. It took a lot of digging to realize that. I didn't realize that I hated myself. I had no clue. Once I realized I had self-hatred, it was like... it was hard.

LS: When you realized it, how did it appear?

LB: Sadness and guilt. I was just depressed and helpless. I had no idea of what was causing my suffering, and it was these false beliefs which I was validating through my own behaviors.

Shame almost. Like, as an intelligent being I was doing that to myself, but I had no idea. I was doing all those behaviors: procrastination, self-sabotage, cutting, bulimia, suicidal ideation... all this stuff to hurt myself because I hated myself. I had no clue.

LS: What's your main interest now? If you had to pick a major, what would you do?

LB: (Laughs) I've been trying to figure that out myself, actually! It's really hard because I feel like psychology is no longer... it's finished.

I've been thinking of, not a life coach per se, but helping people lose weight, help people with their behaviors, and understand their behaviors, and why they create their behaviors. Why they have these emotions to begin with. I don't know exactly what I want to do. I want to help people awaken in the sense of understanding why they are who they are.

I was overweight for 25 years of my life. My mom was overweight, my parents were overweight, it was going to be this way, I couldn't change it. I thought I was going to be overweight forever. I felt really bad. And then I realized that I could, and I did. It's partly recognizing what to do, but also taking the action to do it. It's the action stuff that's often missing.

I wrote the other day... I was playing with the idea of light and dark and how we perceive things. But what if there are totally different realities that we can't understand because we've never perceived them? Like there's North and South, but there are also East and West, other realities. Does that make sense? If we only know light and dark, then we're living in a two-dimensional consciousness.

There's so much I'm interested in. Some of it's more 'out there,' but I don't really care because it's interesting. I'm always learning now. I'm trying to make sense of it, and it's still kind of happening... you know? I don't know. I've rediscovered a passion for learning, and I'm just having fun with it (laughs).

25. JAZ LIN

| History | Early | Born 1986, Austin, Texas |

I met Jaz when I gave her a lift to a meeting I was attending in Western Massachusetts. We met for the second and last time for this interview.

Of all the people I've spoken with, only Jaz has entirely cast off her connections to the past and preconceptions of the future and sailed off to discover the real world on foot. Three years have past, and she's still sailing. She's an inspiration. I love her.

Postscript: Jaz now uses her name Jiling.

Excerpts

> "Everything that I've done has been a journey of exploration, of outer and inner exploration, without any focus or commitment, which I would like to have, but maybe I'm just not ready for it. I'm just 23, I don't know…"
>
> "It's very important to follow your instincts and whatever feels right, because everyone has their own path. Take the experiences as they come, and the people. Remember that every person that walks by is full of stories! Don't look down on anybody for what you see them initially to be, because everybody has something really special and golden inside…"
>
> "I remember sitting on a ridge once and looking out at town, with all of its bright lights and ridiculousness, and then looking at the other side and it was night, and at the darkness and the mountains, and just thinking, like, 'OK, all the people down there, they chose the comfort. They just want to be comfortable. That is why all of this exists'…"
>
> "Looking back, everything makes sense. Everything makes sense all together, and you can't be really, like, 'I didn't really want to go to jail.' I hated going to jail in New York City… It was horrible. And back then, when it happened, it was hell. But if it didn't happen… I wouldn't be who I am today. So everything makes sense all together…"
>
> "You may often be alone, but you're never, ever, ever lonely until you allow yourself to be lonely, because everything's alive. Our ancestors walked under the same sky that we are looking up at… and we're going to live, and we're going to die, all staring at the same sky, under the glow of the same sun, sleeping under the same moon and stars. This earth that we're walking on has been walked on by so many animals, and so many people, and so many spirits blowing through the wind, and that is so special!"

"Arriving at each new city, the traveler finds again a past of his that he did not know he had: the foreignness of what you no longer are or no longer possess lies in wait for you in foreign, unpossessed places."

— Italo Calvino, from *Invisible Cities*

"One never goes so far as when one doesn't know where one is going."

— Johann Wolfgang von Goethe

Interview   Danbury, Connecticut, May 2009

Jaz Lin: I was born in Austin, Texas, where my dad went to school. That's where he got his PhD way back in '87.

LS: That's where I went to school. I got mine in '85, I think. What field was he in?

JL: He was in engineering, I'm not sure which kind exactly. He said he spent all his time in the library. So if you saw a little Chinese nerd sitting in the library with his head always down, that was my dad (laughs).

LS: What's your mother do?

JL: She's a medical technologist. She works in a laboratory. She looks through microscopes, takes blood samples, and makes blood go donk-a-donk-a-donk-a and then looks at them, et cetera.

LS: What did you learn from them?

JL: Both of them are really good with people, and people really like both of them; people just like them. My dad is a leader, and it was like that for me, too, when I was a kid. I was usually the leader of the pack.

But my dad also has a bad temper, and I got that from him also. I tend to blow up really easily. He meditates a lot now, and so he's really, really a lot calmer than he was way back. Still not zunnk! but a lot more chill. From my mum I inherited her... hmm, I'll have to think about that one.

They say that from when I was in the belly, from then until now, I've always been a troublemaker. When I was in the belly I was always kicking and moving around, and causing trouble in the stomach.

When I was born, they say that it was a really difficult birth, like my mum was in labor for a while. The whole time that she was in the hospital, the Challenger (NASA space shuttle) was exploding over and over on the television, and everybody's running around like, "Gaa!" And she's lying there, and I'm in turmoil in the belly, and she's, like, "This really sucks (laughs)." So those were the conditions under which I was born.

It's really interesting to ask my mum about what I was like as a kid, because it sounds like that's pretty much how I am today. She says that I was very independent; I would do whatever I wanted. I was very rebellious, like they would say, "Sleep, sleep, sleep," and I would be like, "No! No! No!" (Laughs) So they would stick me in the crib, and I would pretend to go to sleep, and then once they left the room, I'm out of the crib (laughs) crawling around. And they see me under a table and they're, like, "What are you doing! Get back in there!"

But in school, both me and my sister were really good kids. At home we got in trouble all the time, but in school we were star students. I'm not sure how that happened. I haven't thought about that one before.

My first day in public school I didn't know what to do, so I was sitting and watching everybody, and then the teacher says, "Everybody, look at Joyce!" And I'm, like, "Oh, no!" And she's, like, "Look how she is so good, she's just sitting there with her hands in her lap and her feet crossed. You guys should all sit like that." And I'm thinking, "Oh my god, now everybody's going to hate me." (Laughs) That was pretty funny.

Then up until college: all straight A's because school was easy. School was fun. All of our teachers loved us. I'm not sure how that happened.

And then we started going to meditation group in fourth grade. I was in fourth grade, and my sister was in third grade. My dad had been reading the books of this lady for a while, her name is Ching Hai, and she's of the Sat-Ma tradition. It's sort of like a Hindu-Chinese-Buddhist mix. I was nine years old.

Also in that year I started playing piano and violin, and all of my family became vegetarian, and that year we also entered public school. Before that we were in private school. That year was big.

LS: You mentioned meditation – was it important?

JL: It changed the structure of our lives because now every Saturday night we'd go to the meditation center until Sunday. And then we'd go do group meditation on Wednesday and Friday. So after school, instead of just doing whatever we wanted, we would be with my dad and we'd meditate with him for half an hour, and then go do homework, or play, or whatever. So that was a change.

In the beginning I was really, really into it, but then by seventh grade it became a source of rebellion; it became something I was really, really,... "Ok, life sucks because of that!" Or that was one of the reasons why life sucks. So in seventh grade that was one of the things I pitted against my parents.

LS: Did that become a big battleground? Did you win the battle?

JL: I stopped meditating regularly in seventh grade. Instead of meditating I would pretend to meditate, but instead be reading, or something like that, or somehow entertaining myself while I was sitting there (laughs).

LS: Did you to fake it the whole time?

JL: Yeah, pretty much.

LS: So you never really put your foot down?

JL: No, no. I never, never ever, ever talk back to my parents, because that's totally unacceptable. It's unacceptable in our culture because you are supposed to respect your elders. For example, if my dad and my mom are, like, yelling at us and lecturing us, and if we speak back in some way, then they will get just even more angry and do something horrible to make us not talk next time.

My sister now talks more than I do; she talks back more, and they have more of a dialog, and I've been starting to do it, but still not as much as she can. I just stuff it all in. Like they'll be, like, "Da da da da!" And I'll be, like, "Guhhh…"

LS: Even now?

JL: Yeah still. Even now. I'm learning to express more, but I still can't really talk back, no.

Last time I went back to my parents' place I don't remember what happened, but I do remember conflict. They were yelling at me about something, I don't remember what, and I was displeased about it. My way of coping with it is I'll just let them yell at me. I was just, like, "Yup, yup, yup, yup." And then I'd bike off.

That's how I coped with it in seventh grade, too. They would yell at me, and then I would bike off somewhere and go deal with it on my own, usually up into the mountains. And I would bike further and further distances, and be away from home for longer and longer periods of time. The next day I'd stay at school for as long as possible, and then come home and go off into the mountains, and repeat.

LS: Would you say that your recollection of your life with your family was that they were unsupportive?

JL: I know that my parents loved me very much. I know that they loved me very, very much, and that they've tried their best to be good parents, and they got me through college. They're not totally happy with what I'm doing now, but they're not constantly attacking me, either.

Back when I was really into photography my dad was my greatest fan. And with what I'm doing now, they don't think it's good, they don't think it's healthy, so they're not like, "Yeah, yeah! Go for it!" But they're not, like, completely "Keeek!" about it, either.

My dad's basic thing is, like, "OK, I don't like it, but this is the life you chose, so be it." And my mum says, "Whatever makes you happy! But remember that you can be more comfortable if you want to be." And they leave it at that. But that's because I reminded them that this is a choice, the life that I lead is a choice, it's not a necessity, and that I'm fine. I'm fine.

LS: So tell me about your life. What is your choice? What are you doing?

JL: I am wandering around. Since college I've been bouncing around the country with no real destination or real purpose. I mostly go to communities, and I'm bouncing less than I used to. I don't know how to put it into a nice little nugget. When I first finished college I was on the photo path. I was on the path to becoming a photojournalist. And then I decided I didn't want to do that anymore when I was down in Alabama. And I thought, "OK, I could go back to California and feel like a loser, or I can go somewhere else because I'm in Alabama and I'm close to places I've never been before, so I might as well go check it out."

From there I went to visit a friend in Arkansas, and along the way I met someone really cool in Tennessee, who was, like, "Yo, there's something happening in West Virginia. Do you want to come up with us?" So I'm in Arkansas and I'm thinking, "Do I want to continue West, or do I want to go back East?" And I decided to go back East, and that's the basic path: one thing leads to another, and no real control takes place.

I've definitely tried to take control, many, many times, but plans just don't work out. When I was down in Alabama, for example, I was deciding, "OK, do I want to go check out the Florida Keys, or do I want to go up to Northern Alabama where there's mountains, because I really, really miss mountains. Oh, my gosh, there are all these possibilities and opportunities." And then I'm, like, "I'm going to go down to the Keys."

So I start going and then I think of the mountains and I'm, like, "Never mind, I'm going to go up to the mountains." And then once I hit the mountains and I'm sitting in the woods all by myself and I'm, like, "I'm lonely." I think, "I should visit a friend!" So I decide to go up to Arkansas, and along the way I meet somebody else, and it just turns my direction another way.

A good way of putting what I'm doing right now is that I'm being like the wind. I'll go, and I'll flow, and I'll run into something that I like, and it will push me in one direction. Then I'll run into something I don't like, and it will push me in another direction. Everything I encounter, which I always consider is pretty random – but Daniel doesn't think is random, but to me it feels pretty random – pushes me here and there. So being like the wind.

LS: How did you first get away? How did you "break the strings"?

JL: That's a good question. Someone else asked me that question, "Why did you decide to go." And I was sort of, like, "I don't know." It just sort of happened. Up until I got to Tennessee, there wasn't much direction at all. I'd take out my map in the morning and be, "OK, that place looks good. I'll go there." So it was pretty directionless in the beginning, and I didn't know anything at all.

LS: Were you hitchhiking?

JL: No, I was driving. I started off driving and eventually decided to get rid of my car because gas is expensive. My first time going across the country on my own was the second year of college. I went across the country in the summer for an internship in Delaware. I spent the summer in Delaware, which was a place where I didn't know anyone beforehand, and that was really huge for me. And then I came back. That was a pretty big first bite of the travel bug.

After college it became a whole whirlwind of activity. I bounced over to Hawaii for a photo convention. Bounced back and went up to Utah to check out something, and wandered around Utah for a month. Bounced over to Northern California... Da! Da! Da! Da! All that just contributed to my wandering nature. And then moseying down to Alabama for the photo internship – it was a nice, long mosey down to Alabama – and along the way meeting a lot of people and enjoying a lot. And after Alabama I just kept on going with it, driving.

Driving is a pretty good way to get around because you're totally in control of everything, except you're tethered to the car. So the only difficult thing about it is where to park the car.

I parked my car in Tennessee and roamed around with a friend for a while, down to Alabama to prune apple trees, and then back up to Tennessee to catch a ride up to West Virginia for a week-long convention on mountain-top removal. From there we caught a free bus over to D.C., and from there we caught another free bus up to New York City – I don't remember how we finagled that one – and then hung out in New York City for a while, and caught a ride through Craig's List back down to Tennessee. Drove up to Upstate New York to live in a community for a bit.

Communities are awesome! That was my second community, the one in Upstate New York, and that one is huge. Two hundred seasonal staff that work there for about 3 months at a time, for the summer. I stayed there for three months, which is a really long time for me.

The community-living thing exposed me to all sorts of people from all over the place. That was another thing about college, too, meeting people from all over the place. Ideas from all over the place, and just, like, "Oh, cool! You're from there, and that's what that place has to offer? I want to go there some day." And same thing with Omega (Omega Institute) and all of the people that come through, from the staff to the participants – it's just a full spectrum of color.

By then, that was the longest I had been without my car. I had been living out of my car, which is pretty sweet. The car can hold a whole lot of junk. It was my storage room, and I could sleep outside, and I could fit everything inside of it, and it would take me from A to B to C. But being without the car for such a long period of time made me realize that, "Wow, I don't need it."

While I was at Omega, somebody gave me a book by a guy called Tamarack Song, and it's about primitivism. So I read the book, and it just jived with me so well. At the end of the book there's a website. So I check out the website, and I see that they need people to help out. And I get in touch with Tamarack and we connect, and I'm, like, "OK, I'd really like to come visit." They're in Wisconsin, and I have this strange idea that I'm going to go over to visit them.

I took a Greyhound to Wisconsin and ended up hanging out there for half a year. That was another community. That community was a bunch of people living out in the woods in upstate Wisconsin. That was the first real, real winter of my life, and it was beautiful.

LS: You didn't have trouble adapting to the cold?

JL: Oh, no, because I got there in autumn, so my body adjusted to it. And I'm young… and strong and…

LS: Fat (laughs)!

JL: Yeah (laughs)! Yeah, we ate fat! It was good (laughs).

And then from there I hitchhiked over to Massachusetts, and that was my first time hitchhiking for a long, long journey. I had done some hitching in Hawaii, and some hitching in New Jersey, and some other random places, but it wasn't really standing on the side of the road with my thumb extended.

I was going from Wisconsin to Massachusetts, and Massachusetts was where I spent last summer, that was – I gave myself a month for that journey – it was about a thousand five hundred miles, and I had no idea how long it would take. It was fun and sometimes scary, but not really, because I sort of eased myself into it. When I first left that community, which was the Teaching Drum (Teaching Drum Outdoor School) in Wisconsin, I caught a ride out of there with a friend who was going up to the U.P., the upper peninsula of Michigan.

Hitching is a good way to get to know the people and the area. If you're going slow, you get to know the land. If you catch a really fast ride, then it's just like, Phsst! And you're across. It can be really fast.

LS: That's where I met you. You were living in a tent, or a hut, on the other side of a field. What happened in Massachusetts?

JL: I was working on a farm over there for the summer. And we were also doing a journalism workshop. The first month that I was there I was living on the land all by myself, which was sort of lonely, but it was a good transition from being at the Teaching Drum community back into the normal world.

I came early to help set up, which was fun. So first there was me living on that side of the road and wandering around the woods, and Keith, who was running the program, with his family living on this side of the road. We would take care of the vegetables, build structures for other people, and get things ready for when everybody was going to show up. I found a pretty good balance between town life and woods life.

Within a month everybody else shows up for the program, and life changes because all of a sudden there's a whole bunch of people. Now all the woods aren't just for me to roam in, and there's also more of a schedule, like we all meet together in the morning, and we come together at certain times, and I don't take care of food just for me anymore. It was a fun experiment.

This was really interesting to see… and I didn't really notice it while I was there, but looking back I see myself going through the transition from the primitive Teaching Drum community, back into living on my own, and then into a farm community.

As far as the journalism aspect, the program was sort of scattered. All of us had a main project, and mine had to do with nomadism, actually. It didn't really move forward at all. Daniel was going to be the first person that I interviewed, and our interview didn't get very far. We just started talking about other things (laughs). It was fun, though.

LS: Did it change your direction?

JL: At that time I was really into primitivism, and pretty much everybody at the Teaching Drum is there because they are interested in learning about how to live off the land the way the Native Americans did: building everything on your own, foraging for foods, hunting animals, and that sort of thing. It's a very back-to-the-earth, non-farming thing.

Their philosophy was anti-agricultural. They think that agriculture was this huge tool for civilization to become the way that it is. Without agriculture we would still be out in the woods, pretty much. Now that we have agriculture, we can sit around talking instead of being out foraging for food.

So here I am coming from Wisconsin, working on a farm and going, like, "This is very different from what I've been spending the past half year doing! Do I really want to be here?" The community that happened when everybody showed up knocked me off balance. I loved everybody that I was living with, but we didn't jive completely.

Also, everybody there was more technologically oriented than I was. Back at the Teaching Drum I rarely touched technology, so I came back out feeling a little bit snobby about technology, like, "Pshttt! Computers!" And I'm still a little bit that way, which isn't too healthy.

LS: You think not being technological is unhealthy?

JL: Well, it's not that being not technological is not healthy. The unhealthy part is being snobbish about it. I think being uppity about anything is sort of stupid.

I remember sitting on a ridge once and looking out at town with all of its bright lights and ridiculousness, and then looking at the other side and it was night, and at the darkness and the mountains, and just thinking, like, "OK, all the people down there, they chose the comfort. They just want to be comfortable. That is why all of this exists."

Then I look at the mountains, and it's all dark and mysterious, and it's the unknown, and it's especially unknown for all the people in the town. They have no idea; they know nothing about what's out there. So it's understandable. Everybody has their reasons for doing stuff. I can't be uppity because somebody chooses to live in a cubicle instead of play outside.

I ended up leaving the program and the farm before the program ended. I don't remember how early I left; I think I just left one or two weeks earlier. I was really conflicted about it. Daniel was going down to Florida for a wedding, and I'm like, "Oh, I haven't been down to Florida and I really want to go, but I really want to finish this. I'm so close to finishing." I decided to go with him.

LS: So where are you now? What's next?

JL: Aw, boy. I try not to look too far forward because usually my plans don't walk that far before something comes along to shake 'em. This summer I'm going to be working at Great Hollow, a YMCA-sponsored wilderness school for kids age five through 14; a huge range. I think I'm going to be in the department that teaches kids primitive skills.

I'm really excited to be playing in the woods with kids all summer long. I've heard so many different things about this place, like about kids who are really into it, and then about the teenagers who are just, "Phffft! I'm too good for everything!" I love the little ones, and I love the big ones, and I just love sharing what I'm into. I think there's something to be said about being really, really excited about something, and sharing that excitement, and getting other people… just to see.

One of the cool things about hitchhiking is that you get to meet people from all walks of life. And I get to ask them, "So, what makes you excited to wake up in the morning?" Something I figured out at a party once is that instead of asking people, "Where are you from?" or, "What do you do?" or all those usual boring questions, is to ask them, "So, what are your dreams like?" (Laughs) And watch them go, "Huh? OK." And then go from there.

Looking back, everything makes sense. Everything makes sense all together, and you can't be really, like, "I didn't really want to go to jail." I hated going to jail in New York City.

LS: Did you?

JL: Yeah, I went to jail in New York City. It was horrible. And back then, when it happened, it was hell. But if it didn't happen I wouldn't have stayed longer in New York City, and then I wouldn't have gone to Omega because I wouldn't have learned of Omega, and this and that wouldn't have happened, and I wouldn't be who I am today. So everything makes sense all together.

That's something that's so difficult to remember when times are tough. You know, when something so horrible happens that I'm just sitting there, like, "Oh! Man!" It's really difficult to remember that it's all part of the story. Maybe not now, but it will eventually make sense.

As far as where I'm going right now, this summer's job is going to last until August or September. Right now, after that happens, I want to go back to the desert. I'm visualizing myself going back to the desert when the summer's over, but who knows what the end of the summer will bring.

LS: Is that how you make things happen, by visualizing them and taking the train, or car, or bus that goes in the direction? It sounds like you don't make all these phone calls, and arrange all these things ahead of time, but maybe you do. How did you get this job at Great Hollow?

JL: I learned about this place from a friend that I met three years ago. I got into the wilderness-therapy thing after college – that was the path that I was originally going to walk – and then I decided I was going to walk on the photo path instead. And then, after the photo path, I decided to walk the "unpath."

But there is some direction, and I do try to take control. I would love to… I don't know… that's a difficult one to say. Part of me is, like, "Yeah! I want to know what the future brings." And another part of me is, like, "No, I don't want to know because then it won't be as exciting." I don't know, I really don't know (laughs). I think that there's a definite part of myself that is, "Yeah, I'm going to set this up, and this is going to work." And if it doesn't work, "Oy!" But the other part of me has learned not to wince when things don't go as planned and just to take it as it comes.

LS: Is there any chance that somebody would offer you a stable, long-term thing that involves obligation and responsibility, and would you take it?

JL: Well, hmmm… Actually, Daniel was trying to get me to commit to a relationship. And that was difficult (laughs). Something that's long-term is definitely tempting, because being on the road gets tiring after a while. After not really having anything to hold on to, being offered something secure is really, really tempting.

When I was leaving Alabama, one of my editors said, "Be careful that you don't become one of them." And what he meant is to make sure that I didn't go too much in one direction, because then I might go too much in the other direction, and then I might become somebody who I really don't want to be.

I can see how that happens, and I can see how it has happened to all the old hippies. They walked too far in one direction, and then they walked in the other direction, and now they're the boxes.

Right now I want a base. I want a solid set of roots that I can grow, and that will always be there for me. I have the roots that I had as a kid, but my circle is so different from when I was younger. It's just so different from everything I grew up with. I went back to California and was just looking around and, "Wow! I went to college here? I took all this for granted, and this wasn't surprising to me?" Everything was, like, "Whoa, whoa, whoa, whoa!" Everything was crazy. "How can people live like this? How did I grow up like this?"

LS: Tell me more about Daniel's request for commitment. What did you think he meant when he talked about making a commitment?

JL: Sticking to a certain path instead of being like the wind. That's what commitment means to me. Staying on a path regardless of whatever interesting paths come along the way. I haven't stuck with anything at all since being on this journey.

Everything that I've done has been a journey of exploration, of outer and inner exploration, without any focus or commitment, which I would like to have, but maybe I'm just not ready for it. I'm just 23, I don't know.

LS: That's young, very young.

JL: It is young.

LS: You've done a lot for three years. You got out of college at 20? That's early. Did you do four years of college?

JL: I did it in three years. I was a genius (laughs).

LS: Let me ask you my favorite question: Where do you think you'll be in 10 years? Or maybe a better way to ask it is, can you give me a vision of where you'd like to be?

JL: In 10 years I'll be 33, and by 33... hmm... Where will I be in 10 years?

One possibility is that I will be somewhere in the Southern Utah or Southern Arizona desert, either with red rocks or chaparral all over the place. And I will be living in a community, and I will... do I want one or two... I will have two children, and a very good solid, strong, supporting father to go with the children. And I will be on a plot of land where I can grow foods, and have animals, and be creatively involved in the community and helping people. And I will be knowledgeable about the land, and the plants, and myself, and others around me.

I had a dream once of a bunch of people sitting in a circle, and every so often somebody would go out and doodle around and come back, and then another would go out and doodle around and come back, so in the end it looks like a flower, with all these people rooting out and coming back, rooting out and coming back. And there's this base circle that's moving around all the time, a root community in the center that provides stability for the floating petals of movement.

LS: If you were going to talk to yourself when you were 15 or 16, when the world was so small, and it all seemed so normal, what would you tell yourself to prepare yourself for the future?

JL: What would I tell myself at 15? Oh, boy. I couldn't have plotted my journey way back then. I had no idea that I'd be doing what I'm doing today.

It's very important to follow your instincts and whatever feels right, because everyone has their own path. Take the experiences as they come, and the people. Remember that every person that walks by is full of stories! Don't look down on anybody for what you see them initially to be, because everybody has something really special and golden inside.

My piano teacher said that everybody has a pearl inside, and the purpose in this life is to find that pearl and polish it until it shines like the stars. And when I look at someone and I'm judgmental, I try to remember that that person has a pearl inside, too. What's the pearl? Have they found it yet? Can I help them find it? Everybody is beautiful in some way, and everybody is special in some way.

And another really important thing to remember is that you may often be alone, but you're never, ever, ever lonely until you allow yourself to be lonely, because everything's alive. Our ancestors walked under the same sky that we are looking up at. They went through all sorts of troubles and misfortunes, and they lived and they died, and we're going to live, and we're going to die, all staring at the same sky, under the glow of the same sun, sleeping under the same moon and stars. This earth that we're walking on has been walked on by so many animals, and so many people, and so many spirits blowing through the wind, and that is so special!

It's really important to remember that this life is a gift; it's soooo special to be alive, such a gift. It's all a gift regardless of whether it's a painful hell, or… delicious mangos (laughs)!

Who knows how long we're on earth for. I could die in five minutes, I could die in 50 years, who knows? But it could be any moment. It's all there to be experienced for what it is, and it all comes together in the end as this giant adventure.

A page from Jaz Lin's diary.

26. PHYLLIS SCHLAFLY

History   Late   Born 1924, St. Louis, Missouri

Phyllis Schlafly, ardent opponent of the feminist movement, was known as one of the most right-wing, reactionary voices in 1970's American politics. For this reason I was surprised when John Taylor Gatto, one of the most anti-authoritarian, seditious educators writing today, recommended I speak with her saying, "She's not what the press has made her out to be." I asked her for an interview, she agreed, and as you will discover, there is nothing doctrinaire or preconceived in her view of education.

Not one to shrink from a challenge, Phyllis put herself through college, mothered six kids, earned both a Master's degree and a degree in law, ran twice for Congressional office, has written 20 books, has published a monthly newsletter for 40 years, and is broadcast daily on 500 radio stations. She is the founder and president of the Eagle Forum and the Eagle Forum Education & Legal Defense Fund and, at 85, remains an active lecturer. When Phyllis sees something lacking in the world, she brings attention to it – or fills the need herself.

Postscript: Phyllis passed away on September 5, 2016. She was 92.

SOCIETY

Excerpts

"You asked about my learning process. I believe that once you know how to read, the way you really learn something is to write about it. It's not enough just to read about it; it's only when you write about it that you really have a grasp of what you're talking about…"

"So I wrote a little book called *A Choice, Not an Echo,* and published it myself – who would publish a book by some unknown Alton housewife, as they called me – and I sold three million copies…"

"About a third of our population is basically illiterate. They get all their information from 20-second sound bites on television. They don't read anything, and therefore they don't know much about anything. There is no injustice that was ever done to the minority population in this country as great as letting them go through 12 years of school without teaching them how to read…"

"When I came home from high school, my parents kept right on working. And I thought that's what I was supposed to do… I think what I've done is to simply make use of all my time…"

"How did I become passionate? How did I become an activist? It was one step at a time. I grew up a very shy person. I wasn't a leader… If I can be a leader, then anybody can be a leader. Some leaders are born, and I was not a born social person. I had to learn it all… Why did I have to learn it? Because I wanted to accomplish certain goals. How did I learn it? Basically by running for office…"

"Attitude is the key… (kids) should be so grateful that they live in the greatest country in the world, where they have the opportunity to do whatever they want, where we have so much freedom, where we have so much prosperity. Make what you want of your life…"

"Grievances are like flowers: if you water them they will grow. So little grievances grow into big grievances, and it's so unfortunate! Everybody's got problems, and there's sin in the world, but move on and make your life what you want it to be!"

"Phyllis Schlafly has become one of the most relentless and accomplished platform debaters of any gender to be found on any side of any issue."

— Joseph Lelyveld, in the *New York Times Magazine,* April 17, 1977.

Narrator:	"You just want me to hit you?"
Tyler Durden:	"C'mon, do me this one favor."
Narrator:	"Why?"
Tyler Durden:	"Why? I don't know why; I don't know. Never been in a fight. You?"
Narrator:	"No, but that's a good thing."
Tyler Durden:	"No, it is not. How much can you know about yourself if you've never been in a fight? I don't wanna die without any scars. So come on – hit me, before I lose my nerve."

— *Fight Club* (Film), 1999. From *Fight Club*, by Chuck Palahniuk

"If you hide your ignorance, no one will hit you, and you'll never learn."

— Faber, in *Fahrenheit 451*, by Ray Bradbury

Interview
St. Louis, Missouri, January 2009

LS: I got your name from a guy named John Taylor Gatto...

Phyllis Schlafly: Oh-ho!

LS: ... I asked him who he thought I should speak to, and you were the first person he said.

PS: He's a remarkable guy. Are you going to ask me questions?

LS: As little as I can. There are a couple of approaches that the older people who I interview take. One approach is simply tell me their biography, others tell me about their formative years. You can do whatever you want.

PS: Learning starts with learning how to read. The scandal of our country today is that our expensive educational establishment has allowed kids to go through school and not learn how to read. English is about 85% a phonetic language, and they need to be taught phonics in the first grade. And there is no point in moving to the second grade until they know how to read.

The whole story is told in Rudolf Flesch's book, *Why Johnny Can't Read*, which came out in 1955. That was the year my first child was ready for the first grade. I read the book and believed it. I bought the books that he recommended, taught my child how to read, and then entered him in the second grade, already knowing how to read. I did that with all my six children, and that's why they have done so well. They've all got a couple of degrees and had no problem in school.

In the early 1950s a contrary system came in which was called "Look-Say," and which now is called "Whole Language." Basically, it's teaching the child to memorize a few dozen frequently used words. Now there's a limit to how many words a little child can memorize when he looks at the print on the page; maybe a couple of hundred. This is why, in international tests, you find they score all right in the first and second grades, maybe the third grade, but by the time they get to the fourth grade they're falling way behind. They do not know how to put together the sounds and syllables of the English language.

A child of age five, in a reasonably educated home, will probably know 25,000 words in his oral vocabulary. He'll know words like "grandfather," and "toothbrush," and "upstairs," and "helicopter," and "hippopotamus," and so forth. But if you don't teach him the syllables of the words, then there's a limited number of words that he can memorize. And this is why, as they move along in school and get books with bigger words, they can't read.

I taught my children with a phonics system that was widely used in the Chicago area, and we had no problem. The years went on and, when my grandchildren arrived, I wanted them to learn how to read, too. But by this time there were no phonics books available – they had all been allowed to go out of print. So I ended up writing my own, and here it is. (She presents me with a copy of her *First Reader*, also available in a revised edition entitled *Turbo Reader*. – Ed.) It's the best phonics reader available. And it's an authentic phonics system with which you teach a child to read with only a dozen or so words that they have to memorize, like "the." Basically it works by simply putting the sounds and syllables together.

Up until about 1950, the standard book used in public schools was the *McGuffey Readers*. *McGuffey* wasn't a real phonics book like mine, but it was phonetic. It taught children the sounds of the words, and it taught the American people how to read. But *McGuffey* went out of use, and 90% of the schools in this country adopted the *Dick and Jane* readers, or similar *Look-Say* readers.

The *Dick and Jane* publisher, which I think was Scott Foresman, sent salesmen around the country. The *McGuffey Readers* have no color in them, the print is smaller, and it's a little harder for a kid to relate to. Dick and Jane were full color on every page, with big pictures and a little bit of type in big print. You would have to be a semi-moron not to figure out what the print said after you looked at the picture.

For example, you'd have a see-saw and the line underneath would say, "See Dick up, see Jane down." You'd have to be an idiot not to figure that out. And so the child says, "Look, mother, I'm reading!" But the children aren't really reading, they're guessing. It's a combination of a little bit of memorization, a lot of guessing, and looking at the pictures. Yet, in the first grade, they made the parents and the students think they were reading.

My favorite story about what's wrong with this system happened in the George W. Bush-Al Gore campaign in 2000. There was a big flap about the election in Florida that caused recounting many ballots. They found a significant number of people – it wasn't enough to change the election – had voted for Al Gore for president and had also voted for the Libertarian Party candidate for president. Now, you know if you vote for two people for the same office, you cancel your ballot.

The newspaper did an investigation to find out why in the world anybody would vote for Al Gore and also for the Libertarian Party. Well, some people voted for Al Gore. Then they saw "Libertarian," and they thought it was "Lieberman" – Lieberman was the vice presidential candidate with Gore – and they thought they were confirming their vote for Gore and Lieberman!

If you haven't had phonics, you cannot tell the difference between Libertarian and Lieberman. You look at the beginning and end of the word, and the approximate size, and there it is. Those people couldn't read. These were grown-up people, they had jobs and so forth, but really they couldn't read.

This is what's happened to learning in this country. About a third of our population is basically illiterate. They get all their information from 20-second sound bites on television. They don't read anything, and therefore they don't know much about anything. There is no injustice that was ever done to the minority population in this country as great as letting them go through 12 years of school without teaching them how to read.

LS: There are so many ways you could go with this. Do you want to go to the causes or the consequences?

PS: Well, the consequences are obvious: people can't read. And the causes, well, you can speculate on people's motives. I think one part of it was the marketing plan of the publisher of *Dick and Jane*. In those years, when *Dick and Jane* came in, there was no Federal presence in the public school system. They were all individual school districts, and yet almost overnight, within a couple of years, 80% of the schools had the *Dick and Jane* readers, or the *Alice and Jerry* readers, which was a competitor.

You understand one of the commercial advantages of this: if I sell you my *First Reader*, then I don't have anything else to sell you. I don't have any second reader. But if you buy *Dick and Jane*, or *Alice and Jerry*, you've got to go from first to second to third, and the publisher can sell the series. There's a great commercial advantage in not teaching children how to read. But that's not the whole story. There have to be plenty of people who know what's happened, but who don't do anything about it, and who maybe like the system. Maybe they want people to be dumb so that they can be more easily led around.

LS: That was John Gatto's thesis: tools for dumbing kids down are not just sold, they are enthusiastically bought.

PS: Of course. According to John Dewey, the father of modern education, the whole purpose of public schooling is to socialize children, not to educate them. So there may be different motives, but the result is obvious. The latest adult literacy survey is on the Internet – I pulled it off just about two or three weeks ago – and it's depressing, it's devastating. If you can't read, you can't learn.

LS: Tell me more about what you think learning is.

PS: I think a lot of it is reading the great books, so you get different ideas, different ways of approaching problems, different experiences. You find out what other people did, find out how they accomplished great things. It enables you to cope with life.

LS: Phyllis Schlafly is not your average mid-Western woman, and she didn't become who she was just by reading the books that were available to everyone. How did you become what you are through a learning process that was available to everyone? How did you leverage it in such a powerful way?

PS: I grew up in a very hardworking family. I grew up during the Great Depression, and at the end of the day both my mother and my father had other projects they were working on to finish out the day. My parents worked all the time. I thought that was what I was supposed to do.

I always knew I wanted to go to college; however, we didn't have any money for college. Incidentally, college for women did not just start with the feminist movement; my mother got her college degree in 1920, which I enjoy telling college students.

I went to work on my 18th birthday. In St. Louis we had the largest ammunition plant in the world, the St. Louis Ordnance Plant. I went to work as a gunner testing .30 and .50 caliber ammunition, performing all the tests for the government to accept ammunition: accuracy, penetration, hangfire, all the various tests. Half the time I worked 4pm to midnight, and the other half midnight to eight in the morning, and I went to college in the morning.

I got my B.A. degree from Washington University in St. Louis, and then got a master's at Harvard. I'd saved up enough money to have a year at Harvard. Political science was a subject that fit into my schedule, and I liked it.

I then went to Washington, and I got a job doing various types of tedious research on political subjects, and then I came back to St. Louis and did likewise. Then I got married and started to have a family. My husband practiced law and we lived in Alton, which is about a 40-minute drive from St. Louis.

Everybody knew 1952 was going to be a big Republican year. We lived in a Democratic district. The party came around and asked my husband to run for Congress, but he had no interest. In the course of the conversation, somebody said, "Oh, Phyllis, why don't you do it?" So I did. I ran a kind of an intellectual campaign and won the primary, lost the general election, and have been a volunteer in politics ever since.

My interests and activity grew right along with my children. I was active in Republican women's clubs, and from 1960 to '64 I was president of the Illinois Federation of Republican Women.

One of my hobbies was checking up on Republican National Conventions. I find them quite interesting – I've been to every one beginning in 1952. I've been a delegate to most of them. Most delegates to a Republican convention are first-timers, and they needed to know what happened before. So I wrote a little book called *A Choice, Not an Echo*, and published it myself – who would publish a book by some unknown Alton housewife, as they called me – and I sold three million copies. That's what gave me my national following.

You asked about my learning process. I believe that once you know how to read, the way you really learn something is to write about it. It's not enough just to read about it; it's only when you write about it that you really have a grasp of what you're talking about.

LS: I didn't learn to write until I had to start writing. Reading and writing are wholly different things. It's the difference between looking at a painting, and painting!

PS: Oh, yeah. Yeah. Except that most painters enjoy their work, but most people don't enjoy writing; it's tedious, it's hard work (laughs). But you know the subject after you write about it.

LS: There is still something that's not disclosed in how you learned because either you were extremely capable or lucky... there's a passion thing. It sounds like either you were always passionate in pursuit of something, or you learned to be. How did you go from a normal person to an abnormally capable person? Can other people do it? It's not just reading.

PS: No, no, it's not. (Long pause.) I don't know the answer to your question.

LS: Well… could you restate the question in a way that is meaningful to you?

PS: How did I become passionate? How did I become an activist? It was one step at a time. I grew up a very shy person. I wasn't a leader. That's one of the talks I give: if I can be a leader, then anybody can be a leader. Some leaders are born, and I was not a born social person. I had to learn it all.

LS: Why?

PS: Why did I have to learn it? Because I wanted to accomplish certain goals. How did I learn it? Basically by running for office. I tell people they should run for office (laughs). There are three results of running for office: you win, you lose, or you learn. And I learned a whole lot each time I ran. You learn to relate to people.

LS: You didn't read about it, so there's another kind of learning going on there. Why did you choose to emphasize reading first?

PS: Well, you've got to have something to talk about if you're going to talk to people. You need to read in order to have something intelligent to say (laughs)!

LS: Two things that seem to be the most formative in people's backgrounds are their parents, or some supportive mentor, or reading, as you can appreciate. But not reading in a structured way, rather they just fall into reading for a lack of anything else to do, which is pretty valid if you're a kid, as most of what you're subjected to is pretty trivial.
Tell me a bit more about your parents. Did you have mentors separate from your parents?

PS: No, no… it would be my parents. As I said, we grew up during the Great Depression and my father lost his job. My mother had prepared herself, not only with a college degree but with a graduate degree in library science. When we needed to eat, she got one job after another and ultimately became the librarian at the St. Louis Art Museum, where she was for 25 years. She was the financial mainstay of our family with some pitiful salary all those years.

My father had a few jobs here and there, but I would say my mother was our main support. The mentoring that I had gave me the idea that I had to be prepared to support myself no matter what. That's why I put so much into going to college.

My classmates could have done it. Some of them had parents who could pay for their college, and some of them didn't care and didn't go. But I wanted to go, and I didn't have parents who could pay for it. So I did what I had to do. The goal was to get myself prepared to support myself. It was the goal of having a decent life.

LS: Ultimately, my project is to help people find a reason or a direction. Tell me how other people can find something to draw on… we've got so many kids who don't know where to go.

PS: Don't waste your time. What I tell them is that I was working a 48-hour week at a manual-labor job, and then I was taking a full college course. I cannot understand what college students do with all their time.

This is what I tell the college audiences: "If you're not working a 48-hour week, then I don't understand what do you do with all your time! Why are you wasting your time? These are your most vigorous, healthy, productive years." (Laughs) What are they doing?

LS: What *are* they doing?

PS: I don't know. I can't figure it out! Oh, some of them have a few little part-time jobs, I suppose. Maybe they're partying, but most of it is a waste of time. I think what I've done is to simply make use of all my time.

I remember when one of our sons came home from college, and I said, "Andy, why don't you go out with your high school pals? They'd be glad to see you." "Aw, I don't want to do that." I said, "Why not?" "Well," he said, "all they like to do is go out and drink." "Oh," I said, "how come you don't like to go out and drink?" (Laughs) He's pretty funny, this kid.

He said, "Well, Mother, I've thought about this, and I think that when they came home from high school in the afternoon, they saw their parents, and what did their parents do? They'd sit down, and they'd have a cocktail, and then they'd have a leisurely dinner. And when I came home from high school, my parents kept right on working, and I thought that's what I was supposed to do."

When I was that age, and I came home, my parents kept right on working. After my mother worked her day job, she was writing a social history of St. Louis. Someday I hope to get that manuscript published; it's a wonderful book. And my father worked 18 years sitting at a desk developing a rotary gasoline engine, which he finally did patent, but unhappily never sold. At any rate, in the evenings, we just kept on working.

LS: This is interesting. I'm surprised you don't highlight it more. It sounds like your father had a workshop.

PS: No, it was all done on paper, with drawings.

LS: Really! Amazing. Did your parents encourage you to learn, or read to you, or engage you in their pursuits?

PS: Oh, not particularly. No, they never read to me. I read to myself.

LS: Really? I read to my kid all the time. I think it's kind of standard these days.

PS: How old is he?

LS: I started reading to him, I don't know, when he was five, maybe.

PS: My answer to that is: if you want your kid to be a baseball player, do you sit him down and read him stories about baseball players, or do you go out in the backyard and play ball with him?

LS: I don't know. Tell me.

PS: I think you teach him how to throw and catch a ball. Teach him how to read so that he can read himself. But you've got to give him things he likes to read.

One set of my grandchildren are twin girls and a boy who's a year younger. The girls adapted fine to reading, but the boy saw no utility in learning how to read whatsoever. The girls liked to read about fairies and princesses... and he saw no point in that at all; it was a waste of time. But when he found he could read about adventures and battles, then there was a utility to learning how to read (laughs)!

LS: Can you give me a personal story that's not pedagogy and not philosophy, something illustrative about how you learned?

PS: Something that would illustrate learning? Hmm… I don't know.

LS: How about one of your greatest failures. One learns a lot from them. Or successes.

PS: I don't know what would make a good story. My fight to defeat the equal rights amendment was a very exciting battle.

LS: Preface this by explaining the equal rights amendment. We're talking to kids here, and they won't know what it is.

PS: The feminist movement came into this country and captivated the media in the late 1960s. There are a lot of things wrong with the feminist movement, but the number one thing that's wrong with it is that they teach women to believe they're victims of an oppressive, discriminatory society.

That is so false, because American women are the most privileged class of people who ever lived on the face of the earth. Feminists told women that the solution to their victimhood was a new constitutional amendment, called the Equal Rights Amendment (ERA).

It's a long story, and we'd be here the rest of the afternoon if I tried to tell you all about it. But they put it through Congress, and then it went out to the states, and I took on the battle. It turned out to be a 10-year battle.

Nobody thought we could stick with it for 10 years, but we did, and we finally beat them. We beat everybody. We had Presidents Nixon, Ford, and Carter against us. We had 98% of the Congress, all the Governors, all the media, all the money, even Hollywood, and we beat them all.

One of the main reasons they lost was they were never able to show any benefit. You can wrap up a pretty package and maybe sell it to some dumb person, but over a 10-year period, if there's nothing in the package, then you can't sell it. And they were never able to show any benefit.

Illinois was the front line of the battle. The most dramatic day was in 1980 when we had everything against us. All the media and all the networks were there because the feminists had said that this was the day they were going to pass it.

Jimmy Carter, who was then president, was calling the Democrat legislators, promising them public housing projects if they would vote "Yes." The Governor of Illinois, who was a Republican, was calling the Republicans and telling them they would get dams, roads, and bridges in their districts if they would vote "Yes." And the Chicago mayor, who was then Jane Byrne, was calling the ones who were beholden to the Chicago Machine (the Chicago political establishment – Ed.), threatening that their relatives would lose their jobs if they didn't vote "Yes."

Grown men were weeping on the floor of the legislature that day, especially the Chicago guys who felt they had to vote "Yes" so that their relatives wouldn't lose their jobs.

The pro-ERA feminists had a hunger strike going on in the rotunda of the Illinois capitol, led by an excommunicated Mormon, and they had some experienced hunger strikers left over from the Vietnam War protests. They were lying around on couches on their hunger strike.

The lesbian chain gang chained themselves to the door of the Senate chamber, so that the Senators had to step over them to get into their seats (laughs). Then another bunch of them went to the slaughterhouse and got some plastic bags of pig's blood, and they wrote on our marble floors the names of the people they hated the most.

We'd counted our votes, and we were two votes short. They voted electronically, and when the votes went up on the electronic board, we had won again. God gave us two votes we never had before. It was a dramatic day. It was really tough (laughs)... and we beat 'em all.

Eleanor Smeal, who was the head of the National Organization for Women, was there. ABC put her before the TV cameras in the gallery of the legislature and asked, "Well, Ms. Smeal, you said you had the votes. Why didn't you win?" And she said, "There was something very powerful against us, and I don't mean people." The feminists fought on for a couple more years, but that was the most dramatic day.

LS: Was that a personal victory?

PS: Oh, yeah. It was a personal victory, but I had a lot of good people. I get very embarrassed when people say, "Phyllis single-handedly..." they use that word all the time for some unknown reason, and we had lots of people helping our cause. Every movement has to have a leader. I didn't grow up a leader, but I learned how to become a leader. All I did was raise the flag and say, "Let's march!"

The feminists haven't gotten over their defeat. Hillary Clinton is still calling for the Equal Rights Amendment. Yet they were never able to show one benefit! Not one single good thing that it will do. Of course, when they went on television they'd say it was going to give all women a raise. But that is not true, because the employment laws are already sex-neutral.

LS: Do you see a social need that the ERA catered to?

PS: No, but making people believe that they're oppressed and mistreated and not paid what they ought to be paid is an easy thing to do. I mean, everybody probably thinks he's worth more than he's being paid.

LS: One of the people I've interviewed is Native American. He says his parents bore the brunt of a lot of prejudice and ill treatment. Like a lot of people of their generation, his parents identify themselves as victims. But the current generation rejects this victim attitude. They identify it as a weak, stagnant approach.

PS: Well, they may accomplish something if they get rid of their victimhood attitude. If you wake up in the morning with a chip on your shoulder, you're not going to succeed.

LS: What would you tell kids who are making that transition from being dependent – who are dependents legally and practically, to independence or self-possession – about how they could make the most of themselves?

PS: I think attitude is the key part of it. They should be so grateful that they live in the greatest country in the world, where they have the opportunity to do whatever they want, where we have so much freedom, where we have so much prosperity. Make what you want of your life. I think attitude is absolutely key.

There are an awful lot of people who have the attitude that they are mistreated or unfairly treated. I tell the college students, "Grievances are like flowers: if you water them they will grow." So little grievances grow into big grievances, and it's so unfortunate! Everybody's got problems, and there's sin in the world, but move on and make your life what you want it to be (laughs)!

TRADE

27. TOM KELLOGG

History   **Middle**   **Born 1963, Hartford, Connecticut**

Tom Kellogg, otherwise known as TJ, gives a strong impression: he's observant, soft-spoken, careful in what he says, and always positive, often funny, when dealing with problems. You can sense that he's in control of his time and resources. In contrast, he has some kind of atonia that tenses his fingers and toes, which are always cramped.

Another person could be said to "suffer" from this condition, but that's not how TJ deals with it. His body seems to be just another finicky machine to be coaxed along. Whether he's wrestling a trailer, maneuvering a chainsaw, or digging in a muddy ditch, he works fast, happily, and usually alone. More than once he's tumbled down my front steps; he just laughs, dusts himself off, and succeeds the next time. I find him amazing.

Tom does excavation, which involves clearing and reshaping the land. I worked with him on the last house I built. He and his large, 30-ton excavator can clear a site in dense woods, carve and pave a road, and dig out a perfect basement, all in three days. His skill, speed, and reliability are unmatched. He's also self-taught.

TJ has built a life for himself and his family from the bottom up. He is a testament to what can be accomplished with sensitivity, common sense, and perseverance.

Excerpts

"I decided at a young age that I didn't really like school. It was just boring. I liked it, but… it seemed like if there was one person in the class who didn't understand what the teacher said, he'd just keep saying the same thing until the guy in the back got it. Well, he ain't going to get it: he's been out in the pits smoking pot all day. 'It ain't going to get to him there, sport!' So I would just kind of doze off and think about other things. I just kind of fumbled through school…"

"It's just like 17, 18. High school's coming to an end, and what do I want to do with life? I want to kinda apply myself to machinery. So I decided, well, I'm young and full of energy, so I'm going into the logging business… I learned a lot of lessons through that. It was really good experience. I never would have seen that. I could have been buying an education when I was 50, but I was doing it in my 20s. It taught me a lot about people. I got to say, that was a good time…"

"You've just got to take the time. It's just like I've told you from the beginning: I really enjoyed that farming and logging. Whatever you decide to do in the beginning, make sure you're happy with it. Don't just listen to Mom and Dad. Oh, man, you can make $300,000 a year as a lawyer, and you'll dread every day you're doing it…"

"Take the time and think about what you really want to be, and when you decide what you want to be, pursue it with all you've got. Be the best that you can be… Just always stay focused, Lincoln, always. That would be my advice: whatever you decide to do, stay focused. There are opportunities out there. Anything you want to do."

"Wisdom doesn't come from the lowest depths we may descend to, or the darkest moments we have and will know; it comes from the fall. And when we can look on ourselves and act without arrogance, no matter our material gain, we can be wise. If we can look past the disappointment and the failures and understand why and how they happened, we can be wise."

— Joseph M. Marshall III, from *Walking With Grandfather*

"To attain knowledge, add things everyday; to obtain wisdom, remove things everyday."

— Lau Tsu

Interview   Shokan, New York, January 2008

Tom Kellogg: I grew up in Connecticut. My dad was a manufacturing engineer. We came up here in '67 to work in the Rotron factory. I was about five years old, and, of course, there was nothing up here but a fan-making factory and a bunch of woods! It was like the boonies, it was just... it was scary. We didn't know anybody. You know, the people were nice but they kept to themselves. We eventually made friends with everybody, and they were all great people.

I started out eight, ten years old working on a farm in the summer time. Got introduced to machinery and got to run the stuff by the time I was 10, 12 years old. It was actually Burt Liefeld, the guy that's now our town supervisor. He had a regular working farm: cows, pigs, chickens, the whole nine yards. He was a salesman, and he did this gentleman's farm thing. He was, still is, a real easygoing guy.

His son and I grew up together, and we were always with the tractors, the bulldozer, chainsaw, and stuff like that. We were little kids, 10, 12 years old, riding out through the woods with the bulldozer with no cab. We'd be looking up at the trees going, "Oooo! Don't hit a dead one 'cause that's going to land on us!" We had some really good experiences.

It's not like we had free rein of stuff. When we screwed up, he'd get pissed at us. You know he'd kick us in the ass – he's a big man, he's a good-sized man – and our feet would come right off the ground (laughs)! But, like two minutes after that, it was over. He never brought it up again. If he was pissed at something, he took it out right there, and then that's it, and you didn't do it again. That kind of thing stuck with me. I always respected him for that. You learn; everybody makes mistakes.

When I got older I worked on Al Fox's farm over in Olivebridge. He had a big dairy farm, probably 90 head. Milking cows, that's a full-time job, man. I'd ride my bike four or five miles to the farm. I'd be there five, six o'clock in the morning, clean up all the crap in the calf barn, and then I'd help with milking in the big barn. By then it was 10:30, 11 o'clock, and we were out raking or bailing hay. It was good "work ethic" stuff, that's really all there was around here.

I decided at a young age that I didn't really like school. It was just boring. I liked it, but... it seemed like if there was one person in the class who didn't understand what the teacher said, he'd just keep saying the same thing until the guy in the back got it. Well, he ain't going to get it: he's been out in the pits smoking pot all day. "It ain't going to get to him there, sport!" So I would just kind of doze off and think about other things. I just kind of fumbled through school.

I made it to graduation. My parents were very much of the feeling, "You've got to graduate, and that's what it is. Whatever you want to be – if you want to be a garbage man, you can be a garbage man – but you're going to have your diploma."

My dad being an engineer, that didn't interest me. I respected him for it, but he was in a suit and tie every day. I'd watch him get all dressed up, and I'd go, "Oh, Jesus, I don't want to do that. That just isn't my cup of tea." It was cool work, but as you had to have four or five years of college and then work through various different shops, I wouldn't be to his position for another 10 years. You know? I wanted to get right out there and get my feet dirty.

LS: When were you thinking about this, as a kid?

TK: It's just like 17, 18. High school's coming to an end, and what do I want to do with life? I want to kinda apply myself to machinery. So I decided, well, I'm young and full of energy, so I'm going into the logging business.

I went to work for a local logger running a skidder. It was kind of a screwy situation because he was a trucker, too. He trucked logs and wood for other people in the morning and wouldn't be back until noon. So what do I do while he's not around?

We'd try to set it up so that a whole bunch of trees were cut and topped, and all I had to do was go in with the skidder and pull them out. He wouldn't leave me a chainsaw; I couldn't use his saw alone. I had to trim whatever ones he missed with an ax (laughs)! Like, Jesus, Davy Crockett with an ax! The thing was sharp as could be; I'd rather have the saw!

Eventually I went out and bought a saw but didn't really tell him about it. I kept it in the woods. He'd be, "How'd you get them all trimmed? I don't see any ax marks?" And I said, "Man, you did a good job yesterday. You got every limb." That worked for about a week, and finally he figured it out. He started seeing empty oil and chain cans.

I worked for him for a couple of years, but he led a kind of screwy life. He'd go out and buy a brand new pickup while they were repossessing his car, or they were shutting the electric off in his house. There was always this chaos, and it was always, "Gee, I don't have any money to pay you this week. As soon as I get caught up on my payments, I'll get square." And it just never happened. It was fine because I was living at home; what were my bills? But after a while I started to feel I already bought my education here, I've got to move on.

Then I worked for a large logging company in the area, and that guy did some volume. He probably did 75,000 board feet a week, I mean a lot of wood. I was working with a crew of guys, there were two skidders, and I ran a forwarder. You know the skidders pull them to a landing in the woods, and the guy chops them up into log lengths, and he loads them on a big woods truck, and then you carry them out. It keeps the wood all nice and neat and clean. It's a big thing in the logging business, because dirt and saws don't get along.

I worked for him for about a year, and then decided to go out and buy my own equipment. I started out with an old farm tractor I bought for $1,000 from a guy I knew.

At that time the gypsy moths had hit around here really bad, and there was a lot of standing dead trees. I was comfortable with tractors; I was used to looking up and watching the trees wiggle from the old days! I knew if one of them babies hits you, you're going to lay here. I was very cautious. I did really well with that thing.

I had a guy working with me, and the two of us cut, split, and delivered two cords a day, every day, seven days a week, unless it rained. You know, we wouldn't do it in the rain because that's slippery, nasty shit. I eventually saved up enough money to buy my own skidder and went into the logging business.

My parents had money but I just… what can I say. They would always cover me if I needed money, but I always had to pay it back. It wasn't a free ride, which I respected. If I needed $100 on Monday for fuel, or parts, or something, I'd have the money by Friday to pay them back; it was no problem. Don't think they're going to buy my parts, just endless, you know.

It teaches you discipline, it teaches you to save, and to think ahead about what if something breaks. So if I've got this $1,500 check, then I ought to take half of it and put it away because, when something breaks, I'll have the money to cover it. I got so that I'm… really methodical about that.

I'd always buy stuff so that when times get tough, I'd have the parts to keep going. That's a big part in business, thinking about that. You can't just keep wadding it all in the bank. You might look out at the 50 grand you saved up: "Aw, I'll buy a new pickup." But as soon as you buy a new pickup, the boom breaks off the excavator… and now you've got the new pickup. So learning that taught me a lot, actually, by having that little leash on me money-wise.

I had a couple of different employees, and it just got to be too much. Workman's comp was $42 per hundred of payroll, so for every hundred I would give… let's say I give you $400… it would be $168 for workman's comp. So now I'm paying $568 for a guy who gets $400 a week, so he's not really inspired.

It just got that the overhead was so big. I had guys trucking my logs, and paying ahead for wood lots, and taking lesser-grade lots to keep the guys busy. I did it to get through, but with all the effort I was putting in – working six, seven days a week – I was just keeping up.

It was a good experience. I learned a lot about people in that business, because there's all different kinds of people in the wood business. There's some real "characters" (laughs) – I don't know how to put that so you don't have to edit it! I learned a lot about people in that business.

LS: You mean there are more odd-balls in the wood business than in contracting?

TK: You know, a lot of real shysters. All different kinds. You ain't seen nothing till you go try to sell your wood lot! See what kind of people come up to you, giving you a promise!

I'd cruise a wood lot – cruising is when you go through and estimate how much wood is on a lot. All right, say there's $10,000 worth of wood on it, right? I'll offer you $10,000, with $5,000 to start, and then halfway through I'll give you the other $5,000 so you're not waiting to the end when you've got no wood left. It was all honest and good-intentioned stuff.

Well, one of these other wood lot guys would come along and say, "Oh, no. There's

$15,000 of wood on that lot and I'll give you 10% right now!" And they'd start cutting, and they'd start with the big ones. You know a lot of land owners want to get as much as they can: "Oh, yeah! This guy's the best! He's going to give me $15,000, and that's a better deal!"

So they'd give them 10%, and guy would go through and cut all the big ones first, go around the whole 50 acres. The first couple loads were the Big Dukes, you know? The next load smaller, then next ones smaller still. Well, when it comes time to the last payment, there's no wood left on the land.

So the landowner goes, "Hey, where's my money?"

"Aw, Jezz. I'll get it to you! Next week we're going to square up!"

And as a property owner, they didn't foresee this guy cutting all the big trees. They don't know the scam. They just figure, "Oh, look at all that hard work! He's cutting all them trees. Look at the size of them! Oh, they're beauties!"

Let's say the guy might have ended up getting $5,000 for the whole lot. Here I'd truly paid him $10,000, and he was more attracted to the guy that promised him $15,000, but gave him $5,000. And that's what you're up against in that business: it's whoever has the best line of shit. The handshake and the honest man, that don't mean nothing in that business.

So I learned a lot of lessons through that. It was really good experience. I never would have seen that. I could have been buying an education when I was 50, but I was doing it in my 20s. It taught me a lot about people. I got to say, that was a good time.

Man, I struggled. Financially I was just hanging on. Just paying the electric bill. The cable-vision guy would go up the pole and shut it off, and I'd have the check for him at the bottom, and he'd go up and turn it back on. I had to pay him to go up, go down, and back up again. I had to pay him twice! It's just what I had to do. I was just barely making it.

My equipment was all paid for after a couple of years. Finally, I said, "Ah, shit. I've had enough of this." There was just too many headaches. That's when I got into the construction business.

I went to work for a company down in Kingston, and I'm still very good friends with him, but he was kind of a... how can I say it... he'd give you just enough rope to hang yourself. You wanted to watch what you said. If you said that you could run this piece of equipment, and you want more money, well, the first time you screwed up he'd make it known to everybody: "There's my good operator, he's the best! Now look: he's got fiber optics hanging off the excavator. Now that's going to cost me! That's coming out of your check!"

I had a heads-up about this guy, so I went to work for him just as a shoveler, a laborer at six dollars an hour. I had already run all this equipment, and I could do just as well as anybody, but I didn't want to start out saying, "Oh, yeah, I'm better than anybody you got!"

I started out by getting a feel for everybody. He was a young guy, too, and a couple of his top operators were guys he went to high school with. They were a bunch of jackasses. I hate to say it like that, but one guy who ran the backhoe wore velour shirts all the time. That let you know he was the machine operator, and he wasn't going to get in the ditch. White velour shirt: "Grease my bucket..." Do this, do that. He was just an idiot.

And the other guy, he just kept digging until he got stuff on the end of the teeth: water mains, sewer mains (laughs)! But he must have had some scoop on the boss because the boss never said nothing to him.

I moved the machines around, and he could see that I was really smooth on things. I asked him if I could start coming in on Sundays to practice on the equipment on my own time. Just to get the feel for things.

It was funny. I found out later that he had this back entrance, and he'd be up there watching me with his little binoculars to see how I'd do – he told me this afterwards. And I'd be just… just throwing sand in the air, and trying to catch it before it hits the ground; all kinds of stuff!

I was very finessy. I'm very finessy with the machines. I would always try to do my best. I'd dig a ditch in the sand bank, like from here to your car, pick a point on the bucket that I knew was a certain depth, and then walk back with a ruler to see how level I kept it. I would be within a couple of inches, and that's how you dig a water main: you've got to be at a certain height. You dig a sewer main and it's got to have a certain slope. And that's how I would practice. And he watched all that. I went from $6 to $15 an hour within a couple months!

He did a lot of screamin' and yellin', and I don't take well to the screamin' and yellin' thing. I mean I loved the guy. I get along with him great, but don't scream and yell on the job around other people, because I'm going to scream and yell back.

This guy wasn't the kind of guy you could scream and yell back to. He'd go, "You can't talk to me like that!"

"Yeah, well watch this: I'm going back to cutting logs."

"You leave, and you ain't ever coming back!"

"You got it, that's why I'm leaving."

And then he'd call me up in, like, two days, when I was out in a little wood lot somewhere, and he'd say, "Did you calm down yet?"

"Did I calm down! How about did you calm down!" (Laughs) He'd say, "I really need you." So I'd go back. I did that maybe three, four times and… I didn't think I was getting anywhere… I didn't think I was going any farther with him, at that point.

I had an opportunity to work for this local company that moved road recycling equipment. I got hired as a low-bed operator to move the equipment around. I think I got a five dollar raise right off the bat, so I'm up like 19, 20 dollars to start.

My wife was pregnant with our first child, and the benefits were really good, with three or four months off in the winter so that I could go and do wood and logging. It was just a nice mix. I stayed there for damn near 10 years. But at the same time, kids are 9, 10 years old, and I was missing them growing up, 'cause I was out running this low-bed 80, 90 hours a week. Yeah, man: the money; it was all prevailing wage. My wife was home with two kids, the bills. You know: you've got to make hay while it's shining.

That company covered five states, doing roads and stuff. We'd be in Boston one day, the next day I'd be moving equipment down to New Jersey, and then out to Pennsylvania, and then back. We were all over the place. It was a good gig.

By Wednesday I'd have 40-some hours, and, man, I'd run that truck damn near round the clock. I had a $1,500 expense account, American Express: "Anything you want, just get a receipt for it."

I had the best radio money could buy in that truck. I'd put the windows down, crank that radio up; I could go 24 hours, baby! Wind blowing and the music playing (laughs). I could really stay awake, stay awake, stay awake. Maybe I'd go three, four days, and then I'd have to crash and grab eight hours of sleep.

LS: Jesus, I don't know how you could do that.

TK: Oh, man: go, go, go! I really loved it. I loved that job.

So it was getting… the New York State D.O.T. (Department of Transportation) was getting to change some rules on trucks. And all these different log books: on duty, off duty. All this about how much sleep you're supposed to have, all this stuff was changed to a Federal regulation.

New York State was starting to crack down on all this, so I had a couple of different log books. I showed one when I had eight hours off, and another had eight hours on and eight hours off, and my real log book was like 36 hours on! I think when I left there I was making $22, $24 an hour, plus overtime: time and a half. It was just racking up.

We bought our house; we bought everything. Kaily was eight years old, Evan was six, full-time in school. You know, you've got a wife and two kids at home, and that takes a lot of money. The kids want this, they want that. They had a good childhood.

I was starting to get a little annoyed with these truck rules. Each state had their own different set of rules, so you'd come into Massachusetts and you'd have to pencil whip your log book this way, back up your mileage that way, and then you'd go to Connecticut and it would be another thing. All this paperwork and shit, and then moving all this equipment.

I had a list this long of equipment to move by Wednesday, let's say, and shit, I'm spending half of my time writing out what I did today, and what I think I'm going to do tomorrow. I just want to get it done, you know? So I was getting a little frustrated with trucks.

I got down on the Throgs Neck Bridge in Long Island, and all the loads were over-dimensional: they were over 8'6", they were over-weight, so the state regulations are dawn to dusk as the time you're allowed to move. But inside the five boroughs of New York City, you had to be from 10pm to 6am. So how do you do that! Unless you make it a two-day thing!

I knew a guy that worked on the Thruway, and I'd give him 20, 40 dollars out of my expense account – give him some cash now and again – and he'd give me a permit to run down the Thruway. Who's going to bother you at four o'clock in the morning 'cause you're 10' wide? Take the flags off so the cops don't see it when they go by. They don't know. So that's how I did it. I did it like that for years, the whole time.

So I get down to the Throgs Neck Bridge and it's 10 minutes after six. There was an accident on the Cross Bronx, and I was held up maybe 20 minutes. I used to say to myself when I was a little late like that, that I'd get all the way to the left lane. Then, if the lady gives me any shit, what am I going to do? There are six more lanes over there. Are they going to stop all these cars? No, she'd just say, "You don't do this again." "Yes, ma'am! Yes, OK!"

Well, I'll be God-damned: I pull into this left lane after this accident thing, and there's a bridge authority cop in the booth with this lady. I don't know if it's his girlfriend or something, right? And he says, "Let me see your permit for that. How wide is it?"

"10 feet."

"Let me see your permit."

So I show him my permit. He must have never looked at a permit because he was looking at it for like 10 minutes. "It says here you're supposed to be across this bridge by six o'clock." He said, "I'm going to go out there and stop all that traffic. You back out of this booth, and you wait until 10 am." So he puts his orange rain coat on, and his light, and he's stopping traffic, and I'm thinking, "The first car that hits him, I'm outa here! I'm not sitting around for this act to be my fault!" (Laughs)

I'll be God-damned if that guy didn't stop all those seven, eight lanes of traffic, 100' back. I backed out, went over there, and parked in this area, and waited until 10 o'clock. Lincoln, I never saw that man again, not another cop. About 10 o'clock I went through the nearest toll booth, no ticket, no incident, no nothing. And I thought to myself, "This is a warning to get out of this business." It probably would have been a $1,000 fine for crossing that bridge out of hours, or whatever.

So I got thinking about it, and with missing the kids growing up, and these hours, and I already made all my money, and stuff like that: it's time for change. The next thing you know I quit doing that, and I went to work for this Delroot contractor in Saugerties running equipment.

Delroot was really good, too. It's just that he had a bunch of real characters working for him, and I just couldn't take the nonsense. Everybody… you know they were all "big operators." They'd run the machines right out of fuel, and then call me up on my phone – because I've got a truck that's a mechanic's truck – and they'd say, "Go get me some fuel. I ran my machine out of fuel."

"What's wrong, the gauge don't work?"

"No, the gauge works. I just got no way to get fuel!"

"Well, you better find a way to get fuel, because if you think I'm bringing fuel to you down in Poughkeepsie 'cause you ran it out, you're going to have a long day!" (Laughs) And they had a long wait, I'll tell you that!

It just got so that it was full of all that nonsense. So finally I just went out on my own. And about a year after I did that, I met you!

LS: That's all it was!?

TK: That's it!

LS: I didn't know you were such a greenhorn.

TK: Yeah, well, I don't know about "green" – I had all this experience behind me. I was just riding somebody else's horse.

LS: You'd already bought your equipment, and you've got a lot of it, too: two excavators and trucks…

TK: Yeah, I saved my money. All those 80, 90-hour weeks. I didn't have time to go hang out in the pubs or do vacations and stuff. I just put it in the bank thinking that someday… and that someday came around, and it worked out great.

I'm very happy at this point. I'm 45 and doing well. Not quite to the point of being able to pick and choose my jobs. I've got to keep steady work, but I won't do silly stuff, only stuff I enjoy. It's been a really good run. I can't complain at all.

LS: I thought you'd been independent for 10 years or something. I'd heard about you from my friend Tim, and the way he said it, it sounded like you were a local fixture of some kind.

TK: Actually, I was still working for Delroot when I did Tim's job; I was working nights. That's how I got to meet him. Small world, huh?

LS: All this work has been local. Did you get Delroot to help you get jobs at some point?

TK: No, nope. Everything's word of mouth. Through the years when I worked for these different companies, I always had an old backhoe. And all the kids that I grew up with in school, when they were buying their houses – like when I was buying my house – we didn't have a lot of extra money. You'd buy a house and fix it up as you went.

Their septic would go bad, or their well line would go bad, and I'd go dig it for them and just ask for fuel money. Well, 10, 12 years later these people are all putting additions on their houses, and who are they calling? They're calling me because I'd helped them when they had nothing. Now they all got something, so it worked out great.

The best business is word of mouth. That's why you don't burn a bridge with anybody. If I gave you a price for something – win, lose, or draw – you make it right. If there's an extra thing, then you explain it. If the guy's not happy, you make it right, because a happy customer is the guy who passes your name on to the next guy.

You've got to know what you're doing bid-wise. I can't tell you that I'll do it for $5,000, and it turns into a $40,000 job, and I'm hitting you up for the extra 35. It don't work like that! You've got to explain what this is going to cost up to this point, and this point, and this point, and the total is X amount of dollars. It comes with experience and time. I saw it through all these different contractors, and I took it all in as I was doing it for them.

LS: Were you doing it for them? You must have been hungry to learn about that. Most guys wouldn't know what was going on in the office, would they?

TK: I was very hungry to learn. I didn't do the actual giving the bid. Let's say this McMann who I worked for in Kingston, he would give a bid, and as the job was going on he'd say, "Tommy, we've got to put in this 1,000 feet of sewer main, there's two man holes and they cost this much, and the pipe is this much, and the stone is that much, and I only gave a bid for $60,000, and we've got $45,000 worth of material. We've got $15,000 to make here, so let's do it as cost effective as we can."

He would explain all that to me. If he didn't explain it, then I would have asked. You couldn't come out and say, "Hey, how much you expect to make on this!" But you could say, "How much does all this cost material-wise and stuff?" And he would take the time and explain it to me. It's not like I was taking his information to another contractor in Kingston; I just wanted to know so I could be as efficient as I could on the job.

LS: So what are you doing now?

TK: Just on my own, you know: house sites and road jobs, and all kinds of electrical jobs. I like those mini-excavators. They're nice, they're quick and easy; you're in and out of a job, nice and neat, and on to the next one.

The big machine, like I had at your place, that's almost got to stay with the job from the beginning to the end because to move it is such an expense. The thing is 11-and-a-half feet wide and almost 30 tons. You don't just tippy-toe around with that thing. You've got to pay somebody $300 every time to move it, so you're better to just leave it on the job; finish the job.

This is what makes me a little different from a lot of the guys: they buy the next size smaller machine, and they've got to work the hell out of it to get the job done. Then they throw it on their trailer and move to the next one. I'd saved my money, and I'd bought this bigger machine – bought and paid for – and I just can leave it on a site and do the whole job with that one machine.

Every job's different. I like to stay where I can do the job myself, maybe have somebody help me if I need it. I pretty much work just as one person.

LS: I'd think it was dangerous working alone with these big machines. You ever had any bad accidents?

TK: Nothing. Everybody has mistakes and shit happen, but nothing that really destroyed things. I've had end-dumps where you're riding along, and, you know, you've got 30, 40 tons of mud on the back, and you're going through some place where you've pulled a stump, and it rained and it was filled with water, but you leveled it all back out and forgot the hole was there, and it just goes – whump! – and now it's stuck there. It's not flipped, but it just won't back up, won't go forward.

You've got to go call one of your buddies and get your cable with the big excavator and say, "When I beep the horn it's in reverse, and you back up... but stop before you hit the big yellow machine behind you!" (Laughs) Then you make a road around it, or whatever. Shit happens, that's just part of the business.

LS: You do seem to work by yourself more than most people.

TK: I get frustrated with some of the people in the construction business. Like I was telling you with bringing the dump truck in: Fifty times he never parks in the same spot. "Come on, we've been doing this for a week and a half? That's 300 loads you've backed up and you ain't hit the same spot twice!" How hard is it to back the truck up in the same spot?

And there's a lot of that in the construction business. Unfortunately, you've got a lot of guys that are hard workers but they quit school, or had some bad breaks, or heavy drinkers, or for whatever reason they're running construction equipment because that's what they can do. Some guys are great guys, and some guys are real jack-asses.

LS: Do you want to stay at this level, working on jobs you can do by yourself?

TK: I like it here. I have no headaches. I look forward to wintertime. When things slow down I work in my garage. I like to weld and do all kinds of creative projects. Fix different things, you know. It breaks it up. After doing it for so long, it's just dirt and rocks. It doesn't matter where you are, it doesn't matter what the site is, or how different it looks... it gets real repetitious.

At the end of the year, when that stuff's all done, it's nice to unwind. My garage is right in my backyard, the heat's on, and I just walk out there and start welding, tinkering, fabricating, or whatever I want to do. It breaks it up nice for me.

LS: You have a whole machine shop back there? Do you have a lathe and a milling machine?

TK: I just purchased a lathe. I got the cut-off saws and stuff like that. I'm not some master fabricator, but I've been around a lot of it. I could be.

My dad was a machinist, and he worked in a lot of manufacturing shops. My grandfather was like, a super master machinist. He worked for a company over in East Hartford called Bitterroot, and he could make a clock like nothing. He grew up through the '20s and '30s when everything was cut and filed by hand; you didn't just put it in the CNC machine and say, "OK, I want a clock!"

I remember my dad saying that my grandpa had the patience of a saint, and my dad had half of what he had, and I got half of what my dad had (laughs)! I just weld it together, grind it off, and call it good, you know? "Come on, it's a plow for a tractor. What's the difference if it's off 3 degrees?"

LS: Your kids are 17 and 15. What do you say to kids this age? You know better than I do: what are they looking at?

TK: You've just got to take the time. It's just like I've told you from the beginning: I really enjoyed that farming and logging. Whatever you decide to do in the beginning, make sure you're happy with it. Don't just listen to Mom and Dad. Oh, man, you can make $300,000 a year as a lawyer, and you'll dread every day you're doing it.

All this workforce stuff that's out there, all this equipment stuff, a lot of people aren't interested in it. But somebody's got to run all that stuff. They need the workforce for it, so it's going to be a lucrative thing, as I see it.

So like my son, I'm trying to push him to do that. He has about as much interest in school as I did: he's fumbling his way through 'cause it's boring, and the kids in the back still don't get it! If I can start him out when he's 18 making $50 an hour with a machine. And he's good at it; he's not banging it off your house, or hitting the car and the house… but he didn't mean it (laughs)!

These little machines, he's on them constantly, and that's good. You don't see many 15-year-olds that can do that. I'd trust him working right next to me. He doesn't have the foresight like I have, but I think that comes with experience. Taking the dirt and swinging it to the right instead of the left, because you're going to have to move to the left, and if the dirt's on the left, then you'll have to move it again. But if you swing it to the right to start with, then it's out of your way for step two!

I'm showing him all that, and he's really interested. He likes the mechanic end of things, and hopefully he'll take it and run with it.

No matter what job, even some of the nastiest, crappiest days, you know, always try to grab the most out of it. On days when every bucket of dirt is sloppy mud, it's like, "Ah, shit." It's not going to go back together the way that you're taking it apart. "Well, how can we do it the best? What if we stack these rocks here, and put the mud behind it, and everything stabilizes when it dries out." You come back in two hours and it looks like you were never there, you know? All the jobs are different, even after all the years it's still a challenge.

Take the time and think about what you really want to be, and when you decide what you want to be, pursue it with all you've got. Be the best that you can be. Of course if you're a kid, then there's all kinds of room for change.

Just always stay focused, Lincoln, always. That would be my advice, whatever you decide to do, stay focused. There are opportunities out there. Anything you want to do.

28. CLARENCE W. SEE

History   **Late**   **Born 1922, Baldwinsville, New York**

I'm a slow learner, but I'm really slow when it comes to piloting soar planes: there's something that I'm trying to do that they're not teaching, so I have to learn it myself. That's another way of saying I crash a lot.

The first time I smashed in the nose of my glider, I brought it to Clarence See. I learned a lot about airplane repair and a bit about him. The second time I smashed up the nose of my glider, I sold it without fixing it: it was more than I was willing to handle. I brought it to Clarence to appraise, and I prevailed upon him to provide this story.

Clarence was well known as a mechanic and test pilot in the heyday of the Schweizer Airplane Company in Elmira, NY. He's not one to boast, but I know that an emergency off-field landing is no simple thing even when your engine isn't belching smoke and flames. For Clarence it was just another exciting day at work. Now 86, Clarence is still fixing and flying airplanes and watching college courses that he gets on DVD.

Postscript: Clarence W. See died on December 26th, 2012. He was 90.

Excerpts

"My grandfather was a farmer. He was an inspiration to me my whole life, even though he passed away when I was quite young. Living there on the farm I spent all my time with him… He was a master barn builder. But he made his money raising tobacco. He ran this farm for a captain in the Civil War…"

"One of the things that got me interested in flying was that part of the farm that was on the river flats. They were nice long fields, 3,000 foot long. They would bring students over… and they'd practice approaches and forced landings. When they'd pull up on a missed approach, I'd see the Standards and Wacos going by. I landed in all the fields that I dreamed of landing in as a kid, later on in life…"

"I did the engine installations, worked up the cooling, worked up everything. There was a lot of airplanes out there… Sometimes I had seven or eight airplanes going at one time. I was sometimes flying 10, 12 hours in the day. Start flying at six o'clock in the morning and get through at dark… One summer I had 32 people working for me. The youngest one was 10 years older than I was, and that was quite an education for a kid!"

"The fellow had always wondered how he was going to get the C2 over to the lake. Well, I had the time on the engine, and the water was still out there on the field. So I ran it up to full throttle and the damn thing started to slide. I said, 'Boy, here's a way to get your airplane in the lake!' It was so easy: it started sliding and I just let it go…"

"I'm still going to school… I felt like a 16-year-old every morning that I got up, up until last year."

"Eleven different schools... and there's not one that I've enjoyed. Their memory chafes like a slipping rope against the flesh of childhood... Ten years of school were like that – mining for knowledge, burying life – studying in grade school so I could pass examinations to get into high school – studying in high school so I could pass examinations to get into college – studying in college so... but there I broke the chain. Why should I continue studying to pass examinations to get into a life I don't want to lead – a life of factories, and drawing boards, and desks? In the first half of my sophomore year I left college to learn to fly..."

"Looking ahead at the unbroken horizon and limitless expanse of water, I'm struck by my arrogance in attempting such a flight. I'm giving up a continent, and heading out to sea in the most fragile vehicle ever devised by man. Why should I be so certain that a swinging compass needle will lead me to land and safety? Why have I dared stake my life on the belief that by drawing a line on paper and measuring its azimuth and length, I can find my way through shifting air to Europe?"

— Charles A. Lindbergh, *The Spirit of St. Louis*. Lindbergh made the first nonstop solo trans-Atlantic flight in 1927.

Interview — Whitney Point, New York, August 2007

Clarence See: My grandfather was a farmer. He was an inspiration to me my whole life, even though he passed away when I was quite young. Living there on the farm I spent all my time with him.

He was a master barn builder. A farmer would lose his barn due to lightning, or wet hay, or something, and my grandfather – in wintertime when all he had to do was milk the cows – would cut the framework for a new barn for them.

Course, I was too young to be in on the barn-raising, but my old cousin went to help with the last barn-raising that my grandfather did. He told me the story that all he carried was his auger, a bucket full of wooden pegs, and a mallet to drive them with. He didn't even take a saw with him (laughs)! In two days the whole framework was up, ready for the siding, and my grandfather was done; he would be finished. That last barn that Grandpa built is still standing.

Grandpa was a good mechanic as far as his hands and so forth. But he made his money raising tobacco. He ran this farm for a captain in the Civil War, who was non-resident. He just spent a month or so on the farm in the summertime.

My grandfather had built the house that I was born in between the time that he was 19 and 21. He just got the house done, and Captain Petit came and stayed there for a month or so that summer.

When he got ready to leave, he said to my grandfather, "Why don't you buy this farm from me?"

My grandfather says, "I'd love to buy it, but I haven't got any money."

He says, "You don't need any money." Captain Petit says, "I know you can make the farm pay for itself." So they arrived at a price and my grandfather saddled up a horse and went across the fields and proposed to my grandmother that same evening (laughs)!

He was quite a guy. Tobacco was really great money in the mid-1920s. Then they began to raise tobacco in the South and the demand for the Northern tobacco dropped off. The farm was 130 acres and you couldn't fill a five-gallon pail with the stones on the whole farm; nice loam. You could raise anything on that farm.

I worked there all my years growing up, worked for my uncle during the summer and in the wintertime when he needed me on the weekends. So it was home, and I planned on owning it someday, but my uncle passed away suddenly, and I wasn't in a position to buy it from my aunt.

LS: How did you first get interested in flying?

CS: Probably one of the things that got me interested in flying was that part of the farm that was on the river flats. They were nice long fields, 3,000 foot long. They would bring students over there from the old Syracuse Amboy Airport, and they'd practice approaches and forced landings. When they'd pull up on a missed approach, I'd see the Standards and Wacos going by. I landed in all the fields that I dreamed of landing in as a kid, later on in life (laughs).

LS: By accident?

CS: Yes, at times (laughs)! I was test pilot for Franklin Engine, and I knew these fields, so if I had something I wasn't quite sure of, I'd keep those fields in range.

One of the first exciting things that happened to me in aviation was in 1928 when Lindbergh took *The Spirit* on a tour all over the country. (The name of Lindbergh's plane was *The Spirit of St. Louis*. – Ed.) Kraus Heinz in Syracuse, who up until probably the mid-50s made all the airport lighting that was used in the country, built two huge flood lights – they were I guess 10 foot in diameter, these huge reflectors, of course – and the old Amboy Airport had one on each side of the runway.

I was just a kid, but I can still see just as vividly as if it was last evening: *The Spirit of St. Louis* in a forward slip, coming in to the light, come right down until the wingtip was about a foot above the ground, and then it comes level, and he comes in for a three-point landing. He got out and so forth, and that was it, and my parents took me home.

LS: How did you get started in flying?

CS: Syracuse had an apprentice-training school. If you wanted to become a welder, you could become a welder while you were taking the high school courses. Draftsman, machine shop, and so forth; this was all high school. And in conjunction with all this, they had an aviation school and a mechanics school at the airport.

You spent two semesters involved in other shops – the welding shop, the machine shop, drafting – and after two semesters, if you were still in the class, they started busing you to the airport.

Of course I lived in the country, and my dad who, at that time, was working for Allied Chemical, he went right by the airport. So my bicycle resided in the rumble seat of the Model A, and I'd jump off at Armstrong Road and pedal to the airport. Only time that I'd ride the bus was in wintertime when riding the bicycle was impractical, and I'd catch a ride into Syracuse and then catch the bus.

LS: So what happened after high school – did you go to work for the Franklin Engine Company?

CS: No, I got my ratings. It was apprentice-training school, and you asked me how I had learned to fly. I got acquainted with everyone on the airport, private owners of the airplanes. And Paul Wilcox made me lead boy amongst the students. I guess there was probably 30, and he give me 7 or 8 students, and I was kind of foreman over them. He'd let me bring other people's airplanes into the school to work on; he knew what was going on, and in return they'd give me flying time in their airplanes.

I soloed in a J-2 Cub, but I put a lot of time in other airplanes that were unofficial: Kenner Birds, and Kenner Standards, and the old bi-planes. I had my A&P (Airframe and Power Plant Mechanic Certification) written and passed, and my Private (Private Pilot's License) passed before my 18th birthday. About two or three months later I had my Commercial (Commercial Pilot's License) passed and had enough flying time, because I was getting flying time from half a dozen different private owners at the airport.

A fellow named Otto Enderto was the head of the FAA (Federal Aviation Administration) office in Rochester. He was a bootlegger up until the time he went to work for the FAA. I guess I would have been 10 or 11 years old, because prohibition was 1932 or 33. And I'd hear this airplane way up high, just at dusk, and the sun was just below the horizon, and it got real quiet, and you could see the sun flash off the prop every once in a while. Onondaga Lake was just a mile from where I lived, and I used to pedal my bicycle over to the Hunters' Club where all the seaplanes were, and I knew what was based there – it was this Fairchild Razorback seaplane. It had a J67 Wright engine on it.

In later years I got to know Otto quite well, got talking to him about it. He says, "That was me. I'd always be in gliding range of Onondaga Lake at sunset, and I'd pull the throttle back and land when I had just enough light to touch down." The bootleggers would mostly pick it up on their truck, right there off the dock. Prohibition was over by the time I was old enough to fly.

I passed my Commercial and Flight Instructors rating in one flight. All the universities had CPT (Civilian Pilot Training) courses, and the war was coming. All the contractors at the airports needed flight instructors, so everyone was trying to get their time for an Instructor's rating, so they could go flying for a living.

I was riding with these guys when they were practicing for their Flight Instructors rating. I'm practicing for my Commercial, and riding with them got me doing this stuff that you did for a Flight Instructor's rating. I knew how to do it. We got down and Otto says, "Get your books out and get ready to take your Flight Instructor's written (test), you've just passed your Flight Instructor's practical (test)."

LS: What about your Commercial test?

CS: He just did them together! He says, "I'll write you your Commercial along with your Flight Instructor's Rating next time I come down from Syracuse. It will save a lot of paperwork." (Laughs)

So I studied, and like always he come to Syracuse on a Tuesday, and when the Fairchild taxied up, I come out to meet him. We walked in and he says, "We're in trouble."

I says, "What do you mean, 'in trouble'?"

He says they come out with a multiple choice test; up to this time everything was longhand. You passed more on who you were and what your background was, and the inspectors didn't bother to read it all. But with multiple choice, all they had to do was use the overlay and they'd have it graded.

He says, "I'll lock you in Harry Ward's office. Take all your books so you can pass the son of a bitch; I couldn't pass it! But on one condition," he says, "you run a ground school for all the rest of the guys on the airport so that they're ready to take it when I come back." I passed it. Hell, I don't think I opened a book more than a couple of times, and I passed it all right.

I think I got my seaplane rating on my Private. This fellow had a C-2 Aeronca. He bought a pair of floats for it, and I put them on and overhauled the engine with the kids in the school. We got it all set and then, with kids on each side, we picked the airplane up and carried it across the ramp and set it on the grass.

In those days you always run the engine three or four hours before you flew it after you'd had the cylinders off. So I sat running the engine, eating my lunch, and a hell of a thunderstorm come up, and, boy, did it rain! I was worried about it hailing and raising heck with the airplane. But I sat there with the thing running, in the thunderstorm, until it got through. Holy cats, the grass out in front of me was under several inches of water.

The fellow had always wondered how he was going to get the C-2 over to the lake. Well, I had the time on the engine, and the water was still out there on the field. So I ran it up to full throttle, and the damn thing started to slide. I said, "Boy, here's a way to get your airplane in the lake!" (Laughs) It was so easy: it started sliding and I just let it go. I'd taken half a dozen rides in seaplanes, but I'd never flown one by myself. So that's how I made a landing in the lake before I'd ever made a takeoff (laughs)!

LS: Were you a good student? It sounds like you had no trouble passing those courses.

CS: Oh, no. I never had a problem. I graduated from high school when I was 16. In high school I studied just to get passing grades for sports. I played hockey mostly. I probably would have played some pro hockey if the war hadn't come along. I played with an amateur team for one year. I played three championship hockey teams, and I liked hockey.

I can watch a hockey game on TV, and somebody gets checked into the boards and I can still feel it. "Oh, gee, this is how it feels!" Surprising in hockey, the only time I ever got knocked out was when I caught a puck right above my eyes. I got my glove up to bat it down and missed it, and it got me. The next thing I knew, people were dragging me off the ice (laughs)! Other than closing my eyes up for a couple of days, it didn't hurt me too much.

LS: What do you do at Franklin?

CS: I had the flight test hangar, that was my bailiwick. I did the engine installations, worked up the cooling, worked up everything. There was a lot of airplanes out there – that's how I got to know the Pipers really well.

LS: So this was a mechanics job, not an engineering job?

CS: Well, it was an engineering job in that I worked everything out. One summer I had 32 people working for me. The youngest one was 10 years older than I was, and that was quite an education for a kid!

LS: How did you handle that?

CS: This one fellow was a good mechanic, but he liked to have a drink with his lunch, and I warned him. He was late getting back from lunch one day, and I could smell liquor on his breath. I told Carl Roman, the chief engineer, what I was going to do, and he said, "You do what you have to do." I told him he was done, and he said, "I'll go back to the plant." And I says, "Go ahead." And he goes back to the plant and finds out he doesn't have a job! I had no more problems with the rest of the group after that (laughs)!

LS: Did you ever fly for a living?

CS: Yeah, everything I worked on I flew. Sometimes I had seven or eight airplanes going at one time. I was sometimes flying 10, 12 hours in the day. Start flying at six o'clock in the morning and get through at dark. That was a fun job, believe me! I still flew sometimes for Franklin way up to the 70s. Then I flew for a steel company for 22 years. I was flying a model 18 Beach, an eight-place airplane.

LS: So you were flying people around.

CS: Yeah. Back in the 50s I went to work for Brace-Mueller-Huntley in '49, and Mr. Brace was on the board that controlled who got materials from World War II. And, of course, he had to live in Washington. So I was in and out of Washington often after the war, just overnight often. And we'd usually leave like 2:30 in the afternoon, get home in time for dinner.

We'd get to Washington, and I'd head for the Smithsonian in the morning. And I'd be there in the morning, and I got to know that they unlocked the door at 10 o'clock, and I'd be there at 10 o'clock to get in before there was any crowd in there.

I guess I'd been to the Smithsonian two or three times, but this one morning I got in a conversation with the custodian about *The Spirit*, hanging just inside the door, and he says, "Let me show you something." He went over and here was this screen over in the corner and a chair sitting there. He says, "That's Colonel Lindbergh's chair." He says, "When he's in town, he'll come to the service entrance and I'll let him in, and he'll sit there and look at *The Spirit* for 10 or 15 minutes, until it gets time to open, and then he'll get up and leave. And every time he gets up to walk with me to the door, he'll look up at it and say, 'I still can't believe I made it.'"

Well, I'm there years later, waiting for them to open, and the door unlocks and, my God, who steps out but Colonel Lindbergh! I said, "Good morning, Colonel!" And he draws back – that somebody recognized him kind of set him up – and I say, "You remember landing in the floodlights at the Amboy Airport in Syracuse, New York, in 1928?" "Yes!" he says. I said, "Well, I saw you land there." He says, "Let's sit down!"

We sat down on the steps of the Smithsonian for about 20 minutes until somebody recognized him, and then he left (laughs). He was fine with me, because I was familiar with something that he had done and mentioned it to him. I described watching him land, and he says, "Landing the old *Spirit* without being able to see out the front, that was a little bit of a trick!"

LS: My whole project is about different ways of learning. It's hard to tell how people learn today. So if you were going to tell young people, your grandkids or something, and you were to advise them how to learn, what would you tell them?

CS: Get a good basic education in what they're interested in.

Getting my mechanic's license was a means to an end. I always wanted to fly, but without a lot of money, being a mechanic was a way to learn to fly and not cost anything. I always liked it. I enjoy working with my hands and so forth.

I'm still going to school. I just ordered three DVD's from this Learning Company down in Virginia; they're college lectures. I've had several of them – I've just got kind of fascinated. I have a lot of Jewish friends, and I've always wanted to get the Old Testament and the New Testament cleared in my mind. I just bought *The History of the English Language*. I watch them in the TV. They've got graphics; it's easier to learn if you've got graphics, as you well know. There are math courses, and so forth.

Up until recently – I guess the fact that Betty's getting very, very forgetful – that's probably what's caught up with me. I felt like a 16-year-old every morning that I got up, up until last year.

LS: So you started to feel old just recently?

CS: Yeah, yeah. I've always managed to work even though it was hot. But this summer it just got a little too much for me. It's a whole lot easier to sit inside and read.

29. DONALD DUBOIS

History   Late   Born 1914, Harrisburg, Pennsylvania

Why do I live on Dubois Road? Because Donald Dubois's parents were the first people to live in this area's latest incarnation, so the road is named after them.

I don't recall when I first met Don. I think I knocked on his door soon after I built my house. And then I became interested in him after he showed me his shop, filled with industrial lathes and milling machines. At that time he was in his mid-80s and still pushing finished projects out the door. When I met him for this interview, he was in his mid-90s and still pushing finished projects out the door.

Part of Don's uniqueness stems from there being few nonagenarians with the clarity and enthusiasm of a teenager, but it's more than that. Don has always been a dreamer and a loner. He still drives, cares for his house, his shop, and his garden. He does the yard work on a couple of acres and attends to his wife, Bessie; all by himself as far as I can tell. It must be lonely to be both so young and so old at the same time.

Postscript: Donald Dubois died on October 25th, 2014. He was 100.

Excerpts

"Then I got interested in building gliders, man-size gliders that I could operate, 'cause on my grandmother's farm, where I lived, she had a hill there of about a 30° grade. So I'd pick up this glider and get running, and jump off the edge and glide down to the bottom. Sometimes successfully, sometimes not... It seemed like such a wonderful idea, that you could build a wing, that you could take off and go down the hill. And of course, being that young, a lot of the practical side just went out the window!..."

"The exciting part was coming up with new ideas... You have an idea and in your mind it's beautiful, and you get it on paper, and from paper you go to the actual machining, and the building, and then right there, like they say, you're back to the drawing board (laughs)! That is exciting..."

"I don't know how much the younger people absorb from TV, and the newspapers and whatnot ... whether they're interested in it and get that much into it, but if they are, then just thinking for themselves is the most important thing in the world. Because what's being focused on them, on all of us, is a misguided picture of what it's really like up there. It's really a sad thing that we're getting such a cock-eyed view of the world..."

"Some places you're not going to conclude, you're not going to get a total answer... You proceed, like on an unknown road. You don't know what's out there, but on the other hand, you can't sit down on the side of the road, either... You get into things you never suspect you'd be getting into..."

"When the time comes to exit this life, it's a good idea to go with the smallest possible amount of evil baggage. A person would be well advised not to load yourself up with a lot of stuff you've got to account for. A young person can start working on that right away."

"The student can only learn a difficult action insofar as he can put the teacher inside himself. He must be student and teacher at the same time. He must, more and more, grade his own tasks, get his own feedback, make his own corrections, and develop his own criteria, standards, for doing these things."

— John Holt, from *Instead of Education: Ways to Help People Do Things Better*

"Late, by myself, in the boat of myself, no light and no land anywhere, cloud cover thick. I try to stay just above the surface, yet I'm already under and living within the ocean."

— Jalal ad-Din Rumi, 13th century Persian poet, from *The Illuminated Rumi*, translated by Coleman Barks

Interview   Shokan, New York, November 2007

LS: When did you start learning?

Donald Dubois: I suppose you start your learning from the very beginning by observing what is going on around you. After a while it gets to be a formal situation, when you go to school, and while you're going to school you're picking up along the way, on your own, just by observing what's going on. And, of course, as you get older you begin to analyze different things and try to get everything in perspective: what's most important and what is not. It's a continuing thing. If you're not the type that observes, then you're not going to learn as much.

Along the way you get interested in certain subjects, certain projects. You can get a good deal of learning from what they call "book learning." You can get a good deal of that, but nothing compares with the experience in my line.

From the beginning I liked building things. When I was younger, around 16 or so, I got interested in the idea of flying. I did get up once in the old Waco's open cockpit planes, and then another time I got in a Ford Tri-motor. They had an open field down near Kingston, and for one dollar you got a ride in a Tri-motor, which barely cleared some of those electric lines.

Well anyway, then I got interested in building gliders, man-size gliders that I could operate, 'cause on my grandmother's farm, where I lived, she had a hill there of about a 30° grade. So I'd pick up this glider and get running and jump off the edge and glide down to the bottom. Sometimes successfully, sometimes not (laughs).

And after that I tried building a motorized plane, but I lacked the finances it took to carry it through. Money was always tight then, that was the middle of the Depression. If I saved a dollar I'd go down to the 10-cent store in Kingston and buy nuts and bolts and screws (laughs). For the wings I used muslin, that was the cheapest cloth you could buy, stretched that on, and put on what's call "airplane dope," which would strengthen it. But I never got to take off because the welding was not good in those days, and I'd spin the prop and get it going, and every now and then the welding would come loose and that propeller would land at my feet! I finally decided that wasn't too healthy a procedure. In fact, I have that propeller somewhere here yet.

LS: How did the interest in airplanes come about?

DD: This is a very strange thing, asking me how it came about. In our school up here, our primary school in Ashokan, they had an overhead library with a lot of antiquated books of one kind or another. Somehow I happened to be up in there going through it, and I come across this photograph, or painting, or whatever it was, of one of the very first aircrafts, conceived in the 1700s or 1800s, and it was named *The Ariel*.

I got interested in that, and then I got a hold of some other books. I learned about how the lift of the wings takes place by creating a vacuum on the top, and the shape of the wing, and the controls: the rudder, and the ailerons, and the back elevators. I finally got the theory pretty doggone good. Of course, when it comes to building it, I was restricted to what I could get in the way of money to buy this stuff.

It seemed like such a wonderful idea, that you could build a wing, that you could take off, and go down the hill. And of course, being that young, a lot of the practical side just went out the window (laughs)!

I mean, the idea that I could build a plane by myself, put a motorcycle motor in it in the front with a propeller, and actually take off with it (laughs)! This crazy idea didn't seem so crazy at the time. And I imagine my grandmother and my parents were looking on there and hoping I forget it (laughs)!

LS: Did they encourage you? Were you encouraged by your family?

DD: No, no. I guess they were glad I had an interest in something; it kept me out of mischief. The idea that I might actually try to fly the thing, that must have scared them, which it should have (laughs)!

LS: You didn't have any friends helping you?

DD: No, no. My brothers were younger than I, and they didn't care anyway, I guess. Anyway, they were too young. But other than that, we were rather isolated. There's people around here right now, but you can't begin to know what it was then. There was nobody around here.

The Dubois family was here, and Fred Golnick was up on the corner up there, and other than that, that whole region up there, there was nobody, nobody. And there was nobody down through here, either. The only building was my father's house and my father's garage. It was more or less "Dubois Town." The nearest village was about a mile up the road.

LS: Were you more alone, or were you a loner?

DD: I guess I tend to be a loner. Maybe today, too – I don't know, somewhat. Not that I'm averse to the human population, but that's just the way it was, I guess. When you're interested in building stuff like that, you can be a loner. I've always been a one-man operation, which is no way to get along in this world, especially today.

I didn't really have too much choice. Maybe part of it is because I'm too intense on what I'm doing. I don't know. Of course, you could always think of it from the angle of getting someone to do it with you, to help you, but I've always put all my concentration without wanting outside distraction. And helpers can sometimes be a distraction (laughs), strange as it sounds.

LS: It sounds like your work was more important to you than just making money.

DD: Yes, yes. Yes, it was. My work was also my recreation (laughs).

LS: Did you do anything else besides your work?

DD: Oh, yes. In those early days I played a lot of baseball, and I did a lot of wandering up in these mountains, and so on. I used to like to go up the mountain, Tonche Mountain right behind us there. Many times after school I'd walk up to the top of that mountain.

LS: Did you have an important teacher, someone who inspired you?

DD: I don't know about the inspiration; one of my greatest teachers was in grade school, and that was Harrison Gridley. He was a great teacher. He had all the grades to teach. Aside from the schoolwork, he was quite a man.

In those days there was good-sized kids – you know, bigger than today – they were always getting into some kind of a fight. Well, he had a special way of taking care of that. He brought a pair of boxing gloves, and heavy ones, 16 ounces or so, so if the two guys wanted to fight, OK. He'd take them into the other room and let them fight. Well, after about five minutes with those doggone heavy gloves, they'd had all they wanted (laughs)!

He was very fair in everything that he did. At noontime he'd play baseball with the rest of us. And it was probably that aspect of him, as well as the education side of it, that was a greater memory than anything else.

LS: Was this a one-man school?

DD: Yeah.

LS: How many kids were in the classes?

DD: I'd say 25 in the whole school, from Grades one to eight. He'd take the third grade class up front maybe, for recitation and questions. There was a certain benefit to all the rest of the school: while one group was supposed to be studying, they also absorb some of what was going on up there.

Thereafter I got working in Poughkeepsie in a machine shop. That's where I did most of my machine learning. I was married and had a child when World War II come along, so I wasn't the first choice of the draft.

In the machine shop I was thrown into the middle, sink or swim, and I was one of a good many others, farm boys and city boys and what not, who didn't know anything about machining. That gave me an advantage because, while I didn't know very much, I knew a little bit more than they did.

I got started, and in a couple months I got to be the boss of the machine section. I learned as much from those guys as anywhere else. There was some old-timers in there, too, and of course in those days, jobs being scarce even in the war, the older mechanics were not too anxious to share their knowledge with you. But by observing, again, I picked up a great deal from them.

For 27 years I worked there. I went on from one position to another, and I finally wound up as the manager, I guess you would call it, of the Research and Development machine section.

The company gave me a great deal of latitude in what I could do. I come up with this and that and what not, and then, finally, I retired from there at age 55, I think it was. But before that I had started a machine shop in my basement. That would be around 1955 maybe.

From there I got started on my own, built it a little bit bigger, and finally built a shop down here. And then eventually lost that, and then started the shop that I have here, piece by piece, one building at a time, until I had a combination of about four different buildings put together.

The exciting part was coming up with new ideas; it was the ideas that I had. Out of that I got four US Patents on various items. That's where the excitement comes in: developing something and overcoming the problems that you encounter every time.

You have an idea and in your mind it's beautiful, and you get it on paper, and from paper you go to the actual machining and the building, and then right there, like they say, you're back to the drawing board (laughs)! That is exciting.

After we lost the big shop and I come back here, I still had to make a living because I lost a lot of money on that project. In fact, I was back to zero.

The one item that I developed for the former company that I worked for – I had good relations with them, with their research section actually – I got together with them on one product, and they went for it. That got me out of the hole. I got the patent that I assigned to them with a contract that I would be the exclusive maker of the product over a five-year period. That got me out of trouble financially.

That was a big machine that I called the "Merry-Go-Round Milker." In fact, last year I sent off the last shipment to DeLaval Separator in Kansas City. This was a device like a merry-go-round: it rotates, and as it rotates the cows are milked. They're all standing on this rotary platform, maybe 10 or 12 cows at a time.

LS: It's large then.

DD: Oh, yes, yes. The part that I made was a part that went up on the ceiling. These cows are milked by vacuum, and it requires some electricity to operate it. In order for this to rotate and not wind up the whole detail, you have to have a slip-joint affair up on the ceiling that the vacuum comes through and the electricity comes through. That device was the big one for me.

LS: Tell about the process of succeeding and the process of failing. Do you regret your failures? Are you disappointed with your successes?

DD: Well, nothing is ever 100% in this life in my mind, no matter what angle you tackle it from. Yeah, sure, I'm disappointed that we failed, but I didn't have time to be disappointed too much. I was broke, and I had to start over, start making some money if I could. Sometimes that drives you, it's got to. That's got to drive you.

And as far as the successes are concerned, I always think they could have been greater, I could have done more, but I didn't because along the way... I guess everybody has certain defects, and one of mine is I don't persist long enough. There's a good many items that, had I developed them, I could have been way up yonder. But I didn't. I can't fault myself altogether, either, because those times were tough and you couldn't get money very easy. And then, after that, you've got to have money to push something, no matter how good it is.

For one thing, I made what was probably the first electric wheelchair in the country, as far as I know. That was in '55, I made that for my father because he got muscular dystrophy. I took his wheelchair and motorized it, and he traveled all around the country with that. He could make a four-mile flip around this back road, you know up your road there and down behind the pond, and come back down the state road, and come back on the shoulder of the road. That must have been quite a sight, come to think of it – I thought it was quite normal – to see a guy puttering along the highway in a wheelchair (laughs)!

Now you see what that developed into today. As far as I know, I had the first. Previous to that, according to what I looked through, very rich people in the 1900s could have a gas-powered wheelchair, but it would be a $10,000 job, or something like that. And there's various other things that I did, too – 101 different things that I lost out.

LS: So maybe you like to build things better than to market them? I can understand that.

DD: Yes. And besides, I'd rather admit that I didn't have the skill myself to market. But then again, if you have money, you hire all kinds of guys to do that for you.

LS: What was your experience with schooling? Did you find that school was where you learned the most important things? You said you learned most in the shop.

DD: That's pretty hard to define: the most important, but the important, yes, it was important. But at the time I didn't appreciate it, I didn't care about school, no way – I wanted to be outside, building my stuff. It seemed like such a waste of time when I could be at home making an airplane! But the strange part of it is, though, a lot of what I disdained altogether, I realized later on how valuable it was.

For one thing, among other things in high school, I took French. I didn't care about that at all at the time, but the strange part of it is that today I can recall just about all the French words and phrases. And I can pick up something written in French, and I can get the gist of it.

And the mathematics, too. I didn't care about that; it was just something I had to do. But later on, when I got into the machining and so on, I found out how very important it was that I knew my trigonometry; tremendously important. You think of that in terms of surveying and what not, I mean that's very useful there, too. But you get down to small stuff and the trigonometry is very important.

I remember one man I had working for me in the shop. He never got beyond the third grade, but he was so interested in the work he was doing that I simply showed him the simple parts of trigonometry and how to work the tables, and that totally uneducated guy was so doggone good at that you'd be surprised. It's funny: you never know where the talent lies.

And I suppose, too, the education in English – I didn't care about it at all, and I couldn't see any sense in reading some of these classics, which we had to read. Well, strangely, my English teacher would be horrified to know that I wrote three or four books! Absolutely (laughs)!

LS: Surprised or horrified?

DD: Both, both! Of course, she still might be horrified at some of my English. I never paid any great attention to it. I got no problem in putting out the thought, but the form (laughs), it's something to be desired!

LS: When did that desire arise? Where did that inspiration come from?

DD: Inspiration, I don't know, but I got started in the 1970s, I guess. No particular inspiration, but different ideas would come to my mind and different thoughts, and now and then I'd write them down and put them in the desk over there. And after a while I got an accumulation, so I did the first book and then three more after that.

I think, all in all, one has to have an interest in something. Either that or a number of somethings, 'cause without the interest, and without getting up in the morning and having something you're going to do, it's no good.

LS: So where do you find an interest?

DD: I'm not sure that you find it; I think it comes to you, maybe. I don't know. Of course, self-interest sometimes promotes a lot of that; I mean promoting yourself.

Although, the acquiring of knowledge is all it takes in itself for some people. Sometimes looking for knowledge and getting it is enough in itself. But knowledge, without putting it to some use, is kind of a waste, too.

LS: Bessie tells me that you go to church now. Did you always go to church?

DD: Yes, yup.

LS: Well, that kept you from being too alone, didn't it?

DD: Yes, in a way it did. Yes, yes, sure. My grandmother saw to that. She was quite religious and made sure that all her grandchildren got to church. And of course, we all accepted it to varying degrees. I've been connected with the church, good Lord, about 70 or 80 years.

LS: Do you have any feeling of what life might be for kids these days? Any feeling of what they should do, or shouldn't do?

DD: Well, not really, only the standard "Don't Do's," such as the drugs, and the alcohol, and so on. And of course, if you had the courage to tell them to stay away from sex, it would do no good. When the time comes, things have to happen.

LS: One of the nice things about this project is that I get to talk to younger people at some depth. Some of them tell me that they appreciate speaking with me because they don't get to talk about this stuff to their friends.

DD: Well, this is true. This goes on a lot and even, it seems to me, creates a certain bar with the parents. I think that the children, the kids, the young people, they'll talk with you a great deal easier than they'll talk with parents. What do you find in your experience with them? What they're mostly looking for?

LS: Well, I'm attracted to kids who are energetic, and I mostly talk to kids who are inspired to do something. And I often ask them how they got inspired, and where did it start, or when did it start. Most can't tell me. They don't really know.

It's a thoughtful process, and it seems impossible to explain it to somebody unless they're already doing it. In this project I want to encourage people to use their own thinking, make their own decisions, and not to accept what they're told.

DD: Well, that's the way to go, especially. I don't know how much the younger people absorb from TV, and the newspapers and whatnot, and the magazines, whether they're interested in it and get that much into it; but if they are, then just thinking for themselves is the most important thing in the world. Because what's being focused on them, on all of us, is a misguided picture of what it's really like up there. It's really a sad thing that we're getting such a cock-eyed view of the world.

LS: Where can a person get a good view of the world?

DD: Difficult thing because no individual is able to go out there on his own and canvass the world and take all this in on their own. They've got to accept what's given to them, or not accept it, but they've got to be aware of it. And here is where their own thinking comes in very, very strong, and not too easy, either. I mean, maybe some of us have the idea of the way the world is going, and therefore we tend to accept the part of it that fits into that category, but still, it's very hard to get an honest view of it.

So yes, do your own thinking, and that sometimes bothers me in the area of religion. I've been to that church all my life, and I certainly want to accept a good deal of what's given, especially in the New Testament – the Old Testament I've just come to a bit here and there – but even so, doing your own thinking can get you into trouble (laughs)!

LS: Well, that's an important point. How do you get out of trouble? Do you stay away from it, or do you explore it?

DD: No, it's an ongoing thing, for me anyways. Sure we all like to reach a conclusion on this or that or something. Some things you can't, really, at least not in this world. Maybe we can get a conclusion someplace else.

LS: How do you avoid being frustrated? Doesn't that get you frustrated?

DD: Yeah, that bothers me. I guess I get frustrated. Anything that you cannot conclude and put on a shelf as finished, that's got to bother you, at least it does me. I like to conclude things. Some places you're not going to conclude, you're not going to get a total answer. These people who think they've got it all wrapped up, I take a very dim view of that.

LS: This is important for a young person. How does a person proceed to make decisions when you don't know how things are going to conclude?

DD: You proceed, like on an unknown road. You don't know what's out there, but on the other hand, you can't sit down on the side of the road, either.

LS: If you were 16 again, how would you proceed? Would you be reckless, or would you be cautious and respectful?

DD: I think I'd be a cautious middle-of-the-roader. Actually, if we all knew the outcome – call it the conclusion or whatever you want – it wouldn't be very interesting (laughs).

I suppose young people, when they have a lot of life ahead of them, tend to think it's going on forever. When you get old you begin to wonder what's next? I think even the atheists can't help but wonder what's next. And maybe one might tend to worry about it a little bit, but that's foolish because we have no choice in the matter.

When the time comes to exit this life, it's a good idea to go with the smallest possible amount of evil baggage. A person would be well advised not to load yourself up with a lot of stuff you've got to account for. A young person can start working on that right away.

It's funny how life turns out. You get into things you never suspect you'd be getting into. All in all, it's quite a trip (laughs)!

WRESTLING

30. MIKE SHORT

History   **Early**   Born 1987, Kingston, New York

Mike Short started wrestling as a heavyweight at 13, and for three years he struggled with a lack of self-confidence. Paul Widerman, who became his coach when Mike was a senior, helped him find his strength both in wrestling and in the world.

Seen by outsiders, wrestling appears to be an adversarial sport. It's certainly not for the faint of heart. But as Mike's story shows, it's really about recognizing your weaknesses in order to realize your potential.

Excerpts

"I started wrestling my freshman year, and… I lost every single one of my matches I came upon, and it was a little difficult…"

"I was having my mental conflicts of, 'Do I deserve to win? Do I want to win? Why do I wrestle? I wrestle to win!' And Paul sort of realized that, and a couple of guys that were good, and me especially, that we had the intensity, we had the practice, we had the drills, but we went out on the mat and, somewhere, we faltered…"

"What Paul made me realize is that the person who wants it the most is the one that's going to win. The person that's not afraid to go out there and do it. So wrestling, in my life, even my parents saw it… by the time the end of this season came around they're, like – they didn't know who I was – they're, like, 'Who are you? Where'd you come from?' And I changed…"

"Sometimes I have to wait for the right things to come. I have to wait for things to come to me sometimes, not go to it, or try to. It may sound like the weirdest thing in the world but… I guess that's the way it is in some things."

> "The Zen Master warns: 'If you meet Buddha on the road, kill him!' This admonition points up that no meaning that comes from outside ourselves is real... How often we make circumstances our prison and other people our jailers! At our best we take full responsibility for what we do and what we choose not to do. The most important struggles take place within the self."
>
> — Richard Layton, from a Discussion Group Report entitled "If you meet the buddha on the road, kill him!" April 1996

Interview   Kingston, New York, May 2005

Mike Short: I'm a little slower in the way I think, like I'll be thinking one way and then I'll be, like, "Oh, this is a better way to do it." Like, some friends will go straight to the easiest route. Me, I'll start going off the hard, back to the easy, find an easier route, and that's the way I take.

I spent six and a half hours writing a seven-page essay on something. I didn't want to tell them because the teacher's, like, "How long did you spend on this?" And I just said, "Too long." I didn't want to say that I spent six and a half hours on it.

LS: Well, that's learning! There's more learning in that than getting to the goal of having a paper in your hand.

MS: Yeah. But I spent a lot of time on it. I ended up doing really well, but everyone thinks I spent an hour and a half on it. I'm not the smartest person in class, it's just I work the hardest.

We just got done with our pre-calculus final. Today we got the grades back. I expected to do good on it, because my average throughout the year had been decent – it had been around 80. I got an 85 on it. I was one of the best in my class. I didn't expect to do that well. It came down to what I had, was an 82 average through three quarters, and I end up pulling an 85.

I ended up doing better than most of my class, and they're, like, "You must have spent extra time on it." I said, "No, I spent the same amount of time as you. I was in your class, right there." I used to be... I have ADD, you know what that is, right?

LS: I know about it.

MS: Attention Deficit Disorder. I take Cylert and small doses of Ritalin at night, when I start feeling tired and I need something to help me focus.

I am in Resource. Everybody thinks that Resource is a big place for stupid people. It's not. Some of the smartest people in my school, that I've known, have walked through Resource. I would do good on like a Regents test, or something like that, they are, like, "You must have got more time." "No, I was sitting right there with you. I got the same grade as you."

I realized my freshman year that I didn't have to study... as long as I did my homework and paid attention in class. I found that everyone was cramming the night before, and I was sitting at home watching TV. I pull 90s on tests.

They're like, "How long did you study for this."

"I didn't."

"So how do you do it?"

"I do my homework, I pay attention in class."

I've gone through school without my pills, and I notice a slight change. I have a little harder time focusing when I do my homework, but I'll end up doing my homework. It may not be as good because I didn't focus, but I do it.

I went out, did my SATs this year. I did the awful, worst thing… I got a 300 on the English section. I'm not that good at pulling essays in, like, 55 minutes. I can pull out a good essay, a good page-and-a-half essay, if I've got two hours to read it over, fix my mistakes, reword sentences that were simple that I could reword better. But I got a 300 on the English and I was, like, "Oh, my God!" The average for this is like a 600.

The math sector, the average was 580. I pulled out a 700 on it. I pulled out a 700, so much better than the average. All my friends were, like, "How'd you pull out a 700?" Math is just my easy point; math and science are my simple points in my life.

That's why I want to be an architect. It brings math into my life, and I don't know, but, like you said, you've got to find the simple things and then work out your easier things, work at things you're worse at.

I've been working at English and all that for a couple of years. I'm just telling you this, but for a couple of years my reading level was pretty bad. I came in the high school with like a fifth grade reading level. My reading was awful. I was in Resource because of that, because of my reading disability. Writing wasn't so bad, but reading I was at a fifth grade level.

The English Regents now for 11th grade is you have to write four essays, two days. It's six hours. I took this twice. Mid-year, halfway through 11th grade English, I pulled out a 75 on it. I go, "OK, I can work harder in class, become better." My reading became better over the year, but somehow I pulled out the same grade of a 75. It's like the first essay I put all my time and effort into. I spent like an hour and a half on it, writing it out, rewriting it. And the second one I took like an hour, where I couldn't rewrite it, I couldn't read over it.

That's what Resource was there for. I don't take it any more because my reading is now 11th or 12th grade level. My writing is on, or a little below.

LS: Tell me where the importance of wrestling began?

MS: Wrestling began for me, was eighth grade, and I was, like, "iffy" on it, coming into my first year of high school, because I heard it was really hard. I'm the type of person that doesn't like backing down from things once I start 'em. It's like, I gotta complete 'em.

I started wrestling my freshman year, and I came into the year getting off a broken leg from the football season. I had zero wins through the whole year; I lost every single one of my matches I came upon, and it was a little difficult. I was, like, figuring that I would have been a little better. I thought I would have one win.

Then the next year I'm coming around and I'm, like, "Am I ready to do this again?" I was, like, "Yeah." I had fun, I made friends, it was my new sport. I went through it sophomore year and came out with one win, and I was, like, "OK. There's another win. There's something I did." And I had two coaches that went through with me for three years, up to junior year: Alphonso Favata and his son Christian.

My junior year I came out of it with six wins, nothing big. They were just at meets, and I had wins, and I was becoming better. I could feel myself, I changed myself, and I was feeling it.

My senior year we found out Christian wasn't coaching, and I was, like, "Who's going to coach us? Who's going to be our main coach?" Alphonso is the guy that is there, and our new coach came around, which happened to be Paul Widerman, who had come in years before. He came in a couple of practices and taught us stuff. When we found out about that we were, like, "OK, we'll see what he does."

When Paul came out, it was more of a fun, flowing thing. He taught us different things. He ended up teaching us yoga over the season. We went for outside jogs on one of his properties and had fun. It was a totally different set of mind for practices. When we'd go out and practice for the other three years, it was, like: "Drill, drill, drill! Intensity. Drill, drill, drill. Practice your moves! Intensity." My year ended up being more progressive for me, in that year mentally and physically, than all three… than the other three years for me.

I ended up having a season of 17 and 8. I placed fifth in the New York State Sectionals with a couple of bad losses that I shouldn't 'a had. I should have placed more in a couple of tournaments, which I realized because I was having my mental conflicts of, "Do I deserve to win? Do I want to win? Why do I wrestle? I wrestle to win!" And Paul sort of realized that, and a couple of guys that were good, and me especially, that we had the intensity, we had the practice, we had the drills, but we went out on the mat and somewhere we faltered.

We would have practices where… in one practice he pulled everybody together and he's just like, "This is our practice today: what does everybody fear out here? Why isn't anybody wrestling to their potential?" And I was actually the first one to step up with, "I'm afraid to win. I'm afraid to do my best." And this was about a quarter of the way into the season, and we went on and I got better at it, fighting against that fear of losing, the fear of what my best is, and fulfilling my potential.

At one tournament I lost a match, and I definitely shouldn't have lost. I lost to a guy I should have beaten, and my coach Paul, and Alphonso, pulls me off to the side, and I'm just angry that I lost, and they start talking to me. They went over this with me, that I'm more into this fear thing of winning than they actually thought.

Through the season Paul helped me overcome this. He is, in a way, a mentor to me. He helped me overcome my fear. I'm not really over it yet, but when it comes down to it, when push comes to shove, whether I have to win or lose, I'm going to go out there and try my best. I'm going to win. I'm not going to do anything stupid, I'm not going to be afraid to win, afraid to go to my potential.

What Paul made me realize is that the person who wants it the most is the one that's going to win, the person that's not afraid to go out there and do it. So wrestling, in my life, even my parents saw it… by the time the end of this season came around they're, like – they didn't know who I was – they're, like, "Who are you? Where'd you come from?" And I changed.

Paul is really the person that helped me in wrestling. It was somewhat a change in my attitude towards things, my character. Paul watched you and if he saw something that was bugging you, he would talk to you about it. I wish I had him for other years, but then, I might not be the person I am now. I might be a better person, I might be a worse.

Now that it's over it's like, "Am I good enough to be a walk-on at the college I'm going to?" Do I have enough time, when I go to college my freshman year, to walk on to a wrestling team and spend the time to get beaten around by guys that have been there two, three years? That's now my new fight: "Do I have enough time to go out to college and do it again?"

I wish could go on, but my parents have helped me realize that my Freshman year of college isn't going to be the easiest thing to do, and I don't think that wrestling will be a major thing. I wish it could be, but I don't think it's going to be a major thing in my life.

LS: Why?

MS: I don't know. It's like, other plans. You've got to focus on the real world. That's what everybody… that's what my parents tell me. You've got to focus on what you're going to become – you're not going to become an All American wrestler. You're not going to become an Olympic wrestler. You're not going to make money off of wrestling. So it's like, I've got to focus at what my life is actually going to be.

I got to focus on the future and not childhood things of wanting to keep doing sports. That's my major problem I'm coming in with, is, I want to continue wrestling further, maybe not for the sport of it, but for the physical, healthy aspect of it. I don't like saying this, but I'm afraid of what I could be if I hadn't stuck with wrestling. I'm afraid I would be 325 pounds, 6'2" like I am now, and half the muscle and twice the size I am.

My coaches previous years helped me change, but not until Paul came around did I realize that I could become a better wrestler, that I could do a High Crotch, that I could take someone down, that I could pin 'em.

I lost to a Saugerties kid 3 to 2, stupidly. I had him pinned on his back. I got impatient, as my coaches called it, and the kid got away from me. I had him pinned to the mat, and I tried to do something stupid: I tried to move around out in front of him to hopefully get it tighter, and he got loose, and he ended up beating me 3 to 2 at the end.

Later on, I had another kid in the same situation – he was loose, but he wasn't going anywhere, just like the other kid wasn't. He was stuck on his back, maybe not pinned, but the kid tired out, and I pinned him. I was patient. It took me a minute and a half, it took me about a minute to pin the kid, but I was more patient in my movements, I was more patient in taking my shots. I waited for the right time instead of doing the stupid thing.

Talking about that now makes me realize that Paul helped me with that, too. It made me less impatient in what I had to do. Sometimes I have to wait for the right things to come; I have to wait for things to come to me sometimes, not go to it, or try to. It may sound like the weirdest thing in the world but… I guess that's the way it is in some things.

LS: The things that you're saying are so much bigger than the small stage that you've played them out on. You know that all of these issues apply to everything.

MS: Yeah, that's what my coaches, that's why Paul is bringing them up. My fear to do things, like my fear to take a shot and all that, it may be a small thing there, but that expanded out into the rest of my life. It wasn't that I'm afraid to take a shot, it's that I'm afraid of taking risks. That's how my coach put it. I understood as soon as he said that, that I was afraid to take risks.

All my friends make fun of me because at one point during the season one of my coaches said to me, "You gotta take risks. You can't be afraid your whole life." A lot of people make fun of each other on the team for the small things. They do make fun of me for that. But I just take it as a reminder that that's what I had to overcome at that point in time. That's what I still have to overcome.

Like all my friends, they bug me about asking girls out and stuff like that. And they're, like, "Why don't you have a girlfriend?" It's more the risk of asking them out – I'm afraid to do it. They've all had like four or five girlfriends, and they're like, "Aw, it's simple to do." When you haven't had one yet, it's difficult to ask.

LS: It's all in your mind. It's all how you make it. You're dealing with something that's your own. The one thing that I'll say is that the opposite of fear isn't always bravery. It can be enjoyment, enjoyment in the process. I don't know what the opposite of fear is – foolishness, recklessness, or bravery? You let go of that, too.

MS: It's a fine line between stupidity and bravery.

LS: You could let both of them go and just say, "I enjoy what I'm doing. I'm going to have a good time no matter what happens." Enthusiasm.

MS: Wrestling has been the major role in my life. I know I've said it before, but it really has. It's my turn to make up my choice and whether I want to continue at SUNY Alfred, where I'm going. I don't know if my coach there will be like Paul. I'm afraid that the coach will be the total opposite, like one of my other coaches, Christian, where we just drill, drill, drill: "I don't care what you're thinking, just do it! Go out there and practice. Wrestle tough. The reason you're losing is because you're not good enough yet."

LS: You either take what you're given, or you make up something else. Although, to tell you the truth, in my experience, it's much easier to find what you need than invent what you need. You can't make a stone house out of a bunch of trees, so it's much easier to go where the stones are if you want to make a stone house.

I tried really hard to find out where I would fit in, and I wasn't really able to, because I could never really get a straight answer from people. You know, nobody's going to make a commitment until they know you. So I moved around a lot, between universities, and wasn't very happy with where I ended up, but it played a role, and I take a lot of responsibility in it, both accepting it, and the way I antagonized people, that was me. So maybe it was the right thing, even though it wasn't what I wanted. It's very hard to know.

I guess my conclusion is that in the end what's most important is what you make out of what you have. You never know for sure what you should be doing, where you should be going, whether your decisions are the right ones.

MS: Yeah, my parents, right now, like I want to go to college for architecture. I've really had in my mind that I wanted to become an architect my whole life. What I've heard is they make good money, the good ones do. But when you start off it's like, you don't. And my parents are, like, "You sure you want to do this? Do you really want to go through this?" My parents are trying to change my mind on something that I've always wanted to do. They're not happy with taking the difficult road, that I'm taking the harder road.

LS: Well, one of the most important things about getting ahead in anything, and that they never teach you, is selling. In anything you go into you're always selling something. You're selling yourself at every stage, whether you've got an idea, a project, or something you did, or something you want to do. You have to make your case.

And it's not easy, it's not obvious, and it's not straight-forward. It's hard to say whether it's even honest, because a lot of people don't want the honest answer; a lot of people, most people, they know what they want. They want you to say what they want.

It's the same with asking girls out; asking people to do anything. People generally have an idea of what they want, and they're looking for someone who'll give it to them. And it may not be the right thing. You may know it's the wrong thing, but you have the choice of convincing them to take what you're offering, or give them what they want. And it's like, infinitely, easier to give them what they want.

MS: Yeah, I've heard that.

LS: And if you try to sell them something else, often, the most you'll do is get them to give you a tentative OK, and then they'll switch back to what they wanted. Imagine if you tried to get a girlfriend to be a wrestler, and they weren't a wrestler, and you convinced them to be a wrestler through all kinds of strange arguments. And they bought into it. Well, it wouldn't work for long if that wasn't who they were.

MS: Some of my friends are trying to do that. They're trying to teach their girlfriends to wrestle. And then they have them wrestling each other – it's the funniest thing. And then the girls end up, after doing that, they're like, "We don't want to do this!" Then they end up arguing over it later.

LS: And all the rest of this... It's a mistake to believe that any set of courses and skills is going to get you to a point where you're simply going to be handed a living. Nobody's going to buy what you're selling unless they feel that you are the winner, or the guy who's going to be the winner, for them. And you can never sell them on the basis of some technical details, which they don't understand and don't want to understand.

Architecture is not a corporate thing where you go up the ranks and get a secure position as an architect. It's an independent-contractor's scene. In order to sell an idea, you have to have a number of things that are not part of the standard skill set. You need things that have more to do with wrestling than architecture.

MS: They just want to know how big it is, what it looks like, and how big every room is, and if they have enough space for things. They don't want to know how it's done, or how it's being built, or what it's being built out of; they just what to know what it looks like, and if it's right for them.

LS: If you want to sell yourself as a wrestler in order to get on a wrestling team, or as an architect to get a job, how do you appeal to people? What will they respond to? How can you make it a partnership that's going to work? Each situation is different, and you have to capitalize on your strengths.

But if you had this fear of winning, and this was evident to a coach, then you could spend all the time you want showing them your perfect technique and it probably wouldn't be enough.

MS: It wasn't. That's why I didn't do my best until my senior year, until Paul came around and realized it. My other coaches probably saw it, but they didn't know how to deal with it and Paul did.

Paul learned that sometimes it is in your head. It may be something as simple as an inch in your step, in your penetration step, or it could be something as major as I had: that you think you don't deserve to win, to go out there and take the gold. You deserve to get first place. And that's what Paul sort of taught me, that I practiced probably harder than any wrestler in my weight class.

Sometimes I fell back upon that fear when it came to, "Oh, he's the number one seeded, he must have practiced harder than me." I lost to a kid from Valley Central that I stupidly did a move that I shouldn't have, that I hadn't practiced all year, that I thought I could catch him with. I lost. Later on Paul talked to me about it. Next match I went out there with a little more anger, a little more intensity, and I went out with the moves I knew: I beat him into the ground.

That's how it should have been all year. I should have went out with a little more intensity, a little more anger, and just gone out there with the moves that I had, and not try and do something new. But I realize that sometimes you do make errors like that, that you think you can do something that you can't, and there's consequences to that. I know that from an ATV accident.

I crashed an ATV riding with somebody who was one of my friends. He swerved in front of me, I clipped his front tire, I went down. I ended up breaking three vertebrae, L3, L4, and L5, and my right shoulder blade, and I was in bed for a while. And then I finally could sit up, I could walk lightly, my back was in extreme pain. I've had back problems my whole life because back pain runs in our family somehow, and that threw a knuckleball at me at the end of my freshman year.

When I crashed my ATV, I knew I had done something. I did it by the Fording Place road, in the corn fields down in the Hurley Flats, you probably know. A bunch of my friends were there, and I crashed it, and I was laying there on the ground. I had so much adrenaline pumping through me at the time that I didn't feel anything. I got up and walked away. Mom came down and picked me up. I came home.

I've a very bad scar on the back of my right knee that reminds me of this. Something that hit the back of my right knee left an open wound like this in it, about this deep in some areas, and I've a pretty bad scar and pain in both of my knees on certain days, like on cold days I feel it.

But not until I got home about four hours later I was laying in bed, after I got out of the shower, and I'd sat down on a chair, and I'm like, "I can't stand up, my back hurts." It hurts so much I can't get up. I could not get up and get to the car. Every time I got like this much off, it was, like, "Going back down!"

I ended up being taken off by an ambulance. My friends make fun of me because of that, because I broke three vertebrae and a shoulder blade, and they had to take me off in an ambulance. They make many comments upon that, but I learned, that was another stepping stone in my life, getting over that.

My doctor told me that I should never do sports again. He would be surprised that I would ever become more mobile than I was right after that. I didn't do football until my senior year, this year; went out there, worked my butt off. I wasn't a starter until our final game against the second-place team. We broke three of the records; that was our highlight of the year. We stopped their field goal record, we scored on their home field. Neither of those had been done.

I went out, did wrestling again. Came out with 17 wins. Fifth in sections. Second place when I should have gotten first.

I went out for track. It was my first year out, and I'm throwing shot. I throw nowhere near as good as the guys that throw, but I'm, like, hanging out there with my friends, and for the healthy part of doing another sport. And I did it, but I had major stepping stones from my back.

My doctor said that if I got hit the wrong way, I could have been paralyzed from my waist down. What would I have done if I had listened to him? I talked to many people that listened to doctors for, like, years of their lives. They can't work. What are you going to do with the rest of your time? With your medical insurance you can't live in a house, you can't do nothing. The people ended up going back to work. They're fine. They have slight pain, like I do. They're perfectly fine.

My back, now, my senior year, is stronger than it's ever been. Mentally I've become stronger. I'll notice at nights when I'm getting tired at work, I'll be, like, "Uh! My back hurts!" Subconsciously, in my head I'm just blocking out pain; it shuts off. It's helped in my mental toughness. If I listened to my doctor – I know it's mean to say but – I would end up being like my brother.

I hate thinking about that, that my brother's ending up the way he is. And whenever I try to do something to try to force him to not be the way he is, which makes us conflicted in many ways, he goes to my parents and I can't do anything. This may sound funny to you: there's always the major annoyances in your life and one of them is my brother.

Everyone thinks they don't like their siblings. I like my brother, but I have one annoyance that he has one thing that he's extremely better than me at, which is riding an ATV, because that's what he spends his time doing. And that's all he can ever say that he's better than me at. Like the other day, when we got to school we were arguing about something and he's, like, "I'm better than you at riding an ATV!" And I ended up saying, "That's the one thing that you're better than me at, the ONE thing you've got on me!"

The other major thing that bugs me is skinny people that think they're fat. I hate it when I see a girl that's, like, skinny and she's, like, "I'm so fat!" I just hate people like that.

And the last one's the total opposite: I hate fat people that think they're skinny. I know a couple of people like that, girls especially. I'll see girls that are, like, really big – I admire them for being this brave, but they'll wear the short shirts, with the short shorts, with the low pants, and it's, like, "You just shouldn't be wearing that."

Those are the major things that bug me in my life. They may sound weird, considering that I'm a bigger person, but those are the only things. Sometimes you have weird things that bug you, and those are what they are.

Some people speak their mind toward the things that bug them. I'm one of those people that keep it bottled up. I know that could end up being a bad thing, like someone that goes out and kills a lot of people, but I'm not that type of person. I'm afraid of what could one day happen if I ever release that bottle of rage.

I have never been pushed to that point where I want to hit somebody. Except for one time, and it wasn't even an angry point where I wanted to beat him; it was just like, "Shut up!" And I had to hit him to make him shut up. I have, like, a tolerance, like a really long fuse, as most people call it.

That's always been my nature, but I think it's expanded a little bit through wrestling. My fuse has grown even longer. My friends are like, "Where do you put all the anger and the hate from people calling you names and doing mean stuff to you?" I'm like, "It's in a little bottle over here in my left pocket." And hopefully it will never be opened.

It may not seem like something that wrestling does, but wrestling helps me release it slowly. That's probably one of the reasons why I haven't done something stupid like hit somebody or had a fight. When I had frustration during the season I would hold off during the day, and during practice I would release it into practicing harder and practicing longer. And by the time the end of the season came, when our coaches were, like, "We've got to have an easy practice," I'm like, "Come on. I really need a hard practice!"

My mental state of how I react to people has changed. How I think has changed, in ways. Like our coach had us write out, I can't remember what they're called, but you write out something so many times that it happens. I wrote out, "I could win," like 250 times. I did it before every match toward the end of the season.

It changed my way in thinking. Even something simple like writing down "I could win" a hundred times changes you mentally to believe that you can win. Our coach had the whole team do it together. I ended up winning most of my matches toward the end of the season.

I'd write down, "I'm going to practice harder. I'm going to…" do whatever. And I'd end up doing it, and he taught me that even the simplest things you do can change your whole thought output towards things. So in a way, my coach that one year was really a mentor towards me in my whole life and lifestyle. He was the one that realized that I was going to have problems in my future if I hadn't stopped speaking out. I still do it now, a little, I'll speak out at the wrong times, but I've restrained from it somewhat.

Alphonso brought this up. I would say "No" at the beginning of sentences when I'd ask a question. I'd asked, "Are we going to do something?" And he's like, "We're probably going to do something else." And then I said, "No," and I asked him another question, and he got really angry at me about that, and I didn't understand why he was getting angry because I was asking him a question. Him and Paul brought up the point that before every question I'd ask, after somebody answered another question, I'd say, "No," meaning like, "They're wrong." It was a simple way of how I'd speak, but it changed the whole way that people took what I said to them.

If you heard somebody say "No" after you answered their questions, and then asked you another one, and did that multiple times, it's like, "Why do they keep asking questions if they're just going to say 'No'?" My mom noticed that, too, and not until I brought it up with her and my coach at the same time did I notice that it's when I get nervous, when I'm talking to people, that I say "No" for no reason.

And all the other things they've helped me with, just talking to people, becoming not necessarily a braver person, but a riskier person. I may not be braver in any way, but I won't be as much afraid to take a risk. To some people that might be bravery. To me it's just a higher risk threshold. That's how it's going to be. I've got to work on that, too.

There's a girl that likes me – this is just weird – and I'm "iffy." I like her, she's a friend, and all my other friends are like, "You should ask her out! You should go out with her!" And I'm like, "I don't know." It's the risk of going out and losing a friend. And I don't want to take that risk; I don't like the risk of losing a friend over something like going out with them.

What wrestling has done for me has changed me. It's made me a better person. It's changed the way I am, so I'm going to carry wrestling with me, even though it is over. It's still carrying through everything my coaches helped me with. It's still living on in me.

31. PAUL WIDERMAN

History   Middle   Born 1959, Huntington, New York

I learned of Paul Widerman through a friend whose son was in his high school wrestling program. This interview took place on our first meeting, and as far as we knew we had no common ground: Paul's reticence is evident. It turned out we had many common interests, including our mutual friend Neil Tyson, who is also part of this project.

Only with Paul's help was I able to persuade Lou Giani, Paul's mentor and a private person, to contribute to the project. Paul was instrumental in establishing my connection to Lou's student the Phantom Street Artist, who is interviewed in Chapter 2.

Excerpts

"From a very young age I liked to do a lot of things. I liked to be free. I didn't like to be put in a box, and I didn't like labels. And I liked to go really deeply into things. I liked mind-body, physical things – just naturally liked to move, liked to be in my body... I have something genetic in my body, a mind-body relationship, that I know about. It's just something that... it's just one of my gifts."

"I was pretty accomplished when I was young. I graduated first in my high school class. I was two-time state champion. I was on this fast track that I thought was to fuckin' nowhere. You know? ..."

"Our high school wrestling coach, Lou Giani, was so good and so renowned that there were people who moved to the town to be in his tutelage... That got me in the fold of seeing how he was training people over years. I started to see the discipline with which he approached his craft and how he really developed people over a long period of time. I sort of fell into the fold, kind of accidentally..."

"At this point in my life I'm really looking at wrestling as a movement art... I'm not nearly as interested in the competitive aspect of wrestling as I am in the art of it. It's not so important whether you win or lose, but how you pursue this art form called 'wrestling'..."

"So, to me, your whole life is about finding the things that you're passionate about, that you love, that you're willing to go the distance on. That's how you get fulfillment, that's how you grow, and that's how people really excel, or get great at something..."

"Learning is not something that is done to us, or that we can produce in others. An education is not something we 'get'... it is something we create for ourselves, on a life-long basis. The best learning – perhaps the only real learning – is that which results from personal interest and investigation, from following our own passion."

— Wendy Priesnitz, in "Taking Risks and Breaking Rules," appearing in the May/June 2005 issue of the magazine *Life Learning*

Interview   Kerhonkson, New York, June 2005

Paul Widerman: I would argue that to be great at anything – I don't mean egocentrically great, but, for lack of a better term, like Joseph Campbell's "follow your bliss" kind of great – everything is about personal growth. At some point you're not going to want to spend a lot of time getting good at something if you're not passionate about it or you don't love it. (Joseph Campbell wrote about mythology. See Joseph Campbell Foundation at www.jcf.org – Ed.)

There are not too many Olympic champion wrestlers that hate wrestling. There might be times when they're tired of it, or they're sick of it, or they've been pushed into it for one reason or another, but you don't reach a high level, reach mastery of any activity, if you don't love the activity. It will weed you out.

So, to me, your whole life is about finding the things that you're passionate about, that you love, that you're willing to go the distance on. That's how you get fulfillment, that's how you grow, and that's how people really excel or get great at something.

I don't think that winning's the ultimate goal or the most important thing. So in terms of wrestling, it doesn't really matter to me when I'm coaching somebody whether they become a state champion, or a national champion, or an Olympic champion. It's great if that happens, that's a wonderful thing. So, for a young athlete involved in wrestling, it's really about them being as good as they can be. That's what the sport's about.

Very few people that come out for it are going to do it if they don't like it. I encourage them: "If you're going to be great at this sport, try to learn to love it, and get passionate about it." Then it doesn't matter so much if you win or lose. It's all about growth. Then you can look at your losses more objectively: "Well, why did I lose? What went wrong? What happened? Was he better? Was my technique good or bad? Was this working or not working?" There starts to be a kind of a dispassionate Zen way of looking at the activity, but also a love for the activity.

I remember this experience in college. I really did not like organic chemistry, but I was pre-med and had to take organic chemistry. At some point along the way I realized, "It's not organic chemistry that's boring, it's how I'm thinking about it that's boring. I've got to find a way to make this activity interesting enough so that I'll go in depth into this activity." I started to look at chemistry a whole lot differently once I shifted my consciousness. That was a real shift, and I did fairly well in organic chemistry after that.

LS: Did you like it?

PW: Umm... I'm not sure. I don't think that I ever came to love organic chemistry, but when I realized that molecules were three-dimensional, as opposed to two-dimensional, it made it a whole lot more interesting.

That's how I think about the notion of "follow your bliss" – I don't like the term because it's so clichéd – but the concept is deep. You've got to keep hunting around until you find what moves you.

I've been tremendously influenced by Harvey Fite's "Opus 40." (A monumental, landscape sculpture. See more at opus40.org – Ed.) I was so moved by what Harvey Fite did there. I've been to Opus 40 so many times that I came to know Tad Richards, Harvey Fite's step-son, who lives there in the house that Harvey built. Joseph Campbell and Harvey Fite were friends. Tad told me there was a calm centeredness about how Harvey built Opus 40. To me it is a great example of a man "following his bliss."

I used to run a wrestling camp and would take the kids on field trips to see Opus 40. Before bringing a group of kids there, I'd get a stone out of the woods – a pretty big one, like this big – and I'd put them in a circle and have them pick up the stone and pass it around the circle. That way they'd have a feeling of what it was like to pick up one heavy stone. And then I'd tell them, "Now we're going to go to a place where a man placed stones by hand for 38 years. We're going to see what he did and how he got into working with stone."

And then you go there, and you see what he did. And it completely changes your conception of moving stone, and art, and that kind of thing. So to me, that's kind of what life's about: trying to find things that you like to do enough so that they move you on that level.

Harvey Fite's Opus 40 in Saugerties, New York.

The curriculum of my wrestling camp was quite different. I used to get bored at wrestling camps I went to. I liked wrestling, but I hated the downtime between the sessions because all you did was sit around and talk about wrestling. I got bored; I didn't really like to talk about wrestling that much; I liked to do other things.

In my camp we went on field trips that inspired; the whole idea was to inspire the kids. First we'd go to Opus 40, and then we'd go right from Opus 40 to the Tibetan Monastery. It was very interesting to see how kids reacted to the Tibetan Monastery on the top of the mountain. Then, later in the week, I took them to Nancy Copley's house. She's an architect who's been building her own house for 25 years or so. Nancy is an amazing person... a mentor for me, and another following their bliss. And then we went into Pompey's Cave.

Do you know about Pompey's Cave? It's a cave that was made by a river. However, the underground river is below a dried-out river above it. So, you walk upstream of the dry riverbed, then go down a ladder about 12' underground. Then you can go up or downstream, following the underground river. It is quite an intense experience.

Pompey was a run-away slave girl who was brought up from the South. The legend is that the local farmers hid Pompey in the cave for three days with her infant. Bounty hunters searched for her all over the area, couldn't find her, and moved on. It became Pompey's cave, a place of fear and total blackness, but also of shelter and courage, where you come up against your own mind and thoughts.

The cave is scary. After climbing down the ladder you find yourself in the river, and you're knee to waist high in water, and it's completely pitch black. In some places you have to crawl on your hands and knees, and in some places it's quite vast and cavernous. So it's a dramatic thing to do with a bunch of kids. After Pompey's cave we would finish with a hike in the mountains.

We'd do all of this in between doing yoga, SmartBells, and wrestling. The curriculum ended up being so powerful, in the way that it flowed over the course of the week, that I wanted my whole life to feel like that week. It really moved the kids.

LS: What inspired you to do that? Was there something that you could identify that was important or life-changing?

PW: My relationship to my high school wrestling coach was quite intense. He was a tremendous mentor.

From a very young age I liked to do a lot of things. I liked to be free. I didn't like to be put in a box, and I didn't like labels. And I liked to go really deeply into things. I liked mind-body, physical things – just naturally liked to move, liked to be in my body – so I thought I wanted to be a gymnast, but there was no gymnastics in our town's athletic program.

Our high school wrestling coach, Lou Giani, was so good, and so renowned that there were people who moved to the town to be in his tutelage. One man moved his whole family so that his kids could be coached by Lou.

I got interested in wrestling because I thought I would like it. And the first year actually I hated it! I went out with a team, and I got so pounded that I quit in seventh grade (laughs)! All the tough kids in town went out for wrestling, and I was tough, but I wasn't as tough as them.

The next year this man moved to town who had two sons, and he needed workout partners for his own kids. So he recruited me to be the workout partner for one of his sons. We used to go up to the high school in the summer where they were practicing wrestling, and I would hang around and learn the moves from this other guy who was under the tutelage of Lou Giani.

That got me in the fold of seeing how he was training people over years. I started to see the discipline with which he approached his craft and how he really developed people over a long period of time. I sort of fell into the fold, kind of accidentally.

He was really able to teach people the art and science of approaching something in order to be great at it. He was an Olympian himself, so he knew the different ways to find mastery in yourself.

I've seen many people in other disciplines, like dancers have an understanding of what he was doing and also martial artists. The person I'll bring up very peripherally, because I know you're interested in astronomy and physics, is Neil Tyson. Do you know Neil?

LS: Yes, I went to school with him.

PW: You went to school with Neil?! So did I! Where did you go to school with Neil?

LS: Graduate school, in Texas.

PW: Small world. So you're a friend of Neil (laughs)! A friend of Neil's is a friend of mine (laughs)!

LS: You were an undergraduate with him?

PW: Neil was at Harvard, he was a junior when I was a freshman. He was on the wrestling team. And I'll say this – you can put it on tape – that I was a far better wrestler than Neil was. He was a far better physicist than I'll ever be!

We sort of kind of "glommed" on to each other. He was watching me as a young, blue-chip wrestler – you know Harvard really didn't have any elite wrestlers on the team. It was tricky because I was a light-weight, and I was really too small to be an elite college wrestler. But I could have been on any of the top wrestling teams in the country, but I wanted to go to Harvard.

What happened was, when I was looking at college in high school, I went up there with a friend who was obsessed with going to Harvard, and I was trying to figure out where I wanted to go. One of his mentors said, "Oh, you really should go to Harvard." So we went up there to explore it together.

I remember going into the Freshman Union, the dining room for freshmen, and I just loved the atmosphere. There were students from all over the world – all races, it was very international – just a real mix of people who were good at different things, from academics, to cello, to wrestling. It was such an interesting environment. As soon as I entered that room full of 1,500 so varied and talented… I was, like, "This is where I want to go to college."

I met Neil on the wrestling team, and he tutored me in physics a few times. I will never forget the tidbits of wisdom that he passed on as a senior to a sophomore in college. I remember them to this day.

At that time he was not doing as well in math as the department wanted. I think they wanted him to drop the major and move on to something else. I think he was getting B minuses instead of B pluses or something. And what he told me was that for him to get the grades they want, given the way they were teaching the courses, he would have to regurgitate the material by memorizing the formulas. And that wasn't how he wanted to learn math or science.

He felt he had something creative to contribute, in a real way, and he needed to learn it at a pace where he would own the material, as opposed to regurgitating the material. He was willing to take the heat in order to go at his own pace. He had real confidence once he learned the material; once he knew it, he owned it. And to creatively manipulate the material, he needed to learn it his own way, so he was content to get whatever grades they gave him. I really admired his relationship to science. He inspired me to really learn things at my own pace, my own way.

I'll never be the scientist he is. I think some of us have a natural proclivity for certain things, and he's an innate, true-blue scientist. Well, I'm that way in my body. I have something genetic in my body, a mind-body relationship, that I know about. It's just something that… it's just one of my gifts.

Neil and I connected over something artistically; we both have a sense of art, a passion for intuitive knowledge and art. We found this meeting ground in athletics. At the time he was interested in dance, and there weren't too many other wrestlers interested in dance. We both had this interest in movement for movement's sake.

At this point in my life I'm really looking at wrestling as a movement art, one of many movement art forms. To me it's one of the most interesting – one that I love the most, but I don't look at it as the only one, or the best one. I'm not nearly as interested in the competitive aspect of wrestling as I am in the art of it. It's not so important whether you win or lose, but how you pursue this art form called "wrestling."

In the summers, in high school with Lou Giani, we did wrestling for fun, and we did the art of wrestling. We went to practice, worked out as hard as we wanted. It didn't matter whether you won or lost, you were creative. Then from November to March the idea was to be as good as you could be and to win as much as you could win. So the year was sort of cyclical: you got to be an artist part of the time, and be competitive part of the time.

Wrestling is interesting that way. It gives you this chance to be competitive, and humans seem to like that, focusing on being the champion or being the best. And then at other times you get to be creative, which humans also like. Wrestling gives you the opportunity to do both things.

For me, at this point in my life, I feel like I see the bigger picture, and I'm not as interested in the winning per se. If that were my passion I'd be a college wrestling coach trying to produce Olympic champions.

I was on the path to be the head wrestling coach at Harvard, but I chose not to take that path. I was the assistant there for five years with Jim Peckham, one of the greatest wrestling coaches in the country. When he got ready to retire, he called me to say, "Hey, I'm leaving. Do you want to take the job?" I didn't go back to take the job. I wanted to stay here, in Accord, in the mountains. I wanted to stay on a creative wavelength that felt more important to me.

But now, in coaching high school kids, I try to give them the opportunity to experience both things. To be both as good as they can be, to be competitive – because they like that – but also to look at this as a chance to be creative and work at it like a mind-body, artistic endeavor. I'm going to digress even a little bit more, because these are topics that I've spent a lot of time thinking about.

I was interested in being a dancer, but I became frustrated pretty quickly, and let me tell you why. Dance is interesting in terms of the skill of moving to music and the discipline of how dance works; but to become a dancer in a company, you really become the artistic tool, or medium, of the choreographer.

If you've been a wrestler for your whole life, for 20 years, you're the painter. You get to go out there and decide what's going on on the canvas. You're not used to having somebody tell you what shape to put your body in. And if you get really good at wrestling, then you hold on to that pretty tightly. So I became more and more disillusioned with dance. I realized pretty quickly that intellectually I was finding wrestling way more interesting than dance.

Since that time, people in the dance world have really broken out, and I follow them because I think they're doing amazing work, like Michael Moschen (Contact juggler, dancer, and performance artist, see www.michaelmoschen.com – Ed.). Have you heard of Michael Moschen? If you ever get the chance, get a hold of his video, "In Motion with Michael Moschen." You know he got a MacArthur Award for juggling? He does things with balls, and movement, and pattern making, and physics that are just over the top. Seeing his *PBS* special really influenced me a lot.

You know I'm into this SmartBells stuff, and Michael Moschen's work was one of the things that influenced me regarding the interaction of shape and energies. There's a certain wavelength that Michael is on that really resonated for me, and that I couldn't find in wrestling; couldn't find in dance. Michael made up his own path and explored it both artistically through movement and dance and through science.

SmartBells are way more utilitarian than what Michael is doing, but I'm taking this utilitarian object and doing things on a similar wavelength, pattern-wise. There are other people that are out there on that wavelength – not as much with objects, I think – like there's the Momix Dance Company, and the Pilobolous Dance Company, and Sarah East Johnson. (Three avant-garde dance companies. – Ed.)

I keep an eye out for people in those worlds; I keep a pulse on what they're doing. At this point wrestling is way too small a box – I couldn't fit in the wrestling box – so I've invented my own box. That's why I have a company – it's called THINKFIT – and it gives me a box that I feel comfortable in. In all ways, with movement, creatively, artistically, business-wise… I can move in all of these ways.

To me wrestling is a way – I love wrestling – to transfer knowledge: to teach people things that are not really about wrestling. Wrestling just gives them a way to learn those things.

LS: How much of what you do is focused on teaching and the rewards of teaching?

PW: You mean from coaching wrestling? I have kind of divided it at this point. Teaching wrestling is almost all about the reward of teaching the kids. It's certainly not for the money, though that helps, living out here in the woods.

LS: What's the other part?

PW: I've never wanted to be a teacher in the school system. I really don't have an interest in being there from seven to three every day. That takes up too much time. Wrestling ends up taking up too much time, also, but I feel it's a worthy use of my time because I feel like you can't really match… For me…

You know, the level of this conversation changes completely knowing that you're friends with Neil. That allows me to go to places... You know, I really don't know you, Lincoln, (laughs)!... But if you're doing physics with Neil, then there's a certain level of trust – let's say *simpatico* – about what this is really about.

Like if you're an academic, then you're dealing with the tension between pursuing your gift and passing the energy on to other people: to help open them up to energies in themselves. Some people are different. Some people have no interest in passing on their teaching – they're content to be academics, to study, or be artists, or just abuse their graduate students (laughs)! They have no interest in teaching their graduate students. You know what I'm saying?

To me, that's not what it's about. I see the effect that I have on some of the kids and the effect my teachers have had on me. To me the wrestling season is about the kids, it's not about me. As Coach Giani said to us many times, "I've got all my gold medals at home, boys. I don't need any more. This is your thing. This is not for me; this is for you and your relationship to yourself."

The year before I moved here to the mountains, I was seeing a therapist in Cambridge, trying to figure out what the hell I was doing in my life. When I told him that I wanted to move to the Catskills, I said, "Jeff, I can't really tell you completely. All I can say is that it has to do with modern Japanese architecture."

I'm really interested in architecture, passionately interested in architecture, architecture that has the spirit and depth of a Japanese Zen temple, but modern. The first year that I moved here, I spent the whole winter putting this tiny little addition onto our house. That was sort of a way of expressing this.

I was afraid to use an electric saw, a circular saw, so I cut every piece of wood by hand, in the winter, in the snow. It was all hammers and nails, because I was afraid to use the tools. Now I'm up to using chainsaws and circular saws. You know, living out here you change, but it took years.

That was the first year – I must have been 35 – that I didn't spend every day in the winter going to a wrestling room. I realized that I had spent more years in wrestling rooms than the age of the kids on the local team. They were 17, and I'd spent 20 years in a wrestling room (laughs)! So that year I was passionate. I'm like, "I'm not going to the wrestling room!"

The next year Alphonse, the Rondout Valley High School head coach, came up to me and said, "Will you help me coach the high school team up here?" I was like, "Well, OK." So I go to practice, and he introduces me to the kids on the team, and he goes, "This is Paul. He's an Olympic alternate, and he was the coach at Harvard, and he knows way more wrestling than me, so I'm just going to turn the coaching over to him." And I go, like, "What!" – in my mind, you know, I didn't say, "what" – I said, "That wasn't what I signed up for, Alphonse!"

And then I started to think about it, and you know, I realized that I really didn't get to coach the way I wanted to at Harvard because Jim Peckham was there. So this was an opportunity to use the kids as my laboratory and to teach wrestling the way I wanted to teach it. So I'm trying out all this stuff that I believe. This is my new laboratory!

We lost our first match, and then we won the next seven, and then we went undefeated for five straight years. No, we weren't undefeated, we were 50 and 3 after 5 years. We had three undefeated seasons, and we had a couple of guys place in the States (New York

State Championships). I was teaching them yoga, and every day we had music on. They were wrestling to music, and they were learning yoga.

Then I invented SmartBells. I had been doing movement with barbell plates, and I had all the boys on the team doing the routines with barbell plates. They really liked it, and they were making progress. They started to teach it to other kids in the school, and the girls' field hockey team started doing it, and they were, like, "Wow, these routines were great, but we hate the barbell plates. You need to invent some different weights."

At first I would just say, "Oh, boys, don't complain. Just do it." And then I was teaching a yoga class, and I had everyone doing the routine with their shoe, and that's when I realized, "Oh, I really should invent something to do this with."

My brother was a puppeteer, and he had all this plasticine clay in his puppet studio in New York City. At the time I was going down to work with him, so I brought home about five pounds of clay. I got it into my mind that I was going to invent a weight that was so aesthetic that people would just want to pick it up and work out.

Since my father had been an airplane designer, I knew all about "form follows function," and he would always tell us that if something was beautiful, then it would usually work better in terms of design. So when you design something, you always look for beauty as well as function.

I sculpted the object in clay and tried to make it as sexy as I could with lots of nice curves. Then, I started to do the movements with the clay. I used plasticine, which doesn't harden and allowed the movements to change the shape. It changed into this shape that worked and was unusual. Upside down, it's saddle-shaped. Eventually, a math professor at Stanford pointed out that was one of the three shapes of the universe predicted by the theory of relativity. So, to bring this full circle, so to speak, eventually, years later, I brought it to Neil.

I hadn't seen Neil for 15 years – last time I saw him was at the National Wrestling Championships in Maryland, and he was in grad school – so I punched his name into Google, and I couldn't believe his résumé. I was, like, "Oh my God! Look what Neil has been doing!" (Laughs)

I went down to the Hayden Planetarium and laid all this stuff that I was thinking on him. I said, "Look, Neil, I really don't want to be out here like a quack, making all this stuff up, but look at all of these things. I'm starting to connect some dots. What do you think about this?"

If he had said, "Shelve it," then I would have shelved it, but he was very encouraging about me pushing all these ideas and told me to write a book about it. That has kept me going on ideas like electromagnetic fields, and auras, and quantum mechanics, and SmartBells, and those sorts of things. So Neil came up in my life again, 15 years later, giving a nod on this project.

I see him about twice a year. The last two times I brought Nancy, and he brought his wife, and we went to a wrestling match. I swear, Neil can get more excited about wrestling than physics, and I can get more excited about physics than wrestling. You know what I mean, at this point?

LS: I don't have any overt enthusiasm about physics. I rarely talk about it. It rarely figures in anything that I do with people. But it's what I want to do.

PW: So are you a practicing physicist in some way now?

LS: No, there's nothing in the professional world of physics that attracts me. I consider the professional world antithetical to doing physics in any deep way.

PW: Seems true of a lot of activities, doesn't it? I think architecture is a perfect example.

LS: I know architecture really well. My father was "The Great Architectural Photographer." I spent a lot of time going on trips with him when I was between the ages of 12 and 14. I used to be his assistant. If you now go to the post office you'll see modern architecture stamps that they released just a few weeks ago. Most of them are taken from his photos.

PW: Was there someone in particular that he liked to photograph?

LS: He worked for Frank Lloyd Wright when he was young; he was the only person that Wright would have photograph his buildings. That was before my time.

PW: Is your dad still alive?

LS: No, he died last year.

PW: I'm sorry to hear that. Did you have a good relationship with him?

LS: No, no one really did. He was a very driven person, and he basically wanted the world to stop at the peak of his career. So he decided that he was just going to pretend that it was still 1963 for the rest of his life and treat everybody like that. That's not a way you relate to people. You can't freeze time for everyone else.

PW: It's interesting because having been a Harvard undergrad, living around 1,500 driven people – no, more than that because that's just one class – maybe 15,000 driven people, counting the grad students, undergrads, and the professors. It didn't take me long to realize that I wasn't interested in that mentality.

I was pretty accomplished when I was young. I graduated first in my high school class. I was two-time state champion. I was on this fast track that I thought was to fuckin' nowhere. You know?

LS: When did you decide that?

PW: By the time I was a sophomore.

I took time off after sophomore year. I almost dropped out halfway through. And then I felt, like, "I don't want to waste all my parents' money." It's very socially acceptable to take time off from Harvard, so I thought, "OK, I'll get through the sophomore year, and then I'm out of here."

After that, I spent two months living with a wrestling team in Japan. I worked at the Institute for Aerobics Research in Dallas, Texas. I lived on my own, and traveled, and did things. By the end of the year I felt like I was ready to go back to college, that I wanted to go back. But I felt like, man, they're producing people who end up successful and unhappy.

LS: What did you do with your remaining time there? Did you change direction?

PW: I took every elective in visual studies. I was a biology major and didn't like it. But I didn't drop the biology major, because switching majors at that point would have been too hard. I only needed two more courses to finish the major. So I finished that out and took every elective in visual and environmental studies; it's kind of like the pre-architecture program.

They have a thing called 99-R, which is where you find a mentor and make up your own curriculum. You choose the books that you want to read, study with a mentor, and write two papers: a mid-term and a final. It becomes a course.

Harvard's amazing if you have the gumption to make it what you want to make it. I did three 99-R's, making up my own courses. I studied wrestling, and I did sculpture. Man, I loved that. I was in heaven. It was my last year. Then I took my bio class pass-fail. Almost failed it (laughs a lot)! It was Biochem 10B, and I was like, "Shit, if I fail this I'm not graduating!"

How did you end up out here? You were in Austin at University of Texas?

LS: The University of Texas was kind of a funny mistake. I went there because it was a place I hadn't been yet, but that's like joining the army because you've never been to Iraq, you know? There are various ways to see Texas, and going to the University of Texas Department of Physics is not the best way. It was a war zone.

PW: Is it a good physics department? Is it a renowned department?

LS: Yeah, it's renowned. It's very competitive and also very profit-driven; there's a lot of money flowing in certain veins. A lot of people coming in to follow it: academic money, industry money. Powerful people associated with that, political people. I got a very good education, but I don't give anyone any credit but myself.

Remember that book *All Quiet on the Western Front*, by Erich Remarque? It was World War I, and the main character got a great education about life from the hell of living in the trenches. But I don't think he'd give Germany credit for his education!

I basically did three different dissertations at Texas. Getting failed on each one after I half finished them, until I finally got through on the third time. I learned everything there was to learn there for me: I did a dissertation in every topic that was of interest to me. And I learned all the dimensions of the profession, most of which they would prefer a student never see: the personalities of these people, and the professional consequences of going into the field.

It convinced me that there was nothing there for me, except the topic. The subject is inherent in the field itself, but it wasn't really in evidence in anyone's work. It's like art: you have the choice of being an artist or being a commercial artist. I choose to be an artist in science, but not a commercial artist.

I cannot see any way to make a living in physics without fatally compromising the art. Not only is what I want to do unmarketable, but it's inherent that the project will fail. The real project of science is to investigate the unknown, not to discover the key to the universe, because there isn't any.

All you do is investigate; all you do is ask more questions. If you ever answer a question in science, you've failed, because you've deceived yourself into thinking that there is one. There are always more questions underneath the answers.

The things I want to work on don't have solutions. People aren't interested in them. No one's buying them, but I don't care. I just want to work on these problems for the beauty of running them through my hands, so to speak. I find it beautiful to better understand my relationship to the world.

What about you? What brought you to this area?

PW: I came here from Cambridge and since concluded that men move for one of two reasons: it is either because of love or for money. And there's no money here (laughs)! So

I moved here for love. I moved here to be with Nancy. And then I got roped into coaching wrestling again, or danced into coaching wrestling

What got you interested to write this book?

LS: Basically, I've been a student my whole life. At some point, not long ago, I was taking flight training, and I got so angry at this flight instructor who was putting me in a situation where I was guaranteed never to improve. I felt, "I'm too old to accept this kind of situation."

I recognized that an important element in learning is the decision about what you want to learn, and how you want to learn, and whom you want to learn from. It's crucial that you exercise judgment as a learner.

A lot of people get to a certain point and just teach themselves; they don't rely on teachers anymore. They become experts in their field. But I've always wanted to approach new problems, new fields, so I often find myself in the presence of teachers, at least in certifying situations where I have to meet some standard, as I was doing in flight training. So I thought, "Here's an opportunity to review the skills I've learned about learning and how they can apply to other people."

I first wrote a book in which I complained about all the bad teachers I've had. I decided I could improve on that by focusing on people who are actually learning things. I could do less moralizing and sermonizing by letting people reveal their own experiences. That would also present a broader view than what I could present by myself, and it would be more powerful, too: when people speak with passion, they speak better than I can write. At my best I'm still not a great writer. I can edit, that's what I can do.

PW: So the other book was written once?

LS: Yeah. The other book was psychological background for me, sort of like tilling the soil to get the stones out. Once that was out of the way, I felt I could put down something transcendent. I don't want to present another in the endless series of books about education. I see no point in it.

I think learning is about growth – personal transformation – and it really is your own. There can be education, and people whom you call teachers and mentors, but it's really you realizing that there's a territory in yourself that needs to be born. All the rest is just vehicle.

32. LOU GIANI

History Late Born 1935, New York City, New York

Lou Giani started coaching high school wrestling in Huntington, New York, after wrestling on the 1960 American Olympic team. He coached a record number of New York State champions, is a three-time winner of the New York Wrestling Coach of the Year, and a Distinguished Member of the National Wrestling Hall of Fame.

I was introduced to Lou by his former student Paul Widerman, whom I also interviewed. Paul acted as a liaison between us for the four years it took to produce this interview.

Paul says this project intrigued Lou because he speaks with unusual candor, yet Lou's interview was made difficult by his ambivalence in speaking publicly. We conducted two interviews, editing out many details and deleting whole passages in order to avoid any criticism of school administration.

Lou casts his work entirely in the context of wrestling and competition, yet his ability to build character is magical. He has personally shepherded hundreds of young men who credit him with saving them from lives of poverty and trouble; the Phantom Street Artist was one of his students. Lou is devoted to this task.

Excerpts

"There's hardly any shops in our school system today. All the stuff that I've done as a student in shop class I used in my lifetime, in Grumman, and in my home. I've put rooms on my home, I've built things, and what-not. It's vital for kids to learn, and I can't believe they abandoned it! You're learning something you're never going to learn otherwise, and it's gone: there's hardly any shop classes anymore..."

"I've had so many black kids with no father that they latch on to me. And that's OK, I don't have a problem with that. I love it, it's great. I work even harder with them. I get to know them better. I get to know their family better. I kind of help guide them through their lives..."

"I'm talking with kids all the time, all the time... And they're listening because they know that I am really for them, and it's not only about winning and losing – but I do want them to win, and I want our team to win also. The prime objective here is to make them better kids, stronger kids, and kids who are confident in themselves..."

"We're going to tell him the truth. What he can do. All we've got to do is keep talking about how good he can be, and then work on that. Work with him one on one and talk to him one on one. You keep on building on that until he goes to the top, wherever he can go. He may not ever be a state champion, but he might be able to win 50 percent of his matches, and he knows he did his best. And we've been telling him it, too. So he's been successful, and he feels great about himself. No one's ever going to take that away from him..."

"It is a psychological game, it really is. You need to be right on top of your game with them. You gotta know what to say and when not to say it. In the room, when you're working with them... on the mat right here... you've got a kid that comes off the mat, and he's destroyed. If you go over there and pat him on the back, that friggin' sucks, man. You make him feel worse. Let him go and cry it out for a couple of minutes, do what he wants to do, as long as he don't break anything. Let him get rid of it and then go talk to him after he's cooled down a bit, when the anxiety is gone. That's what makes good coaches ... Where does it come from? I don't know. Half the time I don't even know what I'm doing..."

> "Schools tend to be instruments of our greatest denial by breaking knowledge and experience into subjects, relentlessly turning wholes into parts, flowers into petals, history into events, without ever restoring continuity... the young need some sort of initiation into an uncertain world."
>
> — Marilyn Ferguson, in *The Aquarian Conspiracy*

Note To The Reader: I did a second interview with Lou after we spent a few years talking about the first one. Lou brought notes with him the second time. I spliced the interviews together.

Interview   Suffern, New York, January 2009

LS: Lou, you're the only person I've interviewed twice, so before you start, can you tell me how your thoughts have changed as a result of doing it a second time?

Lou Giani: I changed my approach a little bit. I backed away from a couple of things I said before, that my family would pay for, eventually.

LS: Do you have more clarity?

LG: I hope so, maybe, I don't know. Let's see how it works out. Tell me something to get me started.

LS: Well, the story is about learning, and transformation, and finding the power to become something. It's partly about what you do, but also about how you learned.

LG: I grew up in New York City and went to a Catholic elementary school, and they had no athletics at all at that school. My mom and dad moved to Huntington when I was in the eighth or ninth grade, and once I got out there I started to realize, "Wow, look at this!" They got all these athletic events that I could participate in, and I started to really want to do it. My parents wouldn't let me do it because they were afraid I was going to get hurt, but eventually I got them to go along with me.

I had some great coaches at Huntington, I had some great teachers, and I learned a lot from my coaches. Now the teachers we had, they went out of their way to give me the ABC's, but my coaches were really instrumental in making me a champion and giving me a lot of knowledge about coaching that I still use today.

I felt that as a kid, with the great coaches that I had, they never really brought up athletics as a vehicle to go on through education, which I've done ever since I started to coach.

I left high school after that and never went on to college. I wrestled for the New York Athletic Club for a number of years. I made the Pan-American team, won a couple of national championships, and made the Olympic team. After that I felt that I still needed to do some more competition, and I wrestled another 10 years.

When I look back to the wrestling that I did after coming back from Rome – our Olympic games were in Rome – I now think that... I had a lot of fun doing it, but... I think it was a mistake. I should have started into education. At that time I was working at Grumman trying to raise my family. I had three kids, the whole bit, so I needed to make a living. Grumman made it easy for me to compete as an amateur – at that time you had to be an amateur – and the athletic club paid a lot of our bills for training and for competing.

LS: You mean the company Grumman?

LG: Yeah, I worked for Grumman for 20 years. I worked on aerospace at the end; I was part of the LEM project (Lunar Excursion Module, the Lunar Lander stage of the Apollo project that first put a man to the moon. – Ed.). I was group leader on that LEM project, in charge of thermo-shielding of the descent stage.

LS: So you weren't coaching at that time.

LG: I was still competing. I competed until I was 32 years old. At that point I started to coach at Eastern Military Academy, which was a small school in Cold Spring Harbor. I had to start with a bunch of kids who knew nothing about wrestling. There were three kids on the team that transferred from a public school that knew a little bit. So we started this program together, and we went on. I didn't know too much about coaching, and I learned so much during that period of time. I wound up teaching kids what I did as an athlete and dissecting what I did. I taught that in bits and pieces.

LS: How did that go?

LG: That went fantastically. We built a team in three years that won the private school State's (Private School State Championship) and out of that group of kids we produced three state champions. And from there I went to Huntington High School, my alma mater. A job opened up. I didn't have a degree yet; I didn't even have a teacher's license because I was teaching in a private school.

The athletic director there approached me and talked to me about coaching, and I said, "How am I going to coach? I don't have a degree, I don't have a coach's license?" So he said, "Well, I think I can work something out." So I coached for a few years at Huntington under the title of "Visiting Lecturer." Then I started to realize that I wanted to teach, to become a gym teacher, so I went back to school and went through the normal process of getting a degree. I wound up getting my degree in four years, spending most of my time going to school and working at Grumman.

(Lou consults his notes.)

Problems that I see today is primarily with the way our schools treat disadvantaged kids. I feel that there's a certain element that don't understand what athletics do for minority kids, kids that really have no other way out of the ghetto.

The focus needs to be on having some sympathy for these kids. Maybe that's the wrong word, "sympathy," but have some feelings for these kids and not try to penalize them when they screw up a little bit in school; don't punish them by taking them off the team for a week. If they take them off the team for a week, that don't put them a week behind, it might put them two or three weeks behind.

I also think that there's so many ways that kids can get to college, or to trade school, and I think that's avoided too. A lot of times we try to push a kid to graduate from high school, and he really should be in a trade school, and I've always fought that.

If I felt that a kid should be in a trade school, then I was out there trying to get them to that trade school. Maybe they weren't going to college, maybe they weren't college material, but if I seen a kid that was not doing well in school, and I just couldn't get him to do well, and he just couldn't do well, then my feeling is, "Hey, let's get him in a trade school. We can still have him wrestle, but get him in a trade school where we can teach him a way to earn a living."

The other thing that I see now in education, and it bothers me, is that there's hardly any shops in our school system today. All the stuff that I've done as a student in shop class I used in my lifetime, in Grumman, and in my home. I've put rooms on my home, I've built things, and what-not. It's vital for kids to learn, and I can't believe they abandoned it! You're learning something you're never going to learn otherwise, and it's gone: there's hardly any shop classes anymore.

Let's talk a little bit about wrestling and where we've gone, where everyone's gone with wrestling as far as I'm concerned. When I was wrestling, there was no Peewee program, and today wrestling has changed because of the Peewee programs, and that was developed through USA Wrestling. And we have Peewee programs right to the Olympic games, and a kid from the Peewee program eventually becomes an Olympic champion. That's something that's much different from when I was competing.

My God, I learned how to wrestle with a football coach who was a great motivator, but knew nothing about wrestling. He was teaching us wrestling out of the Navy book and actually showing us: "Oh, look, this is how you do a move…" And he's showing you the book and saying this is how you finish a hold, and he's not too sure about finishing himself. But he was a great motivator, and he would get us to think about that book, and we would eventually learn how to do these things.

Now a kid starts in the Peewees, and when he gets into high school he knows quite a bit about wrestling. You're getting him in real good shape and teaching him some outstanding techniques. It's made better teams, and that really comes from USA Wrestling. They've done a great job with wrestling in this country.

(Lou consults his notes.)

My goal as a coach has always been, "desire, discipline, and determination," and to prepare a kid to go to college, or to prepare him to earn a living somehow.

What do I feel I've done for wrestlers throughout the years? This is how I feel: get them in the best fitness possible; teach them to never give up; motivate them to be the best they can be. Teach basics: techniques that they can learn, that they can learn without being over their heads.

High school, as far as I'm concerned, is basics. You don't have to go into the elite moves; you've got to stay with the basics. Then they've got a great foundation to either go on in club wrestling, or go on in college wrestling. Teach desire, discipline, and determination.

You once asked me, "Do they teach this in a classroom?" I think that in some gym classes they do. In coaching they do, that's for sure. No matter whether you're coaching football or what, they teach all these things or they're not worth their salt.

I also believe that if you come into a real tough program, and I consider our program a tough four-year program, then you'll be successful in the competitive world that we live in. I have no fear that you're going to leave and be successful in our world.

I'm sure that you're thinking, "Well, how did you teach that?" I believe that you teach kids all of that stuff by simply dissecting specific areas in wrestling. I'm just talking about wrestling.

So I walk into my wrestling room, and I've got this youngster, and he's getting beat up all the time, and I want to make him successful. What I do is try to get him to dissect the moves his opponent is always getting on him. Then I try to get him to stop some part of that move. Then, I try to get him to stop more of the move. Finally, I've got a defense worked out. Now I try to score a point. Once I've scored a point, he has some confidence, and from there I just go on and on with that same process.

You said, one time, that kids will not wrestle their whole life; they've got gender and sexuality problems, there are parents' pressure, and what have you. And somewheres along the line they've got to think about making money. After two hours of practice in the Huntington wrestling room, you don't have a gender problem, and you're not worrying about sexuality; you're pretty damn tired.

We demand three months of focus in the program. You come into our program, we want you to be focused for three months. If you have a girlfriend, that's OK. A lot of coaches say no, they don't want that; I don't say no, I've never said no. If the girlfriend is keeping you out on Friday night and you have a tournament on Saturday, I have a problem with that, and we're going to address that. But other than that, as long as you're not dissipating and ruining your conditioning, you can do what you want. The moment you cross that line, then we need to talk.

I'm talking with kids all the time, *all the time*. Even now, as a part-time assistant, I'm talking to those kids all the time. And they're listening because they know that I am really for them, and it's not only about winning and losing – but I do want them to win, and I want our team to win also – the prime objective here is to make them better kids, stronger kids, and kids who are confident in themselves.

Parent pressure. Parents sometimes are a pain in the neck. I haven't had too many problems over the years because I don't let a parent in on me. I never let them get too close. So if I don't wrestle their kid, they're not going to come up to me and say, "I'm your buddy, what are you doing?" I never let them get close enough to do that, with nobody.

LS: Are you guarding against something?

LG: No, I just don't want them to interfere with what I'm doing with their kid. If the kid's on a wrestling team, I'm the coach. We've got three other coaches with us, we're professionals, let us do the job. I'm going to say hello to you, and I'm going to tell you what's going on, but don't step over the line. I'm not going to let you step over the line.

LS: What kind of stepping over the line do parents do? Do they put pressure on you, or on their kid?

LG: They're going to do it both ways. The kid don't want the parent talking to us anyway, OK? The other way that they're going to put pressure on me might be because their kid didn't go to practice for three days, and I've decided, "Hey, you're not going to wrestle this week." They're going to come in and tell me, "Well, we had to go on this skiing trip…" or, "We had to do this…" Stay right there! That's the bottom line.

I feel we build toughness, confidence, and fitness that should last them a lifetime. It's going to make them go forward in life, and I don't think there are too many sports that really do it like wrestling: that one-on-one thing where you really get close to a kid, and he understands what you're talking about. And he understands you as well as you understand him, because you are in close proximity all the time. You know what he's thinking, and you want him to know what you're thinking.

Let's talk about confidence, and we've heard so much about winning: "Winning builds confidence." Yeah, winning does build confidence. I believe that self-confidence is developed through repetition in specific techniques of moves and drills, position scrimmages, and competitive situations.

LS: What does that mean?

LG: Teaching a specific take-down, like a Low Single, we do that through repetition and drill. First you teach it and show it, and then you drill it, and drill it, and drill it, with another member of the team or with a mannequin. Or if I want to do something with a specific kid – like now I'll do it a lot because I'm not head coach, and I've got time to do things – I'll work with a few kids on specific techniques they can handle, OK?

As he gets better at it, he becomes more confident. Then you bring that into the competitive arena, he tries the move, and he gets it: it works. There's your confidence. It's learning a move that you can execute on somebody and make it happen. It's not winning the match, it's, "I know how to get this take-down." That builds confidence.

Lots of times you have a young kid who just never gets over the hill. He gets up there, but just doesn't finish the thing, and you just keep saying to yourself, "If I can only get him through a match and be successful." Then, all of a sudden, through all this repetition, it happens, and he's on his way to winning and being successful. And you can see in his eyes: "Yes, I can do it!"

LS: If you're working on these essential life skills, and you say they're also taught in other sports, then what the hell are people doing in classrooms?

LG: They're teaching them the skills of math, reading, English, the skills of geography, the skills of whatever.

LS: But if those aren't the things that make or break you in terms of being a success, then shouldn't everybody be in athletics?

LG: I think everybody should be in athletics, but I'm an athlete, so I'm biased.

LS: Was your program open to everybody?

LG: The program was certainly open to everybody. Some people came out and they made it, and some people didn't, they just couldn't do it. But it's open to everybody. We never closed the door to anybody.

It's always been open, it's an open try-out. Like in basketball, they've got a certain number of days for try-out. My try-out is the whole season – it's up to you. If you can stay, fine. If you can make it, good. If you can't deal with it, then that's something else.

LS: If you could reshape the way kids learned, what would you do?

LG: We'd have a lot of athletes. But realistically some kids can't be... You know what? I think that I would focus a lot on physical education. I really would. We need to teach some skills – not winning, but being confident in yourself. I don't think we do that enough in Phys. Ed.

LS: You almost said that Phys. Ed. is not for everybody, and I would like to know if that means that you're teaching something that's only right for some people, or is it the way that you're teaching it that's only right for some people?

LG: Wrestling is not right for all people. If you've got a kid that's uncoordinated, how can he ever learn how to wrestle? And you need to get in shape and stay in shape, and you need to believe in yourself.

LS: Yeah, but what about focus, and determination, and the other things you teach? Does he have to find those some other way, and it's not your problem?

LG: Yeah, I do feel that way. But you can do it in physical education. We can teach him self-confidence, focus, and motivation, all that stuff.

I can remember teaching when we had archery and gymnastics – and gymnastics is a great thing to teach self-confidence in – it's not very hard to do, either, on a basic level. But they threw it out because of insurance; we're not allowed to do that, there's no more gymnastics, not at our school.

I think that there are certain lifelong skills that we should be teaching in physical education. You should teach any sport that a kid can do for the rest of his life. You should be teaching fitness.

LS: You say, "Here's my program, this is what I do, this is what we think we accomplish." But many kids are not in your program, or in any program at all. Most kids don't have mentors, they don't have good family situations, their teachers don't really care about their individual accomplishments, and the kid is left to figure out how to navigate through life. What can you say that will help kids find what they need? Very few of them are lucky enough to find a person like you...

LG: But there are others like me out there. They're not everywhere, but they are around. And I think you can teach a lot of the things I'm talking about in a Phys. Ed. class. I really do.

Phys. Ed. What the heck does it mean? Phys. Ed. means getting a kid physically ready, getting his body physically in shape. We got a little bit away from that, and we need to go back to some of that. I'm not saying we got to do calisthenics all the time, but I'm saying we should be teaching fitness, big time.

LS: But it's more than just a physical education course. It's an emotionally empowering thing... People who worked with you in wrestling speak about how important it was to them.

You talk as if you're a sculptor working with good material and how to get the best out of it. And my question is, what about all the kids out there that aren't exactly good material? Most people would not qualify as athletic material. Are they out of your reach?

LG: They're out of my reach. I just think that we need to get more people on the right page, of getting their bodies in shape, and also offer them things that are life-serving. Teach them golf, volley ball, badminton, bowling, archery, anything they can do for the rest of their lives. Teach them how to get in real good shape. I think it's important, and I think that we've got away from it.

LS: Tell me some stories of kids. Give me an example of the transformation, somebody's transformation and how it proceeded in real life. How about that kid who got burned?

LG: That is a good story, that is a positive story. It was out of the ordinary, there's no make-up there.

He got burned pretty bad. I mean, his fingers were burned, there was a burn on his back, his fingers were really burned. They were taking the skin off him by putting him in a whirlpool. Everyday I would go to see that kid down in Huntington Hospital. I went there just about every day. It was so horrible.

It took a year for him to come back, and he had to wrestle with gloves. We had to get the OK for him to wrestle with gloves. He was a good wrestler to begin with, and I always thought the kid would come back because he was so motivated. He just loved the game, he just loved wrestling, and he did come back, and he won the state championship. You know, it's, like, what other kid do you know that did something like that?

LS: Did you make it happen, did he need your support?

LG: I was supportive of him, I definitely was. But the point is that he had such great heart that he was going to come back, and he did come back, and he did a great job. Imagine wrestling with gloves on that came up to your elbows.

LS: Did that have any effect on the team, or on you?

LG: I guess it proved to me that you really can do what you want, as long as you want to do it. The kid had such tremendous drive and determination. I mean, when I first seen him after the fire, "Oh my God, I hope he lives."

I think that it inspired the kids on the team, too, you know. It's quite far back, and I don't remember how that year went as a team, but I'm sure that he was definitely an inspiration to the kids on our team.

Here's another story. A few years ago we had a kid that took All County (championship). So, generally speaking, this kid would have been one of the best kids on my team and could have made this team a better team.

He was a minority kid, and he was a pain in the ass in school. The teachers in the school, and not all of them, but there's a certain group of teachers that didn't want that kid to compete. They were pissed that he wrestled because he dodged the bullet all the time, and no one ever ran interference for him, but we kept talking to him. We, I mean my staff and I, nurtured him through the whole summer of wrestling. Brought him to maybe 12 tournaments. In the fall he started school and got mingled in with a bunch of bozos.

The rule in our school is that if you get thrown out of school three times... Thrown out doesn't mean you have to do something real bad, you could have said to an aide, "Get the hell away from me!" OK? That's good enough to throw you out. He didn't break a window, he didn't beat up somebody, nothing crazy.

So between the beginning of the semester and when our program started, I walk into the office – we had a meeting with all the winter coaches. Right before the meeting's over, I say to the athletic director, I say, "How's Mason doing?" And the director goes, "Oh, he's not going to wrestle for you this year. He's got three suspensions, and one more suspension and he's done." So I go, "What are you talking about? How come nobody was informed? We could have fixed this."

The kid lost a family member last year; it was a very upsetting situation. So the kid is a little off. He's a little off. You can't tell me he's straight 'cause he's not. There's something wrong. He's got to be feeling bad or something. And they haven't done anything for this kid. And then they shelf him in wrestling, the only thing that could have saved him.

He had another year, and we got him back. But suppose he was a senior, what would have happened to that kid? He'd be on the street next year stealing. Whereas maybe we could have changed that whole thing. And we did, we did get him back.

LS: What is it that you're giving him? It seems he's fighting a very different thing from the battle you're fighting.

LG: I'm making him believe that he can make a name for himself in wrestling, that he can win the championship, that he can place high in the county. And people look at wrestling on Long Island as quite a thing. If you can place in the county, you're a pretty good wrestler. So, we're instilling the idea that he can do it.

I would never give you a goal that you could not reach. I want my kids to get goals that they can reach, that are definitely within reach. Our goals are always within reach. You know what I'm saying? We never tell a kid, "Hey, you could be county champion!" when there's no way he could be county champion. We'll tell him something else, but we're never going to tell him that.

We're going to tell him the truth, what he can do. All we've got to do is keep talking about how good he can be, and then work on that. Work with him one on one, and talk to him one on one. Well, (in this case) we were never given that opportunity. And that happens a lot.

LS: Is your relationship with the kids you coach limited to practice time? Or do you become a sort of uncle or father figure?

LG: I think so. I think some kids... yeah. I've had so many black kids with no father that they latch on to me. And that's OK, I don't have a problem with that. I love it, it's great. I work even harder with them. I get to know them better. I get to know their family better. I kind of help guide them through their lives.

We had a kid that won the New York State Championship for us some years ago, and then he screwed up. I got him into Nassau Community College, and he screwed it up. I got him back in, and he screwed it up again.

He came to me again and says, "Hey, coach, I want to go to school, but I don't have any money." So I says, "Yeah, but you screwed up three times! What are you doing?" So he goes, "I know, but what am I going to do?" I says, "Here's what I did: I went to work and went to school." I says, "That's what you've gotta do. This is America, this is what you've got to do. You've got to go to work, get a job, and go to school." And I says, "If you need help doing that, I'll help you."

LS: What was his problem?

LG: He was mixed up. He was really mixed up. I got 25 other kids, and he's graduated. I mean, if he calls I'm definitely gonna help him.

LS: Do you feel bad that you weren't able to get him on the track before he went out of your grasp?

LG: No, I don't feel bad about it because I went out of my way to get him into Nassau Community two different times. I called up the coach, who I knew, and I said, "Come on, stop it. You've got to give him a break. You've got to help him out." And he did. He found some more money and got him back in, and he blew it again. Three strikes and you're out. I think there comes a time where you'd better pick up the ball and run.

LS: I think people misunderstand athletics, and wrestling, in believing that winning is what gets you self-confidence. That's my question. Is it just winning, or is it... ?

LG: No, no. Being successful... first of all it involves going in the room and finishing the practice. There's success there, right? Now you aren't doing well – you're in a group of three guys – and not doing well, every day. Then all of a sudden somebody grabs you aside, and somebody says, "Hey, look, just go for a take-down. Just go for an escape." Success, right? That doesn't mean you won the state championship, but you had success in the room.

You keep on building on that until he goes to the top, wherever he can go. He may not ever be a state champion, but he might be able to win 50 percent of his matches, and he knows he did his best. And we've been telling him it, too. So he's been successful, and he feels great about himself. No one's ever going to take that away from him.

I'm thinking all the time. When I talk to a kid, I always think – I don't just talk – I'm thinking about what I'm going to say. I'm talking about kids, I'm not talking about adults. When I talk to adults, I say what the hell I feel like. But normally, with a kid, I'm always thinking, "Am I going to screw him up psychologically? Am I going to make him feel down?" I don't want to do that. I want to keep him up as much as I can.

It is a psychological game, it really is. You need to be right on top of your game with them. You gotta know what to say, and when not to say it. In the room, when you're working with them... on the mat right here... you've got a kid that comes off the mat and he's destroyed. If you go over there and pat him on the back, that friggin' sucks, man. You make him feel worse.

Let him go and cry it out for a couple of minutes, do what he wants to do, as long as he don't break anything. Let him get rid of it, and then go talk to him after he's cooled down a bit, when the anxiety is gone. That's what makes good coaches, people that know how to do that.

Where does it come from? I don't know. Half the time I don't even know what I'm doing, but I know it works.

LS: People give you an awful lot of credit. Joey's story was interesting because he wasn't in it as a wrestler, he was in it as a person who needed to find himself, and he did. He credits that with saving his life, you know.

LG: He was a great kid. He calls me up every once in a while. We have a lot of kids like that. We do. They never become great wrestlers, but they become pretty good people.

WRITING

33. CAITLIN MCKENNA

History   Early   Born 1988, Bethesda, Maryland

Caitlin became an avid reader in grade school and an avid writer soon after. Writing became her passion far beyond anything that was expected of her, and she has thought about the writing process more than most adults. This has given her a clarity unusual for someone her age.

I met Caitlin in Peru where she was accompanying her father at a week-long conference on shamanism and science. She had come for kind of a growing-up ritual with the Amazon River shamans, to help her in her own journey toward college and independence. After this interview, she went on to attend the University of British Columbia in Vancouver.

Excerpts

"I knew I had an aptitude for writing, but I hadn't thought of doing it seriously until that moment. I can't explain it beyond that. It was a period of time when I was floating... and I was sort of lost as to what to do with my mind. I always need to be doing something with my mind, creating or absorbing, whether I'm reading a book or writing a story. I can't just be idle..."

"The 9/11 attack on the Trade Center... was quite a shock to me. Before that I thought the stuff on the news had little impact on my life, but this did. The whole world seemed to shudder, and I needed to do something in my own world to reflect this shift. I couldn't just let it go; I had to analyze it, to work it over, maybe start doing something different. Writing for me is just what came out of that, I guess... it's hard to explain..."

"My mental world always has to be expanding. I don't like it being static or stagnant. I think people lose their imaginations that way... Imagination is one of the most important things that humans have. It can do so much for us, and it doesn't ask anything in return, except that we use it..."

"You have to start with yourself, because how can you help other people if you can't help yourself? You're the first person that you know, and you're probably going to be the last, so you're the place you have to start..."

"Writing is a way of expanding my world and keeping it from falling still. You can read a lot, but if you expand it on your own, then you can do it anytime you want and you feel the sense of... (sigh)... endless possibility, maybe..."

"The outside world is moving, always moving – maybe not forward exactly, but in all directions. We have to keep up in our heads – and I have to keep up in my head – so I started making my own worlds. I had to record them. That's what writing is for me: recording the worlds in here, in my head."

"The temple bell stops.
But the sound keeps coming
out of the flowers."

— Matsuo Basho, 17th century Japanese poet

Interview   Iquitos, Peru, July 2006

Caitlin McKenna: Before I started writing, I was a big reader. I had this one favorite author called K.A. Applegate; she'd written this long book series. I started reading that in fourth grade, and it went through to seventh grade. Before finishing the series, I'd written a few things for school, mostly short stories, but they didn't amount to much.

In seventh grade I finished reading this huge story that had taken years of my life to get through, and that was when I started writing. I think I was sort of drifting, having nothing to do, and I thought I'd like to create a story like that, I'd like to give something to the world that would touch someone else like her story touched me.

I knew I had an aptitude for writing, but I hadn't thought of doing it seriously until that moment. I can't explain it beyond that. It was a period of time when I was floating, I wasn't reading any story that I could "glom" onto, and I was sort of lost as to what to do with my mind. I always need to be doing something with my mind, creating or absorbing, whether I'm reading a book or writing a story. I can't just be idle.

LS: This is the long series; how long was it?

CM: It was 54 books.

LS: She really kept the plot going for the whole series?

CM: She did. I was so amazed. She's my role model for a writer, basically. I've known a lot of great writers, but she's the one who got me interested in writing because she kept her story going for three whole years, even longer. It was an epic – it was sci-fi.

LS: Do you remember what you felt before you started reading this series?

CM: These books got me interested in science fiction. Before I'd read some fantasy, like Brian Jacques – he wrote what we call "beast epics" where there are medieval settings and where the characters were mice and squirrels and foxes instead of humans.

I hadn't really found a purpose – I didn't like to be idle, but I wasn't as involved in any long reading commitments. There wasn't much to my own artistic endeavors; I was more of a sketcher. Actually, I used to draw a lot of comic strips, and I did that for years. That was sort of my passion when I was younger.

LS: What was the transition like when you ended the 54th volume? It must have been difficult. I mean... I've never read anything that long, but I've read shorter things, and ending them can be a shock.

CM: It was, it really was. I actually cried when I finished it. It was very hard to imagine that it was over even though it made sense, story-wise. It was the culmination, and you could tell. At the same time it was sort of unreal, because it had been a big part of my life, as you can imagine.

LS: When I finished *The Lord of the Rings*, which I did when I was pretty young, I searched at the back of the book for more, and I reread the end and read the footnotes.

CM: Yeah, me too.

LS: It was hard to think that that world was gone. Did you take up writing at that time?

CM: I'd done some school writing. I'd written a short story that was a fantasy about this girl who went to another dimension, a parallel world. I'd liked writing that, and it made me think I might want to write more, but I hadn't written that much prior to this transition.

After I finished this long series, it took me a couple of months just absorbing it and going over it. I didn't actually start writing my own stuff until September or October, because I started eighth grade. I think that was important. Not to speak ill of school, but eighth grade for me was not a very stimulating environment.

LS: How did you feel about the other grades? Did you have a particular attitude towards school at that point?

CM: Well, no… it's hard to describe. Elementary school was very different because I was at a small school. I changed schools at the beginning of seventh grade, but I was still reading this series at that point, so I still had that.

I live in two worlds. A real world and a mental world that's comprised of everything that I've read and written and seen, and everything that isn't in the real world. Because I was still reading the series in seventh grade, I still had that.

My elementary school was very small; I knew everyone in my grade and in the two grades above and below. It was relaxed. There were no cliques. It was very different.

But when eighth grade came along there was a paradigm shift: school got harder and more serious. Plus, since I finished the series, my mental world was seriously lacking something to look forward to (laughs).

That was 2001, and I needed to find something quickly. The 9/11 attack on the Trade Center happened in the second week of school, and that, for me, was quite… well… I didn't lose anyone – which I was glad for – although two of our friends were going to go to see the World Trade Center that day, but they decided not to, who knows why. So they escaped being killed.

That was quite a shock to me. Before that I thought the stuff on the news had little impact on my life, but this did. The whole world seemed to shudder, and I needed to do something in my own world to reflect this shift. I couldn't just let it go; I had to analyze it, to work it over, maybe start doing something different. Writing for me is just what came out of that, I guess… it's hard to explain.

LS: I find writing difficult, but it doesn't seem that it was too difficult for you. What did you get out of it? Did you get a way back into that world that you were in when you were reading?

CM: Yeah, I think that's what it was. My mental world always has to be expanding. I don't like it being static or stagnant. I think people lose their imaginations that way.

I think the imagination is one of the most important things that humans have. It can do so much for us, and it doesn't ask anything in return, except that we use it.

Writing is a way of expanding my world, and keeping it from falling still. You can read a lot, but if you expand it on your own, then you can do it anytime you want, and you feel the sense of… (sigh)… endless possibility, maybe.

The outside world is moving, always moving – maybe not forward exactly, but in all directions. We have to keep up in our heads – and I have to keep up in my head – so I started making my own worlds. I had to record them. That's what writing is for me: recording the worlds in here, in my head.

LS: It's so different than reading.

CM: It really is.

LS: How did you make that transition from reading? When you're reading, it just pours into you. You can do nothing, and just be half awake, and it will pour into you, or you can be very awake. But in writing you have to be peddling, or do you? Can you write stream-of-consciousness and feel that you're rewarded?

CM: It depends. I can do that for my journals. But if I'm writing a story, I try to make it sound real. If I wrote a story from a stream-of-consciousness perspective, I don't think it would make much sense. I could do poetry like that, but with writing I like to have a decent plot and believable characters.

For me, the most important thing are the characters, and I feel like I have to be fully awake to know and talk to them. If you're half asleep in this world, and you're trying to talk to people, then you're not going to get to know half of them. When you're meeting people, you have to be awake. When you're writing, you're meeting people from your subconscious, I think.

LS: Tell me more about the conversations you have with those characters. How do they grow?

CM: Usually the idea has to gestate, you know? The characters have to grow along with the story. It's not like conversations exactly; it's more like having an inner dialog with yourself because characters are aspects of you.

Anyone you create has to come from inside yourself; they can't come from somewhere else, which is kind of scary if you have a character whom you think of as evil. You wonder, "Is that part of me?" Subconsciously, maybe… yeah. But it's OK because we all have things like that in us.

They grow through being written. You introduce them and then, as the plot progresses, you get to see more of their character. Sometimes you're surprised by the turns it takes, and you think, "Oh, I didn't know this about them!" And it seems weird because it's you, but it's a part of you that you don't normally see – a subconscious part of you.

As they grow, you learn things about yourself, but you also learn things about them, because the second you put a character down on paper they become something that's also separate from you. They do become their own person within the reality of the story, and it's just by writing their story that you learn about them. You can't have them fully formed before you put down a single word; that doesn't work. It's impractical. It's like a creationism of writing, and that's not how it works; writing is an evolution. Characters evolve as you take them further in their stories.

LS: Do your characters lead the development of your stories, or do you?

CM: It's sort of a collaborative. You set out different paths – well you set out the paths, but then they choose the path. The choosing is up to them, but the setting up is up to you.

I'm setting up the reality, as far as I know, but maybe I'm just channeling it all from somewhere else.

LS: There are lots of situations that you can set up knowing what you know, but there are many situations you don't have personal experience with, not you or anyone. Do your characters avoid those situations where you feel confused because you don't know what they should do?

CM: I think they might, yeah. If they're part of you, then their character would guide them to avoid situations where they wouldn't fit.

It's like an intuition – there's a lot that you can imagine that you don't have personal experience with. Science fiction runs into this all the time. I can guarantee you that no one who has written science fiction, not the writers I've read anyway, have actually been into space. But they write about it. They write on the basis of what they know from reading about it, and then their own intuition.

LS: How do you deal with characters doing things you are uncomfortable with? Do you censor yourself, do you lock your journal, do you write things and then throw them away, or do you just decide this is going to ruin my day, so I think I'll just have my characters do something else?

CM: It depends on the situation. I have a journal that I've written all in this code that I've invented. No one can read it except me. Sometimes I use this journal to write things that I don't want anyone else to read. I think you need privacy. It's important to record your thoughts, but sometimes you want you, and only you, to be able to read them.

I also have a sketch book that's intertwined with my stories because sometimes I create a creature, draw it, write down its history, and a story will come out of that. I don't usually draw scenes. I prefer words because it's more of a challenge than drawing. I can't draw everything, I can't draw people at all. I can get to the cartoon level, but not to a realistic level. Mostly I draw things that never were.

LS: Does this relationship you have with writing make you feel unusual? Where do you place yourself among your colleagues?

CM: I've a lot of friends who would probably be considered unusual by normal standards, but I've kind of kept my writing personal. I let my friends read a few things, but my writing life really is separate, and in that way I am unusual. I don't know if there are that many people of my age who are serious about writing.

I'd really like to get published, and I'm making steps toward that. I feel like I'm in a chrysalis because not many people have read my words. When and if I get published, it will bring my personal and writing lives together. Then I will be able to show people the product of my efforts and say, "Here, this is what I'm doing. This is the part of my life you don't see."

LS: What do you think about your friends who are on other paths?

CM: Some of my friends are really passionate about things, but they still don't know what they want to do. I think they would like to bring the same passion that they have for, like, reading or music, but they don't know what to do in their own lives.

They don't know if their talent lies in music because they like it, or if they're destined for something completely different. I think college will be good for them because they'll be able to explore their interests. At the same time, I think college will be good for me because I know what I want to do.

LS: Do you think that it's right to say that there are some people who have a public life but no private life, and that you have a private life and a public life?

CM: That's an interesting question. It's appropriate to say I have a private life and a public life. I could go farther and say that I'm living both at the same time. Like when I go to presentations at this conference, and Dad introduces me to all these people, that involves the public part of me, and then when I get bored I go off to think about something.

Thinking for me is part of my private life – it's an interior mental exercise. I carry that with me everywhere I go. If I get bored with the public life, I can retreat. Except sometimes I can't retreat, or shouldn't, or don't want to.

The crisis is that people often don't have enough of a private life. American society is very up on being public and socializing: getting to know people, being gregarious, being social. Except for the extremes, I don't think there is such a thing as being anti-social. I don't think people leave enough time for themselves, their minds, and their own growth – for just being alone with their thoughts. People need to stop and smell the roses; it's cliché but it's true.

LS: Has your traveling been important for your writing?

CM: Oh, yeah, very. I live in a small town most of the time. Travel has helped lend a patina of reality to what I write. I can actually recall smells, and sounds, and sights. I might be describing somewhere I'll never get to, that no one will get to, but I can make it real because I can lend to it the qualities of real cities I've been to. Also, books have been important for expanding my mind. But there is something travel gives you that books can't. The reality is so much greater when you're actually there and you're actually processing this enormous amount of data.

Books describe things in words, which only goes so far. They describe things one at a time, so you can't hold it all in your mind simultaneously, which you need to do for it to be completely real. But if you're dropped onto a street in some city, it's all coming at you at once, and you have to process it, integrate it, feel how it works, deal with the chaos. I think chaos is important to experience because so much of the world is bathed in it all the time. Part of reality involves a certain amount of chaos. It's important to know that not every place is idyllic, small, and provincial.

LS: Are there any other things about writing that you'd like to add that I haven't thought to ask?

CM: One of the most important things in writing is syntax. People don't appreciate punctuation. It's not just the words, it's how you use them, it's the rhythms; writing is almost like singing, or playing music.

The rhythm in what's written can give an impact that words alone can't, and the way you use words. In long series, deciding where to start the books, and where to place each part of the story chronologically, is almost like an expanded version of the syntax that goes in every page. That's something that I value a lot in my own writing, and something that I strive the hardest for.

LS: You speak almost as if you're writing, which makes it easy for me. You're telling me a story with unusual detail. It's like that Bill Cosby joke that begins "I started life as a child."

You started all the way back in fourth grade. It all makes sense; everything worked out so well. Were there periods of depression, chaos, and elation? What about all of the sorrows or… whatever was happening?

CM: Yeah, if I described it all in detail, you'd be hearing the names of a lot of cats. And a lot of things that I just cannot say.

LS: Can't say because they're not sayable?

CM: Well, they are sayable – it would just take too long. It would take hours. You don't want to hear about my life.

LS: That's true, our readers wouldn't tolerate it. On the other hand, maybe my questions cannot be fully answered through dialog. Maybe we can't answer how young people find what you might call their private lives.

If you think about school, one of the reasons I don't like school is that they never teach you to have a private life, they never inspire you to take off on your own. Most of school seems aimed to provide a trade, to prepare you for a job.

CM: So is your son homeschooled?

LS: He's largely homeschooled.

CM: I think that's better. If I could do it again, I'd be, like, "Mom, Dad, homeschool me," just so I could see what that's like. I was writing words before I was reading. My parents would help me write, and then I would read it.

LS: What role did school play? Good and bad.

CM: I can remember writing before I went to any school. I'd have a piece of paper and my mom and dad would teach me how to write letters. I was starting to read words, so when I got to first grade we had these flash cards where we would read words, and I thought this was the dullest, most boring, shit exercise that I'd ever done. It was rote because I knew these words.

In second grade, it was a lot better because we'd have books that we'd read stories out of. Half of the reason that I started reading early was those books. The other half happened at home because that's where I started reading books with my mom. She would read to me, and I would be sitting there looking at the words, so I had that connection.

Third grade was pretty much my least favorite year because we had books that we would read, but we would read them at a glacial pace. We read *Pipi Longstocking*, and I must have read that book in the first day, but it took so much longer for the class to read it. But by that time my love of reading was too strong. If I had been a less enthusiastic reader, that probably would have destroyed my desire.

My favorite part of school was the friends that I had. I made some really good friends whom I liked to hang out with. Classes got more interesting as I got farther into school. Elementary school was a good experience for me overall.

LS: What have you learned from the books you've read? Do you feel that you've understood the material and the people who wrote it?

CM: There's something I've been noticing: this stereotype of authors being alcoholics. I wonder if that's a reflection of that private life you were talking about. I wonder if they get a little absorbed in it.

LS: There's a danger in taking your private life too seriously, and alcohol seems to have a particularly insidious effect on people who do that.

CM: A lot of the time people self-medicate. If they're depressed, they self-medicate with alcohol or drugs.

LS: Yeah, and it's not a successful medication.

CM: Well, no. It doesn't really work, it just makes things worse. Sometimes people might subconsciously be seeking oblivion. Depression makes you do that, like thinking that anything may be better than this; that I'd rather die.

Sometimes people can be completely blind to their own personal life and problems. There are people who have advice for everyone but themselves. I think you have to start with yourself, because how can you help other people if you can't help yourself?

You're the first person that you know, and you're probably going to be the last, so you're the place you have to start. I hope that doesn't sound egotistical.

LS: Why should sounding egotistical weaken your observation?

CM: Maybe egotistical isn't as bad as it's made out to be. You can carry it too far, but you can also carry caring for other people too far, too.

It's a balance. Everything in life is a balance: you have to balance yourself and others. You have to balance the outer world and the inner, the public and the private. It's Anthony Burgess who said that duality is the ultimate reality; it seems that there's truth in that.

34. ALICE PLACERT

History	Early	Born 1982, New York City, New York

Alice Placert is a vivacious, single mother living with her five-year-old son Hunter in lower Manhattan. I didn't know anything about Ali before I met her, and all that I know about her – and all that we have said to each other – is in this interview, except for the doughnut. I bought her son a glazed doughnut, and the two of us bonded immediately.

In mythology, the underworld is the domain of transformation. It lies beyond fear and boredom, somewhere in the big empty hole at the end of the road to nowhere. It's dark and forbidding because moving toward and through a dead end is frightening. Ali's transformation was more frightening than you can imagine.

Excerpts

"My stepmother had Munchausen syndrome by proxy. She would invent mental illnesses and have me medicated for them. It's when you make your children sick to get attention… I spent my late teens in a lot of mental hospitals…"

"For me, the process of becoming an adult was very… abrupt… I got raped, and I got pregnant with my son, at a party by some random guy who I don't know – and I still don't know who he is – and after that I went nuts. I was 20…"

"I wound up sleeping in the park and being in the shelter system. I was raped again. I was stabbed twice while at the shelters. Once in the belly while I was pregnant, and once underneath my arm when I got in a fight with a girl with a knife… I don't remember being upset about it at the time, because there's more important things to worry about than wallowing in self-pity…"

"It always feels better to be able to take care of yourself and to be responsible for your own choices. At the end of the day, when you look back on your life and what you've done, you have to answer to yourself…"

"I feel like a lot of people get stuck in their life… They buy into something that they want without really understanding what it is… because they plan: 'I don't want to have kids until I'm 30, so if I get pregnant before then I'll have an abortion no matter what.' They don't even think about it. You're giving up stuff that may be a good thing in your life because you're so focused on a goal. And then, when you get it, you're not even happy…"

"Just because you have had an idea in your mind about what you wanted to do for X number of years doesn't mean that it's necessarily the right thing to do… a lot of things that seemed like they were the end of the world turned out to be the best things that ever happened to me…"

"I can honestly say that I would not change anything in my life, at all, that has happened, because I'm really happy… I can't imagine a different life. I am, right now, pretty much exactly where I want to be. I don't know how else I would be here."

ALICE PLACERT

"Tommy saw his house on fire,
His mother in the flames expire;
His father killed by falling brick
And Tommy laughed – 'till he was sick."

— Marcus Ordayne, in *Morals for the Young*

Interview   New York City, New York, August 2008

LS: So here's the idea... young people go through a transition around their teenage years, somewhere between 10 and 20. It's when you move out of your parents' circle and find a circle of your own. It used to be a very important transition, and there was a social, family ceremony of growing up, and all kinds of stuff happened. But now there isn't any of that. People get taken away from their parents and get put into school, and then they get turned into robots, or something.

Alice Placert: And they also stay children for a very long time. People are now at the mental age of 15-year-olds when they're 30. They prolong their childhood indefinitely; they never grow up. You see all these people having kids when they're 40 who are awful parents, because it's basically like a teenager trying to raise a kid. Their kids are assholes; it's very annoying, especially when you have to deal with the parents and their children.

I kind of skipped straight into middle age. For me, the process of becoming an adult was very... abrupt.

Basically, I had not a very good childhood; I had a bad relationship with my parents. My stepmother had Munchausen syndrome by proxy. She would invent mental illnesses and have me medicated for them. It's when you make your children sick to get attention. Some people do it and poison their kids. She would say that I was hearing voices, and suicidal, and cutting myself when I wasn't. I was always a "clumsy, slash, active" child, so I would get hurt all the time because I would do stupid shit, like fall down and get hurt, and she would go, "Oh, she hurt herself on purpose!" I had a very twisted childhood.

LS: Where was this?

AP: My father was in the Army, so I grew up all over, mostly in Germany.

And then when I was a teenager, my mother, who I've never had any contact with my whole life, and who passed away in 2002, was actually mentally ill. So my stepmother said, "She's just like her mother. She's inherited it. It's genetic."

When I was in my late teens, she convinced doctors that I had bipolar disorder, which I didn't, obviously: like I'm not on medication for like five years now, and I support a child by myself and take care of him, and have an apartment, and a job, and my child is vaccinated, and... you know what I mean? Like, I take care of the everyday details of life. Clearly, if I had a debilitating mental illness, and was hallucinating, and was cutting myself, you know, there would be evidence of it, and my child would not be OK.

I spent my late teens in a lot of mental hospitals. I almost didn't graduate high school because of it. And then I left college early because she had me hospitalized every semester, and I could never take my finals, and there was no point in going over and over again. I was working to pay for my own college, and it was just insane.

Hunter Placert *(her five-year-old son): I ran through the sprinkler!*

AP: I see that! Go run through again... I'm watching!

I wound up leaving. They were living in Poughkeepsie, so I came back to Poughkeepsie and was working a couple of jobs. I was teaching and running a music program at a Head Start program. I played viola. I wasn't happy, and I didn't like living with my parents, so I wound up quitting and moving to the city.

And then I got raped, and I got pregnant with my son, at a party by some random guy who I don't know – and I still don't know who he is – and after that I went nuts. I was 20.

I knew I was pregnant right away, immediately. I don't know how, I just knew. I'm an atheist, and I'm pro-choice, but I really, really had a feeling that it was the right thing to do, for my life, to keep the baby. It turned out it was the best decision I've ever made in my life. But my parents put me in a mental hospital right after this happened because I was crazy, because I was upset from it, obviously; it was very violent and bad.

HP: What do you have?

AP: I have some pineapple, Sweetheart... and I have your train. So why don't you take your train and your ball on the slide. Go ahead. Hunter, come on, go.

They found out I was pregnant, and they came into this mental hospital and said to me, "If you don't have an abortion, we're never going to speak to you again." And I was, like, "Really! Fine! I'm not having an abortion. Goodbye." It was very difficult because, even though it's a very twisted and bad relationship, it's still your parents, and so it was tough.

Once they found out they were liable if anything happens, they kept me in the hospital. They refused to let me out. They said they were going to keep me for nine months and then take the baby. So I went to court. I took them to court, and they let me out. Then I was homeless for seven months of my pregnancy. I had lost my apartment and my job because I was in the hospital for two months.

I was on the streets. For a few weeks I slept in a cemetery behind a church, because everyone's superstitious and I am not. I was, like, "It's quiet, there's no noise, and nobody's going to bother me here sleeping on somebody's grave." Whatever.

After that I got into a shelter in Poughkeepsie; it was a Catholic shelter. I had only been down in the city for a few months, so my residency wasn't New York City; it was still Poughkeepsie. Battered women's shelters wouldn't take me. They're, like, "Well, you have to go get in a shelter where you were raped." And then I would come here, and, "No, you have to get into a shelter where you have residency." Nobody would take me.

Then I got into this horrible Catholic shelter where their whole goal is to have you never have sex again, for you to be abstinent, which I think by the time you're pregnant is a little too late. It's like you've kind of missed the boat.

They moved me to the Bronx because, like, "You don't know anybody there, so you're not going to be tempted." So they moved me to the Bronx, but they'd already opened a case for me at Social Services in Poughkeepsie.

Then they opened a case for me in the Bronx. There was a lot of violence in the Bronx shelter with this group of girls, so they separated everybody and spread us to different shelters. They moved me to White Plains, and they opened another case for me with White Plains Social Services, without closing any of the previous cases.

***HP**: I lost my ball!*

AP: Where did it go? You've got to run and look for it, Love. Go run and look for it, it's around here someplace. I'm sure you'll find it. Go look.

Because of all the open cases, I got "red-flagged" at Social Services. I was apparently trying to commit fraud, and nobody would give me any services. So then I was screwed. I wound up sleeping in the park and being in the shelter system. I was raped again. I was stabbed twice while at the shelters. Once in the belly while I was pregnant, and once underneath my arm when I got in a fight with a girl with a knife.

LS: So what did you feel about all this?

AP: What a lot of people don't understand about situations like this is that when you're doing it, you don't feel anything. You just have to get through, and you just do what you gotta do. It's like anybody in a very difficult situation: you ask them what was it like when you were there and, like, "What am I going to do: sit here and cry when I'm starving? Or am I going to go out and try to figure a way to eat?" You know what I mean? It's almost easier to be in constant turmoil because you don't have any time to think about it. You just do what you have to do.

I remember landing in the shelter and thinking, "If I get murdered here, nobody's going to know. Who's going to know? I don't talk to anybody. Nobody in the world has any idea of where I am."

The girls in the shelter, some of them were very nice, but because I'm white I had a lot of problems. They wouldn't let me eat. They would threaten me because I'm this white bitch and da-da-da-da-da. And then I would get robbed and stuff. It was definitely... I don't remember being upset about it at the time, because there's more important things to worry about than wallowing in self-pity.

The psychological trauma doesn't happen until after you're OK. And for me, I deal with it very well, but a lot of it doesn't even seem real, like it never even happened. I have scars, I know that it happened, I have medical records, but you kind of disconnect from it in a way. It took me a few years after I was out of this situation to calm down 'cause I was very jumpy.

LS: What could you do while you were in that situation? Could you have a job, could you have a life?

AP: No, there's no way to have a job when you're homeless, because who's going to hire you without an address or a phone number?

I stole food. I got arrested for stealing food – I just cleared the bench warrant now, because I got moved to a different county so I couldn't go to court – I got arrested for stealing yogurt. I would go into restaurants where you get food, and then you go pay, and I would steal the food.

My grandmother in Florida sent me $100 by Western Union, because I still had my driver's license. And I never missed a prenatal doctor's appointment, either – I always had a new hospital when I moved, but I always went to every single doctor's appointment – I did whatever I had to do.

I was seven months pregnant, my grandma sent me $100, and I got a bed in a youth hostel for a week. It just so happened that it was unstaffed at night, so I broke into the office and stole keys. Then I'd let myself in every night, and I'd sleep on the floor.

From there I actually applied for a job at American Ballet Theatre – they were hiring a temporary fund-raising, marketing person for the winter holidays. I used the youth hostel as my address and got the job, which was insane. The first couple of weeks that I was working there, I was sleeping on the floor at this youth hostel.

Then this guy, who was working there, needed a roommate, so I was, like, "All right." I wound up moving in with him, but it turned out it was bad because it was this tiny studio, and he was an alcoholic. He couldn't pay the rent because of the alcohol, and he wound up, like, assaulting me when I was nine months pregnant.

But it just so happened that, across the street from this guy's apartment, a psychiatrist who had taken care of me in one of the mental hospitals when I was, like, 17, had her office. And I wound up...

HP: I need some help. Can you help me find my train?

AP: No, you've got to go look for it. I'm sure you can find it, you're a good looker. Go look. Oh, I see it, it's right there! Right underneath the slide... by one of the green things. Go look.

He assaulted me, and she ended up taking me in, and I lived in her apartment for two weeks. Then, a week before I gave birth to my son, I got a room in SRO in Washington Heights.

LS: SRO?

AP: You share a bathroom in the hall – it's like a tiny room – where I was adopted into this family of Dominicans who lived on the first floor of the building.

She's still like my mom. She doesn't speak any English. I speak fluent Spanish now, I learned Spanish, and that's why I was just in the Dominican Republic, visiting her family. She's like my Dominican mom. Her daughter's like my sister, she's 17 now. I've been helping her.

When I met her she was going to get pregnant and drop out of school. Now she wants to go to Columbia. She's trying to get into school, into college.

LS: How did you do that?

AP: I just became friends with her, and talked to her, for like four years, every day. We talked about stuff and eventually... she's an only child, and she has no father, so it's just like her and her mom. And her mom works all the time.

They had nothing, but when I moved in I had less than them! I was sleeping on the floor, no blanket, no pillow. I had one set of clothes, and that was it. It was amazing, because this is a building in one of the poorest neighborhoods in all of New York. And this building was on a row of buildings in the poorest area in Washington Heights. And the building that I was in, out of all those buildings, was the poorest of all of those buildings. So it was the shittiest apartment on Earth.

When I first moved in, this girl, my friend's daughter, came up with a group of teenage girls who lived in the building and knocked on my door. She knocked on my door with her friends, and they're like, "Oh, hi." I was massively pregnant, and white, and the only white person for miles. It's all Dominicans there.

They're like, "What are you doing here?" I didn't say anything. I was, like, "Well..." I just wanted to lock myself... I had a door with a lock on it, and I just wanted to be alone.

So she looks behind me, and she sees there's nothing in my apartment. So they left, and I went to sleep.

A few hours later I hear a knock on my door and I get up, and they're holding stacks of dishes and sheets. They brought me a microwave. They just randomly collected shit from people in the building.

Basically, I lived in that building for a year after my son was born. I wound up getting a check for 10 grand, because I'd been in a car accident when I was 16. So I paid my rent and all my bills. I had WIC and food stamps – Women, Infants and Children – so you get food vouchers. I was breastfeeding, and they give you extra food if you're breastfeeding.

After that, through very shady means, I wound up getting this enormous apartment on 181st street: a five-bedroom apartment for $1,100 a month. I sublet three of the rooms and lived off of that for a couple of years. I was a dominatrix, and a couple of other things, and now I do editing of books.

LS: Editing of books?

AP: Yeah, I do freelance. I'm applying for more jobs now because, I mean, I was doing fine, and then the economy crashed. Now it's getting tight again.

LS: So where did you learn how to do that?

AP: I just taught myself.

LS: When the opportunity arose, you taught yourself?

AP: Well, I was working in American Ballet Theater doing fundraising and grant-writing for them, when I didn't know how to do that, so… I have a facility for language. I learned fluent Spanish in four months from living in Washington Heights. I just learned it; I woke up one day and spoke Spanish. It was weird.

I suck at math. I feel like all of my brain just goes to language. I'm, like… people go, "I'm bad at math," and I'm, like, "No, I have a learning disability."

LS: Well, have you had much chance to study? It sounds like you've been a little busy since you were 15.

AP: No, I haven't really studied.

LS: When did all this craziness start, when you lost any stability…

AP: After high school. But now I've been living in my apartment here in Soho for two years. I have a good deal. I have a married boyfriend, who I love dearly, and he helps me out if it's an emergency situation. It's actually a very good relationship: very stable and calm. I mean my life is always going to be a little nutty because I'm not a… suburban person. Do you know what I mean? I'm not… I always crave emotion, and I crave… not drama but, like, action, or something going on.

I feel like a lot of people get stuck in their life, do you know what I mean? They buy into something that they want without really understanding what it is: they want to get married, they want to have kids, they want to move to the suburbs. And they get there and it's like, "Holy shit! I've been doing the same thing for the last 15 years, and I'm really not happy."

But for me, I have always tried to do the right thing, whatever it is. I can honestly say that I would not change anything in my life, at all, that has happened, because I'm really happy.

LS: You mean, you wouldn't change it now, but what would you change if you could go back...

AP: I don't think anything, because I can't imagine a different life. I am, right now, pretty much exactly where I want to be. I don't know how else I would be here. I don't know how to explain it.

(Calling to Hunter) What? All right! I'll put medicine on it when we get home! He has eczema; it's very itchy. He has spots on his feet that itch – Put your shoe on! – When he was born... he looked like a tomato.

LS: A tomato?

AP: Yeah, he was covered with eczema when he was born. He has really bad allergies, too.

Everybody would change a couple of things if they could. What would I change in my life, if I could? I don't know. Maybe I would have more kids. I like having kids. But with the married boyfriend situation right now, it's not going to happen anytime soon.

LS: What do you hope to be in 10 years, or where do you hope to be in 10 years? Are you doing something now that you want to continue doing?

AP: I don't know. I have no idea.

Right now, basically, all of my energy goes into my son. So in 10 years, hopefully, I'll have had time to think about what I want to do and figure it out. I'm not much of a planner; I probably could plan a little more than I have already. I just kind of go where life takes me.

Having a goal, especially if there's an interest that you have, is good. But, on the other hand, I think a lot of people over-plan everything to the extent that they pass up a lot of opportunities that would make their life happier, or better.

Again, I'm an atheist, I'm pro-choice, my father was military but he left the military when I was 14, and now he's a lawyer. My parents are lawyers, upper middle class, educated, whatever. I mean, I don't study that much, but I did grow up in a very educated, intellectual household.

I can't think of anyone else – well maybe somebody, but not many people – who would have chosen the path that I chose. I found out I was pregnant when I was five, six weeks pregnant. I could have had an abortion and said, "Well, I'll learn from this. I'll plan better. I'll do whatever..."

I think that a lot of people, because they plan – "I don't want to have kids until I'm 30, so if I get pregnant before then, I'll have an abortion no matter what" - they don't even think about it. You're giving up stuff that may be a good thing in your life because you're so focused on a goal. And then, when you get it, you're not even happy.

I know a lot of people who are middle-aged, suburban people, and overwhelmingly they're miserable! They don't like living in isolation, a lot of them are not happy in their marriages, they're not happy with a lot of the choices they made.

It's like good money after bad: "I've already committed this many years of my life, so I might as well be miserable for another 30 years." And it's so... bad. And it's bad especially if you've got kids, because you want to give your kids a joyful parent, a happy parent.

It's not reasonable to expect to be happy all the time. That doesn't work. But most of the time you should be content and happy. And if you're not, you really need to change whatever it is, you know? You need to figure it out.

Just because you have had an idea in your mind about what you wanted to do for X number of years doesn't mean that it's necessarily the right thing to do. What I've learned is that a lot of things that seemed like they were the end of the world turned out to be the best things that ever happened to me.

LS: What can you tell kids in their teen years about getting their lives together?

AP: I think that people need, hmmm... how do I want to say this. People need to realize that doing what other people expect you to do all the time, and living your life with people telling you what you should be doing, is not, you know... you have to figure out what will make you happy. How can you live your life with no regrets? How can you live your life trying always to do the things that are going to be best for you, without hurting anybody, or anything else?

Like my parents: basically their whole idea was that by having a child with no father and no money, that he was going to be miserable, and that I wouldn't be able to raise him, and we were not going to be happy. But the thing is that you've got to make it work. And if you decide to... I don't know... I feel like I'm talking in circles.

It always feels better to be able to take care of yourself and to be responsible for your own choices. At the end of the day, when you look back on your life and what you've done, you have to answer to yourself.

And the years go by quick! So by doing what everybody expects you to do, and living your life basically as a child because you're taking money from your parents, it's not a good way to live. And if you're doing things because it's what everyone expects you to do, and it's what you're supposed to want, you can get stuck. A lot of times people really aren't happy.

I think the goal of life is to make decisions that make you happy and don't hurt anybody.

35. MATT FORBECK

History   Middle   Born 1968, Milwaukee, Wisconsin

Being a great editor requires Matt Forbeck to be a purse-lipped grammarian and a hawk-eyed perfectionist. But when he speaks, he's on an emotional roller coaster, careening from topic to topic, rarely stopping to complete a sentence.

    When I asked him about the forces that formed him, a hurricane of life spewed forth, leaving me to run in his wake asking, "…and what did that have to do with it?" From typewriters to quadruplets, from parachuting to the Queen's English, from romance to business, it all comes together in his life as an author… I think.

Excerpts

"The most important skill I've learned is typing. As a writer, the best class I ever took was my typing class, and I didn't do very well at it... Learning how to type allowed me to create stories quickly. Without that it would have been too slow, and I would have been frustrated: I would have been pulling teeth the entire time..."

"Writing is something where you can take every class you want, but if you don't have any talent, the skill doesn't do you much good. You have to have raw talent and then learn the skills to apply that talent..."

"I was a very sickly child, I had horrible asthma, and I never thought I was going to live. I never thought I'd make it past my teenage years; I thought I'd be dead by the time I was 17..."

"I hate being afraid of anything. I don't let myself be afraid of things... If something scares me, I make sure to go face it right away and take care of it... I (make) sure that I (stand) up to it. Then you learn, 'Hey, it's not that bad!' It's almost never as bad as you think it's going to be..."

"If you do things out of fear, then you're doing only negative things. You're never going to be building anything; you'll never do anything hopeful..."

"I always wanted to do something exceptional, be exciting, and do cool things. You only get one life, right? So what's the point of sitting back and letting it happen? You have to take charge..."

"I hate rejection, I absolutely hate it, so I try to hedge my bets. As a writer you get rejected constantly, so you try to hedge your bets to make sure that you get rejected as little as possible. But part of life is failing, that's where you learn your best lessons... you learn by your failures..."

"The thing about being a creative soul is that you have to have an ego about it. If you don't think you can do better than what other people are doing, then you probably shouldn't be doing it..."

"If you don't believe in yourself, then why should anybody else? You need to find something that you love, and that you can develop skills for, and passion for... Follow your gut. Follow your heart. See where it leads you."

"I have failed more often, and in a greater variety of attempts, than anyone I know. I also have had some spectacular successes that I would not have experienced if I had not been willing to risk failing. I'll take that a step further and admit that I've learned far more from my mistakes and failures than from any of my accomplishments. You cannot learn without risking failure... Learning requires failure; you won't learn if you are not willing to make mistakes and fail."

— Curtis M. Faith, in *Way of the Turtle*

Interview   Las Vegas, Nevada, April 2007

Matt Forbeck: The most important skill I've learned is typing. As a writer, the best class I ever took was my typing class, and I didn't do very well at it.

When I went to school – this was before computers in a lot of ways – my Catholic high school only had enough electric typewriters for half the class and manual typewriters for the other half. So for half the year I was on the manual and the other half I was on the electric, and I actually sucked at it. I was a straight-A student except for typing; I got C's in typing.

When I was about 14 or 15, I was more heavily into computers than anyone I knew – I had one at home that I'd bought with my own money – but learning how to touch-type opened up the world for me.

I can type 80 to 100 words a minute, and I write somewhere north of 1,000 words an hour when I'm cooking, and if I didn't know how to touch-type I couldn't do any of that. My interaction with the world on a daily basis is through a keyboard, so that skill has proved to be more useful to me than anything else I've learned.

All the other stuff I learned in school: math, science, reading, writing, literary analysis, all that kind of stuff... the most useful thing on an everyday level has been typing by far. Strange (laughs)!

LS: Tell me how this segued into what you became.

MF: I was a computer geek early on, and I was interested in telling stories, but I'm also frustrated by doing things slowly. For instance, I had some artistic skills, but I never sat down and developed them because I knew that the amount of time it would take me to develop those skills was more than I wanted to put into it. I could not sit down and paint models because literally watching paint dry just kills me. I just don't have the patience for it, although I appreciate it when it's done well. I appreciate it a lot.

Learning how to type allowed me to create stories quickly. Without that it would have been too slow, and I would have been frustrated; I would have been pulling teeth the entire time. If I didn't have that, I don't think I would have gone down the road as far as I've gone, which is mostly telling stories in different ways.

LS: How did that start?

MF: When I was a kid, I liked telling stories. I was an early reader; my mother tells me I was a reader at two years old. I was reading *The Jungle Book* when I was four, and not the Disney version but the original Kipling. I read all of Sherlock Holmes when I was five or six, that kind of stuff. I was intrigued by stories, loved stories, loved to read.

In fourth grade my teacher had an essay contest, and I just came up with a silly-ass Star Wars parody called *Food Wars* – it was just completely goofy, goofy, goofy – and I won it, and I'm, like, "Heh! This is stuff that I could do!"

People appreciate it if you write well. I started pursuing that by getting involved in games: *Dungeons & Dragons*, which is a story-telling game at heart. I knew that eventually this is what I wanted to do.

I was very fortunate that I always knew that I wanted to be a writer, or a storyteller of some sort. I know a lot of people who were absolutely confused all the way through high school and college about what they wanted to do with their lives. I was never confused about what I wanted to do, but I was confused about whether I could actually do it, whether I could pull it off.

Being a writer is a very risky thing: there's no clearly defined career path. People don't say, "I'm going to go out and hire writers!" If you get your liberal arts degree in creative writing, you're basically a more highly qualified burger-flipper (laughs).

Writing is something where you can take every class you want, but if you don't have any talent, the skill doesn't do you much good. You have to have raw talent and then learn the skills to apply that talent. I felt very happy that I could do that.

I had many crisis moments in my education – no, not many, a few – where I was listening to my parents, and my parents were saying, "You should do something with engineering, or law, or medicine, or business." That was because I had straight A's in school. I was adept at a lot of different things, and I actually started out in college as an electrical engineer by taking four terms of calculus. My parents wanted me to become an electrical engineer, to do that during the day, and then have writing as a backup.

But you know how this goes: you wake up, and you go to work, and you come back and you say, "I'm tired! I've had a long day doing electrical engineering, and I want to sit back and watch some TV, play a game with my buddies, see my girlfriend, play with my kids..." whatever, and you never get around to writing.

I had actually set up a five-year degree program at the University of Michigan where I was going to do the BS in electrical engineering, and a BA in creative writing at the same time. I woke up one morning about halfway through my second year, and I said, "I just can't do this to myself." I called my parents and told them I was dropping everything, and they said, "No, you're not. It's past the drop-add deadline, and we've already paid for the credits!" (Laughs)

I sat down and I said, "OK, let me figure this out." I looked at my schedule, and I said, "If I finish this term, doing what I'm doing, and take these classes next year, then I can get out of college in three years total with the creative writing degree only." I said, "I'm going to do that!"

I pitched it to my parents as saving them money (laughs). I was going to the University of Michigan, which was not cheap since I was out-of-state. It cost 12 to 15 thousand dollars for tuition alone back in 1990, and I had six siblings behind me, three "bloods" and three "steps." My parents were happy to hear about any money that I could save them.

LS: It sounds like you were a salesman from early on.

MF: Exactly. Well, I try to make it easy for people to see it my way (laughs)!

So I ditched out of electrical engineering, after having done two years, and focused on the straight creative writing degree. I never regretted it.

A creative writing degree doesn't provide an obvious career path. Most employers don't care if you have a creative writing degree or not (laughs)! If they're looking for a writer, they're looking for someone who's talented; they don't really care if you have a degree in it. The degree is just a label to indicate that I got a BA from the University of Michigan. Once I had the BA, I went on to get an education in the real world.

My writing professor, Warren Hecht, was also my student advisor, and I looked at him, and I said, "Should I go on to get a master's now?" He said, "No. If you want to be a writer, then you go out and do things. You live your life, and you see what's out there. If you want to, you can come back later and get your master's, but first you need to have something to write about! Go out there and do something!" OK, that was good advice, so I did that.

I was trying to figure out how I could make a living using and developing my writing skills. That's how I got into games as a professional, because role-playing games involve a tremendous amount of writing. They involve creative writing, and also a lot of something that's similar to technical writing. Games spoke to me both ways because it got both sides of my brain working: the mechanical parts, and the more ephemeral parts of the game. In the gaming industry it's called "crunch" versus "fluff." I like them both, so it suits me pretty well.

When I got out of college, I wanted to go to Europe to visit a buddy of mine named Angel, who was an exchange student from Spain, but I didn't have any money. My parents gave me this speech when I got out of college: they paid for my education – and I really appreciate that – but when I was done, I was done. That was it (laughs)! They weren't going to pay for me to go to Europe.

So I said, "How the hell am I going to get across to Europe?" I looked into it and got a student work visa – because I was going to have to work my way across – but Spain didn't have one of those; they didn't have a student work program. I decided to go to the country that was closest whose language I spoke. So I got a UK work visa, and I went to England.

I flew over in September of 1989. I had $600 in my pocket, which was my life's savings, and a one-way ticket, because I didn't know when I was coming back or where I was coming back from. I didn't know anybody in the entire country. In fact, outside of Angel, I didn't know anybody in the entire continent! But I figured I was young, and stupid, and I could balls my way through (laughs)!

I called up Games Workshop when I landed in London. I'd seen an ad in *White Dwarf* magazine many moons before – that was their "house" magazine – that said they were looking for an editor. I said to them, "I've done a little freelance game design when I was in college, can I have a job interview?" They said, "Yeah, sure. Can you come in Monday?" This was a Wednesday and I said, "Sure."

By Wednesday night I was already running out of money, so I called them up Thursday morning and said, "Can I come in... tomorrow?" They said, "Sure!" The next day I come in, and they're all very casual in T-shirts, blue jeans, shorts, and ripped pants. I show up in a business suit and get laughed at.

They gave me an editing test to take home and said, "Of course you know proper British editing marks, don't you?" I said, "Of course I do! But the American ones are a little different, so it'll take me a little time to catch up." I went back to London and bought myself a Queen's English dictionary and a book on editing marks. I went over the thing with a fine-tooth comb and basically learned the skill on the spot (laughs)!

LS: How did your writing progress after you started as an editor?

MF: I started out editing. Not many people can pull off being an editor, because it requires a very strong command of grammar, spelling, punctuation, and a committed eye to detail. Anybody can string together a sentence and think they can be a writer. It's like everybody thinks they can be on American Idol because we all think we can sing, right? Of course everybody's got that basic level of skill, but to be a professional is entirely different.

I figured a good back door into writing would be editing. I did a lot of editing for TSR when they published *Dungeons & Dragons*. Every time I edited something I'd go, "I could write this. I could write better than this!"

The thing about being a creative soul is that you have to have an ego about it. If you don't think you can do better than what other people are doing, then you probably shouldn't be doing it. Don't waste your time and everybody else's time. Move on to something that you are good at.

LS: Is that sort of like saying that the first person that has to have confidence in you is yourself?

MF: Yeah, definitely! If you don't believe in yourself, then why should anybody else? You need to find something that you love, and that you can develop skills for, and passion for, and just follow it.

There are other things that I could have done for a living. I could have been an electrical engineer. I've got friends who are literally rocket scientists. I've got a buddy who I went to college with who does compression algorithms for the Mars program for NASA. These are brilliant guys. I could probably have gotten into the same kind of thing, but it didn't speak to me in that way.

LS: But you're also a lot more now than just an author. There's a secret life of Matt here...

MF: Which one! Hey, wait a minute, what are you talking about? (Laughs) I have lots of secret lives.

LS: Well, give us one.

MF: I'm a father – which is not much of a secret – a father and a husband. One thing that has shaped my career and that has made me a freelance writer, as opposed to a contract writer on staff someplace, is that I always followed my heart more than my wallet.

When my visa expired at Games Workshop, they offered me a full-time job, and they were ready to help me work out the immigration details. But my girlfriend back home wanted me to come back to Michigan. That was the choice: either my job or my girl; I can't leave her hanging on forever. This was back when trans-Atlantic phone calls were, like, 50 cents a minute and the phone bills were just killing us. We were writing letters everyday because email hadn't really kicked off yet.

It was a choice between my girl or my job, so I said, "Screw my job, I'm going to go be with my girl." I can get another job, but finding another true love is not going to happen, I know that. She meant a lot more to me than any job.

We ended up getting married before she graduated with her master's in social work. Originally, the idea was we'd get married when she got out of college, but we're, like, "Aww, screw it, it's taking too long. Let's get married now!" (Laughs)

Because she was still in college, I was restricted geographically to that location: I couldn't just rip her out of school and take her someplace else. I can't tell you how many job offers I turned down because I had to say, "I can't leave, I'm here with this woman. This is my love, and I'm not going anywhere."

That's informed a lot of my decisions career-wise, and life-wise, over the years. I think that has always done me well. Your job can be very fulfilling, but if you break your heart doing it, then it doesn't mean a damn thing.

My wife and I really wanted to have kids, and we struggled with infertility issues for a long time. After four years of trying, and pissing around one way or another, she became pregnant with our eldest son, Marty. That was eight years ago, and we wanted to have more kids: at least two would be good, maybe three.

We said, "Let's see if we can be a little more aggressive at this point." We were getting older, and we didn't want to wait forever for this to happen. We decided to pony up some decent money and find a fertility doctor who could help us out.

At first my wife had a horrible reaction to the fertility drugs, which caused her ovaries to become overstimulated. The doctor said to us, "We're going to check your ovaries to see that you've only got two eggs that are possible to fertilize." It turned out she had more.

We went in for an ultrasound before Christmas and the doc finds one egg that's been attached, and it's just barely hanging on. She goes, "You'll have to prepare yourselves. This might not work out. Come back after the holidays, and our regular ultrasound technician will be here, and she'll make sure we get this down right."

We come back after the break, and the ultrasound tech says, "Yeah, that one's doing fine, and this one is doing fine, and this one over here is doing fine, and this one over here looks pretty good, too!" Suddenly we had quadruplets on the way. Oh, my God, what did *that* do to our lives (laughs)!?

It will be five years this June 5th that our four babies were born, and that was the most incredible year of my life by far. We are the luckiest people to have these kids in our lives, and my wife is my hero.

LS: How did it go?

MF: The first thing they tell you when you're pregnant with quadruplets is that you should do what's called selective reduction, which is to abort one or more of the fetuses by sticking them with a needle and injecting them with saline. The theory is this makes it so the remaining fetuses are not competing to survive. Anytime you're talking about triplets or more, you're talking about a very high-risk pregnancy. They say, "You need to go in and kill a couple so that the ones that are left will have a better chance."

We're not terribly religious people, but we struggled with that. And another thing is that you have to wait until 13 weeks to do this, so you're at the point where you're actually looking at the ultrasound and seeing... oh, my God! And if you stick a needle into the womb injecting saline, there's also a 10% chance that everything will die.

Here we are – having struggled long and hard, and really wanting these kids – facing the option of losing them all to make one or two of them live, or trying to keep them all and running the risk of having them all die. It could turn into a horrible experience either way.

And also there's the fact that if they're born, then they're going to be born premature...

LS: Is that certain?

MF: Oh, definitely. I think the record for quadruplets is 34 or 35 weeks. (A normal pregnancy has a gestation of 40 weeks. – Ed.) The average is 28. At 28 weeks you're talking about very small children. My wife made it to 29 weeks.

We decided to go through with it, to keep them all. I was reading medical journals that were being published the previous month. We're doing all the research, and we both came to the same decision independently.

Although we're not big believers in God or anything like that, we decided that we'd let fate take care of it: we're not going to kill these children. If it happened that they died, at least we would know that we did our best to make them live.

LS: Is that a form of trusting yourself?

MF: I don't know about trusting ourselves because, you know, a lot of it was out of our control. We were going to do the best we possibly could.

The other horrible options were that the kids could be born deaf, blind, or with horrible cerebral palsy. We could end up not only dealing with having four children at once, but having four severely handicapped children. That was a risk as well.

You don't want that to happen to your kids, but on the other hand, if my kids were handicapped, I would love them just as much. It's not that they wouldn't be more difficult, but you can't make a decision like this based on your own comfort. You can't say, "I'm not going to have this kid because it's going to be inconvenient for me." Ah... I can't do that.

Anyway... umm... I'm getting choked up.

LS: Yeah, I appreciate it! It's a great story.

MF: This is my big story. It's my life's story.

My wife was on bed rest, at home, for 16 weeks. At first she was working half-time as a school social worker, and we rented a wheelchair so she could go to work. I brought her to work everyday, picked her up in that wheelchair, and put her to bed. Then she went to full bed rest. They sent us home with a uterine contraction monitor, something that you put around your waist that detects premature labor that you can't even feel.

On Easter Sunday of that year we sent the data in over the phone line, and they said, "You have to come to the hospital." She spent the next 10 and a half weeks in the hospital in full bed rest, flat on her back, unable to move, drugged up to her eyeballs with magnesium sulfate. This is a muscle relaxer. The idea is to relax the uterine wall so that it doesn't contract. The kids are only 19 weeks old – they don't survive at 19 weeks – they're not viable children at that point. So, in the end, she was on full or partial bed rest for about 26 weeks.

The trouble is that when they give you a muscle relaxant, it relaxes every muscle in your body, not just the uterine wall. She couldn't even focus her eyes! It was just horrible, horrible for her. And every time they'd mess with the dosage, it would make her loopy. I would drop everything I was doing and just sit with her in the hospital.

Then at 29 weeks, pretty much to the day, we had the babies. Pat, Nick, Ken, and Helen came out at 2 lbs 12 oz, 2 lbs 9, 2 lbs 8, and 1 lb 8. My little daughter, she was just a wee bit of nothing. And there were some medical issues.

My son Nick had his lung collapse at 60 hours and had a chest tube put in. I watched them do that. I'm not a very emotional guy – well, I am emotional, everybody's emotional, but I don't show my emotions all that much – but this time I actually got shook watching them do that to Nick. "Oh, my God, I don't know if he's going to make it!" He's doing fine today.

Great kids. Fantastic kids.

My father said, "Why the hell did you watch that!" (Laughs) Like, you know… true: he'll never know that I was there, he was too young, he was barely able to see at 2 lbs 9 oz. But it meant something to me to be there for my kid, no matter what. I wasn't going to back away from it even though it was traumatic for me. I'm sure it was worse for him (laughs)!

After anywhere from 8 to 11 weeks in the hospital, we got to bring the kids home. They had grown to four or five pounds at that point. Once they get out of the woods, they call them "feeders and growers" in the Neonatal Intensive Care Unit.

My son Nick came home on oxygen and an apnea monitor. My daughter Helen had this thing called a hemangioma that was growing on her upper lip; that's basically a wild strawberry birthmark that grew to be larger than her nose and cut off her air supply and her ability to eat. We had to bring her home on an oxygen tank, an apnea monitor, and a nasal-gastric tube, which is a tube that went down her nose. We fed her through a pump that went into her stomach. So while we have five babies, we also have to carry around monitors, oxygen tanks, everything else (laughs).

Helen was on that tube for her first year, and eventually they installed a port in her stomach. A little pop-open thing in her belly that we used to feed her with for the next year. Now she's our best eater. She's still the tiniest thing. I think she's in the third percentile for her age, but she's just a ball of fire. She doesn't let those boys run around at all. She'll be five in about a month and a half.

One of the most amazing parts of the story is that our entire community came out and helped us. Fortunately, when Marty was born we decided to move back to my hometown because we wanted to be closer to the grandparents and the cousins. That worked out really well for us.

Since we're not church-going folks, we didn't have a church to draw on, but in Beloit my parents put out the word that we needed help, and we had 35 to 40 people coming in our house every week to bathe, feed, change the kids, and clean the house. We had this maid service that donated weekly cleanings for the first year. Our neighbors got together and bought us a pallet's worth of diapers: just wonderful people.

LS: This is such a big event. How did this tie in to your life?

MF: Yeah, it's huge. It busted my life down to its barest essentials in many ways.

I ended up taking a job with somebody, which I don't ever do because I like freelancing and being my own boss. I needed a steady paycheck, and I needed benefits.

Being a freelance writer, you don't get benefits, so I took a job with Human Head Studios, a computer game developer in Madison, Wisconsin, for about two years. I had turned that job offer down before, so I had to call them up and ask, "You still got that going?" (Laughs)

I headed their paper game division, and I had a great time. I learned a lot about computer games, but I was eager to go back to being my own boss, charting my own destiny, doing my own thing. I prefer to write novels as opposed to manage projects.

As soon as we realized that my wife was able to go back to work, and our insurance would cover us, I quit. I quit as soon as I could, basically (laughs). I didn't leave them hanging, of course; they were buddies of mine.

LS: Something that I thought was interesting – that you might comment on – was your comment that you felt you could do just about anything in the game industry because it couldn't be that hard...

MF: One of the good things about a liberal arts education is that it teaches you that you can learn things. Right? If you understand how to learn things – if you have the skill of how to learn – then you can do just about anything you put your mind to.

I know how to research anything I want to find out about. I can learn anything I want to learn about. I can develop skills – I know that I can develop skills, even if I don't have them at the moment – I can figure them out. If there's something that I'm not particularly good at, like, say singing or art work, then I can hire people to do that. So I'm not shy of doing just about anything.

I spent four years as a publisher. I was co-founder and owner of Pinnacle Entertainment Group, which was a game company. We did a game called *Deadlands*, a zombie cowboy game, that was our big thing; it was a role-playing game. It also spawned a bestselling miniatures game, a bestselling card game, and a collectible card game. It won awards in every category. We did some good, quality stuff.

If somebody gives me enough of a budget, then I'll pull together any kind of project they can come up with. I know how to project manage, and that's part of it, too. During the four years of running Pinnacle, we produced sometimes 40, 50, or 60 products in a year, and I managed all that, shuffling all the different freelancers and everything else. Once you've learned those kinds of management skills, you can pull off just about any project. Even when you're working as an independent: as long as you know how to learn things, you can pick up whatever you need.

LS: How did you develop this confidence? It's not what you're taught at school where you're rated in terms of specialties, and you're directed into one area or another.

MF: I hate being afraid of anything. I don't let myself be afraid of things. That's what does it. Also, I've done a lot of stupid stuff as a kid: I've jumped out of airplanes, I've done hang-gliding, I've taken piloting lessons, white-water rafting. If something scares, me I make sure to go face it right away and take care of it.

LS: Where did that attitude come from?

MF: I don't know (laughs)! I think it's just a character trait, something you're born with. I know people who are just terrified of everything, and it rules their lives. There are people in my family for whom fear is the main motivating factor in their lives. It's fear of this or that happening.

Our nation right now, because of 9/11, runs on fear; we're motivated by fear. I think that's a horrible thing. You need to face your fears and conquer them, and then you can do something positive. If you do things out of fear, then you're doing only negative things. You're never going to be building anything; you'll never do anything hopeful.

That is where I got my confidence: if I was afraid of something, I made sure that I stood up to it. Then you learn, "Hey, it's not that bad!" It's almost never as bad as you think it's going to be.

The thing that always scared me the most when I was young was talking to girls! (Laughs) People who know me think that I'm bullshitting them because I can talk to anybody. But with the first girl I was interested in, my heart beat like hell, I had a stomach full of butterflies, and it just paralyzed me.

Fortunately my wife was a very kind and forgiving lady (laughs). Through all of my bumbling and stumbling and letting her know that I loved her, and finding out if she would love me back. You can't let yourself be controlled by fear, because it paralyzes you.

I was a very sickly child; I had horrible asthma, and I never thought I was going to live. I never thought I'd make it past my teenage years; I thought I'd be dead by the time I was 17. This sort of colored my reaction to a lot of things. I said to myself, "I may not have a long life…" I never knew, I never really planned for much. I figured I was going to be dead so screw it: I'd do as much as I possibly could in the time I had. This also meant that I couldn't say, "I'll get to it later," or "I'll let it slide for now," or "I'll just have a regular life and not worry about it."

I always wanted to do something exceptional, be exciting, and do cool things. You only get one life, right? So what's the point of sitting back and letting it happen? You have to take charge.

So, like, what did I do last night? I was out until four in the morning with my friends. I do that every time I come to one of these trade shows, even though the smart thing would be to go to sleep at midnight. But I'm not here that often, and I don't see these people that often, so I squeeze every damn bit out of it as I can.

I don't sleep that much, period – having the quadruplets trained me that way. I'm lucky if I get five hours of sleep a night. I just hate the idea of having that down time, time when I'm not able to do anything (laughs)! I'm just kind of crazy driven that way, I guess.

LS: The flip side of being courageous is learning how to land on your feet when the inevitable teaching lesson knocks you down.

MF: Yeah, that's part of the learning process. Actually, failing helps.

I hate rejection, I absolutely hate it, so I try to hedge my bets. As a writer you get rejected constantly, so you try to hedge your bets to make sure that you get rejected as little as possible. But part of life is failing, that's where you learn your best lessons.

In many senses my company Pinnacle Entertainment Group was a failure. When Shane and I were running the company, we never turned a profit. But I can't tell you how much we learned doing that. I managed to apply what I learned to a lot of different things. In that sense I think it was a better education than anything I got in college, or high school, or anything else.

You learn by your failures, but I try not to fail too often!

LS: Tell me the story of one of your failures.

MF: Oww... I don't concentrate on my failures. I can tell you a story about how I almost killed myself parachuting (laughs)! That was stupid!

I had gone parachuting once, and then two years later a buddy of mine decided to go parachuting again. I didn't want to pay for the ground school again, even though I'd forgotten everything I'd learned. I was too cheap to pay the 50 bucks. So when they said, "Have you done this before?" I said, "Yes! I've done this before!"

When I jumped out of the plane and looked down from 3,000 feet – I'm on a static line, so it pulls the cord automatically – I was totally disoriented. I had no idea where the fuck I was. "Where is the target!"

They have a little radio on your front so they can talk to you, but you can't talk back to them. The woman on the ground is speaking to me saying, "Go to your left. Go to your left." I spot a target and I go for it. It turns out to be the expert target, but I didn't realize it. The beginners target is way over here on the other side of the field, and I'm going for the expert target.

The reason that it's the expert target is because it's smaller, and it's right in front of a line of trees (laughs)! As I get closer to this target I realized that I'm going to miss it by, well... enough to hit the trees: "Oh shit!"

The problem was these stunt chutes that we used: when you pull the brakes on your parachute it steals your downward momentum and converts it into forward momentum, but when you take off the brakes, that stolen momentum comes back and whacks you right down. If you time it just right, you can tip toe away like James Bond, but if you fuck it up, you smack into the ground and break your legs!

So I'm like going toward these trees, and I'm thinking, "I can't hit the trees!" So I flared hard – braked hard – and I literally had to pull my legs up so that I didn't get them caught in the tops of the trees. They'd normally be giving me instructions over the radio about when to hit the brakes, but they can't see me because I've gone for the expert target, and I'm on the other side of the trees. I'm thinking, "Oh shit!" (Laughs)

I make it over the trees, and I'm come down as close as I possibly can to the ground before braking. Then I brake as hard as I possibly can, and I end up getting dragged across half of a cornfield by my parachute. The last thing they said to me when they saw that I was not dead was, "Whatever you do, don't let the jump-master see you: he will kill you!" (Laughs)

That was a bit of a failure. It taught me that I should have paid for the refresher course. Don't be cheap when it comes to your life (laughs)!

LS: What can you tell kids these days – in the schools they go to, with tests and the kind of future that they're looking at – about how they might take control of their lives?

MF: Learn what you want to learn, take control of your own education.

I was what they called a "gifted and talented" student in school, which meant that I was always done with everything before everybody else. That meant that I got in trouble because I was always bored out of my mind. I'd be caught reading science-fiction paperbacks instead of the bible in my Catholic school.

If something interests you, follow it. Don't wait for your teachers to bring it to you.

Chase it yourself.

You have down time, you have off time when you're not doing their stuff. You can even work with your teachers to set up independent study programs or projects that you want to work on, or whatever.

When a teacher finds a student who's enthusiastic about something, they're usually happy to support them. It's hard to get kids enthusiastic in school.

Follow your gut. Follow your heart. See where it leads you.

POSTSCRIPT

36. LINCOLN STOLLER

History **Middle** Born 1956, Port Chester, New York

My father was not a happy person. His mother beat him and berated him. He kept no photographs of her – I have only one – and she died in an asylum. All his dreams were nightmares – so, throughout the rest of his life, he said he never dreamed.

My father's deep self-doubt prevented him from understanding love. He never gave emotional support to his family, but he was not rotten. In that very brief moment when he would first see me, in that authentic moment before he started to think, his eyes would light up, and he would exclaim, "Hi, Linco!" And then it was gone, entirely, until we met again after the next long interlude.

I read to my father on his death bed. He was in and out of consciousness. Just before he went into a coma for the last time, he opened his bright eyes and exclaimed "Hi, Linco," and then he was gone. And in remembering him, that is enough, that magic little spark. A lot of strength can come from a very little thing.

This story explores the issue of context. What provides the most important foundation for learning and growing? When you strip off all that you know of your world and yourself, what is left?

"The purpose of seeing through one's own nothingness is to see beyond into what is really there to which one's real self can relate."

— Indries Shah, from *Learning How to Learn*

"... one of the deepest truths about the archetypal energy of the Shadow (is that) everything that is unconscious and not yet clearly manifested and understood in the world of the ego appears nasty, ugly, frightening, 'dark,' and dangerous. However, since the deep unconscious contains all that waking consciousness desires and longs for the most... the dark and frightening mask of the Shadow always hides the thing devoutly wished and sought."

— Jeremy Taylor, from *Where People Fly and Water Runs Uphill*

"... learn by degrees to endure the sight of being, and of the brightest and best of being, or in other words, of the good."

— Plato, from *The Republic*, Book VII, written 360 BC, translated by Benjamin Jowett

Interview with Myself — San Antonio, Texas, August 2008

I tried the herb Salvia divinorum several times, many years before, using a tincture that I held under my tongue. The most I'd achieved was a mildly dissociated state before ejecting what had become a mouthful of bitter spit. Whatever Salvia did, I conjectured, my center would hold. Now I was being offered Salvia in its smokable form – the simple dried leaf – and I accepted it for these reasons:

1. It was guaranteed to have an effect.
2. This professional meeting provided a supportive environment, though it was cold and unemotional.
3. I was familiar with the three psychologists joining me, and our crossing paths seemed fortuitous.
4. Journeying with these people tested whether psychologists could be effective "watchers."
5. It was an opportunity to test my own mettle in less than perfect conditions and to gain deeper insight into the risks of traveling to different realms.

I added some water to a small water pipe. I tested the pipe, tested the lighter, packed its bowl with Salvia's brittle leaves, arranged the pillows, and sat back, unsure of what to expect. The experience would be short, and my three friends would simply and soberly watch me until it was over. I asked one if he expected me to drop the pipe. Would the effect be that rapid? I had a moment of uncertainty, and then I struck the lighter.

The leaf burned quickly. The smoke was easy but became acrid. I held in my breath, poised and watchful, waiting for "The Diviner's Sage" to emerge from her mouse hole in the wainscot of reality. I don't recall exhaling.

I was looking at Kay in the soft light as she sat in a chair at the foot of my bed.

POSTSCRIPT

Moving from bottom to top, I beheld a blue sweater, a deep red bolster, her blond hair, and a cream-colored wall. This stripe of colors narrowed to the width of my central field of vision, surrounded by blackness. As soon as I told myself, "Something's happening…" this stripe repeated twice horizontally, forming a double cross extending from the center of my vision out to the periphery.

The area that surrounded my vision, which we learn as babies may disappear from view but is still there, was no longer there. My vision shrank down to the interior of a straw. All that surrounded me was black, empty, and unknown. All that I knew of myself was foreshortened: the passage of time, the direction of time, and my place in time. I watched my own disintegration, and then lost consciousness.

The EEGs of people experiencing Salvia show gross, global neurological distortions in the first 10 seconds. Slow-wave oscillations dwarf the brain's normal voltages by an order of magnitude; they last one period and quickly diminish. Correlating this distortion to subjective experience is conjecture, but the shape of these oscillations corresponded to the flow of my experience.

I regain full consciousness in an unfamiliar world. I lack perception of anything but my own inner voice. My mind holds only two memories: a snapshot of myself as a child and a memory of three people walking through a hotel lobby. Accompanying these memories is the sense of a whole life's history but, try as I might, as in a lucid dream, I can recall none of it.

My sense of the present is unlike anything in my two memories: it is dark, forbidding, and intangible. I have the dim notion that I am an Aztec soldier wearing some feathered garb, waking from a reverie into a world of struggle and loneliness, and entirely forested with large bulbous things. What are they… giant mushrooms?

I am deeply sad, and I am afraid. The details of the present, which I cannot yet recall, fill me with dread. I need protection; I feel like a child. My sadness arises from realizing these memories are just a reverie, a hopeful daydream, but nothing more. The life that seemed a reality moments before was just a hallucination. The emptiness that now surrounds me, on the other hand, is not a dream.

It dawns on me that I loved that image: that fantasy of what should have been but never was. For a while I struggle with my lack of sensation and memory, aware only of a dark area in front of me. My only certainty is that I am waking from a dream, awaiting a recollection of who I am.

My intellect falters, and a knot forms in my throat. I am overcome with feelings of love and pity. Love, from the realization that I really do love the person I imagined myself to be, a self that could experience a happiness unmatched in this dark world. Pity, from having lost this forever. Like Odysseus tied to the mast, I would give anything to escape the present and regain that paradise. "One, two, three, four…" I count seconds to assure myself that time is passing.

I have glimmers of recollection. Memory fragments suggest the fading past might be more than a total invention. I muse, "Those people in the hotel lobby: had I been in contact with them? Was I involved with those people between then and now? Had something happened?" Perhaps Lincoln Stoller is more than just a reverie imagined from some postcard vision, the invented story of someone else's childhood.

An awful thought strikes me, and I recoil, "Had I retired with some people to a private hotel room to take drugs?" I am stunned by the horrible picture of a witless teenager playing a foolish game of "chicken" and dying. "Could a good person, like me, willingly toss away all that he had ever known? Could the person of my imaginings be such a fool?!" Surely this is nothing more than a sick fantasy. I quickly relax, reassured that no sane person would be so stupid as to take "The Red Pill" and be forever locked out of the dreams of hope, and love, and meaning. And yet…

Where is reality? Why is this hypnopompic state taking so long to clear? Why have I no recollection of other people, family, community, or culture? I rack my brain for some wider context, some connection that will puncture my isolation, something good that I love, my center; but there is nothing.

In my struggle I consider moving my arm and speaking, but neither action seems to have any purpose; I'm not sure how to do those things, anyway. I recall playing my flute in the empty hotel stairwell: how lovely its reverberation. The memory stirs my heart; its sound pierces the silence, and I begin to sing. This is my first utterance, and I sense, rather than see, that it freezes the entities who are watching me like laboratory technicians.

A small window opens out of my darkness, and through this window I perceive people, and I remember. They are the watchers, but we do not love each other. I am still alone. The shock of this hits me, and I shut the window. Then, in a world that is only sound, I begin to speak, and I tell this story.

AFTERWORD

The question of what is learning is ill-phrased, being somewhat inconsistent. It doesn't entirely make sense, which is true of all fundamental questions. Learning is holistic, and holistic questions are best approached using emotions, which express what we feel about the whole.

For 14 years I've been looking for an answer in these interviews. It wasn't until Michelle Murrain said, roughly, "I wish I learned to love myself sooner," that I saw this feeling embedded in every story.

This work is not finished. These explorations have expanded one fundamental question into three: What is transformation? What is love? and, What is learning? This does not complicate anything, in fact it makes the original question clearer. Fundamental reflections reveal new symmetries. Once you understand this, the end of one exploration becomes the beginning of another.

Lincoln Stoller, 2018
www.mindstrengthbalance.com

~

Visit **https://www.mindstrengthbalance.com/learningproject** for additional commentary and to hear extracts from audio transcripts. Follow **@LincolnStoller** and **#TheLearningProject** for additional information.

www.ingramcontent.com/pod-product-compliance
Lightning Source LLC
Chambersburg PA
CBHW080631170426
43209CB00008B/1548